The Madagascar Youths

In 1820, King Radama of Imerina, Madagascar signed a treaty allowing approximately one hundred young Malagasy to train abroad under official British supervision, the so-called 'Madagascar Youths'. In this lively and carefully researched book, Gwyn Campbell traces the Youths' untold history, from the signing of the treaty to their eventual recall to Madagascar. Extensive use of primary sources has enabled Campbell to explore the Madagascar Youths' experiences in Britain, Mauritius and aboard British anti-slave trade vessels, and their instrumental role in the modernisation of Madagascar. Through this remarkable history, Campbell examines how Malagasy-British relations developed, then soured, providing vital context to our understanding of slavery, mission activity and British imperialism in the nineteenth century.

Gwyn Campbell is founding Director of the Indian Ocean World Centre at McGill University, General Editor of the Palgrave Series in *Indian Ocean World Studies*, and Editor-in-Chief of the *Journal of Indian Ocean World Studies*. He held a Canada Research Chair for the maximum tenure (2005–19) and has published widely on Africa and the wider Indian Ocean world, including *An Economic History of Imperial Madagascar, 1750–1895* (2005), *David Griffiths and the Missionary 'History of Madagascar'* (2012), *Africa and the Indian Ocean World from early times to 1900* (2019) and *The Travels of Robert Lyall, 1789–1831* (2020).

The Madagascar Youths

*British Alliances and Military Expansion
in the Indian Ocean Region*

Gwyn Campbell

McGill University

CAMBRIDGE
UNIVERSITY PRESS

University Printing House, Cambridge CB2 8BS, United Kingdom

One Liberty Plaza, 20th Floor, New York, NY 10006, USA

477 Williamstown Road, Port Melbourne, VIC 3207, Australia

314–321, 3rd Floor, Plot 3, Splendor Forum, Jasola District Centre,
New Delhi – 110025, India

103 Penang Road, #05–06/07, Visioncrest Commercial, Singapore 238467

Cambridge University Press is part of the University of Cambridge.

It furthers the University's mission by disseminating knowledge in the pursuit of
education, learning, and research at the highest international levels of excellence.

www.cambridge.org
Information on this title: www.cambridge.org/9781316511718
DOI: 10.1017/9781009053655

First published 2022

A catalogue record for this publication is available from the British Library.

ISBN 978-1-316-51171-8 Hardback

Cambridge University Press has no responsibility for the persistence or accuracy of
URLs for external or third-party internet websites referred to in this publication
and does not guarantee that any content on such websites is, or will remain,
accurate or appropriate.

I Rhiannon, Rhys, a Lludd

Contents

Figures

Maps

Tables

Acknowledgements

Research for this book was supported by the Social Sciences and Humanities Research Council of Canada.

Alternative Names of Madagascar Youths to Britain

Name used	Alternative name/s in this volume
Andrianaivo	Drinave
Ikiotomavo	Rakotomavo, Contamauve
Rahaniraka	Ravoalavo, Volave
Raolombelona	Rolan Balan, Rolam Balam, Roloun Baloun
Raombana	Ratotozy, Rafaralahy, Thotoos
Ratsiorimisa	Shermishe
Razafinkarefo	Zafincarafe, Zafy Coreffe
Verkey	Rainimanana, Ravarika

Glossary of Malagasy Words

andriambaventy	a judge
andriana	highest caste of free Merina
Antalaotra	term for Swahili settled in northwest Madagascar
deka	aide-de-camp
Fandroana	Merina New Year
fanompoana	unremunerated forced labour for the state
fantsika	soldiers living in military garrisons
farara	Malagasy trumpet
filanzana	palanquin
hova	second caste of free Merina, a term also sometimes applied historically to all Merina
jejileva	Malagasy guitar with one to two strings
kabary	public proclamation
Karany	term for Indians settled in Madagascar
lamba	kind of Malagasy toga, usually made of cotton or silk
lokanga	stringed musical instrument
lokanga vava	Malagasy mouth guitar
menakely	a fief granted by the crown
Menamaso	lit. 'Red Eyes', close advisers and followers of Rakoto Radama (Radama II)
mpanjaka	sovereign/ruler
Olomainty	class of royal slave
sampy	traditional Merina talismans
sidikina	English national anthem (played also as the Merina national air)
simbon	loincloth
solifara	sulphur
Sorabe	Malagasy written in Arabic script
tangena	a poison ordeal, and the name of the nut which contains the
trano masina	lit. 'holy house', a house built over generally royal tombs

Tsimandoa	royal messengers and bodyguards drawn from the *Tsiarondahy* sub-caste of royal slaves
valiha	guitar-sounding bamboo instrument
Vazimba	alleged first occupants of the central highlands of Madagascar, killed, assimilated, or chased to the west of the island by proto-Merina settlers
voanjo	Merina military colony
Voninahitra (Vtr)	Merina system of honours or military grades
zazamadinika	'little children', term Laborde applied to his Mantasoa workforce

Abbreviations

AAM	Archives de l'Académie Malgache, Antananarivo, Madagascar
AAMM	*Antananarivo Annual & Madagascar Magazine*
AHVP	Archives historiques de la Vice-Province Société de Jésus de Madagascar, Antananarivo
ALGC	Archifdy Llyfrgell Genedlaethol Cymru (Archives of the National Library of Wales), Aberystwyth
ARM	Archives de la République Malgache, Antananarivo, Madagascar
BAM	*Bulletin de l'Académie Malgache*
BFBS	British & Foreign Bible Society
BFSS	British & Foreign School Society
BL	British Library
CMS	Church Missionary Society
CO	Colonial Office, NAK
HdR	François Callet (ed.), *Histoire des Rois: Tantaran ny Andriana* vols. 1–4 (Tananarive: Editions de la Librairie de Madagascar, 1974) and vol. 5 (Antananarivo: Académie Malgache, 1978) – pages of Malagasy original numbered consecutively throughout
LMS	London Missionary Society
MIL	Madagascar Incoming Letters (SOAS/CWM)
MOL	Madagascar Outgoing Letters (SOAS/CWM)
NAK	National Archives, Kew
NAM	National Archives, Mauritius
PWDRO	Plymouth and West Devon Record Office
RA	Raombana, 'Annales' (1853), AAM
RH	Raombana, 'Histoires' (1853), AAM
SOAS/CWM	School of Oriental & African Studies, Council for World Mission Archives

1   The Context

This is the hitherto untold history of some 100 'Madagascar Youths' who, in the 1810s and 1820s, British authorities accepted for education and training in Britain, on Mauritius, and on British naval vessels. Their agreement to do so followed a diplomatic mission in 1816 to Radama I (r. 1810–28), king of the small landlocked kingdom of Imerina, in the central highlands of the large Indian Ocean island of Madagascar. This mission led first to a draft accord in 1817, which was amended and confirmed in a full Britanno-Merina treaty in 1820 through which the British aspired to suppress the slave trade from Madagascar and secure political and economic hegemony over the island. They promised the Merina king compensation for loss of slave-export earnings, notably in the form of military aid, to enable him to subject the rest of Madagascar to Merina rule, and educational and technical assistance, in the form of British missionary teachers and artisans, as well as secular craftsmen from neighbouring Mauritius. This history is well known.[1] However, there was an additional facet to the Britanno-Merina alliance that is almost completely absent from the historiography. As a result notably of the 1820 treaty, and an additional agreement in 1824, British authorities agreed to pay for 'Madagascar Youths', selected by Radama, to be educated and trained abroad. Accounts of two of these youths, the twin brothers Raombana and Rahaniraka, have appeared in French and Italian.[2] However, what is almost completely unknown is that the twins formed part of a group of about 100 Madagascar Youths selected for training outside Madagascar, under British supervision. The British authorities envisaged that, once they had completed their apprenticeships and returned to Madagascar, these youths would help to cement British

---

[1]   Jean Valette, *Études sur le règne de Radama I* (Tananarive: Imprimerie Nationale, 1962); Hubert Jules Deschamps, *Histoire de Madagascar* (Paris: Berger-Levrault, 1972); Mervyn Brown, *Madagascar Rediscovered: A History from Early Times to Independence* (London: Damien Tunnacliffe, 1978); Gwyn Campbell, *An Economic History of Imperial Madagascar, 1750–1895: The Rise and Fall of an Island Empire* (Cambridge: Cambridge University Press, 2005).

[2]   Simon Ayache (ed.), *Raombana l'historien (1809–1855)* (Fianarantsoa: Ambozontany, 1976); Simon Ayache (ed.), *Raombana: Histoires* (Fianarantsoa: Ambozontany, 1980); Liliana Mosca, *Il Madagascar nella vita di Raombana primo storico malgascio (1809–1855)* (Napoli: Giannini Editore, 1980).

political, economic, and religious paramountcy in the island. However, in 1826, Radama decided to break the British alliance, a decision endorsed by his successor, Queen Ranavalona I (r. 1828–61). This rupture had profound implications for Britanno-Merina relations, the Mauritian and Malagasy economies, and the Madagascar Youths.

This volume comprises seven chapters. This chapter sets the context for the story of the Madagascar Youths. It outlines the history of European interest in Madagascar that led to the first Malagasy visiting Europe and to the emergence of the island as a significant supplier of provisions and slaves to European colonies in the region. It discusses the reasons for a specifically British focus on Madagascar that resulted in the 1816 mission and the Britanno-Merina accord of 1817, and the main authorities involved. It analyzes why that accord was undermined and the fallout of its failure. Finally, it examines the renewal of the alliance and its outcome in the form of the 1820 treaty that included the decision to send a select group of 'Madagascar Youths' abroad for training under British supervision. Chapters 2–4 investigate, in sequence, the histories of the youths sent to Britain, to Mauritius, and for training aboard British naval vessels. Chapters 5 and 6 explore the history upon their return to Madagascar of the youths sent abroad for technical training. The final chapter examines the careers of those Madagascar Youths who, upon their return, were employed for various periods as court officials and diplomats for the Merina crown. Central to this theme were the twins Raombana and Rahaniraka, who in Britain received a liberal education, rather than technical training, and who upon their return to Madagascar served the Merina court, notably as foreign secretaries.

Madagascar in the European Mind

From the time of the 'Voyages of Discovery', Madagascar figured large in the minds of Europeans. It did so for two very different reasons. First, it was considered to be a tropical island Eden possessing exotic animals, plants, and human inhabitants. Second, it was thought to be of significant economic and strategic importance, due to its natural resources and its strategic location on the maritime route to the East.[3]

With a total land surface of 587,041 km², and a coastline of 9,935 km, Madagascar is the world's fourth largest island (after Greenland, New Guinea, and Borneo), approximately the size of Texas or 2.4 times the size of

---

[3] See for example Bruce McLeod, *The Geography of Empire in English Literature, 1580–1745* (New York: Cambridge University Press, 1999); Richard H. Grove, *Green Imperialism: Colonial Expansion, Tropical Island Edens and the Origins of Environmentalism 1600–1860* (Cambridge: Cambridge University Press, 1999); Jason H. Pearl, 'Desert Islands and Urban Solitudes in the "Crusoe" Trilogy', *Studies in the Novel* 44.2 (2012), 125–43.

the British Isles. It is widely believed to hold the world's greatest concentration of unique flora and fauna: 98 per cent of Madagascar's land mammals, 92 per cent of its reptiles, 68 per cent of its plants, and 41 per cent of its indigenous bird species are found nowhere else in the world.[4] Madagascar also possesses a distinctive human population. Early European voyagers noted small communities of Swahili, who they called 'Arab' and the Malagasy termed *Antalaotra*, and Indians, called locally *Karana*, who probably arrived in Madagascar from, respectively, East Africa in the ninth to tenth centuries and India (notably Gujarat) in the eleventh to twelfth centuries.[5] Excluding these groups, Madagascar appeared to be inhabited by two ethnic groups: a lighter-skinned people resembling Malays who inhabited the high central plateau that runs on a north–south axis almost the entire 1,592 km length of the island and a darker-skinned African-looking people who occupied the lowlands. This was confirmed by recent DNA research revealing that, while the island's population is of mixed 'Bantu' (African) and 'Austronesian' (Indonesian) genetic heritage, the degree of African ancestry was less (42 per cent) in the Merina of the central plateau than amongst, for example, the coastal Vezo, Mikea, and Taimoro (62–65 per cent).[6] However, all speak variants of what Europeans commonly called a 'Malay' or 'Malayo-Polynesian' (linguists now use the term 'Austronesian') language. This indicated that the forebears of at least some Malagasy originated from the east, from the broader Malayo-Indonesian-Polynesian region. Additionally, they possessed certain distinctly southeast Asian cultural traits, such as irrigated riziculture and rectangular huts.

The only groups in Madagascar with a clear idea of their origins were the Swahili, the Indians, and the Zafimaniry of the southeast coast who claimed that their ancestors had sailed from Mecca in the fourteenth century.[7] Other Malagasy communities had at most a vague indication that their ancestors had come from somewhere 'overseas'. Indigenous names for Madagascar are as indeterminate. The island was traditionally termed *Izao rehetra izao* ('this whole') in accordance, claimed English LMS missionary James Sibree (1836–1929), with the Malagasy concept that their land was the centre of the universe, *Nosin-dambo* ('Island of Wild Hogs'), or *Ny anivon'ny riaka* ('the

---

[4] Gwyn Campbell, 'Madagascar', in Shepard Krech III, J. R. McNeill, and Carolyn Merchant (eds.), *Encyclopaedia of Environmental History* (New York: Routledge, 2004), vol. 2, 796–8.

[5] Paul Ottino, 'The Malagasy *Andriambahoaka* and the Indonesian Legacy', *History in Africa* 9 (1982), 221–2.

[6] Trefor Jenkins et al., 'ß-Globin Haplotype Analysis Suggests That a Major Source of Malagasy Ancestry Is Derived from Bantu-Speaking Negroids', *American Society of Human Genetics* 58 (1996), 1303–8; Jason A. Hodgson, 'A Genomic Investigation of the Malagasy Confirms the Highland–Coastal Divide, and the Lack of Middle Eastern Gene Flow', in Gwyn Campbell (ed.), *Early Exchange between Africa and the Wider Indian Ocean World* (London: Palgrave Macmillan, 2016), 231–54.

[7] Pierre Vérin, *The History of Civilisation in North Madagascar* (Rotterdam: A. A. Balkema, 1986), 27.

[land] in the midst of the flood').[8] In many Arabic texts it was termed *Kamar* or *Komr* ('Island of the Moon') or 'Bukini'.[9] The famous English explorer Richard Burton (1821–1890) considered that 'Madagascar' derived from 'Mogadishu', after the sheik of that city who had once invaded the island.[10]

Merina oral traditions complicate rather than clarify the issue. They assert that the forebears of the present-day Merina were the last wave of migrants to reach Madagascar, the result of a shipwreck around the start of the sixteenth century.[11] On the coast, they suffered from disease (probably malaria) and encountered hostility from local people, so quickly made their way to the malaria-free highlands where they encountered the Vazimba, a dark-skinned Stone Age population of hunter-gatherers who spoke an unintelligible language. Many Western scholars initially assumed that the Vazimba were either a group indigenous to Madagascar or the earliest immigrants from Africa – possibly related to the Wazimba or the Khoi. The encounter between the two groups was unbalanced as the Merina, equipped with Iron Age technology, swiftly conquered the Vazimba, who they killed, assimilated, or forced to flee west.[12]

Human settlers greatly impacted the environment of Madagascar. The current evidence is that people established permanent settlements in the island from the eighth to ninth centuries CE.[13] They deliberately introduced plants and animals of Southeast Asian and African origin, such as rice, bananas, dogs, and oxen, and, inadvertently, the rat and diseases – including malaria. They probably hunted to extinction the pygmy hippopotamus, a giant tortoise, and several species of giant lemur, some larger than female gorillas.[14] The island's enormous flightless elephant birds, including the world's largest avian species

---

[8] James Sibree, 'Malagasy Place-Names; Part 1', *Antananarivo Annual & Madagascar Magazine* (hereafter *AAMM*) 20 (1896), 404.

[9] Vérin, *History of Civilisation*, 4; Sibree, 'Malagasy Place-Names', 404.

[10] John H. van Linschoten, *Voyage to the East Indies*, vol. 1 (London: Hakluyt Society, 1885), 19.

[11] Ottino, 'Malagasy *Andriambahoaka*'. The possibility of shipwreck off Madagascar was high. Madagascar was first sighted by Portuguese mariners in 1500 and was paid the first intentional visit in 1506. Between 1507 and 1528, at least five Portuguese shipwrecks occurred off the island, almost all on its southeast coast – see Alfred Grandidier et al. (eds.), 'Republication of All Known Accounts of Madagascar', *AAMM* 22 (1898), 234–5.

[12] Gerald M. Berg, 'The Myth of Racial Strife and Merina Kinglists: The Transformation of Texts', *History in Africa* 4 (1977), 1–30; Lin Poyer and Robert L. Kelly, 'Mystification of the Mikea: Constructions of Foraging Identity in Southwest Madagascar', *Journal of Anthropological Research* 56.2 (2000), 163–85; Jean-Claude Hébert, 'Les "sagaies volantes" d'Andriamanelo et les "sagaies à pointes d'argile" des Vazimba: Un problème de critique de la tradition orale merina', *Études océan indien* 31 (2001), 165–89; Sarah J. Dugal, 'What's the Story with Vazimba? Oral History, Social Change, and Identity in Highland Madagascar' PhD, Tulane University (2004).

[13] Gwyn Campbell, 'Africa and the Early Indian Ocean World Exchange System in the Context of Human-Environment Interaction', in Gwyn Campbell (ed.), *Early Exchange between Africa and the Wider Indian Ocean World* (London: Palgrave Macmillan, 2016), 16.

[14] Campbell, 'Madagascar', 796–8.

(*Aepyornis maximus*), probably met the same fate, as did the giant eagle, *Stephanoartus mahery*, which preyed on primates such as lemurs. These birds almost certainly inspired Marco Polo's story of the elephant-carrying *rukh*:

it was for all the world like an eagle, but one indeed of enormous size; so big in fact that its wings covered an extent of 30 paces, and its quills were 12 paces long, and thick in proportion. And it is so strong that it will seize an elephant in its talons and carry him high into the air, and drop him so that he is smashed to pieces; having so killed him the bird gryphon swoops down on him and eats him at leisure. The people of those isles call the bird *Ruc*, and it has no other name.[15]

Voyager accounts of Madagascar stimulated the curiosity of European savants and royalty, some of whom requested the captains of ships visiting the island to return with both natural history and human specimens. Probably the first Malagasy to reach Europe were two boys from the southeast of Madagascar. Seized by the Portuguese captain Ruy Pereira in 1506, following his nation's 'discovery' of the island, they were shipped to Mozambique from where in early 1507 his superior, Tristan da Cunha (c.1460–c.1540), despatched them to Portugal aboard the *Santa Maria*, under the command of Antonio de Saldanha. They arrived in August 1507 and were presented to King Manuel I (1469–1521), who ordered further exploration of Madagascar.[16]

In the mid-seventeenth century, several Malagasy were also taken to France as examples of exotic savages. The first to arrive, in 1655, were brothers, sons of a ruling house, again in southeastern Madagascar, where the French had founded a settlement under Étienne de Flacourt (1607–1660) which lasted from 1643 to 1674. One of the brothers was aged five years, the other was somewhat older. In France, they entered the household of Cardinal Jules Mazarin (1602–1661), chief minister to Louis XIV (r. 1643–1715), who sought to educate them as gentlemen. The eldest boy found difficulty adjusting to life in France and died of 'grief'. However, his brother thrived in his new environment and became standard bearer in the cavalry of the cardinal, accompanying his master when he was appointed governor of Alsace, a region bordering German provinces that France had conquered in 1639. The Malagasy was described in 1675 as

a young man of about twenty-five, very well made, of average height, a perfect dancer. He had . . . the complexion of a negro, but it was not pure black; he was rather of an olive

[15] Marco Polo, 'Concerning the Island of Madagascar', in Henry Yule and Henri Cordier (eds.), *The Travels of Marco Polo* [1298] (Adelaide: eBooks@Adelaide, 2014), bk. 3, ch. 33; see also Anon, *The Arabian Nights: Tales from the Thousand and One Arabian Nights* (London: Hodder & Stoughton, 1924).
[16] Guillaume Grandidier, *Histoire physique, naturelle et politique de Madagascar* (Paris: Imprimerie Paul Brodard 1942), vol. 5, book 1, 8, 12; Pierre Van den Boogaerde, *Shipwrecks of Madagascar* (New York: Strategic Book Publishing, 2009), 28.

reddish-brown colour. What seems to me particular, is that unlike most Moors, he has straight flat hair ... he had only a confused memory of his native country: did not know even two words of his mother tongue; but remembered his abduction well enough.[17]

Of a third Malagasy, who was sent to Nantes, a French nobleman commented in 1658:

We came across a monster ... who, however, is not so ugly or frightful that no woman in Nantes has asked M. de la Milleraye, to whom he came from Madagascar, for his hand in marriage. Avarice is at its peak, and triumphs over love and all that is invincible for those [women] who ask for him want only to run around the country displaying him for money.[18]

This very much set the trend whereby, as part of a pattern of conspicuous consumption intended to reflect their wealth and status, the wealthiest members of the European elite 'collected' and displayed individual non-Europeans.

Madagascar was also considered to be of great strategic importance on the maritime route to the East and rich in natural resources such as tropical hardwoods. Further, contrary to conventional accounts of African gold production which largely exclude Madagascar, the island possesses significant rift and alluvial gold deposits. This was suspected by all early European voyagers and confirmed in the eighteenth century. Thus, English astronomer William Hirst (d. 1769/1770), who visited Madagascar in 1759, supported the 1729 observation by Robert Drury (1687–c.1743–50) that Madagascar produced three sorts of gold – one of which, called 'malacassa', was pale, as easy to cast as lead, and worth up to 20 florins an ounce.[19]

As a result, Madagascar figured in a number of European schemes of colonization. From the time Vasco da Gama (c.1460s–1524) rounded the Cape of Good Hope in 1497 en route to India, the Portuguese sought to supplant Muslim commercial influence in the Indian Ocean, including Madagascar. However, initial projects to colonize the island were quickly abandoned when the Portuguese encountered hostility from its inhabitants and found scant evidence of precious metals or spices. In the seventeenth century, Dutch and English attempts to establish colonies on the island also failed due to local hostility and the ravages of malaria. By the early eighteenth century, the

---

[17] H. de L'Hermine (1675) quoted in Anne Lombard-Jourdan, 'Des Malgaches à Paris sous Louis XIV', *Archipel* 9 (1975), 88–9.

[18] Philippe de Villiers, journal, 22 Mar. 1658, quoted in Lombard-Jourdan, 'Des Malgaches à Paris', 83.

[19] William Hirst to Duncombe, on the *Lenox*, off Madagascar, 6 Sep. 1759, in Biographicus, 'Biographical Sketch of an Old Indian Chaplain', *Oriental Herald and Journal of General Literature* 2 (1824), 405; see also Robert Drury, *Madagascar; or Robert Drury's Journal, during Fifteen Years' Captivity on that Island* (London: T. Fisher Unwin, 1890[1729]), 136; Gwyn Campbell, 'Gold Mining and the French Takeover of Madagascar, 1883–1914', *African Economic History* 17 (1988), 99–126.

British and the Dutch valued Madagascar only as a provisioning base for their East Indiamen– merchant ships sailing to and from the East, notably India.[20]

In 1642, Richelieu (1585–1642), chief minister to Louis XIII of France (r. 1610–43), granted the *Compagnie française de l'Orient* a charter and ten-year monopoly to colonize and exploit Madagascar. In the same year, a settlement was founded in the southeast of the island, governed (from 1648) by Étienne de Flacourt. However, in addition to malaria and the enmity of the Malagasy, it suffered a rupture in supplies from Europe during the Fronde civil wars in France (1648–53), and in 1654 the fourteen remaining colonists were removed to Réunion (called Bourbon from 1642 to 1793). In 1664, Jean-Baptiste Colbert (1619–1683), first minister of state (1661–83) under Louis XIV, created the *Compagnie des Indes*, in emulation of the Dutch and English East India companies. As the French were excluded from large parts of the East by their European rivals, the *Compagnie* sustained a more durable interest in less con-tested fields, such as Madagascar and the Mascarenes. Colbert envisaged trans-forming Madagascar, termed *La France orientale,* into a centre for French imperial and commercial activity east of the Cape (see Map 1.1). The seat of the 'Supreme Council of Trade with India', it would supervise imperial expan-sion in India and China, and cultivate cash crops for export and food crops to provision French fleets. In 1665, a colony was established in southeast Madagascar, but the last settlers abandoned it in January 1676 for Réunion. Internecine conflict, along with malaria, local hostility, and lack of metropolitan support, precipitated its collapse.[21]

---

[20] A. B. Grosbart, 'Madagascar Two Centuries Ago: A Proposal to Make It a British Plantation', *AAMM* 2 (1876), 51–6; William Bontekoe, *Memorable Description of the East Indian Voyage 1618–1625* (New York: McBride, 1929), 7–10; C. Northcote Parkinson, *Trade in the Eastern Seas, 1793–1813* (Cambridge: Cambridge University Press, 1937), 111, 258, 293; Frank Haight, *A History of French Commercial Policies* (New York: MacMillan, 1941), 3–5; Georges Hardy, *Histoire de la colonisation française* (Paris: Librairie Larose, 1953), 45, 52–3; Ralph Davis, *The Rise of the English Shipping Industry in the 17th and 18th Centuries* (Newton Abbot: David & Charles, 1972), 257–8; Jean-Michel Filliot, *La traite des esclaves vers les Mascareignes au XVIIe siècle* (Paris: ORSTOM, 1974), 19–20; Brown, *Madagascar Rediscovered*, 39–48; Malyn Newitt, *The Comoro Islands* (Boulder, CO: Westview Press, 1984), 3, 17.

[21] William Ellis, *History of Madagascar* (London: Fisher, 1838), vol. 2, 44; Conrad Keller, *Madagascar, Mauritius and the Other East African Islands* (London: S. Sonnenschein, 1901), 104; Louis Peltier, 'La traite à Madagascar au XVIIe siècle', *Revue de Madagascar* (August 1903), 105–6; R. E. P. Wastell, 'British Imperial Policy in Relation to Madagascar, 1810–96', PhD, London University (1944), 32; Marcel de Coppet (ed.), *Madagascar* (Paris: Encyclopedie de l'Empire Français, 1947), vol. 2, 288; Patrick Joseph Barnwell and Auguste Toussaint, *A Short History of Mauritius* (London: Longmans, Green & Co., 1949), 41; Raymond Decary, 'Contribution à l'histoire de la France à Madagascar', *Bulletin de l'Académie Malgache* (hereafter *BAM*) 31 (1953), 51; Hubert Deschamps, *Méthodes et doc-trines coloniales de la France* (Paris: Colin, 1953), 35, 43; Hardy, *Histoire de la colonisation française*, 35–42, 45, 52–3, 62; André Scherer, *Histoire de la Réunion* (Paris: Presses universi-taires de France, 1966), 11; Filliot, *La traite*, 21–3, 25–6; Robert Cornevin and Marianne Cornevin, *La France et les Français outre-mer de la première Croisade à la fin du Second Empire* (Paris: Tallandier, 1990), 92, 94, 137–9; Etienne de Flacourt, *Histoire de la*

Map 1.1 The Western Indian Ocean
© IOWC

In 1649, Flacourt had asserted French sovereignty over the Mascarene Islands, east of Madagascar, claims consolidated for Réunion in 1674 and for Mauritius (called Ile de France until 1810) in 1712. The Mascarene economy flourished after Bernard-François de la Bourdonnais (1699–1753) transformed Réunion into a granary to provision both islands and passing ships and Mauritius into a major Indian Ocean entrepôt. He also encouraged the

Grande Isle Madagascar, edited and commentary by Claude Allibert (Paris: Karthala, 1995 [1658]); James Kay, 'Etienne de Flacourt, L'histoire de le grand Île de Madagascar (1658)', *Curtis's Botanical Magazine* 21.4 (2004), 251–7.

cultivation of a variety of cash crops.[22] Nevertheless, local supplies of food and labour proved insufficient, so both were increasingly sought from external sources.[23] The closest and cheapest source was Madagascar. From 1773 to 1810, 77 per cent of the 739 regional maritime expeditions from the Mascarenes charged at Madagascar, most for rice but 56 per cent also for slaves.[24] Following the decisions by Napoleon Bonaparte (1769–1821) that slavery could be maintained in the colonies (in 1802) and that the French slave trade be legalized (in 1803), it is estimated that between ten and twelve Mascarene ships, each carrying on average 100 slaves, made several return trips each year to Madagascar.[25]

Following the collapse of the Flacourt settlement in 1674, French claims to Madagascar were maintained through a series of royal edicts. However, lest it come to be considered more important than the Mascarenes, the white population of Réunion and Mauritius generally opposed plans, periodically hatched in France, to colonize Madagascar. In its turn, Paris blocked Mascarene projects to colonize Madagascar on the grounds of expense and the alleged harshness of Mascarene settlers towards the Malagasy.[26]

British Interest in Madagascar

In the seventeenth century, there was a brief period of English fascination with Madagascar. In 1637, Endymion Porter, a courtier, presented Charles I (r. 1625–49) with a project for the colonization of the island, the virtues of which were subsequently lauded in works published in 1640 and 1641 by passengers who had been aboard visiting English ships. The first of these volumes was written by Walter Hamond, a surgeon on the East India

---

[22] Deschamps, *Histoire de Madagascar*, 43; G. S. P. Freeman-Grenville, *The French at Kilwa Island* (Oxford: Clarendon Press, 1965), 8–10; Derek Hollingworth, *They Came to Mauritius* (London: Oxford University Press, 1965), 1–2.

[23] Deschamps, *Histoire de Madagascar*, 66–7, 69–70; Auguste Toussaint, 'Early American Trade with Mauritius', *The Mariner's Mirror* 39.1 (1953) , 46; Marie-Claude Buxtorf, 'Colonie, comptoirs et compagnie: Bourbon et l'Inde Française, 1720–1767', in *Les relations historiques et culturelles entre la France et l'Inde, XVIIe-XXe siècles*, vol. 2 (Sainte-Clotilde: La Réunion: Association historique internationale de l'Océan indien, 1987), 173; Rafaël Thiébaut, 'An Informal Franco-Dutch Alliance: Trade and Diplomacy between the Mascarenes and the Cape, 1719–1769', *Journal of Indian Ocean World Studies* 1.1 (2017), 130–48.

[24] Ellis, *History of Madagascar*, vol. 2, 70; Albert Lougnon, 'Vaisseaux et traites aux îles depuis 1741 jusqu'à 1746', *Recueil de documents et travaux inédits pour servir à l'histoire de La Réunion* 5 (1940), 27; Auguste Toussaint, 'Le trafic commercial des Seychelles de 1773 à 1810', *Journal of the Seychelles Society* 4 (1965), 20; Auguste Toussaint, 'Le trafic commercial entre les Mascareignes et Madagascar de 1773 à 1810', *Annales de l'Université de Madagascar*, series Lettres et Sciences Humaines 5 (1966), 99–101.

[25] Barnwell and Toussaint, *Short History of Mauritius*, 112, 133; Deschamps, *Histoire de Madagascar*, 95.

[26] Gwyn Campbell, 'Imperial Rivalry in the Western Indian Ocean and Schemes to Colonise Madagascar, 1769–1826', *Revue des Mascareignes* 1 (1999), 80.

Company (EIC) vessel, the *Jonas* (or *Jonah*), who on one occasion spent four months in Madagascar.[27] The second book was authored by London merchant Richard Boothby. After a stopover of three months in Madagascar on a return voyage from Surat, India, Boothby enthusiastically advocated the island to rivals of the EIC as an ideal location for a European colony:

without all question, this country far transcends and exceeds all other countries in *Asia, Africa*, and *America*, planted by *English, French, Dutch, Portuguese*, and *Spaniards*: and it is likely to prove of far greater value and esteem to any Christian prince and nation, that shall plant and settle a sure habitation therein, than the *West Indies* is to the king and kingdom of *Spain*: and it may well be compared to the land of *Canaan*, that flows with milk and honey a little world of itself, adjoined to no other land, within the compass of many leagues or miles, or the chief paradise this day upon earth . . . In further commendation thereof, I will take the liberty of extolling it, I hope, without offence, as *Moses* did the land of Canaan: 'It is a good land, a land in which rivers of waters and fountains spring out of the vallies and mountains; a land of wheat and barley, of vineyards, of fig-trees and pomegranates; a land wherein thou shalt eat without scarcity, neither shalt lack any thing therein; a land whose stones are iron, and out of whose mountains thou mayest dig brass.'[28]

However, an attempt in 1645–6 by wealthy English merchant William Courteen (1572–1636) to found a colony of 145 men, women, and children in Saint Augustin Bay collapsed within a year, following the death of over 50 per cent of the settlers.[29] Efforts in 1649–50 to establish an English colony in northwest Madagascar also failed, due to malaria and the hostility of local Malagasy.[30]

Subsequently, from 1680 to the 1720s, Madagascar commanded English attention because European pirates, chased from the Caribbean, made it their main base for raids on East Indiamen. The pirates included Scotsman William Kidd (c.1654–1701), Englishmen Henry Every (1659–c.1699–1714) and Thomas Tew (1649–1695), and Bermuda-born Creole, John Bowen (d. 1704). Piracy in the Indian Ocean inflicted such losses to European

---

[27] Walter Hamond, *A Paradox. Prooving, That the Inhabitants of the Isle called Madagascar, Or St. Laurence, (In Temporall things) are the happiest People in the World* (London: J. Raworth, B. Alsop, T. Fawcet, and M. Parsons, 1640); Louis B. Wright, 'The Noble Savage of Madagascar in 1640', *Journal of the History of Ideas* 4.1 (1943), 112–13.

[28] Richard Boothby, 'A brief Discovery or Description of the most famous Island of Madagascar, or St. Laurence, in Asia, near unto the East-Indies' [orig. pub. London, 1646], in Thomas Osborne (ed.), *A Collection of Voyages and Travels*, vol. 2 (London: Thomas Osborne, 1745), 628–9, 634.

[29] Gwyn Campbell, *David Griffiths and the Missionary 'History of Madagascar'* (Leiden: Brill, 2012), 416.

[30] See for example Robert Hunt, 'Île d'Asada', in Alfred Grandidier and Guillaume Grandidier (eds.), *Collections des ouvrages anciens concernant Madagascar*, vol. 3 (Paris: Comité de Madagascar, 1905), 264–5.

merchants that, in a rare show of solidarity, the French and British navies combined in a successful effort to drive them away by the early 1720s.[31] Of ultimately greater consequence was the threat that French possession of Mauritius posed to British East Indiamen and the maritime route to India. Ottoman control over the Red Sea meant that Europeans sailing to and from the Indian Ocean arena had to use the Cape route to India, on which Madagascar and the Mascarene islands, notably Mauritius, played increasingly significant roles. Mindful of the significance of Bombay for the British, Bourdonnais, governor of Mauritius from 1735–40, transformed Port Louis, the island's capital, into a major port and dockyard that played a pivotal role in French imperial adventures in the region. For example, during the Wars of Austrian Succession (1740–8), the Mascarene fleet harassed British shipping, annexed the Seychelles in 1743, and in 1746 routed the British squadron under Admiral Edward Peyton (d. 1749) before relieving the siege of Pondicherry and capturing Madras – then Britain's most important Indian possession. Again, from 1780 to 1783, over 100 French ships sailing to India called for provisions at Mauritius, which in 1781 also supplied recruits to fight the British in India. So important had Mauritius become by 1785 that Antoine Joseph de Bruni, chevalier d'Entrecasteaux (1737–1793), commander of the French navy in the Indian Ocean, and governor of Mauritius from 1787 to 1789, successfully argued for the French regional headquarters in the Indian Ocean to be transferred to Mauritius from Pondicherry.[32]

The Revolutionary and Napoleonic Wars proved decisive. In 1793, the disorganized French navy could spare no ships for the Indian Ocean and the British quickly captured French bases in India. In 1796, the British destroyed

---

[31] Charles Johnson [Daniel Defoe], *A General History of the Pyrates* (London: T. Warner, 1724); Hubert Deschamps, *Les pirates à Madagascar* (Paris: Berger-Levrault, 1949); F. D. Arnold-Forster, *The Madagascar Pirates* (New York: Lothrup, Lee & Shepard, 1957); Janice E. Thomson, *Mercenaries, Pirates, and Sovereigns: State-Building and Extraterritorial Violence in Early Modern Europe* (Princeton, NJ: Princeton University Press, 1994), 47–9; R. J. Barendse, *The Arabian Seas: The Indian Ocean World of the Seventeenth Century* (Armonk, NY: M. E. Sharpe, 2002), 40, 271, 471–80; Arne Bialuschewski, 'Pirates, Slavers, and the Indigenous Population in Madagascar, c. 1690–1715', *International Journal of African Historical Studies* 38.3 (2005), 401–25; Malyn Newitt, 'Comoros: Before 1800', in Kevin Shillington (ed.), *Encyclopedia of African History*, vol. 1 (New York: Fitzroy Dearborn, 2005), 289–90; Arne Bialuschewski, 'Thomas Bowrey's Madagascar Manuscript of 1708', *History in Africa* 34 (2007), 31–42; Stephen Ellis, '*Tom and Toakafo*: The Betsimisaraka Kingdom and State Formation in Madagascar, 1715–1750', *Journal of African History* 48.3 (2007), 439–55.

[32] ; Frederick Hervey, *A New System of Geography*, vol. 1 (London: Printed for J. Johnson, and G. & T. Wilkie, 1785) , 351; Barnwell and Toussaint, *Short History of Mauritius*, 58–62, 85–6, 91; Freeman-Grenville, *French at Kilwa Island*, 9; Hardy, *Histoire de la colonisation française*, 87–9; Buxtorf, 'Colonie, comptoirs et compagnie', 170–2; Cornevin and Cornevin, *La France et les Français outre-mer*, 188, 242.

French trading posts on the northeast coast of Madagascar and occupied the Cape of Good Hope, which it then declared it a colony in 1806, in order to prevent the French from using it, as they had in 1778, to supply the Mascarenes.[33] However, Mascarene corsairs inflicted enormous damage to British East Indiamen. For instance, from 1807 to 1809 the EIC lost a minimum of forty ships to Mascarene privateers who, between 1793 and 1810 seized from EIC ships an estimated £2.5 million worth of booty. This transformed Port Louis into a major international emporium, and the Mascarenes were recognized as the maritime 'key to the East'. Given the Russian presence on India's northern frontier, the British considered it vital to secure mastery of the Cape route to India, and in a prolonged campaign from 1809 to 1811 they captured Mauritius, Réunion, and the French posts in Madagascar.

Under the Treaty of Paris in 1814, Réunion was returned to France, but Mauritius was retained by Britain, which subsequently attempted to extend its influence over the region. This inevitably included Madagascar, the chief supplier of provisions and cheap labour to the Mascarenes, and led to a treaty, signed in 1820, between the British and the Merina of Madagascar that laid the basis for one of the most remarkable accords of the early nineteenth century between a European power and an African sovereign, through which the British government paid for the education and training abroad of some 100 Malagasy youths.[34]

The Main Authorities Involved

The main authorities involved in the Madagascar Youths project were, on the British side, Robert Farquhar, governor of Mauritius, and the London Missionary Society and, on the Malagasy side, King Radama of Imerina.

---

[33] Wastell, 'British Imperial Policy', 40; Barnwell and Toussaint, *Short History of Mauritius*, 102, 123–4; Gerald S. Graham, *Great Britain in the Indian Ocean (1810–1850)* (Oxford: Clarendon Press, 1967), 24; Mabel V. Jackson Haight, *European Powers and South-east Africa: A Study of International Relations on the South-east Coast of Africa, 1796–1856* (London: Routledge & Kegan Paul, 1967), 74, 77, 94–5; Hubert Jules Deschamps, 'Tradition and Change in Madagascar, 1790–1870', in John E. Flint (ed.), *Cambridge History of Africa*, vol. 5 (Cambridge: Cambridge University Press, 1976), 398.

[34] Raymond Decary, 'La reddition de Tamatave à l'Angleterre en 1811', *BAM* 15 (1932), 48–9; Barnwell and Toussaint, *Short History of Mauritius*, 102–7, 111; René Sédillot, *Histoire des colonisations* (Paris: Fayard, 1958), 490, 519; Scherer, *Histoire de la Réunion*, 9–31; Graham, *Great Britain*, 18, 42–3, 46; Haight, *European Powers*, 78–9; Jean Valette, 'Documents pour servir à l'étude des relations entre Froberville et Mayeur', *BAM* 16.1–2 (1968), 84; [Jacques Dinan], *Industrie sucrière de l'île Maurice* ([Port Louis]: Le Bureau des relations publiques de l'industrie sucrière, 1972), 10; J. P. Durand and J. Durand, *L'Ile Maurice et ses populations* (Bruxelles: Editions Complexe, 1978), 31–3, 36–9.

Figure 1.1 Robert Farquhar (1776–1830)
Source: https://visa-mauritius.com/mauritius-and-its-culture (accessed 12/02/22).

Robert Farquhar

Robert Townsend Farquhar (1776–1830; see Figure 1.1), first British governor of Mauritius, was born in 1776, the second son of Walter Farquhar (1738–1819), royal physician, and his wife Anne (née Stephenson; d. 1797). He attended Westminster School, and in 1793, aged seventeen, obtained an EIC writership in Madras. He served as British commercial resident in Amboyna (present-day Ambon, Indonesia) from 1798 to 1802, when he was appointed commissioner for adjusting the British claims to the Moluccas, with responsibility for transferring those islands to the Batavian Republic. In 1804–5, he acted as lieutenant-governor of Prince of Wales Island (Penang).[35] During these early years of service in the East, Farquhar acquired a reputation as an efficient, ambitious administrator and gained the approbation and support of Lord Wellesley (1760–1842), governor general of India from 1798 to 1805. On 10 January 1809, Farquhar married Maria Frances Geslip de Latour (1782–1875), one of the two daughters of Joseph François Louis de Latour,

[35] G. B. Smith, 'Farquhar, Sir Robert Townsend (1776–1830), *Oxford Dictionary of National Biography* www.oxforddnb.com/view/10.1093/odnb/9780192683120.001.0001/odnb-978019 2683120-e-9180 (accessed 09.04.21); 'Robert Farquhar', https://mauritiusislandhistory .wordpress.com/robert-farquhar (accessed 09.04.21).

who had left France before the revolution and settled in Madras as a banker and merchant before retiring to Bedfordshire, England.[36] Robert Farquhar and his wife had a son, Walter Minto Townsend-Farquhar (1809–1866), and Farquhar confided to Wellesley, just before joining the Mauritius campaign, that he enjoyed a 'very happy marriage'[37] – to which there is ample testimony during the years they subsequently spent on Mauritius. It appears that Maria fully accepted Farquhar's strong attachment to his illegitimate son, Walter Farquhar Fullerton (1801–1830), born in Calcutta, who was at Eton in 1809, the year his father married Maria.[38]

In 1810, Farquhar sailed to the Mascarenes with the British fleet under Commodore Josias Rowley (1765–1842), which captured Réunion in July that year and Mauritius the following December. Farquhar made Mauritius his base, serving as governor and commander-in-chief in 1810–17 and in 1820–23. He immediately recognized the dependence of Mauritius, as a plantation island, on slave labour imported from Madagascar and East Africa. He also realized the significance of Madagascar as a supplier of provisions. In 1746, before sailing to India to beat the English fleet and seize Madras, Bourdonnais had sought supplies for his fleet in Antongil Bay where later French Vice Admiral Pierre André de Suffren (1729–1788) also provisioned his fleet prior to fighting the English fleet off India.[39] However, while aware of the importance of Madagascar to Mauritius, and of Mauritius in guarding the route to India, Farquhar was also charged with implementing the 1807 ban on the slave trade. The issue was a major concern, as Mauritian planters were dependent on slave labour. Moreover, the prohibition of the slave trade was the prelude to abolition of slavery. It thus raised the problem not only of combatting the slave trade in the region but also how to substitute free for slave labour. In 1807, Farquhar had published 'Suggestions for Counteracting any Injurious Effects upon the Population of the West India Colonies from the Abolition of the Slave Trade', in which he proposed a project for the introduction into

---

[36] 'Lady Maria Frances Geslip Hamilton [née de Latour]', www.lordbyron.org/persRec.php?&s electPerson=MaHamil1875 (accessed 09.04.21); Karina H. Corrigan, 'Chinese Botanical Paintings for the Export Market', *The Magazine Antiques* (June 2004) www .encyclopedia.com/doc/1G1-117878875.html (accessed 30/09/07).

[37] Quoted in 'Townsend Farquhar, Sir Robert Townsend, 1st bt. (1776–1830), of 13 Bruton Street and 2 Richmond Terrace, Whitehall, Mdx.', www.historyofparliamentonline.org/volume/1820-1832/member/townsend-farquhar-sir-robert-1776-1830 (accessed 09.04.21).

[38] David R. Fisher, 'Townsend Farquhar, Sir Robert Townsend', in David R. Fisher (ed.), *The History of Parliament: the House of Commons 1820–1832* (Cambridge: Cambridge University Press, 2009), www.historyofparliamentonline.org/volume/1820-1832/member/townsend-farquhar-sir-robert-1776-1830 (accessed 30/04/19); '*Walter Farquhar Fullerton (b. 1801)), wearing blue Eton suit and white chemise with frilled collar* by William Wood', www .bonhams.com/auctions/20767/lot/117 (accessed 09.04.21); Corrigan, 'Chinese Botanical Paintings';.

[39] Jean Louis Joseph Carayon, *Histoire de l'établissement français de Madagascar pendant la Restauration* (Paris: Gide, 1845), lxvii.

the West Indies of free Chinese labour to be paid for by planters or the government.[40] On Mauritius, Farquhar had the opportunity to implement similar migrant labour schemes. Between 1810 and 1823, he introduced over 1,500 convicts from Bengal, Bombay, and Sri Lanka, who were to be employed chiefly in road building and maintenance in Mauritius.[41] Also, between 1817 and 1840, over 100 Mauritian prisoners, slaves and free, convicted chiefly for theft, were despatched from Mauritius to Sydney, Australia, to work on penal labour projects.[42]

Further, Farquhar authorized the employment of slaves, called 'Government Blacks', in an arrangement first established in 1786 when the French authorities purchased 286 slaves to replace a traditional system whereby slave owners were periodically obliged to supply slaves for public works. After the British seized Mauritius in 1810, they employed Government Blacks in many areas, including servicing the military, and hired them out to individuals. In 1831, the number of Government Blacks stood at about 1,300. Government Blacks were differentiated from Prize Negroes – slaves captured aboard slaving ships by the British Navy – some 3,000 of whom were landed on Mauritius between 1813 and 1827. 'Liberated' from slavery, Prize Negroes were immediately obliged to serve fourteen-year apprentices, most to private individuals but some in the British military and in colonial government departments.[43]

Farquhar developed a strategy of incorporating Madagascar into Britain's informal empire through seeking alliances with Malagasy chiefs and persuading them to ban slave exports, founding a British settlement in Madagascar, and encouraging British missionaries to travel to the island, under his protection, to promote Christianity, the English language, and more generally the values of European civilization (see Table 1.1). To facilitate the realization of his ambitions, Farquhar built up a formidable library of primary and secondary material relating to Madagascar.[44] From the outset, he also envisaged inviting select Malagasy youths – his predilection was for those who as adults would become chiefs – to receive an English education outside Madagascar and return to their native island imbued with civilized values and pro-British sentiments.

---

[40] 'Farquhar, Sir Robert Townsend (1776–1830)', in Leslie Stephen (ed.), *Dictionary of National Biography*, vol. 18 (London: Smith, Elder & Co., 1889), 223.

[41] Clare Anderson, 'The Genealogy of the Modem Subject: Indian Convicts in Mauritius, 1814–1853', in Ian Duffield and James Bradley (eds.), *Representing Convicts: New Perspectives on Convict Forced Labour Migration* (London: Leicester University Press, 1997), 164–6.

[42] Edward Duyker, 'Sydney's People: The Mauritians', *Sydney Journal* 1.2 (2008), 59.

[43] Gwyn Campbell, *The Travels of Robert Lyall, 1789–1831: Scottish Surgeon, Naturalist and British Agent to the Court of Madagascar* (Cham, Switzerland: Palgrave Macmillan, 2020), 245–7.

[44] William John Hamilton, 'Abstract of MSS. Books and Papers respecting Madagascar during the Possession of the Mauritius by the French. Presented by Sir Walter Minto Townsend Farquhar to the British Museum', *Journal of the Royal Geographical Society of London* 20 (1850), 75–88.

Table 1.1 *British intervention in Madagascar, 1811–20*

Year	Event
1811	Capture of French trading posts at Tamatave and Foulepointe, northeast Madagascar – abandoned due to malaria
1814–15	Attempt to establish a settlement in Antongil Bay, northeast Madagascar – settlers massacred by Malagasy
1815	Temporary British occupation of Tamatave and Foulepointe
1815–16	Mauritian settlers attempt to establish plantations near Tamatave – failure (malaria/cyclones?)
1816	Second attempt to establish a colony in Antongil Bay – abandoned due to malaria
1816	Embassy to Imerina returns with two Merina princes for education in Mauritius
1816–17	Embassies to Imerina
1817	Draft treaty with Radama, king of Imerina – General Hall, interim governor of Mauritius refuses ratification
1818	LMS mission to northeast coast fails due to malaria
1820	Britanno-Merina treaty grants right of settlement in Madagascar to British subjects and provides for training of Malagasy Youths in Mauritius and Britain

Note: See Campbell, 'Imperial Rivalry in the Western Indian Ocean'.

In late 1815, Farquhar attempted to found a British settlement at Port Louquez (Lokia), in northeast Madagascar, under the leadership of two army officers, Birch (or Burch) and Bleuman, who renamed the locality Port Farquhar, in the governor's honour. However, after Birch, an inexperienced young man, struck 'Chichipi', a Malagasy chief who had complained about not having received the customary gift of blue cloth, Chichipi's subjects massacred the colonists. Another attempt to settle Port Loquez in 1816 under army lieutenant [Bibye/Bybye] Le Sage (d. 1843), accompanied by British naval lieutenant Vine and a party of volunteer Mauritian Créole soldiers, was abandoned due to continued local hostility and the ravages of malaria which, endemic on the Malagasy lowlands, generally killed about 80 per cent of Europeans who attempted to settle in the island and incapacitated the rest.[45]

In April 1816, acting on reports that the interior of Madagascar possessed a healthy, malaria-free climate, Farquhar sent an embassy to Radama, king of Imerina.[46] The embassy was headed by Jacques Chardenoux (or Chardenaux) (b. c.1766), a former trader to the island, who was instructed to inspect the prospects for a British settlement. Chardenoux, who was well known to

---

[45] Ellis, *History of Madagascar*, vol. 2, 109–11; Samuel Pasfield Oliver, *Madagascar: An Historical and Descriptive Account of the Island and Its Former Dependencies* (London: Macmillan, 1886), vol. 1, 27–9.

[46] Oliver, *Madagascar*, vol. 1, 222–3; James Sibree, 'Imerina, the Central Province of Madagascar, and the Capital, Antananarivo', *Proceedings of the Royal Geographical Society and Monthly Record of Geography* 14.11 (1892), 742.

Radama, opened discussions for a possible treaty with Britain that would include a ban on slave exports, and invited the king to send young members of his court to Mauritius to receive an English education. Radama appeared sympathetic to the idea of an alliance on condition that, if he prohibited slave exports, the British would provide the means to develop alternative export earnings. The two agreed in principle and engaged in a blood-brotherhood ceremony. Chardenoux returned to Mauritius in August 1816, accompanied by three Merina emissaries, Rampola, Ramanohy, and Ratsilikaina; three ministers of Jean René (c.1773–1826), ruler of the main east coast port of Tamatave; and 'two southern chiefs, and a numerous suite' comprising thirty people.[47]

The Malagasy embassy presented Farquhar with gifts comprising mainly 'botanical and other specimens of the products and manufactures of the island, but curiously also a female dwarf, extraordinarily diminutive, being of a race peculiar to the interior of Madagascar'.[48] This may have been in response to Farquhar's request to confirm the reports of Flacourt and others such as Louis-Laurent de Féderbe (1728–1778), governor of Fort Dauphin from 1768 to 1770, of the existence of a pygmy race called Quimos (or Kimos), said to inhabit southern central Madagascar, at latitude 22°S, about 290 km northwest of Fort Dauphin. The Quimos were said to be itinerant, lighter coloured than most Malagasy, with woolly hair and very long arms. In addition, they were excellent craftsmen, and ferocious in defence.[49] There was also widespread belief in forest-dwelling pygmy groups, including the Kalanoro of eastern Madagascar, and the Vazimba and the Mikea in the west of the island.[50]

Delighted at Radama's positive reaction to his first embassy, Farquhar despatched another in November 1816 led by Le Sage. Amongst other things, Le Sage was instructed to discuss with Radama the possibility that 'A boy of

---

[47] Chardenaux, 'Rapport', Port Louis, 13 Sep. 1816, 'Secret', National Archives, Mauritius (hereafter NAM), HB 7; Charles Guillain, *Documents sur l'histoire, la géographie et le commerce de la partie occidentale de Madagascar* (Paris: Imprimerie Royale, 1845), 51; Oliver, *Madagascar*, vol. 1, 29.

[48] *Morning Chronicle* (1 Jan. 1817).

[49] Oliver, *Madagascar*, vol. 2, 34; Samuel Pasfield Oliver, 'Has There Been a Race of Pygmies in Madagascar', *AAMM* 15 (1891), 257–72; Alfred Grandidier and Guillaume Grandidier, *Histoire physique, naturelle et politique de Madagascar* (Paris: Imprimerie nationale, 1908), vol. 4, book 1, 289, 652–4; see also Charles Benevent, 'Notes sur les Kimosy', *BAM* 4 (1905–6), 101–3; André Coppalle, 'Les kimos de Madagascar' [c.1826] *BAM* 8 (1910), 65–7; Antoine Maurice Fontoynont, 'La légend des Kimosy', *BAM* 7 (1909), 51–9.

[50] Richard Baron, 'A Malagasy Forest', *AAMM* 14 (1890), 210–1; Henri Dubois, *Monographie des Betsileo* (Paris: Institut d'ethnologie, 1938), 1119–22; Louis Molet, 'Aperçu sur un groupe nomade de la forêt épineuse des Mikea', *BAM* 36 (1958), 241–3. In addition, there was early speculation as to the existence of other groups of pygmies, such as the 'Tarisbos' and the 'Ola-ala', while in the second half of the nineteenth century the German explorer Carle Liche added to such speculation in the West about Malagasy pygmies with his mythical story of the pygmy Mkodos and a man-eating tree – Oliver, 'Has There Been a Race of Pygmies', 270–1; Anon, 'Man-Eating Tree of Madagascar', *AAMM* 5 (1881), 91–3.

Figure 1.2 James Hastie (1786–1826)
Source: Postcard (source unknown).

9 or 10 years old ... live with the King' and that a school be founded in
Imerina.[51] However, in his haste to secure an agreement with Radama,
Farquhar failed to heed the prevalent advice against travelling to Madagascar
during the rainy season. Of Le Sage's thirty-two-strong party – which included
about twenty artillery men, a surgeon, and two interpreters – Jolicoeur and
Verkey, a slave – twenty-seven died of malaria within six months. Only one of
the survivors remained healthy.[52] Le Sage introduced a number of seeds,
including cotton, pepper, and coffee, but attempts to cultivate them failed due
to a lack of 'husbandry' and appropriate soil. Suffering badly from malarial
bouts, Le Sage soon returned to Mauritius.[53]

Farquhar learned his lesson, and he despatched a third mission to Imerina
in June 1817, during the next dry, and thus healthy, season. It was led by James
Hastie (1786–1826; see Figure 1.2). Born into a Quaker family in Cork,
Ireland, in 1786, Hastie had from an early age thirsted for adventure and,
despite having lost his sight in one eye because of a childhood accident, enlisted
in the British Army. He served in India with the 56th regiment of foot during the

[51] Farquhar, Memorandum to Le Sage, Port Louis, 6 Nov. 1816, HB 7, NAM.
[52] Locke Lewis, 'An Account of the Ovahs, a race of people residing in the Interior of Madagascar:
with a Sketch of their Country, Appearance, Dress, Language, &c.', *Journal of the Royal
Geographical Society* 5 (1835), 237; Campbell, *David Griffiths*, 581, 623.
[53] Le Sage, 'Mission to Madagascar' (1816), 35, Colonial Office (hereafter CO) 167/34, National
Archives, Kew (hereafter NAK); Campbell, *David Griffiths*, 583.

Second Anglo-Maratha War (1803–5), and in 1815, by which time he had risen to the rank of sergeant, Hastie's regiment was posted to Port Louis, Mauritius. There, in September 1816, he distinguished himself in saving Government House in the capital from burning down:

On 25 September 1816 a fire broke out in a government warehouse in Port Louis close to a gunpowder depot. When a volunteer was called for to put out the fire, Hastie offered himself. He drenched a blanket with water and covered himself with it; then using his mouth, he carried water in a bucket, climbed onto an already burning joist, and threw the water onto the flames. After emptying the bucket, he threw it down attached to a rope so that more water could be put in it and remained there until the fire had been extinguished. By risking his life, he saved the city and many human lives.[54]

This exploit led Farquhar to recommend Hastie for a commission and appoint him preceptor to the two Merina princes who Radama had sent to receive British government instruction on Mauritius (see Chapter 3).[55]

In mid-1817, the princes returned to Madagascar with Hastie. On landing at Tamatave, they were met by Radama, who, at the head of an army of 30,000 men, had just established Merina control over the major trade route linking the highland interior to the northeast coast.[56] Only the arrival of Hastie aboard a British warship deterred the king from annexing the port. On 9 July 1817, René acknowledged Radama's suzerainty and signed a 'Treaty of Amity and Alliance offensive and defensive between His Majesty RADAMA King of Ova [i.e. Imerina] and Dependencies on the one part and His Elder Brother JOHN RENE King of TAMATAVE and Dependencies on the other part.'[57] Radama's boldness in marching on Tamatave so impressed Farquhar that he altered his conception of the Merina role within the envisaged British colonization of Madagascar. Thus, he announced Radama to be 'a most powerful and intelligent, but still semi barbarous and superstitious Monarch' who might hold 'the destinies of the vast, populous, and fertile, but ill-treated Island of Madagascar entirely in his hands.'[58] However, he underlined to Radama his protectorate status and emphasized that 'this happy and powerful and flourishing island of Mauritius is but as one drop of rain compared with the great ocean, when

---

[54] François Callet (ed.), *Histoire des Rois: Tantaran ny Andriana* vols. 1–4 (Tananarive: Editions de la Librairie de Madagascar, 1974) and vol. 5 (Antananarivo: Académie Malgache, 1978) (pages of Malagasy original numbered consecutively throughout; hereafter *HdR*), 1081.

[55] J. P. Grant (ed.), *Memoir and Correspondence of Mrs. Grant of Laggan* (London: Longman, Brown, Green, and Longmans, 1844), vol. 1, 192, fn.

[56] James Hastie to Griffiths, Port Louis, 18 Feb. 1821, Madagascar Incoming Letters (hereafter MIL) B.1 F.2 J.B, School of Oriental & African Studies, Council for World Mission Archives (hereafter SOAS/CWM); *HdR*, 1081.

[57] Raombana, 'Histoires' (1853), Archives de l'Académie Malgache, Antananarivo, Madagascar (hereafter RH), 89; see also Pye, 'A summary (6–14 Jun. 1817)', 90–5, CO 167/34, NAK; Hastie, 'Diary' (1817), CO 167/34, NAK; Le Sage, 'Mission to Madagascar' (1816), 33, CO 167/34, NAK.

[58] Farquhar to Stanfell, Port Louis, 7 and 22 Aug. 1817, 97–9, 103–4, CO 167/34, NAK.

considered as a part of the wealth and power and glory of my Sovereign, whose friendship I will obtain for you.'[59]

On reaching Antananarivo in August 1817, Hastie replaced Le Sage in negotiations with Radama. Farquhar instructed Hastie that he would send HMS *Phaeton* to Tamatave towards the end of September that year and that he anticipated that Radama would be there to sign the treaty and would appoint two Malagasy envoys to accompany the treaty to London: a Merina ambassador – Farquhar considered Rampola to be a good choice – and a scribe capable of writing Arabic.[60] In the draft treaty, duly signed in Tamatave on 23 October 1817 by Thomas Robert Pye (fl. 1808–1836), a naval lieutenant serving as chief British agent in Madagascar, Radama pledged to ban the slave export trade – much to the disgruntlement of many of the Merina elite who had become rich on the traffic in slaves. Farquhar upgraded Radama, naming him king of all Madagascar. Further, he promised Radama military aid to subjugate the other peoples of the island, technical assistance to promote the development of legitimate exports, and compensation (called the 'Equivalent') for the ban on slave exports. He also insisted that Radama accept a resident British agent at the Merina court.[61]

The draft treaty was, on the Merina side, written in *Sorabe* (Malagasy written in Arabic script), probably by Andriamahazonoro (d. 1838) and Ratsilikaina, two Taimoro from the southeast of the island where scribes traditionally wrote on handmade paper and Ravinala leaves.[62] It is also worthy of note, in the context of the ban on the slave trade, that Farquhar instructed the first official expedition to Madagascar to assess the potential for the employment there of Indian convict workers, particularly in silk weaving, and dyeing,[63] and assigned convicts to accompany all subsequent missions. For example, in 1816–17, Hastie took with him to Madagascar at least eighteen such convicts, possibly as many as thirty-one. From 1815 to 1817, Farquhar granted various agents he sent on missions to Madagascar a minimum of twelve government slaves.[64]

Hastie returned to Mauritius with the 1817 draft treaty, which Farquhar took to Britain for ratification, unaccompanied by any Malagasy representation. On leaving, he ordered Hastie to return to Imerina: 'you will proceed to Madagascar with the Ministers and suite of King Radama, as soon as

[59] Farquhar to Radama I, Port Louis, 9 Aug. 1817, CO 167/34, NAK; see also Farquhar to Stanfell, 22 Aug. 1817; Ellis, *History of Madagascar*, vol. 2, 140–2, 163–5, 243; Jean Valette, 'Correspondance de Jean René à Sir Robert Farquhar', *BAM* 45.2 (1967), 71–98.

[60] Barry to Hastie, Port Louis, 9 Aug. 1817, HB 13, NAM.   [61] See Appendix 1.

[62] J. T. Hardyman, 'Malagasy overseas from the sixteenth to the nineteenth Centuries', in 'Malagasy Youths and RATEFY TO Gt Britain 1820' PPMS63, J. T. Hardyman file 43, Bx.7, SOAS/CWM; W. E. Cousins, 'Characteristics of the Malagasy Language', *AAMM* 18 (1894), 235; Campbell, *David Griffiths*, 627.

[63] [Farquhar], instructions for Mr Chochot, Port Louis, 23 May 1813, HB 13, NAM.

[64] Campbell, *Travels of Robert Lyall*, 243–5.

a passage can be procured, where you will consider yourself as the Chief Officer of His Excellency's Government.' He was to give Radama the 'Equivalent', comprising articles of 'the first quality'. Moreover, his pay – which as second assistant to the agent for Madagascar had been $150 per month – was from 20 June 1817, the date of his appointment as chief British agent in Madagascar, to be raised to $200 per month.[65] As soon as he reached London, in early 1818, Farquhar met the London Missionary Society directors to discuss the Madagascar mission.[66] However, within a few months, all Farquhar's aspirations had been crushed – for Gage John Hall (1775–1854), his temporary replacement, repudiated the Merina alliance and, abolishing the position of British agent in Madagascar, recalled Hastie.[67]

The London Missionary Society (LMS)

The LMS was founded in 1795,[68] part of an intense upswell of British evangelical interest in converting the heathen in the British Isles and abroad that also extended to Jews and, notably from the time of the French Revolutionary and Napoleonic Wars (1792–1815), to Catholics.[69]

Initially, the LMS supported the view of Anglican evangelical Thomas Haweis (1734–1820) that their overseas missionary endeavour should be concentrated upon heathens 'in an inferior state of knowledge and civilization'.[70] In this spirit, a mission was despatched in 1796 to the Pacific, a field that had caught the public eye after the three voyages of James Cook (1728–1799) between 1768 and 1779, and another mission was contemplated for Africa.[71] However, following the failure of the first South Seas mission, David Bogue (1750–1825), a Scottish evangelical and one of the society's founders, persuaded the LMS to back his viewpoint that missionaries required

---

[65] Barry to Hastie, Port Louis, 15 Nov. 1817, HB 13, NAM.

[66] 'Madagascar', in L'Aristarque Français (18 Apr. 1820).

[67] Barry to Hastie 'Assistant Government Agent, Madagascar', Port Louis, 2 Jun. 1818, HB 7, NAM; see also Barry to Hastie 'Assistant Government Agent, Madagascar', Port Louis, 11 Feb. 1818, HB 7, NAM.

[68] Initially called the Missionary Society, it quickly became referred to as the London Missionary Society, which was adopted as its second title at its general meeting on 14 May 1818; [LMS], *Report of the Directors to the Twenty Fourth General Meeting of the Missionary Society, usually called the London Missionary Society, on Thursday, May 14, 1818* (London: Williams & Co., 1818), 50.

[69] E.g. in the post-Napoleonic era, the Welsh started sending missionaries to Brittany in an attempt to convert Breton-speaking Catholics, a mission that David Griffiths, LMS missionary to Madagascar, contemplated joining; Campbell, *David Griffiths*, 161; Jean-Yves Carluer, 'John Jenkins 1', http://protestantsbretons.fr/protestants/john-jenkins-1 (accessed 15.04.21).

[70] Thomas Haweis, quoted in Johannes Van Den Berg, *Constrained by Jesus' Love: An Enquiry into the Motives of the Missionary Awakening in Great Britain in the Period between 1698 and 1815* (Kampen: J. H. Kok, 1956), 130.

[71] Van Den Berg, *Constrained by Jesus' Love*, 130–1.

special training and that the society should pay greater attention to non-Christian societies that possessed a higher civilization. As director of Gosport Academy, which gave specialist missionary training to LMS candidates, Bogue followed Enlightenment thinking in teaching that there existed a clear global hierarchy of civilization. At the top came Western European Christian societies, followed by literate monotheistic societies, namely Jews and Muslims. Next came non-monotheistic societies that had attained a high level of literary and technical achievement, such as the Chinese, the Japanese, and the Hindus. These were followed by less-civilized non-literate pagan societies, such as the indigenous 'Indians' of the Americas, and finally the barbaric dark-skinned pagan peoples of the South Seas, New Guinea, and sub-Saharan Africa.[72] He subsumed these into two broad categories. The more civilized group were distinguished by populations that were large, spoke a common language, possessed a literature, enjoyed widespread literacy, encouraged mental 'improvement', and promoted significant exchange with other peoples.[73] By contrast, less civilized societies were characterized by small populations and geographical size, minority languages with restricted linguistic range, illiteracy, lack of intellectual activity, limited domestic interactions, and minimal foreign relations and influence.[74] The more civilized mission fields should be reserved for ordained men with a missionary vocation who 'possess superior talents' and 'whose understandings have received considerable enlargement by a previous attention for a longer term to the sources of knowledge' that thereby endow them with 'a high degree of intellectual improvement.'[75] Once in the field, they might apply with advantage not only their classical training but also the 'Useful sciences Mathematics, Natural Philosophy, Geometry, Chemistry &c.'[76] Missionary candidates for more barbaric countries should comprise either industrious students of comparatively poor education, who had nevertheless graduated from the missionary seminary to become ordained, or artisans 'unqualified for the higher branches of Missionary duty',[77] who could

---

[72] David Bogue, 'Lecture 12', People File 18, Bx.10, PPMS63, J. T. Hardyman Papers, SOAS/CWM; see also Emmanuel Chukwudi Eze (ed.), *Race and the Enlightenment: A Reader* (Malden, MA: Blackwell, 2009); Naomi Zack (ed.), *The Oxford Handbook of Philosophy and Race* (New York: Oxford University Press, 2019).

[73] David Bogue, 'Lecture 12,' People File 18, Bx.10, PPMS63, J. T. Hardyman Papers, SOAS/CWM.

[74] David Bogue, 'Lecture 12,' People File 18, Bx.10, PPMS63, J. T. Hardyman Papers, SOAS/CWM.

[75] Report of the committee appointed to 'draw up the outline of a plan for Missionary Instruction' [Meeting of Directors], St Paul's Coffee House, 5 May 1800, LMS Board Meetings, SOAS/CWM.

[76] David Bogue, 'Lecture 20,' People File 18, Bx.10, PPMS63, J. T. Hardyman Papers, SOAS/CWM.

[77] Report of the Committee appointed to 'draw up the outline of a plan for Missionary Instruction,' [Meeting of Directors], St Paul's Coffee House, 5 May 1800, LMS Board Meetings, SOAS/CWM.

instruct in agriculture and the 'Common arts Carpenter, masons, Black-smiths, weaver &c.'[78]

From the outset, Bogue enthusiastically supported the idea of a mission to Madagascar, which the LMS classified as part of Southern Africa.[79] He presented to the first and second LMS general meetings, on 25 September 1795 and on 13 May 1796, a memoir written by Andrew Burn (1742–1814), a fellow evangelical Scot and a retired soldier, advocating the establishment of a mission in Saint Augustin Bay, in southwest Madagascar.[80] In 1799, the LMS sent John Theodosius Van Der Kemp (1747–1811) to establish in South Africa a missionary endeavour that he aspired to extend to Madagascar. From 1805–6, when Van Der Kemp manumitted and married sixteen-year-old Sara van de Kaap/Sara Janse (1792–1861), the daughter of a Malagasy slave woman, this aspiration deepened.[81] In October 1811, following the British capture of the Mascarenes, Van Der Kemp heard from Mauritius that 'the Governor (Farquhar) was very desirous that a Mission sh[oul]d be established on Madagascar that he would give a free passage to that island and also presents for the Chiefs &c.'[82] Van Der Kemp thus determined to found a mission in Madagascar.

Two months later, in December 1811, Van Der Kemp died while preparing to leave for Mauritius.[83] The LMS reacted in 1812 by sending John Campbell (1766–1840) to examine their South African enterprise and 'to obtain information respecting the island of Madagascar, to which the Society are anxious to send a mission'.[84] Campbell received most of his information about

---

[78] David Bogue, 'Lecture 20', People File 18, Bx.10, PPMS63, J. T. Hardyman Papers, SOAS/CWM.

[79] 'Rules for the examination of Missionaries, suggested by the Correspondent Committee, be adopted by this Society', Meeting of Directors, Castle & Falcon, 28 Sep. 1795, LMS Board Meetings, SOAS/CWM; David Bogue, 'Lecture 21', People File 18, Bx.10, PPMS63, J. T. Hardyman Papers, SOAS/CWM.

[80] David Bogue, 'Memoir on a Mission to Madagascar written by Capt. Byrn,' General Meeting, Castle & Falcon, 13 May 1796, 1795, LMS Board Meetings, SOAS/CWM; Olinthus Gregory, J. Handfield, and John Dyer (eds.), *Memoirs of the Life of the Late Major-General Andrew Burn of the Royal Marines: Collected from His Journals, with Copious Extracts from His Principal Works on Religious Subjects*, 2 vols (London: W. Winchester and Son, 1815); James T. Hardyman, 'The London Missionary Society and Madagascar: 1795–1818 – Part I: 1795–1811', *Omaly sy Anio* 7–8 (1978), 48–9.

[81] Van Der Kemp to LMS Directors, Bethelsdorp, October 1810, Meeting of Directors, [Old Swan Stairs], 18 Feb. 1811, LMS Board Minutes, SOAS/CWM.

[82] Van Der Kemp to LMS Directors, Cape Town, 26 Jul. 1811, in Meeting of Directors, [Old Swan Stairs], 18 Nov. 1811 and 3 Oct. 1811, in Meeting of Directors, [Old Swan Stairs], 27 Jan. 1812, LMS Board Minutes, SOAS/CWM.

[83] Emma Corsbie Hardcastle (ed.), *Memoir of Joseph Hardcastle, Esq., First Treasurer of the London Missionary Society: A Record of the Past for His Descendants* (London: Alex Macintosh, 1860), 124; see also Anon, 'Biographical Sketches: Dr. John Theodosius Vanderkemp', *Foreign Missionary Chronicle* (Jun. 1836), 81–2.

[84] John Campbell, *Travels in South Africa undertaken at the request of the Missionary Society* (London: Black and Parry, 1815), 18; see also Andrew C. Ross, 'Campbell, John', in Gerald

Madagascar from William Milne (1785–1822), an LMS missionary appointed to China who sailed there via the Cape and Mauritius in 1812–13. It was a minor miracle that Milne's account reached Campbell. Milne despatched the information in a letter, from Macao, entrusted to the *William Pitt*, an East Indiaman that sank some 240 km off South Africa with the loss of all lives. In his letter, one of a number wrapped in a wax cloth parcel that washed ashore in Algoa Bay and was salvaged, Milne suggested that the best locations for a European mission were in the south and southwest (Saint Augustin Bay) of Madagascar.[85]

In 1814, the LMS appointed Jean Joseph Le Brun (1789–1865) missionary to Mauritius with instructions to prepare the groundwork for an LMS mission to Madagascar.[86] Farquhar asked the LMS to authorize him to send Le Brun to Madagascar, 'promising him protection and assistance'.[87] The LMS instead considered sending to Madagascar George Thom (1789–1842), a missionary in Cape Town.[88] This plan evidently didn't work out, probably due to Thom's marriage in December 1814 to Christina Louisa Meyer (1785–1817).[89] This act ruled him out as a candidate for Madagascar to which, because of the notoriety of 'Madagascar fever' (malaria), the LMS initially determined to send only bachelor missionaries.[90] Subsequently, the LMS resolved to look for other candidates in Britain. They noted in May 1815, 'The Governor [Farquhar] having expressed his earnest desire to promote a mission to the island of Madagascar, the Directors have resolved to commence that work as soon as proper instruments can be obtained, with which they hope soon to be furnished.'[91] This message was reiterated at the LMS general meeting in May 1816,[92] but as they delayed appointing an agent, Farquhar grew impatient and in October that year asked Le Brun directly to accompany Le Sage's expedition to Imerina, due to leave the following month. Le Brun refused to

---

H. Anderson (ed.), *Biographical Dictionary of Christian Missions* (New York: Macmillan Reference USA, 1998), 112.

[85] Robert Philip, *The Life and Opinions of the Rev. William Milne, D.D., Missionary to China* (New York: D. Appleton, 1840), 88–9; Robert Philip, *The Life, Times, and Missionary Enterprises of the Rev. John Campbell* (London: John Snow, 1841), 408; 'Island of Madagascar', appendix 5, in Campbell, *Travels in South Africa*, 379.

[86] [LMS], *Report of the Directors to the Twenty First General Meeting of the Missionary Society, on Thursday, May 11, 1815* (London: J. Dennett, 1815), 6; Richard Lovett, *The History of the London Missionary Society* (London: Henry Frowde, 1899), vol. 1, 674.

[87] Farquhar to LMS, Isle of France, 20 Jun. 1814, in Meeting of Directors, 12 Dec. 1814, LMS Board Minutes, SOAS/CWM.

[88] Meeting of Directors, 28 Nov. 1814, LMS Board Minutes, SOAS/CWM.

[89] Thom to Directors, Cape Town, 27 Dec. 1814, in Meeting of Directors, 27 Mar. 1815, LMS Board Minutes, SOAS/CWM.

[90] Campbell, *David Griffiths*, 38–9.   [91] [LMS],*Report of the Directors* (1815), 6.

[92] [LMS], *Report of the Directors to the Twenty Second General Meeting of the Missionary Society, on Thursday, May 10, 1816* (London: S. McDowall, 1816), 34.

Farquhar's invitation – which was fortunate for him given the ravages caused by malaria to the members of the expedition.[93]

However, in October 1816, the LMS finally appointed two missionaries to Madagascar.[94] In accordance with their policy of reserving the most cultivated and educated missionary candidates for the more civilized pagan realms, such as China and India, and less refined candidates for 'barbarous' regions of the world, the LMS selected for Madagascar, an uncivilized island, David Jones (1796–1841), a native Welsh-speaker of West Walian peasant origins, and Stephen Laidler (1789–1873), an Englishman who came from an ill-educated and impoverished background.[95] They were scheduled to leave Britain in January 1817, but their departure was delayed when Laidler requested to continue his missionary studies at Gosport. He was replaced by Thomas Bevan (1795–1819), who was of rural Welsh-speaking stock, born into a peasant family of 'low circumstances' in West Wales.[96]

Jones and Bevan refused to accept the LMS directive that they go to Madagascar as single men. Facing potential competition from the Methodists, who were investigating the possibility of establishing a mission in Madagascar, the LMS directors relented. The Welshmen and their wives reached Mauritius in July 1818, only to discover that Farquhar, their promised benefactor, had left for London with the draft Britanno-Merina treaty. Hall, the interim governor, refused to honour the draft treaty and broke off relations with Radama. Thus deterred from their intended destination of Imerina, Jones and Bevan attempted to establish a mission under the patronage of Jean René on the northeast coast of Madagascar – with disastrous consequences.[97] In August 1818, Jones and Bevan sailed to Tamatave, leaving their pregnant wives on Mauritius.[98] Hall sent with the missionaries two government slaves as interpreters and two army medical officers 'who understood the treatment of the Malagasy fever' – Dr W. A. Burke (appointed chief of the medical department and physician general on Mauritius in May 1817) and Dr William Sibbald (1789–1853).[99] In Tamatave, the missionaries received an invitation from

---

[93] Jean Le Brun, 30 Oct. [1816], in 'Mémoire Journalière' 2 Jul.–10 Dec. 1816, Madagascar. Journals: Madagascar and Mauritius 1. 1816–1824, SOAS/CWM; Farquhar, Memorandum to Le Sage, Port Louis, 6 Nov. 1816, HB 7, NAM.

[94] Meeting of Directors, 28 Oct. 1816, LMS Board Minutes, SOAS/CWM.

[95] Campbell, *David Griffiths*, 192–3, 588–9.

[96] Meeting of Directors, 13 Jan. 1817, LMS Board Minutes, SOAS/CWM; Campbell, *David Griffiths*, 591.

[97] Oliver, *Madagascar*, vol. 1, 31–2.

[98] Thomas and Mary Bevan [to parents], Falmouth, 4 Mar. 1818, 11646B, Archifdy Llyfrgell Genedlaethol Cymru (Archives of the National Library of Wales), Aberystwyth (hereafter ALGC); [LMS], *Report of the Directors to the Twenty Fifth General Meeting of the Missionary Society, usually called the London Missionary Society, on Thursday, May 13, 1819* (London: F. Westley, 1819), 84.

[99] Oliver, *Madagascar*, vol. 1, 31–2; see also John Rouillard (ed.), *A Collection of the Laws of Mauritius and its Dependencies*, vol. 3 (Mauritius: L. Channell, 1866), 235; Hastie to Griffiths,

Radama to settle in Imerina 'but on account of its distance, the badness of the roads, and the great expense which would have been incurred by the journey, they respectfully declined'.[100] Their refusal to go to Imerina was probably due to political pragmatism, for by 1818 René appeared to be the leading political authority in Madagascar. René was born in Fort Dauphin in about 1773 to an Antanosy female slave and Bouchet, a Mauritian Creole agent of the Compagnie des Indes. He was raised and educated on Réunion or Mauritius before returning to Madagascar, where a devoted guard of 100 Africans helped him seize Tamatave from its ruler, Tsiatana. René subsequently assumed the title of *mpanjakamena* ('red king' – red being the colour of royalty and *mpanjaka mena* meaning, symbolically in this instance, a sovereign both of whose parents were of royal line)[101] and placed Fiche (or Fisatra), his half-brother, as chief of Ivondrona, a settlement a short distance to the south of Tamatave. This enabled René to control the main east coast port and its hinterland. René, who spoke fluent Malagasy and French, sometimes 'put on a Malagasy dress, a cashmir for a simbon [i.e. loincloth] and a kind of muslin tunic' and at other times he 'dressed up like an elegant creole of the period' and 'rode beautiful horses'.[102] André Coppalle (1797–1845), a French painter summoned to Madagascar in 1825 to execute a portrait of Radama, described René in July 1825, six months before his death, as possessing 'a highly bizarre facial appearance; his large head, flat on the top; his patchy red colouring, hollow cheeks, sunken eyes half hidden under thick eyebrows, and moustache like a raptor give him a more savage air than any other native of Madagascar'.[103]

René persuaded Bevan and Jones to start a school, on the Lancastrian plan, at Mananarezo, near Ivondrona, for ten boys, all sons of local chiefs. The pupils included Berora (c.1798–1831), son of Fiche.[104] Shortly afterwards, the missionaries returned to Mauritius for their families. Some Mauritians had warned Bevan and Jones that they were 'going amongst a sort of stealing, poisoning, murdering and savage people who were not looked upon better than stupid wicked brutes'.[105] However, it was malaria that undermined their mission:

Port Louis, 18 Feb. 1821, MIL B.1 F.2 J.B, SOAS/CWM; [War Office], *The Army List for September 1818* ([London: War Office, 1818]), 71

[100] [LMS], *Report of the Directors* (1819), 85.

[101] Henri Lavondès, *Bekoropoka: Quelques aspects de la vie familiale et sociale d'un village malgache* (Berlin: De Gruyter, 1967), ch. 5.

[102] Frappaz (1939) and Siegrist (1937), quoted in Manassé Esoavelomandroso, 'The "Malagasy Creoles" of Tamatave in the 19th Century', *Diogenes* 28 (1980), 58–9,see also 52–3.

[103] André Coppalle, 'Voyage dans l'intérieur de Madagascar et à la capitale du Roi Radama pendant les années 1825 et 1826' (Port Louis, Mauritius, 1827), *BAM* 7–8 (1909–10), 12.

[104] Jones to LMS, Mauritius, 10 Nov. 1818, in 'David Jones: Copies of Letters 1818–39', Madagascar Odds, Bx.4, SOAS/CWM; [LMS], *Report of the Directors* (1819), 85; Ellis, *History of Madagascar*, vol. 2, 208–9.

[105] Jones, Mauritius, 10 Nov. 1820, in 'David Jones: Copies of Letters 1818–39', Madagascar Odds Bx.4, SOAS/CWM.

Jones returned to Tamatave with his family on 24 November 1818 but by the end of the year his child and wife were dead, and he was desperately ill. Bevan arrived with his wife and child in Tamatave on 6 January 1819. By 3 February 1819, all had succumbed to malaria.[106]

In early 1819, following the collapse of the LMS mission, René negotiated an alliance with a French agent, Sylvain Roux (1765–1823), a Mauritian Creole, later French governor of Sainte Marie (1821–3), who called at Tamatave on the French frigate *Golo*, under the command of Baron (Ange René Armand) Mackau (1788–1855). Roux arranged to take Berora, 'Mandit Sara', the child of a local chief's daughter, and Glond, a Portuguese-Indian Creole living on Mauritius,[107] to Paris, where their education was paid for initially by the Ministry of the Marine and from 1830 by the Ministry for the Colonies. Berora went on to receive military training in France, before returning to Tamatave where he died in 1831.[108] The willingness of French authorities to pay for the education of children of Malagasy chiefs in France undoubtedly influenced future plans of Farquhar, the LMS, and Radama.

Radama

Radama I (b. c.1791–5, d. 1828; see Figure 1.3), also known as Lahidama,[109] king of Imerina, played a crucial role in the Madagascar Youths project.[110] Radama's father, Andrianampoinimerina (c.1745–1810), described as 'rather

---

[106] [LMS], *Report of the Directors* (1819), 87; Jones, Madagascar, 17 Apr. 1819, in 'David Jones: Copies of Letters 1818–39', Madagascar Odds Bx.4, SOAS/CWM; *Christian Keepsake and Missionary Annual* (1835), 144.

[107] In 1811, on the capitulation of Tamatave to the British, Glond had been permitted to take ten slaves he owned from Madagascar to Mauritius – 'Noirs declares par Mr. Sylvain Roux', in A. Barry, Avis, Port Louis, Isle Maurice, 10 Aug. 1811, Papers on the subject of the Slave Trade at the Cape of Good Hope, and at the Isle of France, Enclosure 5, Appendix 13 (15 Feb. 1813), *Journals of the House of Commons* 68 (1812–13), 894.

[108] Le Sage, 'Mission' (1816), 26–7, CO 167/34, NAK; Hastie, 'Diary' (1817), 130, CO 167/34, NAK; Hastie, 'Diary' (1820), 466–7, CO 167/50, NAK; Hastie to Farquhar, Tamatave, 11 Sep. 1820, HB 13, NAM; Abel Hugo, *France Pittoresque ou description pittoresque, topographique et statistique des départements et colonies de la France*, vol. 3 (Paris: Delloye, 1835), 320; Ellis, *History of Madagascar*, vol. 2, 210–11; Oliver, *Madagascar*, vol. 1, 150; Henri Le Chartier and G. Pellerin, *Madagascar depuis sa découverte jusqu'à nos jours* (Paris: Jouvet, 1888), 26; Samuel Pasfield Oliver, 'General Hall and the Export Slave Trade from Madagascar: A Statement and a Vindication', *AAMM* 12 (1888), 473–9; L. Aujas, 'Notes sur l'histoire des Betsimisaraka', *BAM* 4 (1905–6), 108–11; Raymond Decary, 'Documents historiques relatifs à l'établissement français de Sainte-Marie sous la Restauration', *BAM* 13 (1930), 59; Decary, 'La reddition de Tamatave', 59–60; Campbell, *Economic History*, 69.

[109] Susan Kus and Victor Raharijaona, 'The 'Dirty' Material and Symbolic Work of 'State' Building in Madagascar: From Indigenous State-Crafting to Indigenous Empire Building to External Colonial Imposition and Indigenous Insurrection', in F. G. Richard (ed.), *Materializing Colonial Encounters* (New York: Springer, 2015), 215.

[110] Oliver, *Madagascar*, vol. 1, 222–3; Sibree, 'Imerina', 742;.

Figure 1.3 Radama I (r. 1810–28)
Source: Campbell, *David Griffiths*, 502.

tall, bony and sinewy',[111] is popularly considered to have been the founding
father of the nineteenth-century Merina kingdom. One of a number of contending princes in the Merina civil wars of the late eighteenth century, he staged
a coup d'état in 1787 to become king of Ambohimanga, which secured for him
domination of northern Imerina, the largest market for slaves exported to the
Mascarenes in exchange for gunpowder, arms, and specie. This in turn laid the
basis for military success against rival princes and his domination of all Imerina
by about 1794. He subsequently established his administrative capital in
Antananarivo and set about raiding neighbouring highland provinces for both
slaves and cattle, which were also in high demand in the Mascarenes. Under
his rule, Imerina became the economic centre of Madagascar and attracted
significant numbers of foreign traders, Swahili traders from the northwest

---

[111] Raombana, quoted in Thomas Lord, 'The Early History of Imerina based upon a Native
Account', *AAMM* 24 (1900), 475.

coast, and European and Créole traders from the northeast coast. When Andrianampoinimerina died in 1810, he was succeeded by Radama.[112]

There is dispute as to the year of Radama's birth. Raombana, court secretary under Ranavalona I, who as a child had known Radama, asserted that he was born in 1782, while Europeans familiar with the king considered that he was born sometime between 1791 and 1795.[113] Radama was one of the younger children of Andrianampoinimerina, who had many wives (if not the ritual 'twelve' royal spouses), and numerous offspring. Rambolamasoandro (d. 1828), Radama's mother, enjoyed sexual liberty and had several children by different men, including two half-brothers of Radama, who, when he became king, sent them to Mauritius for a year to be educated (see Chapter 3).[114] In c.1800–4, Andrianampoinimerina summoned Andriamahazonoro (d. 1838) and Ratsilikaina, two Taimoro sages from the southeast of the island, to inaugurate a palace school where, by 1817, they had taught *Sorabe* to five or six royal children, including Radama.[115] By 1820, according to Jones, Radama had also mastered the French language.[116] This was probably Créole French, which Radama had learned early in life from the Mascarene slave traders who visited Imerina every dry season between May and October.

Radama was the favourite son of Andrianampoinimerina, who, to ensure he inherited the throne, had his eldest son, Rabodolahy, killed, rejected the claims of his second eldest boy, Rakotovahiny, on the grounds that he had failed as a military leader, and had a third son, Ramavolahy, and many of his

---

[112] Regis Rajemisa-Raolison, *Dictionnaire historique et géographique* (Fianarantsoa: Librairie Ambozontany, 1966), 55–9; Campbell, *Economic History*, 18–58.

[113] Griffiths to William Griffith, [Antananarivo, 1821], 19157E, ALGC; Carayon, *Histoire de l'établissement français*, 93; Charles Theodore Hilsenberg and Wenceslaus Bojer, 'A Sketch of the Province of Emerina, in the Island of Madagascar, and of the Huwa, its Inhabitants; written during a Year's Residence' (1823), in William Jackson Hooker (ed.), *Botanical Miscellany; containing Figures and Descriptions of such Plants as recommend themselves by their Novelty, Rarity, or History, or by the Uses to which they are applied in the Arts, in Medicine, and in Domestic Economy together with occasional Botanical Notes and Information*, vol. 3 (London: John Murray, 1833), 268; Joseph John Freeman and David Johns, *A Narrative of the Persecution of the Christians in Madagascar with details of the Escape of the Six Christian Refugees now in England* (London: John Snow, 1840), 7; RH, 76, 175; Coppalle, 'Voyage dans l'intérieur de Madagascar', 31; Francis Riaux, 'Introduction: Notice historique sur Madagascar' (1862), in Ida Pfeiffer, *Voyage à Madagascar* (Paris: Librarie Hachette, 1881), xvi; Jean-Pierre Razafy-Andriamihaingo, *La Geste éphémère de Ranavalona Ire: L'expedition deplomatique malgache en Europe 1836–1837* (Paris: L'Harmattan, 1997), 15.

[114] RH, 61; Raombana, 'Annales' (1854), Archives de l'Académie Malgache, Antananarivo, Madagascar (hereafter RA), B1, Livre 10–11, vol. 8, 24.

[115] Hardyman, 'Malagasy Overseas', in 'Malagasy Youths and RATEFY TO Gt Britain 1820' PPMS63, J. T. Hardyman file 43, Bx.7, SOAS/CWM; Cousins, 'Characteristics of the Malagasy Language', 235; Campbell, *David Griffiths*, 627.

[116] Jones, quoted in the *Manchester Times and Gazette* (2 Jun. 1832).

Table 1.2 *Radama's wives*

Inherited from Andrianampoinimerina:	11. Ramiangaly
1. Rasendrasoazokiny	12. Ravoandriana.
2. Rasendrasoazandriny	
3. Rasamana	**Arranged by Andrianampoinimerina**
4. Ramatoaramisa	13. Ranavalona: senior wife
5. Ravolamisa	
6. Razafitrimo (4–6 were sisters)	**Chosen by Radama:**
7. Rabodomirahalahy	14. Rasalimo (Sakalava Menabe princess)
8. Rafostsirahety	15. Ramoma
9. Razafinamboa	16. Ravo
10. Rasoamananoro	

Source: HdR, 1086.

allies assassinated for allegedly plotting a coup.[117] While they were still children, Andrianampoinimerina arranged for Radama to be married to Rabodo/Ramavo (c.1780–1861), daughter of Andriantsalama, a close ally of Andrianampoinimerina.[118] Rabodo thus became Radama's first and senior wife. After Radama succeeded to the throne in 1810, he followed royal tradition and, with the exception of his mother, Rambolamasoandro, married all his father's wives.[119] He also married a further three women (see Table 1.2).[120] Radama divorced at least two of his wives,[121] two or three of his other wives lived until at least 1880.[122] Radama also maintained in Antananarivo palace a harem of select slave concubines with whom he spent considerable time.[123]

In the 1820s, Radama was described by Aristide Coroller (1799/1802–1835), a close counsellor, as about 1.6 m tall, 'slender and small in his limbs

---

[117] Freeman and Johns, *Narrative of the Persecution of the Christians*, 8–9; RH, 71–3; Thomas Trotter Matthews, *Notes of Nine Years' Mission Work in the Province of Vonizongo, North West, Madagascar, with Historical Introduction* (London: Hodder and Stoughton, 1881), 7; Jean Valette, 'Contribution à l 'étude de la succession d'Andrianampoinimerina', *Revue française d'histoire d'outre-mer* 59.214 (1972), 115–17; Bruno Hübsch (ed.), *Madagascar et le Christianisme* (Paris: Agence de coopération culturelle et technique, 1993), 221.

[118] RA, 172.   [119] RH, 78.

[120] Hilsenberg and Bojer, 'Sketch of the Province of Emerina', 259; Guillaume Grandidier, 'Le mariage à Madagascar', *Bulletins et Mémoires de la Société d'anthropologie de Paris* 4.1 (1913), 38–9; see also Guillaume Grandidier, 'A Madagascar, anciennes croyances et coutumes', *Journal de la Société des Africanistes* 2.2 (1932), 183–4.

[121] *HdR*, 521, 599.

[122] James Sibree, 'Relationships and the Names Used for Them among the Peoples of Madagascar, Chiefly the Hovas; Together with Observations upon Marriage Customs and Morals among the Malagasy', *Journal of the Anthropological Institute of Great Britain and Ireland* 9 (1880), 44.

[123] Coppalle, 'Voyage dans l'intérieur de Madagascar', 54–5.

and body, his figure in general being well-proportioned ... [and somewhat contradictorily] He was broad and square across the shoulders but very small in the waist. He had a pretty hand, small feet, and fair skin.'[124] French voyager and planter, Jean-Louis Carayon (b. 1794), stated that he had an expressive face and eyes, possessed a commanding presence, and was an excellent orator.[125] Merina men traditionally wore their hair long, but in April 1822, when at his 'country-seat' of Mahazoarivo, Radama employed 'an Englishman' to cut his hair short in emulation of the British military style.[126] Naturalists Karl Hilsenberg (1802–1824), a German, and Wenceslas Bojer (1795–1856), from Bohemia, sent by Farquhar to study and collect natural history specimens in Madagascar, provided an intriguingly detailed description of the king:

He possesses considerable natural understanding and extraordinary shrewdness; he is as gay and amiable as he is hasty tempered, but susceptible of much sensibility and affection. He is very desirous of instruction, and is fond of the society and manners of Europeans, whom he does all that is possible to attract to his court, and takes pleasure in their conversation, especially on the subject of war. His chief delight is in hearing anecdotes of heroes who have distinguished themselves, and whom he neglects nothing that lies in his power to imitate. Since the period that Europeans have frequented the country, King Radama has much changed his manners, he wears their costume, adopts their manner of living, and has learned the French language, which he writes with tolerable accuracy. He is a great amateur of music, and as we can both of us play on the German flute, we often have the pleasure of his society, and of moving him and all his family, even to tears.

But all these pleasing qualities are eclipsed by his great self-love, pride, and distrust, which unfortunately have increased since the British Government has kept up an intercourse with him. He has little gratitude for friendship shown him, because he looks upon it as his rightful due; he is sometimes generous, and even capable of giving largely and granting unexpected favours, but at other times his avarice is most sordid and degrading.[127]

Radama loved horse-riding, Malagasy and European music, and dancing.[128] He was also very fond of drink. Raombana asserted that intoxication with brandy influenced Radama's decision in 1822 to execute the ringleaders of the female protest against the cutting short of his, and his officers', hair.[129] André Coppalle, who painted a portrait of Radama, noted in 1825 that Radama preferred gin to wine, while others considered that alcohol consumption

---

[124] Coroller, quoted in Ellis, *History of Madagascar*, vol. 2, 400; see also Hilsenberg and Bojer, 'Sketch of the Province of Emerina', 268; Carayon, *Histoire de l'établissement français*, 32.

[125] Carayon, *Histoire de l'établissement français*, 32.

[126] Griffiths, 'Journal', quoted in *Missionary Register* (Apr. 1823), 179; see also Keturah Jeffreys, *The Widowed Missionary's Journal* (Southampton: Printed for the author, 1827), 37–8; Montgomery, *Journal of Voyages and Travels*, vol. 3, 245 HdR, 1078.

[127] Hilsenberg and Bojer, 'Sketch of the Province of Emerina', 268–9.

[128] See e.g. Coppalle, 'Voyage dans l'intérieur de Madagascar', 80.

[129] RH, 106. See also Chapter 7.

hastened Radama's death. Thus Coroller commented that 'Towards the latter years of his life, he was addicted to feasting and drinking to excess.'[130]

Radama was a child during the last engagements of the Merina civil wars: Andrianampoinimerina captured the town of Antananarivo in 1795 or 1796, Ambohidratrimo in 1801, Anosizato in 1802, and Antsahadinta in 1803 – when he finally became ruler of what was then considered to constitute the territory of Imerina.[131] By the time of his father's death in 1810, Radama too had become a competent military commander, leading expeditions against Ambositra in the highland province of Betsileo, to the south of Imerina, and against the Menabe Sakalava of western Madagascar. When Andrianampoinimerina died, a number of subjected towns and regions rose in rebellions that Radama ruthlessly suppressed. For example, he captured the rebel town of Ambatomanga, which commanded the eastern approach to Imerina, burnt all its dwellings, and deported its surviving inhabitants.[132]

To consolidate his economic position, Radama expanded the western frontiers of Imerina through obtaining the peaceful submission of the large neighbouring provinces of Imamo and Vonizongo, rich in silk and in cattle respectively.[133] His armies overran Vakinankaratra, a significant slave supply centre to the immediate south of Imerina, and rival trade routes, such as the one in Antsihanaka, the highland province to the north, forged by the Swahili to link the west and the northeast coasts.[134] He also ordered devastating attacks upon the Bezanozano of the Ankay, to the east of Ambatomanga, to eliminate them as intermediaries in the trade with Europeans on the northeast coast. Further, he established Merina military colonies (*voanjo*) on the rich agricultural lands of north Betsileo and the Lake Alaotra region of Antsihanaka. By 1814, Merina-ruled territory had quadrupled in area to about 18,000 km^2, creating the core of the future Merina empire. From it, a series of cattle and slave raids were launched on other peoples. In 1816, one such expedition returned from south-west Madagascar with a booty of 2,000 slaves and 4,000 cattle.[135] A few years

---

[130] Quoted in Ellis, *History of Madagascar*, vol. 2, 401, see also 394; Coppalle, 'Voyage dans l'intérieur de Madagascar', 32; Grandidier, *Histoire physique* (1942), 216

[131] Jacques de Lasalle, 'Mémoire sur Madagascar'. *Notes, reconnaissances et explorations* 2.2 (1898 [1797]), 591; J. C. Herbert, 'Les tribulations de Lebel, "négociant-voyageur" sur les hauts plateaux malgaches (1800–1803)', *Omaly sy Anio* 10 (1979), 119, 136, 1431.

[132] *HdR*, 1067; RH, 80.

[133] Sibree, 'Imerina', 744; Campbell, *Economic History*, 31–2, 67; see also RH, 4; Rajemisa-Raolison, *Dictionnaire historique et géographique*, 162–3.

[134] Guillaume Grandidier, *Histoire physique, naturelle et politique de Madagascar* (Paris: Hachette, 1928), 268, 335; Daniel Couland, *Les Zafimaniry, un groupe éthnique de Madagascar à la poursuite de la forêt* (Tananarive: Imprimerie Fanontam-boky Malagasy, 1973), 106–14; Alain Delivré, *L'histoire des rois d'Imerina: Interprétation d'une tradition orale* (Paris: Klincksieck, 1974), 225–6.

[135] Hastie, 'Diary' (1817), 147, 211, CO 167/34, NAK; RH, 21, 67; Raombana in Ayache (ed.), *Raombana (1809–1855)*, 13; Oliver, *Madagascar*, vol. 1, 221–2, 227–9; *HdR*, 120, 441–2, 658; [Émile] Prud'homme, 'Considérations sur les Sakalaves', *Notes, reconnaissances et*

later, Radama likened himself to Napoleon, who he considered 'my model . . . the example that I want to follow'.[136] However, the destruction wrought by his military campaigns often created famine conditions and resulted in rampant insecurity along the main trade arteries, including that to Tamatave, Imerina's most important foreign trade outlet.[137]

The opportunity of an alliance with the British thus came at an opportune moment. At first, Radama resisted British pressure to ban slave exports. The slave trade financed the court and its expansionist policies and was the chief source of revenue for the Merina elite, whose support had been critical to Andrianampoinimerina's success in the civil wars and who, from 1810, comprised the most important segment of Radama's council.[138] Nevertheless, Radama felt that members of his royal council were too powerful and wished to increase the crown's authority at their expense. A ban on slave exports would certainly diminish the wealth of his councillors. In order to avoid it similarly undermining royal revenues, it was imperative that Imerina develop alternative export staples and secure an immediate outlet to the coast. In June 1817, a 30,000-strong Merina force marched on Tamatave, where Radama accepted the submission of René.[139] Subsequently, the British negotiated a draft treaty in which Radama agreed to ban the slave export trade in return for annual compensation from the British, who also promised him military aid to conquer the entire island, over which, for the first time, they declared him sovereign.[140]

Hall's decision to cancel the alliance with Imerina completely undermined Radama's new policy. It obliged him to renew the slave traffic to the Mascarenes that amounted, according to Hastie, to 'between three and four

explorations 6 (1900), 41; Grandidier and Grandidier, *Histoire physique* (1908), vol. 4, book 1, 233, 235, 249–52, 268; Grandidier, *Histoire physique* (1928), 235, 268, 335; C. Savaron, 'Contribution à l'histoire de l'Imerina', in 'Notes d'histoire malgache', *BAM* 14 (1931), 57–66; Georges-Sully Chapus, 'Le soin du bien-être du peuple sous le règne d'Andrianampoinimerina', *BAM* 30 (1951–2), 1; Valette, *Études sur le règne de Radama I*, 19; Delivré, *L'histoire des rois*, 208, 225.

[136] Antoine Jully, 'Notes sur Robin', *Notes, reconnaissances et explorations* 3 (Mar. 1898), 515.

[137] Chazal, 'Notes' (1816), 24, Add. 18135, British Library (hereafter BL); Le Sage, 'Mission' (1816), esp. 61–2, 85, 91–139, CO 167/34, NAK; Chardenoux, 'Journal du voyage fait dans l'intérieure' (Tamatave, 17 Aug.), Add. 18129, BL.

[138] Gwyn Campbell, 'Role of the London Missionary Society in the Rise of the Merina Empire 1810–1861', PhD, University of Wales, Swansea; Ludvig Munthe, Simon Ayache, and Charles Ravoajanahary, 'Radama I et les Anglais: Les négociations de 1817 d'après les sources malgaches ("sorabe" inédits)', *Omaly sy Anio*, 3–4 (1976).

[139] RH, 89; see also Le Sage, 'Mission' (1816), 33, CO 167/34, NAK; Pye, 'A summary (6–14 Jun. 1817)', CO 167/34, NAK; Hastie, 'Diary' (1817), CO 167/34, NAK; Le Sage, 'Mission' (1816), 33, CO 167/34, NAK.

[140] Farquhar to Stanfell, Port Louis, 7 and 22 Aug. 1817, CO 167/34, NAK; 'Treaty between Radama and Governor Farquhar', Tamatave, 23 Oct. 1817, in *Papers Relating to the Abolition of the Slave Trade in the Mauritius, 1817–1820*, vol. 18, *House of Commons Parliamentary Papers* (1821), 356–7; Ellis, *History of Madagascar*, vol. 2, 140–2, 163–5, 243; Jean Valette, 'Correspondance de Jean René et Sir Robert Farquhar', *BAM* 45 (1967), 71–98.

thousand souls, at the lowest computation every year'.[141] Consequently, Tamatave quadrupled in size from 1818 to 1820, at which time it housed sixty European slave traders.[142] In 1819, in order to ensure his control over the trade, Radama despatched a Merina army to the northeast coast that killed Fiche and massacred his men at Ivondrona.[143] The Merina force was commanded by John Brady (c.1795–1835), a Jamaican Creole of Irish extraction who, as a British corporal, had accompanied the 1816 Mauritian expedition to Imerina and remained behind in Radama's service.[144] In 1819, Brady also obliged René to again swear allegiance to Radama, although Coppalle later commented that René was 'polite with the French whose company he enjoys, flattering to the English whom he needs, fearful of and submissive to Radama whom he dreads and hates'.[145]

Further, Radama engaged Robin (fl. 1812–1830), a Frenchman, to establish a school at court instead of the one Farquhar had envisaged supervised by British missionaries. Robin was born in France where he studied medicine before, in 1812, enlisting in Napoleon's army. Following peace in 1815, Robin travelled to Réunion. There, in 1817, he was jailed for theft, but he escaped and fled to Tamatave where Lagadière, a French trader, and René, hired him to visit Imerina – presumably to purchase slaves. In Antananarivo, Robin was engaged by a wealthy Merina cattle merchant to teach his children French. He learned Malagasy and, in 1819, married one of his Merina pupils – a fifteen-year-old called Augustine. Impressed with his teaching abilities and his military service under Napoleon, Radama hired Robin to teach him arithmetic and metropolitan French – Robin used the French versions of the *Life of Napoleon* and *History of Tippo Saib* to teach the king.[146] Robin also formed a school in Masoandro (a house in the royal compound in Antananarivo) comprising three classes, two for academic and one for military instruction.[147]

---

[141] Hastie to Griffiths, Port Louis, 18 Feb. 1821, 19157E, ALGC; Le Sage, 'Mission' (1816), 26–7, 61–2, CO 167/34, NAK; Hastie, 'Diary' (1817), 130, CO 167/34, NAK; Hastie, 'Diary' (1820), 466–7, CO 167/50, NAK; Oliver, 'General Hall', 473–9; Aujas, 'Notes sur l'histoire des Betsimisaraka', 108–11; Jean Valette, 'Rainandriamampandry, historien de Jean René', *BAM* 48/1–2 (1970), 1–3.

[142] Campbell, *Economic History*, 69.

[143] John Holding, 'Notes on the Province of Tanibe, Madagascar', *Proceedings of the Royal Geographical Society of London* 14.5 (1869–70), 368.

[144] Campbell, *David Griffiths*, 68.   [145] Coppalle, 'Voyage dans l'intérieur de Madagascar', 14.

[146] Campbell, *David Griffiths*, 699.

[147] Coppalle, 'Voyage dans l'intérieur de Madagascar', 32; see also Hastie, 'Diary' (1820), 484–484b, CO 167/50, NAK; 'letter', Roads at Tinling, 27 Sep. 1829, quoted in the *Morning Chronicle* (1 Mar. 1830); Paul Ackerman, *Histoire des revolutions de Madagascar, depuis 1642 jusqu'à nos jours* (Paris: Librairie Gide, 1833), 47–50; Jully, 'Notes sur Robin', 513; Adrien S. Boudou, 'Petites notes d'histoire malgache', *BAM* 23 (1940), 68; Oliver, *Madagascar*, vol. 1, 33. Robin was also the first to take and administer quinine to counter malaria – James Cameron, *Recollections of Mission Life in Madagascar during the Early Days of the LMS Mission* (Antananarivo: Abraham Kingdon, 1874), 27.

In sum, it appeared that Farquhar's long campaign to establish an alliance with the Merina crown of central Madagascar that would result in a ban on slave exports and secure durable British hegemony in the island, had failed. Hall, interim governor of Mauritius during Farquhar's visit to Britain, annulled the draft treaty, and despatched the newly arrived LMS agents to the east coast where all bar one succumbed to malaria. Radama immediately renewed the slave trade and swung the Merina realm, incorporating the central highlands and eastern seaboard around Tamatave, the single most important port in the island, into French not British imperial sway.

Renewal of the Britanno-Merina Alliance and the Madagascar Youths Project

In mid-1820, Farquhar returned to Mauritius. He immediately ordered Hastie, who Hall had demoted, to return to Antananarivo, in the company of the LMS missionary David Jones to attempt to renew the Merina alliance. Farquhar instructed Hastie,

You will inform Radama that it is the intention of the Government to send him some good Artificers with their Tools, and that if he wishes it, we shall receive several of his free Subjects here, for the purpose of instructing them in the most useful handicraft trades. But you will by no means encourage any idea of an enlistment of Apprentices by Individuals, as People here and at Bourbon [Réunion] have spoken of, which appears rather to lead to a concealed Slave traffic, however pure the intentions of those who propose it may be supposed.
The Persons whom Radama may choose to send should be placed under the care of Mr. Jones, the Madagascar Missionary, for their instruction, and not be considered as bound to any individual, but under the special care of the Government, on the same footing exactly as those sent up by you before, on the execution of the Treaty, and who were returned to Madagascar by the Person then holding the Administration [Hall].[148]

Jones informed the LMS that Farquhar had instructed him, upon reaching Antananarivo, 'to request Radama to allow Missionaries to settle within his dominions, and, in case of his consent being obtained, to determine upon the most eligible places for Missionary Stations; to open a regular communication between Ova, Radama's capital, and Tamatave, and to obtain his permission for some Malegache boys to return with the Deputation to the Mauritius, in order to be there instructed, under the patronage of the Governor'.[149]

On 9 September, Hastie and Jones reached Tamatave. There they were well received by René, who informed Hastie that he wished Farquhar to send him 'Indians, Chinese and, in fact, sons of every nation, and giving these

[148] Farquhar to [Hastie] [Aug. 1820?], HB 13, NAM.
[149] Jones to [LMS], Port Louis, 19 Aug. 1829, in *Missionary Sketches* 12 (1821).

people permission (subject to his approval) to obtain concession of ground here'. Influenced by his recent instructions from Farquhar, Hastie responded by ridiculing such 'wild schemes' and informing René that each family resident in Tamatave should place one to two boys as apprentices to mechanics in Mauritius, who, upon completion of their training, would return to Tamatave.[150]

On 16 September, Hastie and Jones left Tamatave and, en route to the high plateau, passed a convoy of about 1,000 slaves, including many children, being marched to the coast for export.[151] On 3 October, they reached Antananarivo, and on 7 October entered into negotiations with Radama and his counsellors, in which Robin, who had also been appointed royal secretary, assisted. The negotiations were conducted in French,[152] a testament to Robin's teaching ability and to Radama's knowledge of the language.[153] On 8 October, Hastie, known locally as 'Andrianasy' (from *Andrian* – '*Andriana*' and *asy* – '*Hastie*'),[154] informed the king that 'Farquhar would receive Radama's free subjects for instruction' in response to which, on the following day, Radama 'requested permission to send some of them to England, for that purpose'.[155] Overnight the king's resolve cemented. David Jones recorded that, on 10 October, Radama informed Hastie that he would agree to a treaty on the condition

that he should be allowed to send some of his people to the Mauritius and England for instruction, and that artificers should be sent to him. Mr. Hastie said, that he was authorised by his excellency to promise artificers, and to take back some of his people for instruction, but beyond this he had no authority. The king sent again, requiring that twenty persons should be sent to England for instruction, as he was persuaded nothing but instruction could reconcile his people to the abandonment of the slave traffic. In this dilemma, Mr. Hastie consulted with me. I observed, that as the treaty would tend to open a door for the secure residence of missionaries in Madagascar, I thought it probable the Missionary Society itself would not object to take some of the proposed Malegaches under its care, for education. It was now agreed by Mr. Hastie, that six of the free subjects of Radama should be sent to England for education. This proposal was sent to the king, and his reply was, that he would again see Mr. Hastie in the evening. In the

[150] Hastie to Farquhar, Tamatave, 11 Sep. 1820, HB 13, NAM.

[151] Hastie to Barry, Port Louis, 20 Aug. 1820, HB 21, NAM; *Missionary Register* (1822), 35; 'Extracts from Jones' Journal (1820)', in Thomas Smith. *The History and Origin of the Missionary Societies: Containing Faithful Accounts of the Voyages, Travels, Labours, and Successes of the Various Missionaries who have been sent out, for the purpose of Evangelizing the Heathen, and other Unenlightened Nations, in different parts of the Globe / compiled and arranged from the authentic documents*, vol. 2 (London: Thomas Kelly & Richard Evans, 1825), 366–70.

[152] Jones, quoted in the *Manchester Times and Gazette* (2 Jun. 1832).

[153] 'Extracts from Jones' Journal (1820)', in Smith, *History and Origin of the Missionary Societies*, vol. 2, 372.

[154] Campbell, *David Griffiths*, 582.

[155] 'Extracts from Jones' Journal (1820)', in Smith, *History and Origin of the Missionary Societies*, vol. 2, 372–3.

interval, we prepared a paper, containing translations into French of what the society has published relative to Madagascar in its Annual Reports, and stating, that I was sent by the Missionary Society, to ask Radama's permission and protection for missionaries to settle in his country, and that, if he consented to grant these, I was authorised to promise, that the society would send out more missionaries to civilize, as well as to Christianize his people. I sent also, with this document, a copy of the Society's Report for 1819, and the Missionary Sketch, which represents the people of Otaheite destroying their idols, and building a chapel. I requested the king's secretary to explain these to his majesty, in like manner as I had explained them to *him* . . .

The next morning [11 October 1820], at eleven o'clock, his majesty sent to communicate his final determination, which was, that the treaty should be signed this day, and that he would republish his former proclamation, requiring the immediate cessation of the slave traffic, provided Mr. Hastie would agree to take twenty of his subjects for instruction, ten to proceed to the Mauritius, and the other ten to England. The moment was now arrived when the welfare of millions was to be decided. Mr. Hastie came to me and asked what was to be done, and whether the Missionary Society would take some of them under their charge. Having no authority, I could not go beyond what I had said yesterday; on which Mr. Hastie said, that he would agree to the king's proposal, even if he himself should bear the expenses of the ten Malegache youths who were to be sent to England. The agreement was accordingly made, a *kabar* held, and a proclamation published.[156]

The agreement formed the substance of a supplementary clause to the 1820 treaty, which Robin helped draft, in which it was agreed that 'Mr. Hastie engages on the part of his government, to take with him, twenty free subjects of his Majesty King Radama, to be instructed in, and brought up to different trades, such as mechanicians, gold and silversmiths, weavers, carpenters, blacksmiths; or placed in the arsenals, dock yards, &c. &c. &c. whereof ten shall be sent to England, and ten to the Island of Mauritius, at the expense of the British Government'.[157] This accord formed the foundation of the Madagascar Youths project whereby, in the 1820s, the British authorities paid for the training abroad, in Britain, in Mauritius and on British naval vessels, of some 100 Malagasy youths. The next chapter explores the history of those selected to go to Britain for education and training.

---

[156] 'Extracts from Jones' Journal' (1820), in Smith, *History and Origin of the Missionary Societies*, vol. 2, 373–4.
[157] *Papers Relating to the Abolition of the Slave Trade*, 356–8.

2   Britain

This chapter presents the history of the Madagascar Youths chosen to undergo craft apprenticeships in Britain. It examines their selection, reception, education, and training under LMS supervision; their trials, tribulations, and successes; and how they changed British perceptions of the Malagasy. The two Madagascar Youths who received a liberal education in Britain form the core focus of Chapter 7.

British Informal Imperialism in Madagascar

After the signing of the Britanno-Merina treaty in Antananarivo, in October 1820, Hastie took it and a select group of Madagascar Youths to Mauritius. For Farquhar, the renewal of the treaty was a major triumph. Firstly, it resulted in a ban on slave exports for which, on 27 July 1821, Farquhar was granted a barony.[1] Secondly, Farquhar considered that the treaty secured British ascendancy in Madagascar, which he planned to incorporate into the informal British Empire through a number of strategies. A central goal was the rapid promotion of British-backed Merina military conquest and political domination of the island. To this end, Farquhar despatched warships to the French colony of Sainte Marie in 1821 with the message that Madagascar was an independent British ally; to Iboina in 1822 and in 1824 to warn the Sakalava king Andriantsoly not to entertain a French alliance; and to assist a Merina expedition that in 1823 crushed the rebel 'Tanambe' chiefs on the east coast between Fenoarivo and Antongil Bay.[2]

---

[1] Gwyn Campbell, *David Griffiths and the Missionary 'History of Madagascar'* (Leiden: Brill, 2012), 581.

[2] Samuel Pasfield Oliver, *Madagascar: An Historical and Descriptive Account of the Island and Its Former Dependencies* (London: Macmillan, 1886), vol. 1, 150–1; M. L. G. Gourraigne, 'Les relations de la France avec Madagascar pendant la première moitié du XXe siècle', in *Conférences publiques sur Madagascar faites à l'École Coloniale pendant l'année scolaire 1908–1909* (Paris: École Coloniale, 1909), 20; Raymond Decary, 'Documents historiques relatifs à l'établissment français de Sainte-Marie sous la Restauration', *BAM* 13 (1930), 70, 73–85; R. E. P. Wastell, 'British Imperial Policy in Relation to Madagascar, 1810–96', PhD, London University, 1944, 150–1, 154, 187; Jean Valette, *Études sur le règne de Radama I*

Farquhar also appointed Hastie as British political agent to the Merina court to secure British paramountcy, to advise the king on domestic and foreign policy, and to oversee the establishment of a British colony in Imerina, the first members of which would comprise the technical and educational experts envisaged in the 1817 draft treaty. In this, Farquhar's ambitions were facilitated by the LMS. Following the signing of the 1820 treaty, David Jones, the sole survivor of the first LMS venture in the island, had intended to return to Mauritius with Hastie. However, at Radama's request, he remained in Antananarivo, where the king assigned him a house, teachers of Malagasy, and sixteen pupils who were to receive an 'English education' in a 'Royal College' that Jones opened in the palace. Three of his students, including Rakotobe, the heir to the throne, were Radama's nephews. The others were all children of the court elite.[3] Further, in October 1820, Radama had authorized Jones to write to the LMS requesting 'as many Missionaries as I please, provided the number contain some good artificers, that his people may be taught in civilization as well as in religion'.[4] A notice from Radama, published in the *Mauritius Gazette* of 3 March 1821, inviting planters, traders, and craftsmen of British nationality to settle in Madagascar, drew little response. However, delighted with the prospect of patronage by both Farquhar and Radama, the LMS sent out a number of missionaries, both clerical and artisan. The first group of missionary craftsmen comprised Englishmen Thomas Brookes (1793–1822), a carpenter; John Canham (1798–1881), a tanner and leather worker; and George Chick (1797–1866), a blacksmith.[5] By the end of 1822 the British community in Imerina numbered approximately twenty, including two missionary clerics and their wives and eleven artisans.[6] However, while Farquhar made it clear to Radama that the missionaries should be 'perfectly free, and masters of their own actions',[7] he left the missionaries in no doubt about their status as British agents, supplementing their salaries from the Mauritian treasury and supplying them with as much material assistance as he could. Moreover, he instructed Jones, after mastering Malagasy, to return to

(Tananarive: Imprimerie Nationale, 1962), 52; Mabel V. Jackson Haight, *European Powers and South-east Africa: A Study of International Relations on the South-east Coast of Africa, 1796–1856* (London: Routledge & Kegan Paul, 1967), 122–45.

[3] David Jones to Miss Jane Darby, Gosport, Tananarivoo, 14 Mar. 1822, in 'David Jones: Copies of Letters 1818–39', Madagascar Odds Bx.4, SOAS/CWM; 'Madagascar', *Missionary Register* (1822), 35.

[4] Jones to Telfair, Antananarivo, 14 Oct. 1820, quoted in *Quarterly Chronicle of the Transactions of the London Missionary Society* 2 (1821–4), 93.

[5] Richard Lovett, *The History of the London Missionary Society 1795–1895* (London: Henry Frowde, 1899), vol. 1, 801.

[6] Campbell, *David Griffiths*, 45.

[7] Farquhar to Hastie, Mauritius, 30 Apr. 1822, CO 167/63, NAK.

Mauritius in order to teach the language to future British agents to Madagascar, envisaging that other clerical missionaries would assist Hastie and educate the children of the Merina elite.[8]

Although larger than the French community in Imerina, Farquhar considered that the British contingent was too small to counter French aspirations in the island:

The establishment [i.e. of a British colony] in Madagascar is yet comparatively small and in its infancy. It is but the seed and germ that time will develop and extend, and it is necessary to look forward and provide against contingencies, so liable to occur and which, unless prudently met, might prove highly disadvantageous if not fatal to the British interests in the island.[9]

In 1822–3, in an attempt to expand the basis for a British settlement in Imerina, Farquhar commissioned studies on Malagasy resources from two botanists, Hilsenberg and Bojer. He also persuaded Radama to issue a second proclamation, emphasizing that British settlers would enjoy both full royal protection and the freedom to travel, build, and cultivate within his territories.[10]

However, more pivotal to Farquhar's designs to secure British hegemony in Madagascar were the 'Madagascar Youths'. In the governor's mind, they would learn the English language and imbibe British culture and key skills, such as textile manufacture, that upon their return might form the basis of export industries to replace the slave trade. Additionally, the Madagascar Youths under British supervision would be exposed to Protestant worship and teaching, and some might convert. All would desire to retain the British alliance. Farquhar persuaded the British government to cover the costs of travel, accommodation, and training of the Madagascar Youths, while the LMS directors agreed to supervise the training of those sent to Britain. This was, in turn, to have significant consequences for the way the LMS, the government in London, and British society in general viewed Madagascar.

---

[8] William Ellis, *History of Madagascar* (London: Fisher, 1838), vol. 2, 355; Oliver, *Madagascar*, vol. 1, 36; Ludvig Munthe, *La Bible à Madagascar* (Oslo: Forlaget Land og Kirke, 1969), 71.

[9] Farquhar to Hastie, Mauritius, 30 Apr. 1822, CO 167/63, NAK.

[10] Barry to Hastie, Port Louis, 28 Mar. and 27 Apr. 1822, CO 167/77, NAK; Hastie to Farquhar, Port Louis, 19 May 1823, CO 167/66, NAK; Farquhar to Wilmott, Madagascar, 6 Jun. 1823, CO 167/66, NAK; 'Proclamation de RADAMA Ier relative au commerce avec l'extérieur' (Mahajanga, 28 Jul. 1824) in Jean Valette, 'Un plan de développement de Madagascar: Le projet Bergsten (1825)', *BAM* 40.2 (1966), 24; Hastie, 'Diary' (1824–5), CO 167/78, NAK; David Griffiths, *Hanes Madagascar* (Machynlleth: Richard Jones, 1843), 26, 28–9, 30–1; [Edward Baker], *Madagascar Past and Present* (London: R. Bentley, 1847), 196–8; Wastell, 'British Imperial Policy', 200; *HdR*, 1074.

Selection of Madagascar Youths to Serve Apprenticeships in Britain

On 14 October, three days after the treaty was signed, Radama selected the first batch of youths to be sent to Mauritius and Britain for instruction. Jones recorded of the event,

the people entered into a high discussion as to who should have the king's permission, and the honour, to send their children to be instructed. One man said that he would give three thousand dollars for permission to send his child. – 'Well,' said the king 'give me one thousand five hundred dollars, and he shall go.' The man hesitated a little, and then answered that he would give that sum. 'Well,' rejoined the king, 'as you are in earnest, he shall go for nothing.' The place was, on Saturday, crowded by the richest and most respectable people in the capital, from among whose children a selection has been made for instruction.[11]

Radama chose nine Malagasy youths to travel to Britain, rather than the ten originally envisaged, and assigned to seven of them the crafts he wished them to learn (see Table 2.1).[12] Of the seven, five belonged to the top *andriana* caste: Raolombelona, Razafinkarefo, Ikiotomavo, Ramboa, and Andrianaivo; one, Ratsiorimisa, was of the *hova* or second-ranked caste; and one, Verkey, was, in contravention of the treaty, a slave. The parents of all, except Verkey, contributed to the purchase of outfits for their sons.[13]

A Malagasy embassy of four travelled with Hastie and the boys to Mauritius: Andriamisetra and Ratefy (d. 1828), both brothers-in-law of Radama, and secretary Andriamahazonoro – and Antaimoro, scribe.[14] Rafaralahy, another of Radama's brothers-in-law, asked that he and his wife accompany the group to Britain. However, as he had protested vehemently against the anti-slave trade clause of the 1820 Britanno-Merina treaty, the king refused.[15] On 1 November 1820, the convoy arrived in Tamatave where, to the disappointment of the captains of the fifty-five slaving ships in port awaiting fresh cargoes, as also probably of the Swahili traders there, Ratefy proclaimed the renewed ban on slave exports. Even though it was only the start of the rainy season, some of the Madagascar Youths caught malaria before, on 5 November, they sailed from Tamatave aboard the *Eliza*. On 24 November, they reached

---

[11] 'Extracts from Jones' Journal (1820)', in Thomas Smith, *The History and Origin of the Missionary Societies* (London: Thomas Kelly & Richard Evans, 1825), vol. 2, 377.

[12] Hardyman, 'Malagasy Overseas', PPMS63 J. T. Hardyman file 43, Bx.7, SOAS/CWM.

[13] Edward Baker, 'Restraint upon the Diffusion of knowledge under the Madagascar Queen's Government', La Chausée, Maison Mabille, Port Louis, 13 Sep. 1836, NAM, HB 9; Campbell, *David Griffiths*, 638.

[14] Hardyman, 'Malagasy Overseas', PPMS63 J. T. Hardyman file 43, Bx.7, SOAS/CWM.

[15] Guillaume Grandidier, *Histoire physique, naturelle et politique de Madagascar* (Paris: Imprimerie Paul Brodard 1942), vol. 5, book 2, 188.

Table 2.1 *Madagascar Youths sent to Britain to learn artisanal skills*

Name	Father	Notes	Education/skill assigned by Radama
Raolombelona (1810–1851), known in Britain as Rolan Balan/Rolam Balam/Roloun Baloun	Endrien Asule [Andrianasolo?]	Joint heir with brother to chieftainship of Mangasuavina [Mangasoavina], in Analamanga region of Imerina that has, as its capital, Antananarivo.	Making calico
Razafinkarefo/Zafincarafe (1814–after 1861), also called Zafy Coreffe in Britain	Endrien Ralal (Andriandralala), 1st instructor of Radama, chief treasurer, and 2nd to king in absolute power	Razafinkarefo's grandfather was Ralala, one of Radama's judges.	General school education
Ikiotomavo/Rakotomavo (1810–1821), also called Contamauve in Britain.	Endrien Sihoov [Andriantsihova?] chief of Bootathancaud [Ambatonankady?], a judge, a minister and a distant relative of Radama	Ikiotomavo, his mother, was of equal rank to his father.	Silverwork
Ramboa (1806–1826, also known as Romboa in Britain	Andriamatsa Rasikiha, deceased, member of a leading Andriana clan from Marovatana, who had gained fame and wealth for his ability and inventiveness as a craftsman.		Gun-making
Andrianaivo (1809–1824), known as Drinave in Britain, brother of Ramboa (above)	Andriamatsa Rasikiha (see above)		Make calico
Ratsiorimisa (b. 1799), known as Shermishe in Britain	Farlah Sasul (Faralahisolo), a *hova* man of some property from Anosizato	The only one of the group who was married when they left for Britain. He was a skilled carpenter with some knowledge of silver work. In August 1816 he had accompanied Radama's half-brothers, Ramarotafika and Rahovy, to Mauritius to learn to be a gunsmith (see Chapter 3).	Cannon founding

| Verkey (1799–1854), known in Madagascar as Rainimanana and Ravarika | Mancawn [Mancana?] of Tassimo [Tatsimo] in the Anosy region of SE Madagascar | As a child, he was exported to Mauritius as a slave. He had knowledge of tin work and, by 1816, spoke Malagasy, Creole French, and English. In 1816, he accompanied Le Sage's embassy to Antananarivo as an interpreter. In August 1817, Hastie acquiesced to Radama's request that he retain Verkey as an equine instructor and make him an *olomainty* (lit. 'black person') or royal slave. | Learn to manufacture gunpowder |

Source: Hastie, 'Diary' (1817);Meeting of Directors, 11 Jun. 1821, LMS Board Minutes, SOAS/CWM: RH, 40–1, 96–7; 'List of Malagasy sent to Britain', Casgliad J. Luther Thomas, ALGC; Hardyman, 'Malagasy Overseas' PPMS63 J. T. Hardyman file 43, Bx.7, SOAS/CWM; L. Nogue, 'Étude sur l'école professionnelle de Tananarive', *Notes, reconnaissances et explorations* 1.1 (1900), 418; Ellis, *History of Madagascar*, vol. 1, 217–18; Simon Ayache (ed.), *Raombana l'historien (1809–1855)* (Fianarantsoa: Ambozontany, 1976), 1–2, 71, 77, 87, 99, 359; Campbell, *David Griffiths*, 638.

Port Louis, Mauritius, to a warm reception by Farquhar and Hastie's wife, Mary (née Yates).[16]

Hastie handed Farquhar a letter from Radama giving the governor the final choice over which Malagasy should lead the delegation to London. Farquhar confirmed the wishes of the king, who subsequently wrote to him:

I fully approve of the choice you have made of the two subjects I sent you to go to England. Ratefe [Ratefy] is better suited in every respect for this trip than the other [Andriamisetra]; he is also the first ranking prince in my Kingdom. I could not choose anyone better than him. He alone knows my true intentions. He is also provided with my full powers.

As far as Indrientsimestre [Andriamisetra] is concerned, I judged him too young still to engage meaningfully in our affairs, even though he ranks in the highest class in my court. He is also my brother-in-law and my good friend. His good qualities speak to the latter. I expect him at the end of April or May in the company of your Agent, as you informed me and as Mr. Hastie promised me.[17]

He added, 'I forgot to mention to you Diamasanor [Andriamahazonoro], the secretary of Ratefe. It was me who commanded him to accompany Mr. Hastie to Mauritius and Ratefe to England.'[18]

Ratefy was thus confirmed as leader of the embassy to Britain. Ratefy (Ratefinanahary) was the son or nephew of Andriamary, prince of Imamo, a principality west of Antananarivo that was renowned for the production of silk, cotton, iron, and hemp. During the Merina civil wars of the late 1700s, Andriamary submitted to Andrianampoinimerina, who in consequence gave his eldest daughter, Rabodosahondra, in marriage to Ratefy. Radama thus became Ratefy's brother-in-law. Rabodosahondra and Ratefy had a daughter, 'Rassa' (b. 1815), and a son, 'Coutaboy' (b. 1816).[19] On Andriamary's death, Ratefy inherited Imamo, but he continued to live at court in Antananarivo where he and Radama forged a close friendship. Following Radama's ascension to the throne in 1810, Ratefy led an army to conquer Betsileo.[20] By 1820, Ratefy, who, like Radama, had been taught at the royal school to write *Sorabe*, was commander-in-chief of the Merina army, second in command only to Radama.[21]

By June 1821, Andriamisetra had returned to Antananarivo; Radama commented to Farquhar,

my brother-in-law Adrien Simiset who is back here, informed me of all you did for him, his colleague, and the people in their suite. He gave me exact details of all the goodness

[16] Hardyman, 'Malagasy Overseas', PPMS63 J. T. Hardyman file 43, Bx.7, SOAS/CWM; Grandidier, *Histoire physique* (1942), vol. 5, book 2, 189.
[17] Radama to Farquhar, Tananarivoo, 11 Feb. 1821, HB 21, NAM.
[18] Radama to Farquhar, Tananarivoo, 11 Feb. 1821, HB 21, NAM.
[19] Ayache (ed.), *Raombana (1809–1855)*, 13.   [20] *HdR*, 521, 1072–3, 1100.
[21] 'List of Malagasy sent to Britain', Casgliad J. Luther Thomas, ALGC.

and care you gave them during their stay with you. I also learned from him that the persons destined for England left last January, all praising your kindness, and under the supervision of respectable persons of your Government.[22]

The Malagasy contingent travelling to Britain was the largest ever to have done so. The first indication of someone from Madagascar visiting Britain is in 1793, but nothing is known of this individual.[23] In late 1817, Rahanafa and 'Ovah' [meaning 'Hova' or Merina], two Malagasy male apprentices, almost certainly ex-slaves, who served as household servants, accompanied their respective masters, Farquhar, governor of Mauritius, and his chief secretary, Colonel G. A. Barry, to England to ratify the draft Britanno-Merina treaty.[24] The group left Port Louis on 16 January 1821 aboard the *Columbo*, commanded by Captain Richardson, under the supervision of George Harrison, a Mauritius government officer chosen by Farquhar. The governor stated that Harrison 'has been entirely dependent on me since his earliest infancy', indicating an intimate father–son relationship. Harrison also carried from Farquhar letters of introduction for Ratefy to George IV (1762–1830) and to Farquhar's family members in England.[25]

Arrival in Britain

The Madagascar Youths were not the only representatives of exotic regions of the globe brought by missionaries to Britain. Such people included at least sixteen inhabitants of the Pacific islands, which since the voyages of James Cook had been the focus of intense scientific and evangelical missionary attention.[26] However, when the Malagasy reached Britain, in mid-May 1821, they caused a public sensation. First, their visit was a result of a treaty, a core clause of which was a ban on slave exports from Madagascar. By the mid-1790s, slavery had largely ended in Britain, which in 1807 had also passed a parliamentary act banning the slave trade.[27] The arrival of the Madagascar Youths was therefore of signal symbolic significance to what Zoë Laidlaw

---

22 Radama to Farquhar, Tananarivoo, Jun. 1821, HB 21, NAM.
23 Hardyman, 'Malagasy Overseas' PPMS63 J. T. Hardyman file 43, Bx.7, SOAS/CWM.
24 Farquhar had earlier that year sent Hastie to Madagascar with a Malagasy apprentice tasked with teaching the Merina the use of the plough and generally improving local agricultural methods – Peerthum Ally Hossen Orjoon Satyendra, 'Liberated Africans in Nineteenth Century Mauritius', *L'Express* [Mauritius], 2 Feb. 2005 – www.lexpress.mu/article/liberated-africans-nineteenth-century-mauritius (accessed 16/12/18).
25 Hardyman, 'Malagasy Overseas' PPMS63 J. T. Hardyman file 43, Bx.7, SOAS/CWM.
26 Bernard Smith, *European Vision and the South Pacific 1768–1850: A Study in the History of Art and Ideas* (Oxford: Oxford University Press, 1960); Sujit Sivasundaram, 'Natural History Spiritualized: Civilizing Islanders, Cultivating Breadfruit, and Collecting Souls', *History of Science* 39.4 (2001), 417–43.
27 Norma Myers, 'Servant, Sailor, Soldier, Tailor, Beggarman: Black Survival in White Society 1780–1830', *Immigrants & Minorities* 12.1 (1993), 49.

terms the 'humanitarian network' that bound prominent British parliamentarians and evangelicals in the late 1700s and early 1800s.[28] At that time, there were in Britain thousands of non-Europeans, generally termed 'Black', although they comprised people of both African and Asian origin. The majority, including almost all non-European females, were in domestic service. A minority belonged to the 'black labour aristocracy' of skilled workers, entertainers, and boxers,[29] although they were outnumbered by African and Asian beggars – a phenomenon of growing parliamentary concern.[30] Again, many Asian and African males had served in the British Army or Navy, or had deserted from merchant vessels. They were concentrated in major ports, such as London, Liverpool, Cardiff, and Bristol.[31] Black seamen, unlike Lascars and other Asian sailors, were regarded as 'British', as were Black soldiers. If they fell on hard times, they were theoretically entitled to poor relief, which some claimed.[32] Some non-Europeans in Britain, such as Dean Mahomed, who had served in the EIC's Bengal Army, married local women.[33]

The Madagascar Youths were considered part of the 'Black' community, although most were of highland Merina origin and had Indonesian colouring and features. Certainly, they differentiated themselves sharply from Africans. Thus Raombana, one of the youths stated,

The English were surprised, but very agreeably . . . by the appearance of these strangers: for I am certain that in England it was thought that the Malagasy would facially and physically resemble Mozambicans or Hottentots, and that they were cannibals; but now it was found that all (except Verkey) were different [from Africans] and with their olive complexion, and European-type noses looked much more like Europeans, not at all like flat-nosed frizzy-haired Mozambicans or Hottentots.[34]

Members of London society, who had implicit faith in the supremacy of the monarchical system, were also surprised to learn that the Malagasy had a sovereign, who had sent a prince (Ratefy) to Britain as his ambassador. The British were further taken aback by the fact that the Malagasy elite were literate. The ambassadors carried a letter written by Radama, presumably in French, and at least two, possibly three, of the party – Ratefy, Andriamahazonoro, and, according to Ludwig Munthe (1920-2002), Verkey – were literate in *Sorabe*.[35] All these factors put the Malagasy visitors to Britain on

[28] Zoë Laidlaw, *Colonial Connections, 1815–45: Patronage, the Information Revolution and Colonial Government* (Manchester: Manchester University Press, 2005), 27–30.
[29] Myers, 'Servant, Sailor, Soldier, Tailor, Beggarman', 48, 68.
[30] Myers, 'Servant, Sailor, Soldier, Tailor, Beggarman', 59.
[31] Myers, 'Servant, Sailor, Soldier, Tailor, Beggarman', 54–9.
[32] Myers, 'Servant, Sailor, Soldier, Tailor, Beggarman', 61, 66.
[33] Michael H. Fisher, *The First Indian Author in English: Dean Mahomed (1759–1851) in India, Ireland, and England* (Delhi: Oxford University Press, 1996).
[34] RH, 779–81. Raombana's case is examined in detail in Chapter 7.
[35] RH, 96–7; Munthe, *La Bible à Madagascar*, 12.

a separate footing from sub-Saharan Africans and Pacific Islanders and obliged London society, and British evangelicals in general, to re-evaluate Madagascar and the Malagasy in their classification of civilized places and peoples.

Ratefy duly met George IV, celebrated abolitionists Thomas Clarkson (1760–1846) and William Wilberforce (1759–1833), and leading evangelicals. He visited and was much impressed by the Woolwich Armoury, which annually produced 24,000 cannons.[36] Ratefy transmitted to the LMS directors Radama's desire for both educator and artisan missionaries. They, in turn, invited him to their 27th annual general meeting on 10 May 1821, where evangelical preacher Rowland Hill (1744–1833) successfully proposed a motion that

the Meeting presented to Prince Rataffe, its most respectful acknowledgements for the honor of his presence, and begs that he will express to King Radama, the lively gratitude which the Society feels for the gracious reception which he has given the Revd. David Jones, one of its Missionaries and that he will assure His Majesty, of its earnest desire to meet the wishes which are contained in the Letter which he has done the Directors the honor of addressing to them.[37]

The visit of a Malagasy royal sparked off enormous interest in Madagascar and in the LMS mission in the island. The LMS AGM was packed, and members of the London elite inundated Ratefy with invitations.[38] He also had his portrait executed (see Figure 2.1).

The LMS were so impressed by a non-Black, literate prince, and by Andriamahazonoro, Ratefy's secretary, who was not only literate but 'possesses skill as a Physician and has obtained Rank in Ovah, he is patronized by the King',[39] that they immediately upgraded Madagascar from the category of a savage African island to a semi-civilized eastern pagan island. Consequently, in addition to the artisan agents Radama had called for, they selected the English missionary John Jeffreys (1792–1825), rather than another Welsh peasant like David Jones or David Griffiths (1792–1863), who had been sent out in 1820 as a replacement for Thomas Bevan.[40] Jeffreys was a graduate of the elite Blackburn Independent Academy, where he had received both a classical (Latin, Greek, and Hebrew) and a conventional (Moral Philosophy, Theology, French, Geography, Music, and Dancing) education, as well as some medical training. In mid-1821, Jeffreys and his wife, Keturah

---

[36] RH, 96–7; Ayache (ed.), *Raombana (1809–1855)*, 75; Campbell, *David Griffiths*, 638.

[37] Twenty-Seventh General Meeting of the Society, Great Queen Street Chapel, Lincoln's Inn Fields, Thursday 10 May 1821, LMS Board Minutes, SOAS/CWM.

[38] Simon Ayache, 'La découverte de l'Europe par les Malgaches au XIXe siècle', *Revue française d'histoire d'outre-mer* 73.270 (1986), 11.

[39] CO 167/56, NAK; see also 'List of Malagasy sent to Britain', Casgliad J. Luther Thomas, ALGC.

[40] RH, 103; Ayache (ed.), *Raombana (1809–1855)*, 77; Campbell, *David Griffiths*.

Figure 2.1 Prince Ratefinanahary (mid-1821)
Note: Engraved by Samuel Freeman (1773–1857) and published by Frederick
Westley, 10 Stationers' Court, London, in January 1822; courtesy of ALGC.
Freeman (1773–1857) was a famous London-based portrait engraver. He
studied under Francesco Bartolozzi (1727–1815), born in Italy, the son of
a goldsmith, who studied painting in Florence, trained as an engraver in
Venice, and worked in Rome before moving to London in 1764 to work as
engraver to George III. Freeman, whose independent career started in 1807,
specialized in stipple engraving and in crayon portraits. He produced some
fifty-seven portraits of England's early-nineteenth-century elite, and some
based on previous artists work – such as that of Don Cervantes, following the
designs of William Kent (London: Tonson, 1738) and José del Castillo
(Madrid: Ibarra, 1780), published in Charles Jarvis, *The Life and Exploits of
Don Quixote De la Mancha* (London: W. Wilson, 1821), vol. 1; see also
'Samuel Freeman (1773–1857), Engraver', National Portrait Gallery.
Frederick Westley (who later in the 1820s became Frederick Westley and
A. H. Davies) published much anti-slavery and pro-missionary literature,
including James Montgomery (ed.), *Journal of Voyages and Travels by the
Rev. Daniel Tyerman and George Bennet*, 2 vols. (London: Westley & Davis,
1831) and Mary Prince, *The History of Marchy Prince, a West Indian Slave*
(London: Frederick Westley & A. H. Davis, 1831).

(née Yarnold) (1791–1855), accompanied Ratefy and Ratsiorimisa back to Madagascar.[41]

The impact made by Ratefy lingered. Thus, in the first week of November 1823, the 'Madagascar Dress' became 'a source of unrivalled attraction' 'eagerly sought after by Ladies of the first eminence', and men in elite circles started to dress as 'Madagascar chiefs' at fancy-dress balls.[42]

Initiation and Preliminary Instruction

Henry Bathurst (1762–1834), third Earl Bathurst, secretary of state for war and the colonies from 1812 to 1827, agreed that the British and the Mauritian authorities would bear the cost of travel, lodging, provisions, and instruction for the Madagascar embassy and youths. Thus, on 17 April 1821, Farquhar agreed that the Mauritius treasury pay $1,569 towards the subsistence of Ratefy and his suite.[43] In all, from 1821 to 1825, the Mauritian government paid 5,318.46 currency dollars (a money of account, the rate of exchange for which was constantly in flux)[44] and the British government almost £3,658 on the travel and expenses of the Madagascar Youths sent to Britain (see Tables 2.2 and 2.3).

Table 2.2 *Expenses in England of Madagascar embassy and youths (£)*

1821	1822	1823	1824	1825	Grand total
1225.5.1	393.15.0	531.4.0	593.3.6	914.4.8	£3657.12.3

Source: Kelsey, 'Abstract of the Expense'.

[41] *Morning Chronicle* (21 Apr. 1821); James Hastie to David Griffiths, 18 Feb. 1821, in Ayache (ed.), *Raombana (1809–1855)*, 258; *Missionary Register* (May 1821), 193; *Missionary Register* (1822), 34; Keturah Jeffreys, *The Widowed Missionary's Journal* (Southampton: Printed for the author, 1827), 33; RH, 96; Gerald M. Berg, 'Virtù, and Fortuna in Radama's Nascent Bureaucracy, 1816–1828', *History in Africa* 23 (1996), 45–6, 49, 52.

[42] *Morning Post* (4 Nov. 1823); *Leeds Mercury* (24 Sep. 1825); for examples of early nineteenth-century European concepts of Malagasy dress, see Martinus Stuart, *De mensch, zoo als hij voorkomt op den bekenden aardbol* (Amsterdam: Johannes Allart, 1806),vol. 5, 243; Johann Andreas Christian Löhr, *Die Lander und Volker der Erde; oder, Vollstandige Beschreibung aller funf Erdtheile* (Leipzig: Fleischer, 1819), vol. 3, 14.

[43] Barry to Hastie, Port Louis, 17 Apr. 1821, HB 13, NAM; Henry Goulburn to George Burder, Downing Street, 6 Jun. 1821, in Meeting of Directors, 11 Jun. 1821, LMS Board Minutes, SOAS/CWM.

[44] See N. J. Kelsey, 'Abstract of the Expense incurred by the Government of Mauritius on Account of Madagascar' (26 Nov. 1827), in 'Slaves in Mauritius' 40–44, *Papers relating to the Slave Trade* 26.2 (House of Commons, 1828); Saunders & Co. to Duke of Wellington, 11 Leadenhall Street, London, 31 Aug. 1830, in Duke of Wellington (ed.), *Despatches, Correspondence and Memoranda of Field Marshall Arthur Duke of Wellington K.G.*, vol. 7 (London: John Murray, 1878), 218–22.

Table 2.3 *Expenses in England of Madagascar Youths (£)*

Dates	Item	Education (incl. board)	Sum
Jul.–Dec. 1821	Nine youths	BFSS	£249.0s.0d
12 Jan. 1822		BFSS	£106.11.0
1 Jan.–3 Apr. 1822		BFSS	£112.10.2
Jul.–Oct. 1822		BFSS	£76.7.7
Jan.–Apr. 1823		BFSS	£63.3.10
Jul.–Dec. 1823	Education of the five Madagascar Youths, Manchester	Dr Clunie	134.18.1 (For Andrianaivo: £26.15.8; Raolombelona: £27.7.0; Rahaniraka: £26.5.7½; Raombana: £26.13½; Razafinkarefo: £26.16.9½)
Jan.–Jun. 1824	For the education &c., of the Madagascar Youths, Manchester	Clunie	£199.16.0
Jul.–Dec. 1824	Education, Clothing &c. of four Madagascar Youths, Manchester	Clunie	122.7.6 (Razafinkarefo: £29.13.2; Raombana: £28.5.10; Rahaniraka: £28.16.8; Raolombelona: £35.11.10)
	Sundry Expenses incurred by C Vanderkemp, Madagascar Youths, and the youth from Africa lately deceased	BFSS	£62.0.1

BFSS = British & Foreign School Society. Source: Meeting of Directors, 14 Jan., 24 Jun., and 14 Oct. 1822, 14 Apr. and 29 Dec. 1823, 12 Jul., and 27 Dec. 1824 – LMS Board Minutes, SOAS/CWM.

Bathurst, who kept Radama regularly updated about the welfare and progress of the Madagascar Youths,[45] initially asked the Church Missionary Society (CMS), representing the evangelical wing of the established Church of England, to assume responsibility for the supervision of the Madagascar Youths in Britain:

The expense of these Youths devolving on Government, a proposal was made to the Church Missionary Society to take the charge of them. The Committee expressed their readiness to accept the charge; and to avail themselves of the facilities thereby offered,

[45] See e.g. Barry, Chief Sec to Govt, to H, Port Louis, 6 Jun. 1825, HB.4, NAM.

of prosecuting their purpose of establishing a Mission in Madagascar, which had been for some time in contemplation.[46]

However, the CMS deferred to the LMS because of its established connection to Madagascar.[47]

Consequently, at a board meeting on 14 May 1821, after reading David Jones' account of the circumstances leading to the 1820 Britanno-Merina treaty, the LMS directors resolved

that it is the indispensable duty of the Missionary Society, to take under their care, if practicable, the tuition of the Nine Madagascar Youths who are sent to the country for Instruction and that the Treasurer and Secretary confer with the Secretary of State for the Colonies and all other persons concerned in this subject.[48]

The directors took into consideration Radama's wishes for the youths, as expressed by Harrison, and received a government commitment to pay 'Fifty Guineas pr. Annum. for each youth, and when their Education is completed, Government to defray the Cost of their removal to their own Country.'[49] They then agreed that their aim should be

to give to the Youths a plain English Education, including a strict attention to the inculcating of religious and Moral principles, and (when qualified to enter upon it) instruction in certain Mechanical Arts, and some branches of Science; according to a Minute to be handed to the Society by Mr. Harrison.[50]

The LMS directors added that

The Society is to be entitled to consider itself vested with full authority over the Youths, with liberty to make any application to His Majesty's Government on all subjects relating to them.

Should it become needful either on account of health, or any other cause, to send any of them back to Madagascar, before the termination of the period had in view, the Government will find the means, or the expenses of conveyance, outfit &c. &c. – the Society will once a year make a Report on the progress of the Youths to the Government to be communicated to Radama King of Madagascar, through the Governor of the Mauritius.

The expenditure will be of an economical kind, as it regards Board, Lodging and Clothing, it being understood that it is in habits of industry and frugality, as Artificers; that they are to be brought up; but it will be necessary, considering their former Stations, and for the purposes of health, that their Clothing and Diet be somewhat liberal.[51]

The emphasis was initially on teaching the youths English. Hence it was decided that,

---

[46] *The Missionary Register* (Jan. 1822), 34–5.   [47] *The Missionary Register* (Jan. 1822), 35.
[48] Meeting of Directors, 14 May 1821, LMS Board Minutes, SOAS/CWM.
[49] Meeting of Directors, 21 May 1821 and 11 Jun. 1821, LMS Board Minutes, SOAS/CWM.
[50] Meeting of Directors, 11 Jun. 1821, LMS Board Minutes, SOAS/CWM.
[51] Meeting of Directors, 11 Jun. 1821, LMS Board Minutes, SOAS/CWM.

with a view of instructing them in the English Language, those Youths ... be placed under the care of the British & Foreign School Society [BFSS], for whose accommodation arrangements have been made by the Treasurer and Secretary – and that Messrs. Holehouse and Oldfield with Revd. Messrs. Hill, Innes and Townsend be a Committee of superintendence during their residence in the Borough Road, and that they attend divine Worship at <u>Surrey Chapel</u>.[52]

The supervisory committee comprised prominent evangelists, engaged in missionary and other humanitarian causes. Charles Holehouse (1757–1834) was an enthusiastic supporter of not only the LMS, but the CMS and all other evangelical missionary societies. T. P. Oldfield was an LMS director from at least 1816 to 1834.[53] Rowland Hill and John Boutet Innes (1783–1837) were leading evangelical clerics.[54] Rev. John Townsend (1757–1826) was a founder of the London Asylum for the Deaf and Dumb (now the Royal School for Deaf Children, Margate) in 1792, of the LMS in 1794, and of the British & Foreign Bible Society (BFBS) in 1802, and in 1807 of the London Female Penitentiary – which accommodated and helped to rehabilitate repentant prostitutes.[55]

Further, in order to cater for the health of the Madagascar Youths, the LMS directors requested 'Wm. Gilham, Surgeon, to pay attention to their health during their residence at the above School.'[56] William Gilham was possibly a relative of G. A. Gillham of Blackfriars Road, also a surgeon, who had gained celebrity in 1808 by saving a Tahitian youth, Tapeoe, from abuse by a man called Kelso. Tapeoe had been sent to Britain in 1806 by Captain W. Wilson and subsequently attended Borough Road School.[57]

Borough Road had its origins in a school that Joseph Lancaster (1778–1838), an English Quaker and educational innovator, opened in 1798 (see Figure 2.2). Based on the monitorial system, whereby the older taught the younger children,

---

[52] Meeting of Directors, 11 Jun. 1821, LMS Board Minutes, SOAS/CWM; see also *Missionary Register* (Jan. 1822), 35.

[53] 'List of Directors' in [LMS], *Report of the Directors to the Twenty Second General Meeting of the London Missionary Society, 10 May 1816* (London: S. McDowall, 1816); [African Institution], *Seventeenth Report of the Directors of the African Institution* (London: Ellerton and Henderson, 1823), 97;Proceedings of the Church Missionary Society for Africa and the East (1825–6), 10; 'List of Directors 1834' in [LMS], *The Report of the Directors to the Fortieth General Meeting of the Missionary Society, usually called the London Missionary Society* (London: Westley & David, 1834), xii; Charles Hole, *The Early History of the Church Missionary Society for Africa and the East to the end of AD 1814* (London: CMS, 1896), 399.

[54] John Browne, *History of Congregationalism and Memorials of the Churches in Norfolk and Suffolk* (London: Jarrold and Sons, 1877), 272.

[55] H. Dominic W. Stiles, 'Rev John Townsend (1757–1826), Founder of the London Asylum', https://blogs.ucl.ac.uk/library-rnid/2012/09/07/rev-john-townsend-1757-1826-founder-of-the-london-asylum/ (accessed 23.04.21).

[56] Meeting of Directors, 11 Jun. 1821, LMS Board Minutes, SOAS/CWM.

[57] Review of Joseph Fox, *An Appeal to the Members of the London Missionary Society, against a Resolution of the Directors of that Society; dated March 26, 1810; with Remarks on certain Proceedings relative to the Otaheitan and Jewish Mission* (London: Darton and Harvey, 1810), in *Critical Review* 21.1 (Sep. 1810), 62–5; Sivasundaram, 'Natural History Spiritualized', 435.

Figure 2.2 Borough Road School (1821)
Source: *Evangelical Magazine and Missionary Chronicle* 29
(Oct. 1821), 476.

he intended it to help educate poor boys living in his Southwark neighbour-
hood. In 1808, the BFSS, also founded by Lancaster, took over administration
of the establishment. Further, in 1817, Borough Road College, a teaching
institution, was also established in the vicinity.[58]

In 1821, the LMS reported of the school:

The common means of instruction being far too expensive to be adopted for the education
of the poor upon a great scale, Mr. Joseph Lancaster, about the year 1798, devised
a method by which a school, however large, might be managed by one master, and one
set of lessons, thus diminishing the expense for each individual child to a mere trifle; while
at the same time the plan communicated instruction with astonishing celebrity.[59]

As noted in the case of Tapeoe, a number of non-European children were
enrolled in Borough Road School. A few years previous to the enrolment of

[58] Iris Turner, *The History of Borough Road School/College from Its Origins in 1798 until Its
Merger with Maria Grey College to Form West London Institute of Higher Education in 1976*
(London: Brunel University Press, 2015), esp. 58–65, 89–101 – http://bura.brunel.ac.uk/handle/
2438/11435 (accessed 27.01.22).

[59] *Evangelical Magazine and Missionary Chronicle* 29 (Oct. 1821), 477–8; see also
Thomas Coates, 'Report of a Visit to the Model School of the British and Foreign School
Society in the Borough Road', in Central Society of Education, *Papers* (London: Printed for
Taylor & Walton, 1838), 329–31.

Table 2.4 *Foreign male students, Borough Road School, 1810–30*

Year	No.	Non-British	Origin	Year	No.	Non-British	Origin
1810	16			1821	19	Shermish	Malagasy
1811	20			1822	33	Rolan, Drinave,	Malagasy
						Contamauve	n.a.
						Boo Poihena,	
						N. Twaana	
1812	55	Williams, George	African	1823	27	Verkey, V. Ramboa	Malagasy
1813	35	James Reid,	African	1824	50	12?	Greek?
		James Coy					
1814	27	James Coy, African	African	1825	15	1?	Greek?
1815	28			1826	31		
1816	29	Jeffries	African	1827	33		
1817	25	Soemeske,	Russian	1828	28		
		Tymayoft,	French				
		Busse	African				
		E. Fossard					
		African					
1818	36	Joseph Naudi	Maltese	1829	37	Bryieux	French
		Samuel Piper	Antiguan			Lemue	?
1819	26			1830	34	2	Greek?
1820	29						

Source: 'Borough Road College – Student List', www.brunel.ac.uk/about/Archives/Documents/ Excel/Male-Students-at-BRC-Read-Only.xlsx (accessed 27.01.22)

the Madagascar Youths, pupils at Borough Road included between two and four African youths who accompanied Daniel Sutherland (d. 1818) and his wife as missionary teachers to Sierra Leone, West Africa.[60] One official register gives an indication, albeit incomplete, of its non-British students in the 1810s and 1820s (see Table 2.4).

The 1822 BFBS report stated of Borough Road,

The male and female central schools in London receive, the one 500, the other 300 scholars. These are always full and numbers are waiting for admission. Since their establishment in 1798, 28,086 have been admitted; and many of these are now discharging the duties of their several stations in life, in a far better manner than they probably would have done, had they not received the benefits of early scriptural instruction.[61]

---

[60] [African Institution], *Eighth Report of the Directors of the African Institution read at the Annual General Meeting on the 23rd of March, 1814* (London: Ellerton and Henderson, 1814), 24; see also [African Institution], *Ninth Report of the Directors of the African Institution read at the Annual General Meeting on the 12th of April, 1815* (London: Ellerton and Henderson, 1815), 64.

[61] 'Abstract of the Eighteenth Report of the British and Foreign School Society', *Missionary Herald* 20 (Apr. 1824), 122.

The LMS placed the Madagascar Youths in Borough Road School on 25 June 1821,[62] and on 16 July 'Resolved, that it be referred to the committee for superintending the education of the Madagascar youths to provide them with clothes &c. &c. as occasion in their opinion may require.'[63] However, Ratsiorimisa who, aged twenty-two, was by far the eldest of the Madagascar Youths, and had left a wife and family in Madagascar, 'soon manifested a reluctance to remain in England and returned [to Madagascar] with Prince Rataffe' in mid-1822.[64]

The eight remaining Madagascar Youths made good progress at Borough Road under the tutorship of Charles Picton/Pickton (1796–1827). One of Lancaster's first apprentice teachers, Picton had in 1818 helped to establish the Lancastrian system in New York.[65] The Scriptures formed the basis for all Borough Road students to learn to read and write English. The report for the exam held on 26 January 1822, which Wilberforce attended, and which was chaired by Joseph Butterworth MP (1770–1826), treasurer of the Methodist Missionary Society, noted,

The company were then gratified with a most interesting exhibition of the progress made by Eight Youths from Madagascar ... These lads, who in June last knew not a word of English, and were thereby detained from entering the School nearly six weeks, have notwithstanding acquired considerable proficiency. They can now read easy lessons, and both write and spell words of two syllables ... They possess considerable talent, and are amiable in their dispositions and manners; and evince an aptness at learning, which promises to render their visit to London completely successful.[66]

However, as noted, Verkey, already possessed considerable knowledge of English.

Shortly after the examination, the youths lost another of their number, Ikiotomavo, almost certainly to 'consumption' (tuberculosis, the 'White

---

[62] Meeting of Directors, 25 Jun. 1821, LMS Board Minutes, SOAS/CWM.

[63] Meeting of Directors, 16 Jul. 1821, LMS Board Minutes, SOAS/CWM.

[64] *Missionary Register* (Jan. 1823), 18; see also *Missionary Register* (Jun. 1822), 228; RH, 96–7; Rabary, *Ny Daty Malaza: Na Ny Dian' i Jesosy Teto Madagaskara* (Tananarive: LMS, 1930–1), 42; 'Borough Road College – Student List', www.brunel.ac.uk/about/Archives/Documents/Excel/Male-Students-at-BRC-Read-Only.xlsx (accessed 27/01/22).

[65] *Missionary Register* (Jan. 1823), 18; *Evangelical Magazine and Missionary Chronicle* (Nov. 1824), 505; John Franklin Reigart, *The Lancasterian System of Instruction in the Schools of New York City* (New York: Teachers College, Columbia University, 1916) 18; Ayache (ed.), *Raombana (1809–1855)*, 80; Jennifer Muller, '"Engines of Educational Power" – The Lancastrian Monitorial System and the Development of the Teacher's Role in the Classroom: 1805–1838,' PhD, Rutgers State University, New Jersey (May 2015), 69, 98, 105 fn 67, 122.

[66] *Missionary Register* (Jun. 1822), 228–9; see also George John Stevenson, *Methodist Worthies: Characteristic Sketches of Methodist Preachers of the several Denominations with Historical Sketch of each Connexion* (London: Thomas C. Jack, 1885), vol. 4, 561–4; Simon Ayache, 'Un intellectuel malgache devant la culture européenne: L'historien Raombana (1809–1854)', *Archipel* 12.1 (1976), 107–8.

Killer'—so named due to the extreme paleness of those affected). Most Pacific Islanders brought to Britain had also died, probably of tuberculosis, which was rampant in early nineteenth-century British cities.[67] Concerned about Ikiotomavo's health, the LMS had contacted the Colonial Office, which, in mid-January 1822, offered Ikiotomavo passage aboard HMS *Andromache* to the Cape, from where he would be sent via Mauritius to Madagascar. The LMS first requested the opinions of surgeon J. A. Gillham (d. before 1845) and George Darling (1783–1862), an Edinburgh University–trained physician of renown, who, for example, also treated John Keats (1795–1821) and Charles Lamb (1775–1834).[68] Gillham and Darling concurred that moving Ikiotomavo in winter might endanger his life. The LMS conveyed their opinion to Bathurst, who accepted that Ikiotomavo should remain in Britain until the following summer.[69]

However, by early February 1822, Ikiotomavo's health had deteriorated significantly, and 'seeing that the advance and mildness of the season will now admit of it, without the risk formerly apprehended', the two doctors urged the LMS to send him home without delay.[70] Bathurst agreed and arranged for Ikiotomavo to sail that March aboard HMS *Andromache*, under Joseph Nourse (1779–1824).[71] The *Andromache* was a thirty-eight-gun ship captured from the French in 1799; it was renamed first *Princess Charlotte* and, in 1812, *Andromache*. In January 1822, Nourse was appointed as commodore in charge of the vessel, along with Thomas Goble (1780–1869) as purser, and James Rutherford and William Guland as, respectively, surgeon and assistant surgeon. Darling and Gillham supplied Rutherford with Ikiotomavo's full medical history, and the LMS purchased '3 doz. of Shirts' for the youth's use on the voyage – a reflection of a persistent 'consumptive' coughing up of blood.[72] On 11 March 1822, the board was informed that Ikiotomavo

---

[67] John V. Pickstone, *Medicine and Industrial Society: A History of Hospital Development in Manchester and Its Region, 1752–1946* (Manchester: Manchester University Press, 1985), 225–9; Sivasundaram, 'Natural History Spiritualized', 430; Jennifer L. Boxen, 'A Spirit of Benevolence: Manchester and the Origins of Modern Public Health, 1790–1834', MA thesis, Florida Atlantic University (2013), 1–2, 57–8, 83–4.

[68] Meeting of Directors, 14 Jan. 1822, LMS Board Minutes, SOAS/CWM; *Proceedings of the Royal Medical and Chirurgical Society of London* 4 (1864), 194–5; Arthur Foss and Kerith Lloyd Kinsey Trick, *St Andrew's Hospital Northampton: The First 150 Years, 1838–1988* (Cambridge: Granta Editions, 1989), 126.

[69] Wilmot to Hankey, Downing Street, 17 Jan. 1822, in Meeting of Directors, 21 Jan. 1822, LMS Board Minutes, SOAS/CWM.

[70] Meeting of Directors, 11 Feb. 1822, LMS Board Minutes, SOAS/CWM.

[71] 'Commodore Joseph Nourse C.B.', in *Asiatic Journal and Monthly Register for British India and its Dependencies* 21 (Jan. 1826), 34–8; 'Joseph Nourse', www.thepeerage.com/p15954.htm (accessed 04/10/2009).

[72] Meeting of Directors, 25 Feb. 1822, LMS Board Minutes, SOAS/CWM; see also Helen Bynum, *Spitting Blood: The History of Tuberculosis* (Oxford: Oxford University Press, 2012).

had arrived at Portsmouth, but that the ship not being ready to sail the Revd. Mr. Griffin had taken him to his house for a few days. In the meantime, by the directions of Capt. Nourse, a cabin would be fitted up for his reception, in order that he might have the benefit of being on board the Vessel.[73]

Taking advantage of the delay, the LMS forwarded to Nourse 'a Letter to Radama, king of Madagascar, respecting Coutamave'.[74] Shortly afterwards, Ikiotomavo died aboard the *Andromache*,[75] which the same month (March) sailed from Spithead for the Cape of Good Hope and Madagascar. On 8 December 1822, Nourse wrote to the LMS directors informing them

that he had delivered all the effects belonging to Countemaive the Madagascar Youth Deceased to his Grandfather Prince Rafala the Chief of Foul Point, Madagascar who appeared deeply sensible to the attentions which had been paid to his Grand Son – that he had also written to the King, Radama informing him of the Death of the youth and the disposal of his effects.[76]

The *Andromache* then returned to the Cape from where Nourse was instrumental in the recruitment of more Madagascar Youths as naval apprentices (see Chapter 4).

Training

On 21 May 1821, the LMS directors appointed William Alers Hankey (1772–1859), LMS treasurer, and John Arundel (1778–1848), LMS home secretary, to meet Henry Goulburn (1784–1856), Bathurst's secretary, in order to determine the precise conditions governing LMS supervision of the Madagascar Youths selected to be apprenticed in crafts. As a result, they noted,

The Rank which these Youths held in their own Country will make it proper that situations more select, than those of common English Apprentices, should be found; and that their Clothing and maintenance shall be superior in comfort to that usually enjoyed by such persons.
   When these Youths are sent back to their own country, if the end of their residence in England has been adequately effected, they shall be furnished, at the expense of Government, with such Tools, Instruments and Books, as the Society shall judge necessary for the communication of the knowledge which they have acquired to their Countrymen.[77]

---

[73] Meeting of Directors, 11 Mar. 1822, LMS Board Minutes, SOAS/CWM.
[74] Meeting of Directors, 11 Mar. 1822, LMS Board Minutes, SOAS/CWM.
[75] Meeting of Directors, 8 Apr. 1822, LMS Board Minutes, SOAS/CWM; *Missionary Register* (Jun. 1822), 228; RH, 96–7, Archives de l'Académie Malgache, Antananarivo, Madagascar (hereafter AAM); Rabary, *Ny Daty Malaza*, 42.
[76] Meeting of Directors, 14 Apr. 1823, LMS Board Minutes, SOAS/CWM.
[77] Meeting of Directors, 11 Jun. 1821, LMS Board Minutes, SOAS/CWM.

It is of note that the LMS considered the six Madagascar Youths concerned to be of superior rank to 'common English Apprentices' and assigned them to learn skills in which non-Whites represented only 0.8 per cent of total craftsmen.[78] By the early 1820s, conditions for most apprentices in Britain were parlous. From 1562, when it was first enacted by parliament, the Statute of Artificers ensured that the main avenue for young men to enter a specific craft or trade or industry was an apprenticeship organized by a craft guild. This entailed a formal contractual relationship, generally of seven years' duration, between a master craftsman and the apprentice. The master provided the apprentice with formal training in a specific craft and in the appropriate manners and wider skills necessary to conduct business, as well as with a small amount of money. At the end of a successful apprenticeship, the trainee could establish his own business. The Statute of Artificers was repealed in 1814 because of abuses of the system by masters and the emergence of new trades, notably those, from the late eighteenth century, associated with the Industrial Revolution that were not provided for by the conventional apprenticeship regulations. From then, until the rise of trade unions in the latter half of the nineteenth century, the guilds lost their power to regulate apprenticeships, and in the new laissez-faire economic environment, no legal requirements existed for craft training. This was particularly significant for the Madagascar Youths, who were apprenticed in the English capital where a corporation ruling had in 1731 forbidden the apprenticeship of Black males.[79] Only with the establishment of trade unions did regulated apprenticeships again became significant. It is estimated that there were over 340,000 apprentices in England in the early 1900s.[80]

The LMS supervisory committee considered that, by mid-1822, the Madagascar Youths would have acquired sufficient English to start their apprenticeships. Consequently, in February 1822, the LMS board asked the committee

to make inquiries for suitable Masters under whom they may acquire the knowledge of those arts and trades, which their friends in Madagascar pointed out for them, and to use their best endeavours to place them in pious families, where attention will be paid to

---

[78] Myers, 'Servant, Sailor, Soldier, Tailor, Beggarman', 58.

[79] Myers, 'Servant, Sailor, Soldier, Tailor, Beggarman', 48.

[80] Thomas Deissinger, 'Apprenticeship Systems in England and Germany: Decline and Survival', in Wolf-Dietrich Greinert and Georg Hanf (eds.),*Towards a History of Vocational Education and Training (VET) in Europe in a Comparative Perspective: Proceedings of the First International Conference, October 2002, Florence*, vol. 1 (Luxembourg: Office for Official Publications of the European Communities, 2004), 33–6; 'Apprenticeships', in Richard Evans, *A Short History of Technical Education*, https://technicaleducationmatters.org/2009/05/13/chapter-3-the-guilds-and-apprenticeships (accessed 23.04.21); James Mirza-Davies, 'A Short History of Apprenticeships in England: From Medieval Craft Guilds to the Twenty-First Century', House of Commons Library (2015), https://commonslibrary.parliament.uk/a-short-history-of-apprenticeships-in-england-from-medieval-craft-guilds-to-the-twenty-first-century (accessed 23.04.21).

their religious instruction, and that they be requested to endeavour to accomplish this object by or before Midsummer next, when it is expected that then, at least some of them, will leave the Borough School.[81]

Ikiotomavo died in late March or early April 1822, but the LMS directors decided on 12 August 1822 that, 'being fully prepared for leaving the School,' Verkey, Ramboa, and Andrianaivo, three of the five remaining Madagascar Youths destined for craft training, should start their apprenticeships.[82] By December that year, the other two youths were also ready. Thus, Holehouse wrote to the LMS,

Eighteen months have passed away since you received into your care certain youths from Madagascar, and appointed a few friends to superintend them. Being one of those friends, I have fulfilled your wishes, and visited the school once every week, with few exceptions. I have the pleasure to declare, that Mr. and Mrs. Picton, the master and mistress of the School, have exercised unremitting attention to these lads, always thoughtful for their comfort and Instruction. I have the pleasure to say, that if the same number of youths were selected from any sphere of English Society, they would not, I am persuaded, excel those from Madagascar in good Temper, pleasing behaviour, and Mental Capacity.[83]

The LMS directors recognized that their agents lacked the competency to supervise Ramboa and Verkey in learning the arts of, respectively, gun and gunpowder manufacture but appear to have been untroubled about the morality of training them in the use of items used both in war and with reference to guns and gunpowder, commodities that helped to fuel the slave trade in Africa.[84]

Verkey

In August 1822, the LMS requested Robert Howard & Co. of 115 Old Street Road, one of the largest producers of tin ware in London, if Verkey – who had been raised in southeast Madagascar with a knowledge of tin work – could be

[81] Meeting of Directors, 25 Feb. 1822, LMS Board Minutes, SOAS/CWM.
[82] MS 11936/447/830309, 27 Apr. 1809, National Archives, www.nationalarchives.gov.uk/A2A/ records.aspx?cat=076-sun_2-0-447&cid=-1&Gsm=2008-06-18#-1 (accessed 02/09/2009); Meeting of Directors, 12 Aug. 1822, LMS Board Minutes, SOAS/CWM; Thomas Curtis, *The London Encyclopaedia* (London: Printed for T. Tegg, 1829), vol. 22, 118–19.
[83] Charles Holehouse to LMS, 30 Dec. 1822, in Meeting of Directors, 30 Dec. 1822, LMS Board Minutes, SOAS/CWM.
[84] For the gun–slave debate in the context of the African slave trade, see e.g. Gwyn Campbell, *An Economic History of Imperial Madagascar, 1750–1895: The Rise and Fall of an Island Empire* (Cambridge: Cambridge University Press, 2005); Chapurukha M. Kusimba, 'The Impact of Slavery on the East African Political Economy and Gender Relationships', in Lydia Wilson Marshall (ed.), *The Archaeology of Slavery: A Comparative Approach to Captivity and Coercion* (Carbondale: Southern Illinois University Press, 2014), 230–54; Warren C. Whatley, 'The Gun–Slave Hypothesis and the 18th Century British Slave Trade', *Explorations in Economic History* 67 (2018), 80–104.

placed there to learn 'the art of manufacturing Tin Goods'.[85] Robert Howard (1738–1812), founder of the company, a Quaker, and a founding member of the BFBS, had become wealthy through tin plate manufacturing.[86] However, the company declined the request, possibly because Verkey's intention to learn gunpowder manufacturing offended the firm's Quaker sentiments (many were pacifists). On 9 September 1822, the directors asked Arundel 'to look out for suitable situations in which Verkee [sic] the Madagascar Youth who is to learn the manufacture of Gunpowder and Tin Working, may be instructed in those arts, with due attention to the preservation of his morals'.[87] In the interim, the directors employed Verkey in 'learning the system of teaching'.[88] Finally, on 19 February 1823, the Colonial Office authorized Verkey to go to either Waltham Abbey or the Royal Laboratory, Woolwich Arsenal.[89]

Verkey was sent to Waltham Abbey, located on the River Lea, in Essex, some 30 km northeast of Borough Road School. The Second Anglo-Dutch War (1665–7) had stimulated the government into converting an oil mill at Waltham Abbey into a gunpowder manufactory, and, from 1702, William Walton (d. 1711) and his family developed it into a principal supplier of gunpowder to the Board of Ordnance. By the 1730s, the centre was described as 'the largest and completest [gunpowder] works in Great Britain';[90] in 1804, it was classified as one of the top three (alongside Faversham, and Ballincollig in southwest Ireland), and again in 1810 as the best gunpowder manufactory. Set in 170 acres of parkland, Waltham Abbey gunpowder works was kept top secret.[91] In 1806, a canal system that ensured the safe delivery of raw materials and collection of gunpowder was extended to enable barges to convey gun-powder to the Warren, an ordnance storage depot at Woolwich arsenal on the south bank of the River Thames, and the royal arsenal at Purfleet, also on the

[85] MS 11936/447/830309, 27 Apr. 1809, National Archives; *Commercial Directory* (1841), 437; Meeting of Directors, 12 Aug. 1822, LMS Board Minutes, SOAS/CWM; Curtis, *London Encyclopaedia*, vol. 22, 118–19; [Robert Howard & Co.], *A Catalogue of Tin, Japanned, & Zinc Wares: Sold by Robert Howard & Co* (London: J. H. Banks, 1842).

[86] Jim Burton, 'Howard, Luke (1772–1864)', *Oxford Dictionary of National Biography* (1 Sep. 2017), www.oxforddnb.com/view/10.1093/ref:odnb/9780198614128.001.0001/odnb-978 0198614128-e-13928 (accessed 13.07.21).

[87] Meeting of Directors, 9 Sep. 1822, LMS Board Minutes, SOAS/CWM.

[88] Charles Holehouse to LMS, 30 Dec. 1822 in Meeting of Directors, 30 Dec. 1822, LMS Board Minutes, SOAS/CWM.

[89] Meeting of Directors, 24 Feb. 1823, LMS Board Minutes, SOAS/CWM.

[90] www.royalgunpowdermills.com/historicpast.htm (accessed 04/10/2009); see also 'Waltham Holy Cross – Economic History and Local Government', www.british-history.ac.uk/report .aspx?compid=42719&strquery=powder (accessed 04/10/2009); 'The Royal Gunpowder Mills – Waltham Abbey', www.glias.org.uk/news/193news.html (accessed 04/10/2009).

[91] In the course of the nineteenth century the works expanded to become a complex of twenty buildings. At the end of that century, it switched from gunpowder to cordite, the mills producing a wide range of explosives and chemical propellants up to 1991; see www .royalgunpowdermills.com (04/10/2009).

Thames, where five gunpowder magazines had been established from 1760 following an explosion at Woolwich.[92]

Gunpowder production at Waltham Abbey, fuelled by the French wars, reached 30,000 hundred-pound [45.36 kg] barrels in 1813, when the works employed 260 people,[93] and in 1816 a Royal Small Arms Factory was erected nearby, manufacturing military rifles, muskets, and swords. However, the onset of peace in 1815 resulted in a sustained fall in production. Consequently, in March 1823, Joseph Hume (1777–1855), MP, an avid reformer, objected in Parliament 'to the unnecessary expense of the establishments at Waltham Abbey and Faversham, which had cost the country £150,000 in the last ten years, and where little or no gunpowder had been manufactured'.[94]

Dr Parker of Woolwich Arsenal, an enthusiastic supporter of evangelical causes, advised the LMS that 'Verkey must go to Waltham Abbey to acquire the art of manufacturing [gunpowder]' and that 'when he is perfectly instructed in this, he should be sent to Woolwich to acquire knowledge of the methods of application'.[95] However, it appears that Verkey only attended Waltham Abbey. In 1823, when Verkey commenced his apprenticeship, a bizarre event occurred at Waltham. Its inhabitants, and those in neighbouring Cheshunt, annually performed a ritual 'perambulation' of their respective parishes during which certain slight liberties were taken, and which ended in the two groups engaging in rival banter. However, in 1823, the people of Cheshunt reiterated a complaint, dating back to 1601, that parish boundaries should be redrawn to give them all of Waltham 'west of Powder Mill Lane'. Bedlam resulted: 'This created great sensation in the town and the men of Waltham met their antagonists at the Marshgate, where a desperate battle ensued and when heads were fractured and other personal injuries sustained.'[96]

Verkey served his apprenticeship under John Braddock, 'Master Refiner of Saltpetre',[97] whose son and namesake gained renown as author of a book on

[92] Mick Sinclair, *The Thames: A Cultural History* (New York: Oxford University Press, 2007).
[93] John Maynard, *The Parish of Waltham Abbey, Its History and Antiquities* (London: J. R. Smith, 1865), 87; 'Waltham Holy Cross'.
[94] Anon, 'Ordnance Estimates', HC Deb (14 Mar. 1823) *Hansard*, vol. 8, cc598.
[95] Meeting of Directors, 24 Feb. 1823, LMS Board Minutes, SOAS/CWM; see also John Seely Stone, *A Memoir of the Life of James Milnor, DD: Late Rector of St George's Church, New York* (New York: American Tract Society, 1848), 357–9.
[96] James Carr, 'An Account of the Perambulation of the Parish of Waltham Holy Cross, taken in 1823', quoted in William Winters, *The History of the Ancient Parish of Waltham Abbey, or Holy Cross* (Essex: W. Winters, 1888), 45; see also William Winters, *Our Parish Registers; being three hundred years of curious local history, as collected from the original registers, church-wardens' accounts, and monumental records of the parish of Waltham Holy Cross* (Waltham Abbey: W. Winters, 1885), 55.
[97] H. A. Young, *The East India Company's Arsenals & Manufactories* ([Luton]: Andrews UK, 2012), 95.

gunpowder production.[98] In February 1824, Braddock informed the LMS that Verkey had made significant progress and would complete his training by the close of March that year.[99] However, Dr John A. Gillham (b. 1774) warned the LMS that Verkey was in poor health – possibly another reference to tuberculosis – and might not survive another winter.[100] Gillham, who in 1797 had served for a few months as an LMS missionary doctor in Tahiti, returned to become chief surgeon to the Coldstream Guards, then established a practice at Clapham and served as physician to the LMS.[101] Gillham's observations persuaded the LMS board to advise Bathurst to send Verkey back to Madagascar.[102] In August 1824, they granted Verkey's request that he 'be furnished with a certain quantity of weights which he should require, on his return to Madagascar, in applying his knowledge of Gunpowder to practical uses'.[103] The following month, the directors reported that although 'Verkey is of opinion that he has learnt everything we have shown him in the Art of making Gun Powder' and was 'a Youth of very able parts and understanding' who 'has paid the greatest attention to acquire information', they were apprehensive that 'when he returns to Madagascar he will be much at a loss for the necessary machinery and various utensils used, and also not having the Chemical Knowledge to ascertain the purity of the ingredients for the component part of Gun Powder'.[104]

British evangelicals placed great emphasis on converting pagans under their care to Christianity. The most important signal of this process was baptism, during which converts adopted new, 'Christian' names.[105] On Friday 8 October 1824, shortly before his departure for Madagascar, Verkey, alongside Ramboa and Razafinkarefo, was baptized by the Rev. John Angell James (1785–1859) of Birmingham. For James, 'a national authority on matters spiritual', the baptism of the Madagascar Youths was a major victory for Christianity in its fight against the heathen world of Chinese, Hindu, and native

[98] John Braddock, *A Memoir on Gunpowder, in which are discussed the Principles both of its Manufacture and Proof* (London: Richardson, 1832).

[99] Meeting of Directors, 3 Feb. 1824, LMS Board Minutes, SOAS/CWM.

[100] Pickstone, *Medicine and Industrial Society*, 225–9; Boxen, 'A Spirit of Benevolence', 1–2, 57–8, 83–4.

[101] Rhys Richards, 'Manuscript XVII: Who Taught Pomare to Read? Unpublished Comments by a Missionary Surgeon on Tahiti in May 1807 to October 1810, and Journal Entries by an Able Seaman at Tahiti in 1811', *Journal of Pacific History* 40.1 (2005), 105.

[102] Extract from a despatch of the Earl Bathurst [to governor of Mauritius], 20 Jul. 1824, NAM, HB 4.

[103] Meeting of Directors, 9 Aug. 1824, LMS Board Minutes, SOAS/CWM.

[104] 'Report from the Ordinance Dept. relating to Verkey (one of the Madagascar youths) who has been instructed in the process of making Gun Powder' transmitted in a letter from Mr W. Horton, dated 30th Sep. 1824, NAM, HB 4.

[105] Myers, 'Servant, Sailor, Soldier, Tailor, Beggarman', 61–2; Sivasundaram, 'Natural History Spiritualized', 418.

American idolaters, and African barbarians.[106] The baptisms took place in Rowland Hill's chapel on Blackfriars Road in what the directors called a 'deeply interesting and numerously attended' service.[107] It was reported that

About eleven o'clock the chapel doors were opened, and the interior soon filled with a highly respectable congregation, the majority of which were composed of elegantly dressed ladies, all of whom seemed to take a deep interest on the occasion. The three youths, the eldest of whom appeared to be about 18 years of age, were conducted into the Chapel by the Rev. Mr. James, and took their seats immediately under the pulpit. The young men were dressed in European fashion, and possessed open and pleasing countenances, none of their features, except their colour, resembling the natives of that part of the continent of Africa which is contiguous to Madagascar.[108]

The directors presented Verkey, who had taken the baptismal name 'Joseph',[109] with a parting gift comprising £5 worth of books and, at his request, a case of mathematical instruments, a watch, and a fowling piece.[110] On 30 October 1824, the three youths sailed from Gravesend aboard the *Alexander*, under Captain Richardson, for Mauritius, where they arrived on 19 February.[111] There, they planned to wait until April, when Hastie was expected to arrive from Madagascar, and subsequently accompany him back to Tamatave.[112]

Ramboa

Radama requested that Ramboa learn the art of gunmaking. In consequence, the LMS sought to place him in Birmingham, which in the late eighteenth century had surpassed London as the gun-producing centre of Britain.[113] In August 1822, they asked Rev. Timothy East (c.1784–1871) of Ebenezer Chapel, Birmingham, to secure an apprenticeship for Ramboa with a local gunmaker.[114] East, described by radical George Jacob Holyoake (1817–1906) as 'a saintly and popular preacher',[115] had in 1814 converted John Williams (1796–1839), a celebrated LMS missionary to the South Seas. In 1822, East

---

[106] Catherine Hall, *Civilising Subjects: Metropole and Colony in the English Imagination 1830–1867* (Chicago: University of Chicago Press, 2002), 301–2.

[107] Meeting of Directors, 11 Oct. 1824, LMS Board Minutes, SOAS/CWM; see also 'Baptism of Three Madagascar Youths', *Morning Chronicle* (12 Oct. 1824).

[108] 'Baptism of Three Madagascar Youths', *Morning Chronicle* (12 Oct. 1824).

[109] *Missionary Register* (1824), 519.

[110] Meeting of Directors, 26 Sep. 1824, LMS Board Minutes, SOAS/CWM.

[111] *Evangelical Magazine and Missionary Chronicle* (Dec. 1824), 549.

[112] Meeting of Directors, 27 Jun. 1825, LMS Board Minutes, SOAS/CWM.

[113] 'The Birmingham Gun Barrel Proof House', www.gunproof.com (accessed 05/10/2009); Joseph McKenna, *The Gun Makers of Birmingham, 1660–1960* (Jefferson, NC: McFarland & Company, 2021), 27–95.

[114] Meeting of Directors, 12 Aug. 1822, LMS Board Minutes, SOAS/CWM.

[115] George Jacob Holyoake, *Sixty Years of an Agitator's Life*, vol. 1 (London: T.F. Unwin, 1909), 46.

preached a sermon entitled 'Christianity Contrasted with Hinduism', and in 1825 published *Lectures on Moral and Religious Subjects, addressed to Mechanics*.[116] In November 1822, East informed the LMS that he had found an opening for Ramboa, but on terms which made the directors write to Radama 'apprising him of the impractibility, of rendering any one person perfect in the art of Gunmaking, on account of the variety of its branches, and as each branch requires an apprenticeship'.[117] In February 1823, Thomas Harris, a Birmingham merchant, accompanied Ramboa from London to place him 'under the care of a proper person, who shall teach him the art of Gunmaking'. Shortly after reaching Birmingham, Harris announced the 'safe arrival of himself and the youth' who 'was in good health and perfectly cheerful and happy when he resigned his charge of him' to East.[118] Ramboa lodged with a Mr Jacques, who charged a rent of about £22.10s a month,[119] probably in the vicinity of St Chad's Cathedral, where gun production was concentrated.[120]

However, a year later, Ramboa fled Birmingham. This and Ramboa's subsequent behaviour indicate that a distressing incident had occurred. On 8 March 1824, Jacques informed the LMS that 'Romboa, the Madagascar youth ... had left his house on Sabbath [29 February] and had not since been heard of'.[121] The directors learned that Ramboa 'had arrived in London on Wednesday evening [3 March] having walked greater part of the way from Birmingham to town – that he was now under the care of Mr. Picton at the Boro' Road School'.[122] In his journey to London, Ramboa had covered just over 200 km, averaging 51 km a day. While it is intimated that he might have been offered an occasional short ride, in a cart or on a horse, he walked most of the way. The sight of a coloured youth travelling alone and long distance would have aroused the interest of all he passed but was by no means a unique occurrence. Slavery had largely ended in Britain by the mid-1790s, and many former slaves abandoned their 'masters' to seek independent existences, often in the major cities.[123]

On hearing of Ramboa's arrival at Borough Road School, the LMS board despatched a delegation, which included the LMS foreign secretary, Rev.

---

[116] George Yates, *An Historical and Descriptive Sketch of Birmingham* (Birmingham: Beilby, Knott, and Beilby, 1830), 138; Ebenezer Prout, *Memoirs of the Life of the Rev. John Williams, Missionary to Polynesia* (Andover: Allen, Morrill & Wardwell, 1843), 13; David Murray, *Biblical Student's Assistant* (Edinburgh: Oliver & Boyd, 1844), 10, 129; John Sibree and M. Caston, *Independency in Warwickshire: A Brief History of the Independent or Congregational Churches in that County* (Coventry: G. & F. King, 1855), 186.

[117] Meeting of Directors, 9 Dec. 1822, LMS Board Minutes, SOAS/CWM.

[118] Meeting of Directors, 24 Feb. 1823, LMS Board Minutes, SOAS/CWM.

[119] Meeting of Directors, 22 Dec. 1822, LMS Board Minutes, SOAS/CWM.

[120] 'Gunmakers of Birmingham'; 'The Birmingham Gun Barrel Proof House'.

[121] Meeting of Directors, 15 Mar. 1824, LMS Board Minutes, SOAS/CWM.

[122] Meeting of Directors, 15 Mar. 1824, LMS Board Minutes, SOAS/CWM.

[123] Myers, 'Servant, Sailor, Soldier, Tailor, Beggarman', 49–50, 59.

George Burder (1752–1832), and Holehouse, to see Ramboa and 'ascertain from him the true state of the case'.[124] The delegation reported 'their unanimous opinion that he should not return to Birmingham'. In consequence, the LMS settled their account with Jacques.[125] However, failing to find 'a suitable situation' for Ramboa in London, the directors wrote to the 'Revd. Messrs James and East of Birmingham respecting his case and the expediency of his returning to Birmingham – but not to the same situation in that town'.[126] East replied on 5 April 1824, 'urging upon the Directors the propriety of his returning not only to Birmingham but also to Mr. Jaques the person under whose care he had been previously placed'. Consequently, on 12 April 1824, the board authorized Arundel, LMS home secretary, 'to embrace the earliest opportunity which may offer for a return of Romboa to Birmingham'.[127]

The prospect of returning to Birmingham apparently caused Ramboa to go insane. Picton urgently contacted the LMS board, who, fearful of the youth's 'aberration of mind', requested Dr J. A. Gillham to examine Ramboa.[128] In his report of 24 April, Gillham made no reference to symptoms of phthisis, thus ruling out tuberculosis – which had long been associated with madness – as a possible cause of Ramboa's derangement.[129] He stated that

he had visited Romboa at the British and Foreign Free School – where he had found him in an Insane State of Mind which was progressively increasing to stronger acts of violence, endangering both his own safety and that of others around him – that he had deemed it necessary to place him in a Lunatic Asylum and accordingly had proceeded with him to the Retreat, Clapham Road, licensed to Dr. Burrows, where he is safely lodged and where he can visit him and treat the case as circumstances may require.[130]

The LMS sent Gilham's report to Bathurst, who informed them that he had confidence in their decision and wished Gilham to continue treating Ramboa.[131]

The 'Retreat', newly opened in 1823, was a private lunatic asylum situated in large grounds west of St John's Church and the British Home for Incurables on Clapham Rise (High Street).[132] It was directed by George Man Burrows (1771–1846), who applied 'scientific psychiatry', modelled after Parisian hospital

---

[124] Meeting of Directors, 15 Mar. 1824, LMS Board Minutes, SOAS/CWM.
[125] Meeting of Directors, 22 Mar. 1824, LMS Board Minutes, SOAS/CWM.
[126] Meeting of Directors, 29 Mar. 1824, LMS Board Minutes, SOAS/CWM.
[127] Meeting of Directors, 12 Apr. 1824, LMS Board Minutes, SOAS/CWM.
[128] Meeting of Directors, 19 Apr. 1824, LMS Board Minutes, SOAS/CWM.
[129] E. R. N. Grigg, 'Historical and Bibliographical Review of Tuberculosis in the Mentally Ill', *Journal of the History of Medicine and Allied Sciences* 10.1 (1955), 58–108.
[130] Meeting of Directors, 26 Apr. 1824, LMS Board Minutes, SOAS/CWM.
[131] Meeting of Directors, 26 Apr. 1824, LMS Board Minutes, SOAS/CWM; R. M. Horton to Directors, Downing Street, 1 May 1824, LMS Board Minutes, SOAS/CWM.
[132] From an 1880 Ordnance Survey map – 'The 1832 Madhouse Act and the Metropolitan Commission in Lunacy from 1832', http://studymore.org.uk/3_06.htm (accessed 18/04/09); 'Sibella Road Conservation Area Appraisal', www.lambeth.gov.uk/sites/default/files/CA58Si bellaRdAppraisal.pdf (accessed 28.01.22).

practices. Until 1829, Burrows enjoyed the reputation of being one of London's most successful psychiatrists.[133] The Retreat accommodated from twenty to thirty inmates, including the geologist William Buckland (1784–1856),[134] most of whom were transferred there in 1823 from a smaller asylum in Chelsea that Burrows had directed from 1816, and which had accepted its first resident inmate in 1821. Patients in 1829 included a surgeon, a silversmith, a tea dealer broker, a wine merchant, a silver chaser, a tobacconist, a merchant, a servant, a bricklayer, four clerks, and two army officers.[135]

The LMS chose carefully, for they wished to avoid the abuse of lunatic asylum inmates that was disclosed as being widespread by a parliamentary select committee from 1815–16, which led to a series of legislative reforms in the committal of lunatics and the maintenance of asylums.[136] Commissioners who inspected the Retreat in October 1829 found it generally satisfactory but advised Burrows to 'prevent such a great intermixture of the sleeping rooms of the two sexes'.[137] The LMS directors were possibly impressed by Burrows holding religious services in the asylum each Sunday and his belief that 'Madness is one of the curses imposed by the wrath of the ALMIGHTY on his people for their sins'.[138] Somewhat contradictorily, he also considered insanity to be a disease, detectable by an odour similar to 'henbane in a state of fermentation',[139] that could be treated and sometimes cured. Burrows' fortune waned from 1829 when he was involved in two successive cases of wrongful confinement. Although in neither case did Burrows act out of ill intent, the media painted him as unscrupulous. The *Quarterly Review* even coined for him the phrase 'burrowsed', meaning 'wrongfully confined'.[140]

Most asylum inmates were removed from familial surroundings to be committed to the care of 'specialists'.[141] However, Ramboa was twice removed, first from his original Malagasy family and secondarily from the Madagascar Youths, who, since leaving Madagascar, had become his second 'family', and

---

[133] George Man Burrows, *An Inquiry into Certain Errors Relative to Insanity and Their Consequences, Physical, Moral and Civil* (London: Thomas and George Underwood, 1820); Akihito Suzuki, *Madness at Home: The Psychiatrist, the Patient, and the Family in England, 1820–1860* (Berkeley: University of California Press, 2006), 43–50, 60.

[134] 'William Buckland (1784–1856)' – www.oxonblueplaques.org.uk/plaques/buckland.html (accessed 28.01.22).

[135] '1832 Madhouse Act'.   [136] Suzuki, *Madness at Home*, 15, 20–1.

[137] Charles Ross, Thomas Turner, and H. H. Southey, 'Report' (1829), quoted in '1832 Madhouse Act'.

[138] George Man Burrows, *Commentaries on the Causes, Forms, Symptoms, and Treatment, Moral and Medical, of Insanity* (London: Thomas and George Underwood, 1828), 1; see also '1832 Madhouse Act'.

[139] Burrows, *Commentaries*, 297; Suzuki, *Madness at Home*, 46.

[140] Suzuki, *Madness at Home*, 50–61; Akihito Suzuki, 'Burrows, George Man (1771–1846)', in H. C. G. Matthew and Brian Harrison (eds), *Oxford Dictionary of National Biography* (Oxford: Oxford University Press, 2004), www.oxforddnb.com/view/article/4114 (accessed 18/04/09).

[141] Suzuki, *Madness at Home*, 1–4.

to whom he could relate in his mother tongue. Again, whereas British inmates, upon being committed, were temporarily deprived of their civil rights, Ramboa, as a juvenile Malagasy in Britain, enjoyed no 'civil rights', nor any possible claim on property. This considerably facilitated the ability of the LMS to commit Ramboa as they were not obliged, as in most cases concerning adult British subjects, to proceed via a commission of lunacy.[142] It is worth considering if the LMS were also motivated, as it appears were many family heads in relation to children falling under their authority, by the desire to suppress 'juvenile rebellion'.[143]

Further, the case of Ramboa raises the issue of how race and madness were perceived by nineteenth-century Europeans. There had been previous cases of individuals from the Indian Ocean World travelling to Europe and being committed to lunatic asylums. One example is John Hu, a Chinese convert to Catholicism, who was taken by Jesuit missionary Jean-François Foucquet (1665–1741) to France in 1722. In France his behaviour, including 'escapes' and the desire to walk instead of taking a coach from Orléans to Paris, led to him being confined in May 1823 in Charenton lunatic asylum (where the Marquis de Sade was detained from 1801 until his death in 1814). Hu remained in Charenton for two years, before being returned to China in 1726.[144] For all the publicity given to Ratefy in 1821, most people considered Ramboa to be 'African', and thus from a place of overlapping savagery, violence, overt sexuality, and insanity.[145] Despite Ramboa having received an elemental English education in Borough Road School,[146] Burrows noted of his encounters with the youth in the Retreat,

I have met with two facts which favour the position, that natives of the torrid zone upon becoming *acclimaté* in England, may be soon affected by mental derangement. One was a youth of Madagascar, not arrived at puberty, who had been brought over by the Missionary Society to be educated and instructed in the principles of Christianity. He could read a little, but could not speak English. He was in a state of melancholia, and after being in my establishment three or four months, recovered and went home. The other was a native of South America, and a well-educated young man. He also sunk into melancholia. There was no apparent cause in either case to occasion insanity.[147]

On 21 June 1824, Holehouse reported that Ramboa's health had improved and recommended that he be removed from the asylum. The LMS board had

---

[142] Suzuki, *Madness at Home*, 14–38.   [143] Suzuki, *Madness at Home*, 9.
[144] Jonathan D. Spence, *The Question of Hu* (New York: Knopf, 1988).
[145] Richard C. Keller, *Colonial Madness: Psychiatry in French North Africa* (Chicago: University of Chicago Press, 2007). For sexuality, see e.g. Johannes Fabian, *Out of Our Minds: Reason and Madness in the Exploration of Central Africa* (Berkeley: University of California Press, 2000), 79–86.
[146] *Missionary Register* (Jun. 1822), 228–9.   [147] Burrows, *Commentaries*, 237.

Gilham re-examine Ramboa and forwarded his report to the Colonial Office.[148] Further, they sought the advice of East on the propriety of returning Ramboa to Birmingham. East responded that 'in the opinion of the person who had the Instruction of the Madagascar Youth in the Art of Gunmaking, he [Ramboa] would not be able to acquire a knowledge of the various branches unless his time was considerably extended'.[149] Consequently, the directors advised the Colonial Office that Ramboa should be sent back to Madagascar, and Bathurst authorized the move, informing Lowry Cole (1772–1842), who in 1823 had succeeded Farquhar as governor of Mauritius, of Ramboa's 'symptoms of mental derangement'.[150] The LMS presented Ramboa with £2.10s worth of 'useful books'[151] and, on 30 October 1824, he sailed for Mauritius aboard the *Alexander*, in the company of Verkey and Razafinkarefo.[152]

Andrianaivo and Raolombelona

Andrianaivo, earmarked for training in textile production, had like Ikiotomavo fallen seriously ill before the close of 1821, and the LMS contemplated sending both home.[153] Ikiotomavo died soon after, but Andrianaivo's health improved sufficiently for the LMS to enrol him that year in Borough Road School.[154] In August 1822, the directors asked Rev. William Roby (1766–1830) of Grosvenor Street Independent Chapel, Manchester, a fervent LMS supporter, to find Andrianaivo an apprenticeship to learn 'the art of manufacturing calico'.[155] A little later, they requested the same favour for Raolombelona. Roby duly obliged, writing to the directors in November 1822,

that one of his friends had offered the gratuitous use of a room in his factory, entirely separated from the other workmen – that looms might be purchased for two or three pounds each – that a suitable person may be provided to teach and superintend the youths at the rate of Fifteen Shillings pr. Week – and that he could provide suitable accommodations for them at the rate of twelve or Fourteen Shillings pr. week.[156]

---

[148] Meeting of Directors, 28 Jun. 1824, LMS Board Minutes, SOAS/CWM.
[149] Meeting of Directors, 30 Jun. 1823, LMS Board Minutes, SOAS/CWM.
[150] Extract from a despatch of the Earl Bathurst [to Governor of Mauritius], 20 Jul. 1824, NAM, HB 4.
[151] Meeting of Directors, 26 Sep. 1824, LMS Board Minutes, SOAS/CWM.
[152] *Evangelical Magazine and Missionary Chronicle* (Dec. 1824), 549.
[153] Meeting of Directors, 14 Jan. 1822, LMS Board Minutes, SOAS/CWM; Wilmot to Hankey, Downing Street, 17 Jan. 1822, in Meeting of Directors, 21 Jan. 1822, LMS Board Minutes, SOAS/CWM.
[154] 'Borough Road College – Student List'.
[155] Meeting of Directors, 12 Aug. 1822, LMS Board Minutes, SOAS/CWM.
[156] Meeting of Directors, 18 Nov. 1822, LMS Board Minutes, SOAS/CWM; see also Meeting of Directors, 11 Nov. 1822, LMS Board Minutes, SOAS/CWM.

The board accepted these terms, determining 'that the two youths ... be sent down to Manchester under the care of Mr. Wilson, who leaves Town for that place this week'.[157]

Andrianaivo and Raolombelona left London on 20 November accompanied by LMS missionary, Samuel Sheridan Wilson (1797–1866). Sheridan, who was from Manchester, where he had joined Roby's congregation, was in 1818 appointed to the Greek mission and sent to Malta. However, because of the turmoil that followed the Greek Revolution of 1821, he spent from September 1822 to early 1824 in England.[158] Two months after he returned to London, the LMS directors ordered him to Manchester, with a letter for Roby containing 'full instructions ... respecting the care of their [the two Madagascar Youths'] health and morals [and] requesting him to send a report to the Directors quarterly of their state'. Wilson deposited the youths with Roby 'in Safety, though fatigued' on the evening of 21 November. A few days later, Roby informed the directors,

After a night's rest at our house, they said they were as well as when they left London. Having ascertained their proficiency in Arithmetic &c. &c. I felt the weight of your Instructions in reference to the Continued improvement of their Education. In the lodgings which I had procured for them, I found this could not be the case. Except by private Tuition which would have involved additional Expense. Having applied to the Revd. Dr. Clunie to know if he could possibly accommodate them, he immediately consented to receive them at the reduced terms of thirty three Guineas pr. Annum, affording them for this sum, Board, Lodging, and Education, morning and evening among his pupils. – The terms are lower than I had contracted for their board and lodging. They cannot be more advantageously situated. Mrs. Clunie's care and Tenderness will be more likely to preserve their health than the weekly visits of a physician; but I confidentially expect that Dr. Jarrold will superintend their farther purpose and we have two or three Surgeons who will be equally ready to give their attendance.[159]

John Clunie (1784–1858), a close friend of Roby, was born in London and educated at Hoxton Academy and Glasgow University. He was the founder, and from 1812–37 the principal, of elite Nonconformist academies in Leaf Square and Seedley Grove, Manchester.[160] In 1822, John Morrison (1814–1843), son of Robert Morrison (1782–1834), the first Protestant (LMS) missionary to China, entered Clunie's academy, probably shortly before Andrianaivo and Raolombelona. John later returned to China, where he had been born, and became

---

[157] Meeting of Directors, 18 Nov. 1822, LMS Board Minutes, SOAS/CWM.

[158] James Sibree, *London Missionary Society: A Register of Missionaries, Deputations, etc. from 1796 to 1923* (London: LMS, 1923), 19.

[159] Meeting of Directors, 25 Nov. 1822, LMS Board Minutes, SOAS/CWM.

[160] Josiah Thomas Slugg, *Reminiscences of Manchester Fifty Years Ago* (Manchester: Simpkin, Marshall & Co, 1881), 275; Benjamin Nightingale, *Lancashire Nonconformity, Or, Sketches, Historical & Descriptive, of the Congregational and Old Presbyterian Churches in the County* (Manchester: John Heywood, 1893), 212.

a renowned translator of Chinese.[161] John was evidently intrigued at the presence of the Madagascar Youths, who he and the other British boys studying under Clunie got to know well, for in 1824 Robert Morrison wrote to his son in Manchester: 'It is gratifying to me that Mary and you feel interested in missionaries and the Madagascar boys, because Missions are the cause of God.'[162]

On 22 December 1822, the LMS wrote to Radama I:

in conformity to the wish of your Majesty and the friends of the Youths . . . we have now the pleasure of stating, that Drinave [Andrianaivo] and Rolam Balam [Raolombelona] have been placed under the care of a very respectable friend of the Society at Manchester, in which town they will be instructed in the art of making and dying (or printing) Calicos, at one of the Factories there, while they will have the opportunity when at home (place of their residence in Manchester) of improving their learning under the instructions of the Friend above mentioned, who will also pay the greatest attention to their moral conduct.[163]

And shortly afterwards, Hankey, the LMS treasurer, requested from the Colonial Office an increase to 40 guineas a year in the government living allowance for Andrianaivo and Raolombelona.[164]

In January 1823, the LMS directors were delighted to hear from Roby that Andrianaivo and Raolombelona 'had woven two pieces of calico about [80] yards each'. They immediately requested Roby 'to have the said pieces bleached, dyed, and printed, according to the judgement of the person under whose superintendence they have been made, and afterwards sent up to the Missionary Rooms'.[165] Roby attended the LMS general meeting in May 1823, and at the board meeting on 19 May 'presented several Pieces of Calico worked by Drynave and Rolam Bolam the two Madagascar Youths – which were reported on examination by two Directors to be highly credible to their diligence and improvement'. The directors then decided 'that the said pieces be forwarded to Madagascar with the next goods forwarded to that Station accompanied by a letter to Radama – explanatory of the particulars regarding their production &c.'.[166]

However, in a paper read before the Literary and Philosophical Society of Manchester, celebrated Manchester physician Thomas Jarrold (1770–1853), while lauding the 'semi-barbarous' as opposed to barbarous nature of the

[161] J. Barton Starr, 'Morrison, John Robert (1814–1843)', *Oxford Dictionary of National Biography* (3 Jan. 2008), www.oxforddnb.com/view/10.1093/ref:odnb/9780198614128 .001.0001/odnb-9780198614128-e-19327 (accessed 14/07/21).

[162] Quoted in William John Townsend, *Robert Morrison: The Pioneer of Chinese Missions* (London: S. W. Partridge, [1890]), 176.

[163] Hankey and Burder to His Majesty the King of Madagascar, [London], 23 Dec. 1822, Madagascar Outgoing Letters (hereafter MOL), SOAS/CWM.

[164] Meeting of Directors, 30 Dec. 1822, LMS Board Minutes, SOAS/CWM.

[165] Meeting of Directors, 17 Jan. 1823, LMS Board Minutes, SOAS/CWM.

[166] Meeting of Directors, 19 May 1823, LMS Board Minutes, SOAS/CWM.

Madagascar Youths, sounded a note of warning about them to the British public, in relation to Andrianaivo, Raolombelona, and Razafinkarefo in particular:

The king of Madagascar has sent several youth to this country for instruction; three of them are placed under the care of my friend, Dr. Clunie. They have acquired a knowledge of our language; they imitate our manners, and copy every thing they are desired. In school talents, they equal the European children of the same age; but their first impressions were received in Madagascar; and though they were not more than nine years old when they arrived in England, they have not lost their national character – and national character is dependent on early impressions. They take a certain station among their school-fellows; and though there is much affection felt for them, and much attention paid them, yet there is a want of assimilation; – they and their school-fellows are evidently of two countries, and have been brought up under different impressions . . .

I have not particularized the influence of early impressions on the nations just mentioned, because the character of a people so far advanced in civilization as they, is more complex than in a more barbarous age: but to meet the subject fully, I have included the semi-barbarous with the civilized, and have taken our own country as the example. I may here remark, that, when early impressions are mentioned, it is intended to be understood, that influence which the mental and moral character of the individual who has the care of a child has on its instinctive faculty.[167]

In July 1823, Clunie informed the LMS that 'Rolam Balam and Drinave, were in perfect health, and afforded him, by their attention and behaviour, entire satisfaction';[168] while the following month Raolombelona detailed to the directors 'the objects of trade and learning in which he and Drinave are receiving instruction'.[169] In January 1824, Clunie sent the LMS a report of the health and general improvement of the Malagasy under his care and requested that 'a small carding machine may be provided for the Madagascar Youths to take with them when they leave this Country' – to which the LMS board assented.[170]

However, by mid-May 1824, Clunie felt the need to inform the directors that Andrianaivo had contracted a 'dangerous illness' – tuberculosis; news they immediately passed on to Bathurst.[171] Manchester in the 1820s was an unhealthy place to live. During that decade, as its cotton textiles sector boomed, Manchester became the 'paradigmatic industrial city',[172] attracting thousands of immigrants: From 1821 to 1831, the population of Manchester, Salford, and their suburbs grew from 162,000 to 238,000 (a 47 per cent increase).[173]

---

[167] Thomas Jarrold, 'Of the Influence of Early Impressions on the Future Character', *Monthly Magazine or British Register* 59.409 (1825), 301–2.
[168] Meeting of Directors, 21 Jul. 1823, LMS Board Minutes, SOAS/CWM.
[169] Meeting of Directors, 8 Sep. 1823, LMS Board Minutes, SOAS/CWM.
[170] Meeting of Directors, 3 Feb. 1824, LMS Board Minutes, SOAS/CWM.
[171] Meeting of Directors, 17 May 1824, LMS Board Minutes, SOAS/CWM.
[172] Pickstone, *Medicine and Industrial Society*, 42.
[173] Pickstone, *Medicine and Industrial Society*, 43.

However, in such a dense urban population, poor living and work conditions resulted in high rates of illness. In the 1820s, children aged under ten accounted for over half of the city's deaths,[174] while most adult patients suffered from gastro-enteric diseases, typhus, catarrhal fever, rheumatism, coughs, asthma, and dyspnoea (laboured breathing).[175]

Andrianaivo died at 7 a.m. on 19 May 1824, aged fifteen. Just prior to his death, he had asked to be baptized, at which event he showed 'pleasing evidence of real conversion'.[176] It was commented that 'His remains were interred at New Windsor, the pall being supported by the four remaining Madagascar youths, and the whole of the students of the academy joining in the funeral procession, with black crape and white favours on their arms'.[177] In July 1824, Bathurst alerted the governor of Mauritius:

From the difference of the Climate, the health of most of the Madagascar youths has been very materially affected, and one named Drinave, I regret to state, has fallen victim to a decline probably engendered from this cause ... The Disease of which the unfortunate young man died had assumed no character of fatality till a very short period before his death. Its progress was then so rapid as to preclude the possibility of removing him from this Country.[178]

Raolombelona, the eldest of the Madagascar Youths still in Britain, continued his apprenticeship and studies. In November 1824, David Griffiths, a Welsh LMS missionary in Madagascar, acknowledged a letter, forwarded by the LMS, from Raolombelona to Radama, but commented that it was so familiar in tone that the missionaries would change it before sending it to the court.[179] Nevertheless, on 21 June 1825, J. Chenie, a tutor at Leaf Square Academy, Pendleton, near Manchester, informed Arundel that during the previous six months, Raolombelona

has pursued his Study of English Grammar, Geography, and Chemistry, and has added to them a considerable part of the first Book of Euclid's Elements.[180]

Chenie continued,

He has also practised Weaving almost the whole of the half year, and is considered a very good workman, and far better acquainted with the principles of the art and preparation of the work than many who earn their livelihood by weaving. His is now

---

[174] Pickstone, *Medicine and Industrial Society*, 54.
[175] Pickstone, *Medicine and Industrial Society*, 55.
[176] Charles Williams, *The Missionary Gazetteer* (London: Frederick Westley and A. H. Davis, 1828), 325; see also 'Character and Obituary of Drinave', *Missionary Register* (1824), 465; RH, 96; Ayache (ed.), *Raombana (1809–1855)*, 87.
[177] *The Gentleman's Magazine* 94. 1 (Jun. 1824), 646
[178] Extract from a despatch of the Earl Bathurst [to governor of Mauritius], 20 Jul. 1824, NAM, HB 4.
[179] Griffiths to Arundel, Tananarive, 4 Nov. 1824, MIL B.2 F.1 J.C, SOAS/CWM.
[180] Barry to Hastie, Port Louis, 25 Apr. 1826, NAM, HB 4.

about to change his employ by recommencing the art of dy[e]ing, and to attend to it exclusively during the present holidays: this last will enable him to see the whole process every day, as during school time he only attends to his mechanical employment in the morning and his other studies in the afternoon. He also continues to show great attachment to the duties of religion, which I hope may render him a blessing to his countrymen.[181]

In late 1825, when Roby informed the LMS board that Raolombelona had become 'sufficiently acquainted with the arts of weaving and dying', the directors decided to send him back to Madagascar.[182] As Roby also told them that Raolombelona 'has expressed a wish to be baptized before he leaves this country . . . there is very good reason to believe that he is a real Christian',[183] the board gave their approval. On 8 February 1826, in Grosvenor Street Chapel, Manchester, Roby baptized Raolombelona, who took the baptismal name 'John'. The *Evangelical Magazine* commented,

We understand that the dear youth has since been unanimously admitted a member of the church at new Windsor [near Manchester], under the pastoral care of the Rev. James Priddie [1786–1873], and that peculiar interest was felt, both at the church meeting and at the administration of the Lord's supper. May this prove one of the '*the first fruits*' of a glorious harvest in Madagascar, for which we earnestly entreat the prayers of all the friends of missions.[184]

On 11 May 1826, Raolombelona sailed from Gravesend aboard the *Alexander*, under Captain Richardson. He was accompanied by LMS agents freshly recruited for Madagascar: David Johns (1796–1843), a clerical missionary; James Cameron (1799–1875), a carpenter; and John Cummins (1805–1872), a spinner; and their wives, Mary Johns, née Thomas (d. 1867); Mary Ann Cameron, née McClew (1804–1864); and Matilda Cummins, née McCroby (d. 1873).[185] On 20 July 1826, they reached Mauritius, from where, together with James Hastie, they were granted a free passage aboard HMS *Wizard* to Madagascar, reaching Tamatave on 2 August.[186]

Razafinkarefo

In June 1823, the LMS board recorded that Razafinkarefo, together with the twin brothers Rahaniraka and Raombana (for whom see Chapter 7), 'now at Borough Road School, had accomplished all that they would learn, in that

[181] Barry to Hastie, Port Louis, 25 Apr. 1826, NAM, HB 4.
[182] Meeting of Directors, 3 Jan. 1826, LMS Board Minutes, SOAS/CWM.
[183] Roby to LMS, Manchester, 3 Jan. 1826, in Meeting of Directors, 16 Jan. 1826, LMS Board Minutes, SOAS/CWM.
[184] *Evangelical Magazine and Missionary Chronicle* (Mar. 1826), 129; see also 'Christian Missions', *Derby Mercury* (15 Feb. 1826).
[185] Campbell, *David Griffiths*, 45–6.   [186] Campbell, *David Griffiths*, 676.

Institution, and that it was important that they should be introduced to higher pursuits and better Society more suited to their destination'.[187] Accordingly, the directors asked Clunie to admit them into his Leaf Square Academy after the midsummer recess.[188] Clunie agreed, notice was given to the BFBS,[189] and the youths despatched to Manchester, where they arrived on 24 July 1823.

Nine months later, in April 1824, Roby reported that the Madagascar Youths were progressing in both education and morality,[190] but Clunie informed the LMS that Razafinkarefo had received medical attention.[191] In early May, after Clunie advised the directors that 'it was the opinion of the Medical Gentleman who attended him that sea-bathing would be of service', they authorized Clunie to send Razafinkarefo to the coast.[192] He had returned to Manchester by the time of Andrianaivo's death on 19 May, when 'the Medical Gentleman who had attended him urged the importance of Zafincarafe being sent home to Madagascar without any unavoidable delay'.[193] Alarmed, the LMS notified Bathurst, who arranged that Razafinkarefo leave with Verkey and Ramboa, informing Lowry Cole on Mauritius that Razafinkarefo 'is affected with a tumour under his Arm, from which very serious consequences are apprehended'.[194] On 13 August, the board met the 'three Madagascar Youths who are to embark on board the *Alexander*' to decide how they should be equipped for the return voyage[195] and presented Razafinkarefo with a farewell gift of £2.10s worth of books.[196]

On 30 October 1824, the three youths embarked for Mauritius.[197] The following month, while they were still at sea, LMS missionary Griffiths presented to the LMS a very complimentary picture of Razafinkarefo's siblings in Madagascar. He reported that Razafinkarefo's two brothers and two sisters attended the mission school and that the two brothers paid visits to their home town as assistant teachers.[198] He stated further that three more of Razafinkarefo's relatives attended mission schools, including Rakoutou [Rakoto], Andriantana, and Ratsitouvana [Ratsitovana], who were all employed as assistants at mission schools in Ambohimanga and Ambohidrabiby.[199]

[187] Meeting of Directors, 9 Jun. 1823, LMS Board Minutes, SOAS/CWM.
[188] Meeting of Directors, 9 Jun. 1823, LMS Board Minutes, SOAS/CWM.
[189] Meeting of Directors, 30 Jun. 1823, LMS Board Minutes, SOAS/CWM.
[190] Meeting of Directors, 26 Apr. 1824, LMS Board Minutes, SOAS/CWM.
[191] Meeting of Directors, 11 May 1824, LMS Board Minutes, SOAS/CWM.
[192] Meeting of Directors, 11 May 1824, LMS Board Minutes, SOAS/CWM.
[193] Meeting of Directors, 24 May 1824, LMS Board Minutes, SOAS/CWM.
[194] Extract from a despatch of the Earl Bathurst [to Governor of Mauritius], 20 Jul. 1824, HB 4, NAM.
[195] Meeting of Directors, 9 Aug. 1824, LMS Board Minutes, SOAS/CWM.
[196] Meeting of Directors, 26 Sep. 1824, LMS Board Minutes, SOAS/CWM.
[197] *Evangelical Magazine and Missionary Chronicle* (Dec. 1824), 549.
[198] Griffiths to Arundel, Tananarive, 4 Nov. 1824, MIL Bx.2 F.1 J.C, SOAS/CWM.
[199] Griffiths to Arundel, Tananarive, 4 Nov. 1824, MIL Bx.2 F.1 J.C, SOAS/CWM.

Postscript: Plans for Training Madagascar Youths As Medical Doctors in Scotland

It is of note that three years later, in September 1827, Radama asked Lowry Cole on Mauritius to arrange that three Madagascar Youths be sent to Edinburgh for medical training:

Desirous of sending three of my young subjects to Scotland to learn medicine, surgery & c., I beg you to be my mediator with the British Government, to ensure that my desires are fulfilled . . .

Mr. Anderson, Medical Doctor of the frigate HMS *Samerang*, promised me that if your Government would do me this favour and would permit him to do so, he would care for and supervise my aforesaid subjects in Scotland.[200]

This request may have reflected Radama's rapidly deteriorating health. In the event, Lowry Cole decided that it should not be forwarded to London until commented on by Robert Lyall (1790–1831), an Edinburgh trained surgeon shortly expected to reach Mauritius and replace Hastie as British agent in Madagascar.[201] On 30 October 1827, during a brief visit to Madagascar, when he met Radama at Tamatave, Lyall enthusiastically pursued the king's idea, but cautioned him,

my opinion was that it would be useless to send any young man to Edinburgh without a previous education, because all the lectures are delivered in English; and that I would advise, in preference, that a well-educated medical man should be engaged to proceed to Tananarivou, and to act as Surgeon to the Army and the People, while I would attend the King, His Court, and His Staff &c; and that he should also undertake the preparatory education of a number of young men for three years; at the end of which period, the three most distinguished of them might be sent to the University of Edinburgh, while the others might become the assistants of the Surgeon, and be capable of doing much good in a Country in which there is no regular medical person. I added that I had occasion to believe that Mr. Edington, assistant Surgeon of the *Samarang*, would be glad to have such an appointment.[202]

Lyall noted further that 'As this plan was contingent – i.e. depended upon the arrangement of other affairs – the King seemed to approve it, but at the same time changed the subject.'[203] Lyall then sailed for Mauritius, returning to Madagascar in mid-1828. However, by the time he reached Antananarivo in late July 1828, Radama was dead.[204]

---

200   Radama to Lowry Cole, Tamatave, 1 Sep. 1827, HB 4, NAM.
201   Radama to Lowry Cole, Tamatave, 1 Sep. 1827, HB 4, NAM.
202   Lyall, journal entry for 30 Oct. 1827, CO 167/116, NAK.
203   Lyall, journal entry for 30 Oct. 1827, CO 167/116, NAK.
204   Gwyn Campbell, *The Travels of Robert Lyall, 1789–1831: Scottish Surgeon, Naturalist and British Agent to the Court of Madagascar* (Cham, Switzerland: Palgrave Macmillan, 2020), 118.

In all, as a product of the 1820 Britanno-Merina treaty, seven Madagascar Youths were sent to Britain to be apprenticed in armaments and textiles. These, Radama envisaged, would provide the basis for establishing domestic industries that would both reduce Merina dependence on outside sources and, in the case of textiles, promote 'legitimate' export staples to replace slaves. Radama planned that, upon their return, these youths would supplement, and eventually replace, the missionary and other European craftsmen active in Madagascar. One of the seven Madagascar Youths returned immediately to Madagascar, two died in Britain, and two became so ill the LMS sent them back to their homeland. However, another two Madagascar Youths apprenticed in crafts profited fully from their experience and subsequently helped shape the history of Madagascar and Malagasy–British relations (see Chapter 5). The next chapter focuses on the history of the second major group of Madagascar Youths selected to train abroad under British supervision – those sent to Mauritius.

3   Mauritius

This chapter focuses on those Madagascar Youths sent to the neighbouring Indian Ocean island of Mauritius. This group has received scant attention in the literature although they constituted the second largest group of Madagascar Youths despatched abroad for training under British supervision in the two decades following the British capture of the island in 1810. They numbered about thirty-five; they were mostly males but the group included at least four females. Upon their return, some played surprisingly significant roles, notably in Merina royal and military ritual (see Chapter 6).

Mauritius is a small island, 2,040 km² in area, almost elliptical in form, measuring roughly 52 km from east to west and 64 km from north to south. It is located at longitude 20.35° S, latitude 57.55° E; it is some 5,900 km west of Perth, Australia, 226 km east of its sister island of Réunion (then called Bourbon), 880 km east of Tamatave on the northeast coast of Madagascar, and 1,800 km east of continental Africa. Initially uninhabited, it was colonized by the Dutch from 1638 to 1710, and by the French from 1715 to 1810, when, during the Napoleonic Wars, it was, with Réunion, seized by the British to prevent hitherto frequent attacks by local privateers on British ships in the Indian Ocean. Under the Treaty of Paris (30 May 1814), marking the end to French wars, Britain handed Réunion, an 'island without a port', back to France but retained Mauritius (called Isle de France under the previous French regime), which possessed in Port Louis a port and shipyard of major significance, in order to safeguard the maritime route to India (see Figure 3.1).[1]

In late 1824, Robert Montgomery Martin (c.1801–1868), assistant surgeon on the 1823–4 expedition of HMS *Leven* and HMS *Barracouta* under William

---

[1] Robert Montgomery Martin, *Statistics of the Colonies of the British Empire* (London: Allen, 1839), 497–8; Jean Louis Joseph Carayon, *Histoire de l'établissement français de Madagascar pendant la Restauration* (Paris: Gide, 1845), 1; Jean Baptiste Thiriot, *L'Ile Maurice, La Réunion et les productions de l'Inde, 1785*, edited by E. Génin, (Douai: Imprimerie O. Duthillœul, 1882), 41; Patrick Joseph Barnwell and Auguste Toussaint, *A Short History of Mauritius* (London: Longmans, Green & Co., 1949), 125; Hubert Jules Deschamps, *Méthodes et doctrines coloniales de la France* (Paris: Colin, 1953), 96–7.

Figure 3.1 Port Louis c.1830
Source: https://sites.google.com/site/crumbleholmefamilyhistory/john-c
(accessed 29.01.22).

Fitzwilliam Owen (1774–1857) to southeast Africa and Madagascar (see Chapter 4), stated that

The Mauritius is one of the most picturesque and romantic looking islands in the eastern hemisphere; the land rises from the coast to the middle of the island, and chains of mountains intersect it in various radii, from the centre to the shore; there are however, three principal ranges, in height from 1,800 to 2,800 feet above the sea, mostly covered with timber, and few presenting, except at their very summits, bare rock.[2]

The Madagascar Youths sent to Mauritius could not have failed to have observed, and been influenced by, the dramatic changes the island experienced in the early nineteenth century. First, the island's physical environment underwent major transformation. From the 1720s the French exploited its rich volcanic soil, cultivating a variety of cash crops, including sugar cane, pepper, cinnamon, cloves, nutmeg, coffee, tea, cocoa, annatto, cotton, spices, and indigo – the main crop in in 1794. However, Mauritius lies in a major cyclone

___
[2] Martin, *Statistics*, 498.

Table 3.1 *Mauritius: major adverse events 1816–24*

Date	Event	Impact
25 Sep. 1816	Fire	Destroys 25% of buildings in Port Louis
1816–17	Measles	Epidemic
25 Jan. 1818	Cyclone	Damaged Royal College; wrecked five ships in harbour
28 Feb. 1818	Cyclone	Much damage to buildings and plantations
29 Mar. 1819	Cyclone	Much damage; lives lost
Apr. 1819	Cyclone	Much damage; lives lost
16 Nov. 1819-	Cholera	Epidemic: started in Port Louis; many dead; population flee
13 Apr. 1820		to countryside. In total some 10,000 dead
1821	Dysentery	Epidemic
1823	'Pestilence'	Affected humans and horses
23 Feb. 1824	Cyclone	Much damage to buildings, sugar factories, plantations and animals; many deaths from collapsing buildings
6 Dec. 1824	Cyclone	Much damage to animals
1824	Epizootic	

Source: Charles Telfair, *Some Account of the State of Slavery at Mauritius, since the British Occupation in 1810; in refutation of anonymous charges against Government of that Colony* (Port Louis: J. Vallet and V. Asselin, 1830), 79, 87; Daniel E. Anderson, *The Epidemics of Mauritius* (London: H. K. Lewis, 1918), 33; Holmberg, 'Mauritius', *Economy and History*, 5.1 (1962), 8; Burroughs, 'Mauritius Rebellion of 1832', 11; S. B. De Burgh-Edwardes, *The History of Mauritius (1507–1914)* (London: East and West, 1921), 36, 57–9, 61; Charles Alexander Gordon, *An Epitome of the Reports of the Medical Officers to the Chinese Imperial Maritime Customs Service from 1871 to 1882* (London: Ballière, Tindall, & Cox, 1884), 373.

zone, and suffered major crop damage, notably to cotton, coffee, and cloves (see Table 3.1). The impact of cyclones, possibly accentuated by the fallout from the 1815 eruption of Tambora, pushed planters to switch increasingly to cultivation of sugar cane – which generally survived cyclonic storms. From 1816 to 1826, sugar production grew fivefold and, following the British government decision in 1825 to lower the duty on the import of Mauritian sugar into Britain to the level enjoyed by West Indian sugar producers, Mauritius experienced a further acceleration in sugar production: from 1825 to 1830 the area under sugar cane almost doubled, increasing from 112.5 km^2 to 218 km^2, and sugar exports almost quadrupled from 10.66 million kg to 40.93 million kg. [3]

[3] Albert Walter, 'Climate', in Allister Macmillan (ed.), *Mauritius Illustrated: Historical and Descriptive, Commercial and Industrial, Facts, Figures, & Resources* (W. H. & L. Collingridge: London, 1914), 188; Lars Holmberg, 'Mauritius: A Study in Disaster', *Economy and History* 5.1 (1962), 8; Peter Burroughs, 'The Mauritius Rebellion of 1832 and the Abolition of British Colonial Slavery', *Journal of Imperial and Commonwealth History* 4.3 (1976), 246–7; Richard B. Stothers, 'The Great Tambora Eruption in 1815 and Its Aftermath', *Science* 224.4654 (1984), 1191–8; William Kelleher Storey, *Science and Power in Colonial*

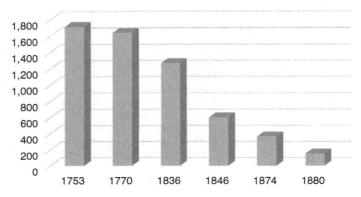

Figure 3.2 Mauritius: area under forest 1753–1880 (km²)
Source: Albert Walter, 'The Sugar Industry', in Allister Macmillan (ed.),
*Mauritius Illustrated: Historical and Descriptive, Commercial and
Industrial, Facts, Figures, & Resources* (W.H. & L. Collingridge: London,
1914), 210; see also John Mauremootoo, 'African Case Study II: Mauritius –
A History of Degradation and the Beginnings of Restoration', 6, www
.researchgate.net/publication/267937347_African_Case_Study_II_Mauritiu
s_-_a_History_of_Degradation_and_the_Beginnings_of_Restoration
(accessed 08/05/19).

The enormous increase in sugar cane cultivation had a dramatic impact on
land cover. By the end of the French period, in 1810, a diverse range of crops
was grown on about a quarter of the island's area. However, the sugar boom
resulted in a hitherto unprecedented deforestation – one augmented after
abolition in 1835 when ex-slaves fled the plantations to settle and clear
unclaimed land. Indeed, by 1880 most original forest on Mauritius had disappeared (see Figure 3.2).[4]

It also severely impacted the production of other agricultural produce, including
vegetables. As John Newman (1795–1848), director from 1825 to 1848 of the
Royal Botanic Garden at Pamplemousses, near Port Louis, stated in May 1829,

Mauritius (Rochester, NY: University of Rochester Press, 1997), 26–7; see also Richard
H. Grove, *Green Imperialism: Colonial Expansion, Tropical Island Edens and the Origins of
Environmentalism, 1600–1860* (Cambridge: Cambridge University Press, 1997), 168–263.

[4] George Bidie, 'Effects of Forest Destruction in Coorg', *Journal of the Royal Geographical
Society* 39 (1869), 82; Paul Koenig, 'Economic Flora', in Allister Macmillan (ed.), *Mauritius
Illustrated: Historical and Descriptive, Commercial and Industrial, Facts, Figures, & Resources*
(W. H. & L. Collingridge: London, 1914), 102; Anthony Cheke and Julian Hume, *Lost Land of
the Dodo: An Ecological History of Mauritius, Réunion & Rodrigues* (London: T. &
A. D. Poyser, 2008), 117–18.

The sugar cane being cultivated as the most profitable production to the planters, Horticulture has fallen off to an alarming extent, and unless some measure is adopted to have the Market in Town supplied with abundance of vegetables, I feel persuaded very injurious consequences will ensue. It is almost out of the power of the poor inhabitants to purchase vegetable food. Were there an abundance of vegetables at the market, there would always be a check upon the rise of the necessaries of life, the prices of which have become very exorbitant.[5]

The transformation of the island's economy to monoculture sugar production also resulted in a surge in demand for labour. After the 1810 British conquest of Mauritius, Farquhar, the first British governor, found himself in a dilemma, for he was expected to implement the 1808 ban on the slave trade, on which the island's white population depended to secure a cheap servile workforce for their plantations. As early as 1813, Farquhar alerted authorities at the Cape of Good Hope that he lacked the necessary ships to suppress the maritime traffic in slaves.[6] At the same time, he realized that British rule required the collaboration of the white Francophone population, numbering about 8,000, which held a monopoly of land, were resident and not (as in the Caribbean) absentee landlords, and resented any assault on what they considered to be their slave property rights. Moreover, they had been emboldened by major concessions the British had made in 1810 when, as in Quebec, the British on Mauritius granted legitimacy to the Roman Catholic church and to French as an official language.[7]

Indeed, there was after 1810 a significant illicit import of slaves, chiefly from Madagascar and Mozambique, although there is considerable debate about the numbers and the time period involved (see Figure 3.3 and Table 3.2).[8] However, the evidence is that from the 1780s, internecine ethnic rivalry and the pillaging of trade caravans in Madagascar regularly interrupted the trade from Imerina, the chief source of slaves.[9] The 1809–11 British blockade and occupation of the Mascarenes further disrupted foreign trade in the region, as

---

[5] John Newman, 'Remarks relative to the Agriculture of the Colony' (May 1829), in Newman to George Murray, Mauritius, 1 Jun. 1829, CO 167/107, NAK.

[6] Farquhar to Rear Admiral [Tyler], Naval Commander in Chief, Cape Town, Port Louis, 20 Nov. 1813, CO 167/151, NAK.

[7] Farquhar to Captain Curran, Port Louis, 9 Sep. 1816, CO 167/151, NAK; Burroughs, 'Mauritius Rebellion of 1832'.

[8] George Stephen, letter to the editor, *The Times* (19 Jun. 1835); Richard B. Allen, 'Satisfying the "Want for Labouring People": European Slave Trading in the Indian Ocean, 1500–1850', *Journal of World History* 21.1 (2010), 56; Vijayalakshmi Teelock and Abdul Sheriff, 'Slavery and the Slave Trade in the Indian Ocean', in Vijayalakshmi Teelock (ed.), *Transition from Slavery in Zanzibar and Mauritius* (Oxford: African Books Collective, 2016), 32.

[9] Nicolas Mayeur, 'Voyage au pays pays d'ancove, autrement dit des hovas ou Amboilamba dans l'intérieure des terres, Isle de Madagascar' (1777), 167, 180, 186, BL Add. 18128; Nicolas Mayeur, 'Voyage au pays d'ancove, par le pays d'ancaye autrement dit des Baizangouzangoux,' related by Dumaine (1785), 204–5, 207–8, 212–16, BL Add. 18128; Nicolas Mayeur, 'Réflexions sur l'établissement et l'amélioration du commerce de Madagascar' (1802), 42, BL

Table 3.2 *Mauritius: children in the slave population, 1821–6*

Year	Total slave population	Slave children aged under seven	Slave children as % total slave population
1821	66,162	7,528	11.38
1822	63,099	7,221	11.44
1823	63,076	7,456	11.82
1824	65,037	7,903	12.15
1825	63,432	12,644	19.93
1826	61,988	8,906	14.37

Source: Valentine, 'Dark Soul of the People', 40.

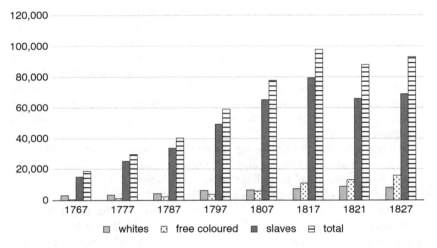

Figure 3.3 Mauritius: estimated population 1807–27
Source: Martin, *Statistics*, 503; Telfair, *Some Account of the State of Slavery*, 14; Barbara Valentine, 'The Dark Soul of the People: Slaves in Mauritius, 1835', BA thesis, Rhodes University (2000), 38.

was reflected in Madagascar by sharp falls from 1810 both in the domestic money supply and in domestic slave prices – which halved between 1810 and 1817 from $90 to $45.[10] From his ascension to the Merina throne in 1810,

Add. 18136; Gwyn Campbell, *An Economic History of Imperial Madagascar, 1750–1895: The Rise and Fall of an Island Empire* (Cambridge: Cambridge University Press, 2005), 64.

[10] Le Sage, 'Mission to Madagascar' (1816), 121–2, CO 167/34, NAK; Hastie, 'Diary' (1817), 150; Auguste Toussaint, *La route des Îles: Contribution à l'histoire maritime des Mascareignes* (Paris: SEVPN, 1967); Jean-Michel Filliot, *La traite des esclaves vers les Mascareignes au*

Radama continued his father's policy of military expansion and by 1814 had quadrupled the extent of Merina-ruled territory in the central highlands. However, his attempt in 1815 to conquer the trade route from the plateau to the ports of the northeast coast created devastation and famine conditions that undermined rather than promoted commercial security.[11]

In mid-1817, Radama's armies gained control of the trade route to the northeast coast for the first time. This permitted unhindered slave exports from Imerina, numbers reaching an all-time peak of 4,000 slaves a year in 1820. However, after the Britanno-Merina Treaty, signed in October that year, slave exports stopped in all regions controlled by the Merina, whose armies waged relentless war against neighbouring peoples of Madagascar, while British naval ships patrolled coastal waters. This effectively ended slave exports to Mauritius, although a lively disguised trade, that of indentured labour, continued to Réunion.[12]

The Madagascar Youths on Mauritius would have immediately noted that it was a slave society, in which slaves engaged in multiple tasks. Daniel Tyerman (1773–1828) and George Bennet (1775–1841), who formed a two-man LMS deputation to Mauritius in 1828, commented of slavery there,

Slavery exists in this island to such an extent that its miserable victims are met in droves, or singly, every where, performing all kinds of base, penal, and brute labour. In Port Louis the domestic servants are almost entirely bond-men and bond-women ... In the streets they are seen dragging carts and drays like beasts of burthen. But it is on the sugar-plantations that these helots swarm, and blacken the face of the country. Such estates are rather numerous than large, and are tilled by bodies of field-drudges, from one to three, four, and even five hundred.[13]

Moreover, the relentless decline in slave imports pushed Mauritian authorities into employing various forms of unfree labour. For instance, during his governorship between 1810 and 1823, Farquhar introduced over 1,500 convicts from Bengal, Bombay, and Sri Lanka to be employed chiefly in the building and maintenance of roads.[14] Some penal labour was employed in British missions to Madagascar. In 1816–17, at least eighteen convicts, possibly as

---

XVIIe siècle (Paris: ORSTOM, 1974); Gwyn Campbell, 'Madagascar and the Slave Trade, 1810–1895', *Journal of African History* 22.2 (1981), 203–8.

[11] Chazal, 'Notes' (1816), 24, BL Add. 18135; Le Sage, 'Mission' (1816), esp. 61–2, 85, 91–139.

[12] James Hastie to Griffiths, Port Louis, 18 Feb. 1821, MIL B.1 F.2 J.B, SOAS/CWM; Campbell, 'Madagascar and the Slave Trade', 208; Campbell, 'Labour Migration to the French Islands of the Western Indian Ocean, 1830–60', in Gwyn Campbell and Alessandro Stanziani (eds.), *The Palgrave Handbook of Bondage and Human Rights in Africa and Asia* (Basingstoke: Palgrave MacMillan, 2019).

[13] James Montgomery (ed.), *Journal of Voyages and Travels by the Rev. Daniel Tyerman and George Bennet* (London: Westley & Davis, 1831), vol. 2, 493.

[14] Clare Anderson, 'The Genealogy of the Modern Subject: Indian Convicts in Mauritius, 1814–1853', in Ian Duffield and James Bradley (eds.), *Representing Convicts; New Perspectives on Convict Forced Labour Migration* (London: Leicester University Press, 1997), 164–6.

many as thirty-one, accompanied Hastie to Madagascar.[15] Further, the government of Mauritius employed slaves, called 'Government Blacks', an institution first established in 1786 when the government purchased 286 slaves to replace a traditional system whereby it obliged slave owners to periodically supply slaves for public works. The British also employed them to service the military. Tyerman and Bennet commented of these slaves in 1828, 'Government possesses much of this questionable kind of property, and not only employs slaves upon its own necessary works, but lets out individuals for hire to private persons having temporary occasion for them; a practice common also with other holders of human livestock.'[16] In 1831, the number of Government Blacks stood at about 1,300.[17] Government Blacks were differentiated from Prize Negroes – slaves captured aboard slaving ships by the British Navy – some 3,000 of whom were landed on Mauritius between 1813 and 1827. 'Liberated' from slavery, Prize Negroes were immediately subjected to fourteen-year apprenticeships, most to private individuals but a minority in the British military and in colonial government departments. In June 1829, the Commission of Eastern Enquiry concluded that Prize Negroes generally were treated worse than Mauritian slaves.[18] In 1825 and 1829, experiments were also made with imported Indian indentured labour, but these failed and the Indians were quickly repatriated. Significant Indian indentured immigration started only from the second half of 1834, as abolition in 1835 approached.[19]

All 'free' inhabitants of the island of sufficient means employed servile labour of some kind. F. E. S. Viret, secretary to the governor of Mauritius, commented in 1833 of Port Louis, where most of the Madagascar Youths were apprenticed,

some of the best and most airy parts of Port Louis (the 'Champs de Mars and Delort' for instance) are unsupplied with water in the houses – and that very indispensable requisite, in a hot climate the more especially so, has to be sent for to the nearest public fountain – this is attended with much trouble and expense, it being in large Establishments almost the work of one or two people, and is a labor which domestic slaves do not like to have imposed upon them. Another serious evil, and I fear an insurmountable one, prevails

[15] Madagascar was not the only recipient: from 1817 to 1840, over 100 convicts were transported from Mauritius to Sydney, Australia. However, the latter comprised people, slaves and free, convicted of crimes – chiefly theft – on Mauritius: Edward Duyker, 'Sydney's People: The Mauritians', *Sydney Journal* 1.2 (2008), 59.

[16] Montgomery (ed.), *Journal of Voyages*, 493.

[17] 'Government Blacks' (27 Jan. 1831), CO 167/102, NAK; Dick, 'Memo in regard to some of the Taxes stated to have been imposed at Mauritius by the British Govt.' [n.d. 1831?], CO 167/158, NAK.

[18] Satyendra Peerthum Ally Hossen Orjoon, 'Liberated Africans in Nineteenth Century Mauritius', *L'Express* [Mauritius] (2 Feb. 2005), www.lexpress.mu/article/liberated-africans-nineteenth-century-mauritius (accessed 16/12/18).

[19] Aapravasi Ghat Trust Fund, 'The Indenture Experience', www.aapravasighat.org/indenture.htm (accessed 30/06/14).

throughout the Town of Port Louis: there is not a common sewer to carry off the filth and dregs of the place, which have therefore to be removed in Tubs, before day-break, to particular spots on the seashore; and I know not how this disgusting work can continue to be performed under the state of things about to be introduced at Mauritius.

Slave servants were generally to be hired at from 7 to 10 Dollars a month, or about £20 or £25 a year each – the person hiring them being at [bearing] the expense of their food and clothing: a free servant was much more expensive. A single man can hardly manage with less than two servants – families require them in numbers, and so do all whose means permit of their keeping house and seeing company . . .

those persons who obtained apprentices from among the captured and condemned negroes, have no doubt been supplied with servants of a certain class at a less expense than the rates I have just mentioned – but the periods of service of these people have now nearly all expired, and I regret to think that among them (and their numbers are considerable) there will be found comparatively few who are likely to do well as free persons. In a great many instances, the fault may be with the apprentices themselves, and in others it has proceeded from the want of due attention to them, on the part of their former masters.

During my residence at the Mauritius, I had, at different times, six of these people in my service, by whom I endeavoured, tho' I fear not very successfully, to do my duty: one suffered death by sentence of the Tribunals; a second died in the Civil Govern. Hospital from an inveterate habit of drunkenness; a third was so bad a subject that I could not keep him about me; a fourth, whom I brought up from a boy, gave me so much trouble, but having some good qualities I hope he will yet do well; a fifth was an excellent servant and, before I left the Mauritius, I took to have his name borne on the 'Etat Civil' as a free man; the sixth was a good but poor creature who, if left to himself, would never be able to gain a livelihood.[20]

The Madagascar Youths would certainly have encountered Malagasy slaves. It is estimated that, by 1826, some 19 per cent of slaves on Mauritius were of Malagasy origin, compared to 19 per cent of East African and 3 per cent of Southeast Asian origin (see Figure 3.4).[21] However, Malagasy slaves on Mauritius were drawn from a minimum of thirteen ethnic groups, who occupied different regions of the world's fourth largest island. This was recognized by French naturalist and artist Jacques-Gérard Milbert (1766–1840), during his visit to Mauritius from 1801–3, who referred to the several 'nations' of Madagascar.[22]

Some of these groups spoke mutually unintelligible dialects of Malagasy. In the late nineteenth century, the Merina even experienced difficulty understanding the people of southern Betsileo, a neighbouring

---

[20] Viret, 'Memorandum on the Expenses of Living at the Mauritius &c', 26 Nov. 1833, CO 167/173, NAK.

[21] Teelock and Sheriff, 'Slavery', 28, 34; see also Megan Vaughan, *Creating the Creole Island: Slavery in Eighteenth-Century Mauritius* (Durham, NC: Duke University Press, 2005), 46, 49.

[22] Vaughan, *Creating the Creole Island*, 104.

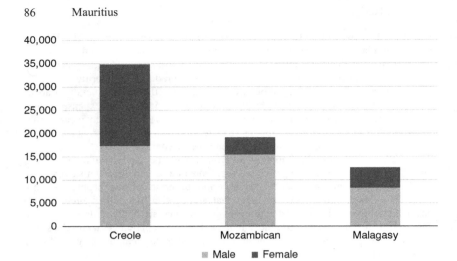

Figure 3.4 Mauritius: Creole and slave population, 1826
Source: Teelock and Sheriff, 'Slavery', 34.

highland province, who they had conquered and subjected to their administration in the 1810s:

Although it is generally understood that the language spoken throughout the island of Madagascar is essentially one, yet the dialects of the several tribes, and even of different clans, vary considerably. People from adjacent provinces have often great difficulty in understanding one another; and so great is the difference between the dialects of Imerina and South Betsileo, that a Hova [Merina] hearing the latter for the first time can only catch the general drift of the speaker's remarks, and probably will fail to do even this if the Betsileo are excited and speak rapidly.[23]

The dialectical differences between the Merina and the coastal peoples of Madagascar was even greater. For example, LMS missionary David Jones, who in 1818–19 started learning the Betisimisaraka dialect of the northeast coast, commented in August 1821, 'While I remained at the capital of Ova [Imerina] from October 1820 until last June, I devoted a part of every day to study the dialect of that Province and I found an immense difference between it and what I had formerly learned.'[24] Even today, only the Merina dialect is commonly understood (but not spoken) in most of the island.[25] Thus, contrary

---

[23] Thomas Rowlands, 'Notes on the Betsileo Dialect (as spoken in the Arindrano District)', *AAMM* 10 (1886), 235.

[24] Jones to Farquhar, Port Louis, 11 Aug. 1821, HB 21, NAM.

[25] See e.g. Maurizio Serva, Filippo Petroni, Dima Volchenkov, and Søren Wichmann, 'Malagasy Dialects and the Peopling of Madagascar', *Journal of the Royal Society Interface* 9 (2012), 54–67.

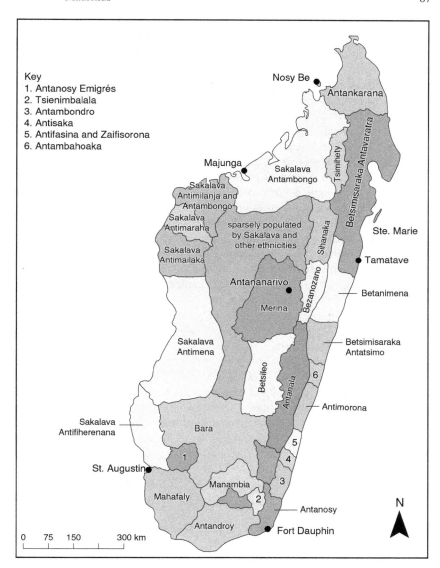

Key
1. Antanosy Emigrés
2. Tsienimbalala
3. Antambondro
4. Antisaka
5. Antifasina and Zaifisorona
6. Antambahoaka

Map 3.1 Madagascar: ethnic divisions
Source: Drawn by Kareem Hammami, © IOWC.

to the claims of Larson, who asserts that all Malagasy on Mauritius at the time spoke a mutually intelligible Malagasy,[26] most Malagasy who had spent any time on Mauritius would have more naturally spoken Mauritian Creole to each other.[27]

Thus, the majority of Madagascar Youths, who were Merina, would not have been able to communicate with a substantial proportion of Malagasy slaves on Mauritius. Moreover, it is highly unlikely that they would have wished to socialize with them. For the most part, the youths that Radama sent to Mauritius came from wealthy slave-owning families that regarded slaves as a servile caste irrespective of whether or not they were of Merina origin. Moreover, the ruthless military expansion engaged in by Merina forces from the late 1790s, in which they enslaved many non-Merina, had engendered among the Merina feelings of ethnic superiority to non-Merina, and among the latter significant animosity to the Merina. Similarly, the Madagascar Youths would have found nothing untoward in the use of convict and other forms of forced labour which, if not as widespread as it became from the 1820s, was common in early nineteenth-century Imerina.[28]

These general observations form the context to the experiences of the Madagascar Youths sent to Mauritius.

The Two Princes

Chardenoux, who led the first Mauritian embassy to Imerina in 1816, returned to Mauritius in August that year with a Merina embassy comprising over thirty people, including several youths who Radama wished to receive instruction on Mauritius. Of these, two were Merina princes, Ramarotafika (Ratafikia) and Rahovy, of the first ranking *andriana* caste. Another was Ratsiorimisa, of the second-ranking *hova* caste, whose father was a landowner, and who had been trained in what historian Simon Ayache (1927–2017) termed the 'noble' art of the goldsmith.[29] Radama sent Ratsiorimisa to be apprenticed as a gunsmith.[30] A fourth youth was 'the son of one of the nobles of the Betanimena' of the northeast littoral of

---

[26] Pier M. Larson, 'The Vernacular Life of the Street: Ratsitatanina and Indian Ocean Créolité', *Slavery and Abolition* 29.3 (2008), 327–59; Pier M. Larson, *Ocean of Letters: Language and Creolization in an Indian Ocean Diaspora* (Cambridge: Cambridge University Press, 2009).

[27] Philip Baker and Chris Corne, *Isle de France Creole: Affinities and Origins* (Ann Arbor: Karoma, 1986).

[28] Gwyn Campbell, 'Slavery and Fanompoana: The Structure of Forced Labour in Imerina (Madagascar), 1790–1861', *Journal of African History* 29.3 (1988), 463–86.

[29] Simon Ayache (ed.), *Raombana l'historien (1809–1855)* (Fianarantsoa: Ambozontany, 1976), 71.

[30] Ludvig Munthe, Simon Ayache, and Charles Ravoajanahary, 'Radama I et les Anglais: Les négociations de 1817 d'après les sources malgaches ("sorabe" inédits)', *Omaly sy Anio* 3–4 (1976), 31, fn. 49.

Madagascar.[31] Radama's interest in sending Malagasy youths to be educated and trained on Mauritius prompted Farquhar to instruct Le Sage, who in November 1816 led another embassy to Imerina, to negotiate with Radama for 'A certain number of Children of all the chief men to be sent here [Mauritius] for instruction in all the arts and sciences.'[32]

In the meantime, Farquhar appointed James Hastie preceptor to Ramarotafika and Rahovy. Half-brothers of Radama, the princes were products of extramarital relationships engaged in by their mother, Rambolamasoandro, one of the wives of Andrianampoinimerina[33] (who in order to control his harem, Raombana claimed, had thirty of his wives executed – on the charge of being unfaithful to him).[34] The position of instructor to the two princes was a major promotion for Hastie. The princes were welcomed into the Farquhar household in Government House at Reduit. This residence was established in 1749 by Pierre Félix Barthélemy David (1711–1795)), French governor of the Mascarenes from 1746 to 1753, in a 1.5 km^2 estate that included a 'French' garden.[35] The princes were, at least occasionally, entertained by Farquhar, his wife, Maria, and their seven-year-old son, Walter.[36]

Raombana, a contemporary of the princes, and later royal secretary and chronicler, stated that in the year they spent on Mauritius, Farquhar wished the princes to become literate in English, and to impress upon them the power of Europeans so that they might influence Radama to respect British might.[37] This was undoubtedly the case. Farquhar's instructions to Hastie reveal an emphasis on discipline, physical exercise, learning English, and imbibing the precepts of Christianity and English class distinctions. They were, for example, to avoid any social intercourse with Malagasy 'servants' in his household.

Reduit, 19 November 1816[38]

Sir,

His Excellency the Governor has chosen you to fulfil an important duty towards the two young Madagascar Princes, intrusted to your charge for their education, and is desirous that your conduct, in the performance of this duty, should be guided by the following principles.

---

[31] Charles Guillain, *Documents sur l'histoire, la géographie et le commerce de la partie occiden-tale de Madagascar* (Paris: Imprimerie Royale, 1845), 51; Samuel Pasfield Oliver, *Madagascar: An Historical and Descriptive Account of the Island and Its Former Dependencies* (London: Macmillan, 1886), vol. 1, 29.

[32] Farquhar, Memorandum to Le Sage, Port Louis, 6 Nov. 1816, HB 7, NAM.   [33] RH, 61.

[34] RH, 70.   [35] Koenig, 'Economic Flora', 107.

[36] Farquhar to Ramaroutafique, Port Louis, 1 Jul. 1820, HB 21, NAM; Farquhar to Hastie, Instructions, Port Louis, 4 Sep. 1820, HB 13, NAM; J. P. Grant (ed.), *Memoir and Correspondence of Mrs. Grant of Laggan*, vol. 1 (London: Longman, Brown, Green, and Longmans, 1844), 192, fn.; Gwyn Campbell, *David Griffiths and the Missionary 'History of Madagascar'* (Leiden: Brill, 2012), 582–3.

[37] RH, 82.   [38] Farquhar to Hastie, Reduit, 19 Nov. 1816, HB 7, NAM.

In the first place, your object must be to gain the esteem and regard of those persons, by a careful, watchful, and fatherly attention to them, in every respect – being particularly attentive to their personal cleanliness, and their clothing, lodging, bedding, and apartments – taking care to teach them punctuality and exactness, even in the minutest points regarding these objects, which are so essential to comfort, to health, and to the convenience of those persons with whom they are to associate.

You will be careful, in your every conduct, not to admit that familiarity which is inconsistent with strict and prompt obedience to all your directions – so that you shall by the correctness of your own behaviour give an example to them, and that any want of respect or carelessness or disobedience be sufficiently repressed by the expression of your disapprobation, without having recourse to severe measures.

You will send in a report upon a card, every day, of the conduct and progress of the young persons, stating the lessons they have taken, the attention they pay, and the progress they make. These cards are to be given to each respectively, to curry His Excellency the Governor, who will examine them, and take such notice as they may require.

You will cause these young persons to acquire a habit of early rising. After having dressed, you will make them repeat with you the morning prayer, and afterwards study an hour before breakfast. At Breakfast they may be allowed an hour, and afterwards return to school. In the middle of the day, they may be allowed two hours of relaxation – then dress for dinner. After dinner, they are to walk and take exercise and, in the evening, to repeat from memory such pieces as they may have learnt in the morning. In the evening, after washing, and changing their linen, they are to repeat the evening prayer before going to bed.

Such is, generally speaking, the routine to be followed.

You are to teach them English, as the primary step and for this purpose, you are to prevent their intercourse (as much as is convenient) with the servants who speak the Madagascar tongue.

You will for this purpose also take an English vocabulary and put opposite each word, the word of Madagascar, of the same meaning, and you will make them practice this vocabulary in writing, and repeating, so that you may also yourself acquire such a knowledge of their tongue as will enable you to communicate with them without difficulty.

You will once a week present these young persons to His Excellency in person, and receive his orders for their course of studies.

You will be careful that no persons interfere with them in their studies, or strikes or molests them in the slightest degree – nor allow them to interfere with others, either white or Black – nor let them learn any trick of annoying or troubling servants or others; but on the contrary, teach them to do everything for themselves, as much as possible, and to be as little dependent as possible on servants for the fulfilment of their wants or wishes.

You will be careful that their diet is plain and wholesome, for which purpose they will dine with you generally. When their conduct merits the distinction, His Excellency will invite them to his own table, during the week – either one or both according to their conduct.

You have nothing to attend to but these young persons. You will therefore associate with no Soldier or other person, whom it would be improper for those who are committed to your charge to know – but you will keep a respectable distance equally from your Superiors, from those of your own class, and your inferiors.

His Excellency has selected you for this charge from the good character given you by the Commandant of the Troops, and your officers, and His Excellency has no doubt but your Conduct will be such as to justify the confidence reposed in you.

From time to time, you will receive further written directions, either to point out the Course you are to take, or to Correct any errors you may fall into.

You will not interfere, or allow the young persons to interfere, with any of the Servants of the house or others than those appropriated to Serve them, and you will have your own Servant to attend on yourself.

The rations for yourself and the young persons shall be each per day –

    1 lb Beef, or mutton or Pork
    2 lb Bread
    1 Bottle milk
    2 lb Vegetables
    Tea and Sugar and Coffee per week

Your own pay will depend in its future amount upon your conduct, and the progress of your pupils. For the present it is fixed at 40 Dollars per month exclusive of your rations and 8 Dolls. per month for a Servant.

The Reverend Mr. Le Brun, Protestant Missionary, has been directed to attend at Reduit two days in the week for the purpose of instructing your young pupils in the principles and practice of our holy religion.

You will give him every assistance and facility in your power and second his instructions by your own conduct and example, and by shewing every due attention and respect to the character of the Reverend teacher.

Hastie considered his tutorship of the princes to be a success. They made some progress in education, learned British discipline, and dressed in European fashion – spectacularly so when having their portraits executed (see Figures 3.5 and 3.6). They were also given two ponies.[39]

[39] RH, 90.

Figure 3.5 Ramarotafika (c.1805–1828)
Source: www.facebook.com/ArisivaMalagasy/photos/ratafika-sy-rahovy-18
05-1828sary-ratafika-sy-rahovy-album-a-foibenny-arisivam-pi/1670493276
612456, open access (accessed 29/01/19).

Figure 3.6 Rahovy (c.1805–1828)
Source: www.facebook.com/ArisivaMalagasy/photos/ratafika-sy-rahovy-18
05-1828sary-ratafika-sy-rahovy-album-a-foibenny-arisivam-pi/1670493276
612456, open access (accessed 29/01/19).

In June 1817, as 'Tutor to the Madagascar Princes', Hastie accompanied Ramarotafika and Rahovy back to Madagascar with instructions from Farquhar to keep a diary detailing all events.[40] In August 1817, they reached Antananarivo where the freshly acquired British values of the princes were immediately challenged by a case in which four slave girls were accused of having caused the illness of one of the princes' sisters. The slave girls were forced to take the *tangena* poison ordeal. Addressing Welsh readers, Griffiths described the *tangena* as follows:

the priest prepares a poison from the *tangena* – which is a nut as large as a walnut. It contains a highly noxious kernel which, by means of a stone, is ground to a powder, which is mixed with clean water in a bowl. He next releases a little juice from a branch of a *Banana* tree into another dish, and rolls into it three pieces of chicken skin, each about the size of a crown. The accused is subsequently required to consume all these things without delay.

The priest then lays his hand upon the head of the afflicted creature and calls on the *tangena* as all-knowing, omnipresent, upright and just, without deceit or dishonesty, to instantly strike the wretch dead should he be guilty. However, the *tangena* is appealed to preserve the life of the accused should he be innocent, by assisting him to instantly vomit the three slivers of skin. This would be accepted as a sign of his innocence before the queen and people. Should the accused fail to regurgitate all the pieces of fowl skin, and instead retain one or two in his stomach, or should he refuse to swallow more warm water, or chance to incline his head towards the south, he is considered a '*m[p]amosavy*.'

The word *m[p]amosavy* signifies someone possessed by an evil spirit. Any such person must be beaten with sticks or stoned to death.[41]

The four girls failed the test, and consequently had their limbs severed and their body parts thrown off a clifftop in Antananarivo. It was reported that children, including the two princes, subsequently spent an hour throwing stones at the mangled corpses.[42] Missionary William Ellis (1794–1872) records in his *History of Madagascar* (1838) that

A few days after they had taken a part in this barbarous and inhuman pastime, the elder of the youths not appearing at the usual time in the morning, his tutor sent to request his attendance, and, on being told that he was still asleep, went himself to arouse his young pupil, prompted partly by curiosity to see the interior of his dwelling. He found him in a small and mean apartment, his sleeping-place within a yard of the fire-place, and presenting a picture of idleness and filth scarcely to be surpassed in the meanest dwellings of the common people. The tutor remonstrated with his pupil upon this deviation from the habits he had acquired in the Isle of France [Mauritius]; to which the young prince could only reply, that dirt was warm, and the weather cold, and he chose the former because it was customary.[43]

Farquhar left Mauritius in November 1817 for Britain, returning in July 1820. In September 1820, he sent Hastie to Antananarivo with presents for the two princes

---

[40] Wm Blane, Chief Sec's office, to Hastie, Port Louis, 28 Jun. 1817, HB 13, NAM; *HdR*, 1081.

[41] David Griffiths, *Hanes Madagascar* (Machynlleth: Richard Jones, 1843), 23–4.

[42] William Ellis, *History of Madagascar* (London: Fisher, 1838), vol. 2, 176–7.

[43] Ellis, *History of Madagascar*, vol. 2, 177.

that included 'caps engraved Ramaroutafique and Rahove as a present from this Government',[44] and two almost identical letters, dated 1 July 1820 and written in French (the translation of the first is given below):

My dear Ramaroutafique [Ramarotafika,][45]

I hope that you will accept with Satisfaction, in this letter that I charge Mr. Hastie to transmit to you, as a testimony of my Remembrance and my constant friendship, a piece of silver engraved with your name. Although I am separated from you by great distances, and since you left me have been very occupied by affairs of the highest importance, I have never ceased to think of you as a son whom I love tenderly and whom I wish to see again.

To this end, I have charged Mr. Hastie to seek the approval of the King your brother, so that if your wishes are in accordance with mine, you may come to spend some time with me, either on your own or with your brother, in the assurance that you will, with Madame Farquhar and myself, always find the Sentiments and attentions which are due to you as the brother of a King whom we honor, and as if you were one of our children.

Walter, whom we left in England, has not forgotten you, and asked me to remember him to you when the occasion presented itself.

As soon as I know the intentions of the King and your own preferences regarding the journey that I am proposing to you, I will provide you with the means to travel here.

In the meantime, please accept, Dear Ramaroutafique, the assurance of the sincere friendship in which I am and always will be

Your affectionate
R. J. Farquhar

Farquhar's motives in inviting the princes to return to Mauritius were not purely filial. He had informed Hastie,

I intrust you with a Letter of invitation to the two young Princes who were here three years ago, residing for their education in my Family, under your tuition, to return with you, one or both, for a short Visit to Mauritius, and you will express my desire to see them, and I also write a letter to Radama to obtain his Concurrence. These Princes may probably be induced to repeat the Visit often, and may be made useful in many ways, to the saving also of many European lives and much expence on going and returning from the interior. Radama may even be induced to fix on one or other of them here, as his Ambassador, and he would thus share with us the expence and trouble of constant communication.[46]

By 'saving ... European lives', Farquhar was referring to the toll exacted by malaria, which had killed many of the British agents sent to Madagascar.

---

[44] Farquhar to Hastie, Instructions, Port Louis, 4 Sep. 1820, HB 13, NAM.
[45] Farquhar to Ramaroutafique, Port Louis, 1 Jul. 1820, HB 21, NAM.
[46] Farquhar to Hastie, Instructions, Port Louis, 4 Sep. 1820, HB 13, NAM.

Hastie arrived in Antananarivo in early October, and on the thirteenth of that month, two days after the signing of the Britanno-Merina treaty, Rahovy responded to Farquhar's letter:[47]

My Dear Sir,

For my Brother and myself I beg to acknowledge your Kind invitation and present delivered us by Mr. Hastie and to assure you that we remember with great pleasure your Fatherly care of us.

With best wishes to Mrs. Farquhar and Walter,

Believe me Sincerely
your Friend
Rahove

Rahovy's letter makes no reference to the princes returning to Mauritius. Nevertheless, Mauritian government accounts indicate that it expended on 'Madagascar Princes on Mauritius', $12,312.08 (currency) between 1817 and 1824 (see Table 3.3), and a further £16 in 1826, indicating that, if not Ramarotafika and Rahovy, other junior members of the Merina royal family spent time on Mauritius, under Mauritian government instruction, during that period.[48] These included a Prince 'Simisate': on 12 February 1821, Hastie informed Farquhar that 'the Madagascar Prince Simisate is now recovering from an illness that has confined him for some time to the House' and recommended as part of his convalescence that the prince take up horse-riding. In response, Farquhar authorized the purchase of a horse for $350.[49]

Table 3.3 *Mauritius: expenses, Madagascar princes, 1817–24 (currency $)*[50]

Year	Expense
1817	4189.90
1819	0
1821	3235.75
1823	420.00
1818	0
1820	0
1822	4409.58
1824	56.85

[47] Rahove to Farquhar, Tananarive, 13 Oct. 1820, HB 21, NAM.
[48] N. J. Kelsey, 'Abstract of the Expense incurred by the Government of Mauritius on Account of Madagascar' (26 Nov. 1827) in 'Slaves in Mauritius' 40–4, *Papers Relating to the Slave Trade* 26.2 (House of Commons, 1828).
[49] Wm Blanes to Hastie, Chief Sec's Office, Port Louis, 13 Feb. 1821, HB 13, NAM.
[50] Kelsey, 'Abstract of the Expense incurred by the Government'.

Apprentices

The Britanno-Merina treaty stipulated that the youths sent to Britain and Mauritius should be non-slaves. However, Verkey, one of the youths sent to Britain, was an *Olomainty*, a class of royal slave, and Raombana claims that those sent to Mauritius included both *Olomainty* and *Tandonakai,* who were of Hova (second-ranking free caste) origin.[51] Rainandrianampandry, a Merina statesman executed by the French in 1896, noted another three who were 'sent oversees', undoubtedly to Mauritius, for training: Iandrasana, son of Andriantseheno, 'whose feet were unnaturally large', Ramboavao, and Rahidimaso.[52]

While in principle favourable to Radama's demand that the Mauritian government pay for the training of a select group of Malagasy youths on Mauritius, Farquhar required authorization from London. Thus, in April 1821, he informed Radama,

> The plan which you have submitted for sending apprentices from Madagascar to this Island to learn the Arts of European Life appears to be worthy of your advanced Knowledge in the progress of civilization, and altho circumstances prevent the adoption of it on my own Authority, I consider it a duty on my part towards Madagascar to submit it to His Majesty's Ministers. But for this purpose, it will be necessary that you enter into a more complete development of the System, and I shall then forward your letter with all the explanatory circumstances attending it for the consideration of the competent authorities in England.[53]

Table 3.4 *Madagascar Youths sent to Mauritius as apprentices from 1821*

AndrianMandasuale	Tharats Meena (f)
AndrianMesarak	Tharats Whaynik (f)
AndrianRadealifout	Tharats Feetrahana
AndrianHainingan	Eheeza Fiena Simaloum
AndrianMandisearivou (Nandingarivou/Amboanarivou)	Eheeza Fiena Wanteta
Meakalou or AndrianSuanarivou	Eheeza Semavaty Annietsuk
Matiendrarivou	Eheeza Semavaty Soul
Navahien	Mak Nafehi
Drinilets	Ratefe alla
Scemandraha (Cimandresse /Cimadresee / Cimandrake)	Nithanarivou
Maroufaly Ravahiry	Tarata (f)
Maroufaly Hanorana	Teraka (f)
Tharats Eheeza (Arnansue)	Kele Sambi

Note: All male except those marked 'f' = female. Source: [dated c.June 1824?], HB 5, NAM.

[51] RH, 11, 96.
[52] Rainandrianampandry, quoted in L. Nogue, 'Étude sur l'école professionnelle de Tananarive', *Notes, reconnaissances et explorations* 1.1 (1900), 419.
[53] Farquhar to Radama, Port Louis, 20 Apr. 1821, HB 21, NAM.

In the meantime, however, he accepted responsibility for the youths. Following the 1820 Britanno-Merina treaty, ten youths according to Ellis, seven according to Griffiths, formed the first cohort sent to Mauritius. There, they were apprenticed to learn the arts of carpentry, tailoring, tinsmithing, mulberry and silk-worm cultivation, and coffee production (according to James Cameron); carpentery, gold and silver smithing, iron smithing, painting, and shoemaking (Ellis); and, additionally, house-building (Rabary).[54] By mid-1821, eight Madagascar Youths were serving apprenticeships on Mauritius, it being noted by Hastie in 1824 that

With reference to the Estimate dated 20 July 1821 for the apprentice fees of eight free subjects of King Radama sent here agreeable to treaty to be instructed as mechanics, I beg that you will do me the favor to acquaint H.E. the governor that half the [Cremieux] or apprentice fee was paid by the Government at that time, and as the period of apprenticeship is expired on 20 Feby. last year, and the Boys appear to have made a fair proficiency in their respective trades, I have to solicit that H.E. will be pleased to authorize the balance of the fees agreed on, amounting to five hundred dollars, ... be now placed in warrant for payment.[55]

In mid-1821, Radama wrote to Farquhar to ask 'if it would be possible for me to introduce several [additional] persons from the respectable homes of my country to Mauritius to learn some trades'.[56] Farquhar agreed, and Abraham Latsaka asserts that Radama included among those sent three girls to learn home economics (see Table 3.4).[57]

In January 1822, G. A. Barry, Farquhar's chief administrative secretary, informed Hastie that 'in consequence of the Shoemaker Folk's clandestine departure from the Colony, that the Boy belonging to king Radama who was apprenticed to him to learn his Trade, may be now placed with Mr. Durand, and that you may be authorized to incur an expense of 50 Dollars for the payment of the apprentice fee to that person'.[58] The 'Folk' referred to was probably the same shoemaker, called 'Tolk', who in September 1816 had earned acclaim for assisting Hastie in extinguishing a fire that threatened to destroy Government House in Port Louis.[59] In October 1822, Hastie calculated the 'Subsistence and clothing of Eight native Madagascar Lads who are apprenticed to Tradesmen at the Mauritius at 8 Drs. Per

[54] Ellis, *History of Madagascar*, vol. 2, 413; Griffiths, *Hanes Madagascar*, 26; James Cameron, *Recollections of Mission Life in Madagascar during the Early Days of the LMS Mission* (Antananarivo: Abraham Kingdon, 1874), 4; Rabary, *Ny Daty Malaza: Na Ny Dian' i Jesosy Teto Madagaskara* (Tananarive: LMS, 1930–1), 16–18.

[55] Hastie to Sec. to Govt Mauritius, 5 Jun. 1825, HB 4, NAM.

[56] Radama to Farquhar, Tananarivoo, Jun. 1821, HB 21, NAM.

[57] Abraham Latsaka, 'Politiques scolaires et stratégies concurrentielles à Madagascar de 1810 à 1910', doctoral thesis, University Lyon II (1984), 52.

[58] Barry to Hastie, 'Govt. Agent for Madagascar', Port Louis 17 Jan. 1822, HB 7, NAM.

[59] 'Robert Farquhar', https://genealogie.mu/index.php/en/?option=com_content&view=article&id=225:login-register&catid=7&Itemid=321&lang=oc (accessed 12.09.19).

month each. £768.'[60] In all, the sums paid out for the Madagascar Youths apprenticed to various trades on Mauritius amounted to $550 in 1822 and $510 in 1825.[61]

Some of the Malagasy apprentices died on Mauritius. In June 1824, it was reported that 'the Boy named Cimandrasse, who was apprenticed to the Trade of a Jeweller here died on the 5th instant of a Chronic disease of long standing of the Thoracic and abdominal viscera'.[62] Thoracic refers to the lungs and heart, and abdominal to probably the liver, pancreas, spleen, adrenals, and kidneys.[63] Shortly after, Hastie was informed that

J. B. Nicolas, a Jeweller to whom a Black named Cimandresse belonging to King Radama was apprenticed, having on the death of the said Black, which took place on the 29th of May last at the Civil Hospital, stated that a sum of one Hundred Dollars remains due to him as the apprentice fee and no document bearing on the subject appearing on record in this office, I have received His Excellency's directions to desire that you will furnish every necessary information on the subject and also a copy of the authority for the purpose of being laid before His Excellency.[64]

It appears that the sum claimed was paid, and additionally Hastie authorized the payment of $10 to cover the 'expense incurred by J. B. Nicolas for the internment of the Boy named Cimandrake'.[65] In November 1824, Barry reported to Hastie the death of another of the Madagascar boys: 'I have the honor by direction of His Excellency the Governor to state to you for the information of King Radama that a Boy named Farla, belonging to him, and who was placed in apprenticeship with Nelson D'Emmerez, died in the Civil Hospital of an attack of Tubercular Phthisis [tuberculosis] on the 2nd Instant.'[66]

Musicians

From the time he ascended the throne of Imerina in 1810, Radama, who engaged in a ceaseless campaign of military expansion within the island, took Napoleon as his idol. Fond of celebration, dance, and music, he would also have been impressed by Napoleon's use of music to inspire his troops. As Napoleon wrote in July 1797,

Among all the fine arts (writes the young commander-in-chief), music is the one which exercises the greatest influence upon the passions, and is the one which the legislator

---

[60] Hastie to Barry, Foul Point, 14 Oct. 1822, HB 7, NAM.
[61] Expressed in 'currency dollars' – Kelsey, 'Abstract of the Expense incurred by the Government'.
[62] Barry to Hastie, Port Louis 11 Jun. 1824, HB 5, NAM.
[63] Craig Hacking and Daniel J. Bell, 'Solid and Hollow Abdominal Viscera', https://radiopaedia.org/articles/solid-and-hollow-abdominal-viscera (accessed 17.07.21).
[64] G. A. [Newry] to Hastie, Port Louis, 23 Jun. 1824, HB 5, NAM.
[65] Hastie to Sec. to Govt Mauritius, 5 Jun. 1825, HB 4, NAM.
[66] Barry to Hastie, Port Louis, 8 Nov. 1824, HB 5, NAM.

should most encourage. A musical composition created by a master-hand makes an unfailing appeal to the feelings, and exerts a far greater influence than a good work on morals, which convinces our reason without affecting our habits.[67]

From his first encounter with the British, Radama wished them to train a significant number of Malagasy youths on Mauritius in European military music so that, upon their return, they might form a military band. Indeed, Mauritian government accounts show expenditure on the teaching of music to Madagascar Youths from 1813 to 1826 (see Figure 3.7). This has to be mistaken, for the first British contact with Radama was in 1816 – unless it takes into account the teaching of music to Malagasy slaves on the Belombre Estate of Charles Telfair (1778–1833), who was Farquhar's secretary, a planter, and a major supporter of the LMS. It also marks the beneficiary as being Archibald Kyle (b. c.1785), quarter-master and music master of the 82nd regiment of the British Army, which only arrived on Mauritius in 1819. Otherwise, the first indication of Madagascar Youths being sent to Mauritius for musical instruction was after the signing of the draft treaty in October 1817, when Radama requested that Hastie take six Merina youths back to Mauritius for that purpose.[68] Hastie agreed, and in November 1817 deposited $20 with the bandmaster of the 22nd regiment on Mauritius 'For Music Boys'.[69] However, in February 1818, Gage John Hall, Farquhar's temporary replacement, repudiated the Merina alliance and, in 1819, sent back to Imerina the six Malagasy youths who had recently arrived.[70]

On the signing of the Britanno-Merina treaty in October 1820, Hastie promised Radama that he would take to Mauritius both the youths destined for an education in Britain and the eight Madagascar Youths 'to be instructed in music, for the purpose of being formed into a band for the regiment of guards of his Majesty the King of Madagascar'.[71] However, Rainandrianampandry named ten youths, all 'former slaves', that were sent to Mauritius to learn music: Rakitonga, Raboniakatra, Ramanankoazy, Rafihivatoma, Rasome, Rabetrano, Rasody, Rabenjaro, Rabemiakatra, and Rainimpasava.[72] It appears that although they did not accompany Hastie on the *Eliza* they arrived shortly

---

[67] Bonaparte to the Inspectors of the Conservatoire, Milan, 26 Jul. 1797, quoted in J.-G. Prod'homme and Frederick H. Martens, 'Napoleon, Music and Musicians', *Musical Quarterly* 7.4 (1921), 584.

[68] James Hastie to Griffiths, Port Louis, 18 Feb. 1821, MIL B.1 F.2 J.B, SOAS/CWM. Ellis incorrectly states that they were four in number – Ellis, *History of Madagascar*, vol. 2, 180.

[69] Cash Account of James Hastie, Asst Agent at Madagascar (1817–18), HB 7, NAM; see also Hastie, 'Diary' (1817), CO 167/34, NAK; Hardyman, 'Malagasy Overseas' PPMS63 J. T. Hardyman file 43, Bx.7, SOAS/CWM.

[70] Hastie to Griffiths, Port Louis, 18 Feb. 1821, MIL B.1 F.2 J.B, SOAS/CWM.

[71] No. 2, Additional Articles, in *Papers Relating to the Abolition of the Slave Trade in the Mauritius* (1821), 360; BL Add. 20131 f. 116.

[72] Nogue, 'Étude sur l'école professionnelle de Tananarive', 418.

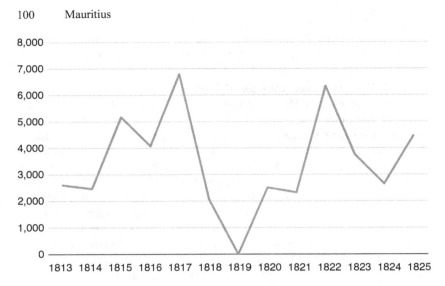

Figure 3.7 Mauritius: expenses for teaching music to Madagascar Youths
1813–25 (currency $)
Source: Kelsey, 'Abstract of the Expense incurred by the Government'.

afterwards and were placed for instruction with the band of the 82nd regiment.
Thus, in April 1821, Hastie informed Farquhar's secretary,

I have the honor to request that you will be pleased to acquaint H.E. the Governor that
the likelihood of the Regiment's doing duty in the Colony soon changing quarters, as
well as my expected departure for Madagascar, renders it necessary that a new arrangement should be made for the eight Boys sent here by Radama to be instructed in Military
Music, and as I am aware that Radama attaches much importance to this object, I beg
leave to suggest that they may be placed in care of Mr. Kyle, the Master of the band of
the 82d. Regt., who has been favored by his Commanding Officer with a permission to
undertake such charge and has in repeated instances proved his skill in the instruction of
Music and always supported such moral character as makes it particularly desirable that
these Boys whom it is highly necessary witness a good example, receive some school
education, may be placed with him.[73]

From 1820 to 1821, Kyle instructed four household and two field slaves from
Belombre Estate, placed with him by their owner, Telfair, with the authorisa-
tion of Farquhar.[74] As Telfair commented:

Believing in the influence of music in civilizing mankind, a vocal and instrumental band
was formed among the Slaves, who, for above three years, learned the principles of this

[73] [Hastie] to Barry, Port Louis, 9 Apr. 1821, HB 13, NAM.
[74] Barry to Hastie, Port Louis, 14 Apr. 1821, HB 13, NAM; Telfair, *Some Account of the State of
Slavery*, 182–3.

art, from the best European masters. During this time I gave up their services, for they were thirty miles [48 km] distant from the estate. This band assisted in teaching the musicians of Radama, king of Madagascar, under the superintendence of Mr. Kyle, the respectable Quarter-Master of His Majesty's 82nd Regiment.[75]

In June 1821, after he had returned to Antananarivo, Hastie informed Farquhar

Radama enters warmly into the plan of placing apprentices with the inhabitants of the Mauritius and says he will write to his Excellency on the subject requesting that his intercourse with the isle of France [Mauritius] may be on the same footing as that existing between European nations where it is customary for parents to send their children to neighbouring countries for education or instruction in arts or trades.[76]

Moreover, Radama immediately selected five more youths to be sent to Mauritius to learn martial music, Hastie informing Farquhar in July 1821, 'I shall send the boys to be instructed in Military music as soon as possible.'[77] These had reached Mauritius by January 1822, when Kyle reported to the governor,

at the request of Radama and under sanction of His Excellency's letter dated 4 septr last, I have brought five boys with me to be added to the Madagascar 'band' to be placed under the 'Music Master' and clothed and fed in same manner as those already under his tuition.[78]

In all probability, of the five, one was called 'Benea', who later became leader of the Mauritius-trained band in Madagascar.[79] In early February 1822, Hastie noted to the governor that

the Madagascar Boys under charge of the Band master of the 82d Regiment have also been under the tuition of the Schoolmaster Serjeant and have made such progress as proves that much attention has been paid to their education ... and as it is a most desirable object that these boys, now thirteen in number, should devote all their time to study, I beg leave to recommend that a female Black from the Matricule department may be attached to Mr. Kyle to wash and mend their cloth[e]s.[80]

Hastie's request was approved.[81]

In March 1822, Radama informed Hastie that, in response to Hastie's request for another six to eight boys to learn military music on Mauritius, he would select and send another eight, in two successive groups of four.[82] That April, Jean Réné informed Hastie that

---

[75] Telfair, *Some Account of the State of Slavery*, 64.
[76] Hastie to Farquhar, Tananarive, 8 Jun. 1821, HB 21, NAM.
[77] Hastie to Farquhar, Bank of the River Bayuana, 100 miles WSW of Tananarive, 9 Jul. 1821, HB 21, NAM.
[78] Kyle to Barry, Port Louis, 8 Jan. 1822, HB 7, NAM.
[79] Ellis, *History of Madagascar*, vol. 2, 422.
[80] Hastie to Barry, Port Louis, 7 Feb. 1822, HB 7, NAM.
[81] Barry to Hastie, 14 Feb. 1822, HB 7, NAM.
[82] Radama I to Hastie, Tananarivou, 6 Mar. 1822, HB 7, NAM.

During your absence, King Radama sent me four young men to be forwarded to you [on Mauritius], asking me to arrange their passage – Monsieur [Scarvelle] was able only to take aboard the two that weren't ill. Please be so kind as to inform His Excellence, Governor Farquhar, and you will receive from the same Captain a letter addressed to you.[83]

On 24 April 1822, Farquhar agreed to pay Sergeant Kyle 'for teaching Military music to the five Madagascar Boys last arrived and delivered over to him, in the same proportion as that allowed to him for that purpose for the Eight boys previously placed under his charge'.[84] In October 1822, Hastie calculated the cost of the Malagasy youths undergoing musical tuition: 'Subsistence, clothing, cost of Instruments and salary of Tutor of Fourteen Lads under instruction in Military Music at Isle of France to form a Band for King Radama at 18 Drs. Per month each. £ 3024.'[85] In total, it appears that the last Madagascar Youths being instructed in music completed their instruction in 1826 and returned to Madagascar in either 1826 or 1827. In total, the Mauritian government spent on them $45,163.85 currency dollars from 1813 to 1825, and a further sum of £882 in 1826.[86]

However, as indicated in the quotation above, the Madagascar Youths learning music suffered considerably from health issues. They were so often sent to the Civil Hospital that, in mid-1822, A. Montgomery, the surgeon in charge from 1821–5,[87] advised Hastie that their diet should be changed to include, at least three days a week, fresh instead of salted meat. Hastie conveyed the message to Farquhar who acquiesced to Montgomery's request.[88]

The Ratsitatanina Affair

The Madagascar Youths sent to Mauritius would all have been affected by the Ratsitatanina affair of 1822. Ratsitatanina was a high ranking *andriana* general in Radama's army, who, in a moment of inexplicable folly during a military campaign against the Sakalava, threatened Radama's life. Had Ratsitatanina been of lower rank, he would have faced execution, but Radama and Hastie decided it would be better to send him into exile on Mauritius. Ratsitatanina arrived on 3 January 1822 aboard HMS *Menai*, commanded by Captain Fairfax Moresby (1786–1877), escorted by a company of Merina soldiers and Rafaralahy Andriantiana, a royal envoy. The ship was also carrying five

[83] J. Réné to Hastie, Tamatave, 20 Apr. 1822, HB 7, NAM.
[84] Barry to Hastie, Port Louis, 24 Apr. 1822, HB 7, NAM.
[85] Hastie to Barry, Foul Point, 14 Oct. 1822, HB 7, NAM.
[86] Kelsey, 'Abstract of the Expense incurred by the Government'.
[87] W. Draper Bolton, *Bolton's Mauritius Almanac, and Official Directory for 1852* (Mauritius: Mauritian Printing Establishment, 1852), 129.
[88] Hastie to Barry, Port Louis, 22 Aug. 1822 and Barry to Hastie, Port Louis, 27 Aug. 1822, HB 7, NAM.

Madagascar Youths sent to be instructed in military music. Hastie gave clear instructions to the Mauritian authorities that Ratsitatanina 'the state Prisoner sent here by Radama' should be securely confined.[89]

In Port Louis, Ratsitatanina was sent to the Bagne, a prison founded in 1766 close to Port Louis harbour. Its initial purpose was to house slaves who were subjected to hard labour; from 1810, under British rule, it also held convict Prize Negro apprentices (it had over 5,000 inmates in 1836 and 9,000 the following year).[90] On 17 February 1822, aided by fellow prisoners, Ratsitatanina escaped the Bagne and fled up the Pouce, a local mountain, where he attracted to his cause a motley band of about twelve slaves and apprentices. Before the 1820 Britanno-Merina treaty, Ratsitatanina, like Radama, had been a major slave trader and, through contact with Mascarene slave traders, undoubtedly spoke some Creole.[91] Farquhar despatched some soldiers against the band on the Pouce, causing its members to disperse, and on 20 February Ratsitatanina was captured on a sugar plantation. A trial was held, and on 15 April Ratsitatanina and two accomplices were beheaded in Jardin Plaine Verte, Port Louis, and their heads publicly displayed. The rest of his band were permitted to return to their prospective masters and employers.[92]

The authorities executed Ratsitatanina and his two band members less because of the threat they posed, which was negligible, than to calm local white settler anxiety about slave revolt. Fear of slave rebellion was widespread among slave owners in a plantation colony where slaves comprised about 75 per cent of the population and whites only 10 per cent, and where the reported number of maroons, or runaway slaves, averaged over 6,000 annually between 1821 and 1826 (see Figure 3.8).[93] Moreover, many slaves and others subject to bonded labour on Mauritius, regardless of whether or not they were of Malagasy origin, dreamed of – and sometimes attempted – escape to Madagascar as the nearest independent land where they believed that they might regain freedom.[94]

Thus, in the popular imagination of both the slave and the free population, a fugitive Merina noble might succeed in seizing a vessel and sailing to Madagascar. This was certainly the conviction held by the fervently anti-British

[89] Hastie, 'Diary' (9 Oct. 1821), in Hastie to Barry, Port Louis, 8 and 14 Jan. 1822, HB 7, NAM.
[90] James Backhouse, *A Narrative of a Visit to the Mauritius and South Africa* (London: Hamilton Adams & Co., 1844), 19.
[91] See e.g. Radama to Hastie [1824?], HB 5, NAM.
[92] Larson, 'Vernacular Life', 327–8, 331–3; Clare Anderson, 'The Politics of Punishment in Colonial Mauritius, 1766–1887', *Journal of the Social History Society* 5.4 (2008): 411–22.
[93] Martin, *Statistics*, 14; Richard B. Allen, 'Marronage and the Maintenance of Public Order in Mauritius, 1721–1835', *Slavery and Abolition* 4.3 (1983), 219; Valentine, 'Dark Soul of the People', 38; Richard B. Allen, 'Maroonage and Its Legacy in Mauritius and in the Colonial Plantation World', *Outre-Mers: Revue d'histoire* 89.336–7 (2002), 140.
[94] See e.g. the case of two Malagasy and nine Malay runaway slaves from Mauritius found in 1789 in a pirogue in open seas hoping to make Madagascar – Allen, 'Maroonage and Its Legacy', 144.

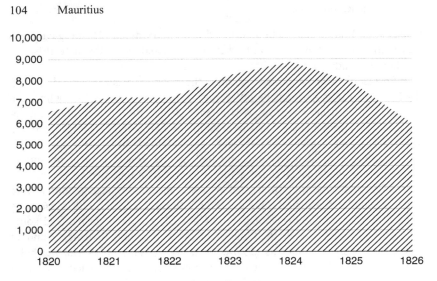

Figure 3.8 Mauritius: reported maroon cases, 1820–6
Source: Adapted from Allen, 'Marronage and the Maintenance of Public
Order', 219.

and pro-Ratsitatanina French writer, B.-F. Leguével de Lacombe, who recorded
the events a few years later. He stated that Ratsitatanina's fellow prisoners in the
Bagne,

> Knowing his hatred for the English . . . told him that he would die in servitude if he failed to
> break from his chains; but that in the event that he succeed in escaping, which they
> considered an easy task, they would take him to Madagascar on one of those large boats
> that he could see through the bars of a prison skylight, from which one could see the port.[95]

However, Ratsitatanina was aware that, had he succeeded in fleeing to
Madagascar, he would almost certainly have been captured and killed either
by Radama or by one of the coastal peoples hostile to the Merina. The affair,
albeit small-scale, non-violent, and short-lived, assumed in the local imagination the dimensions of a slave revolt. As British colonial official, S. D. De
Burgh-Edwardes (1895–1968), recorded,

> In February, 1822, some slaves assembled on the Pouce Mountain and appointed
> a Malagasy named Ratsitatane as their leader and decided to come down to Port
> Louis, when they hoped the other slaves would revolt to fight for their independence.
> Laizaf, one of the ringleaders, denounced the plot to the police. On the 22nd, at 4 p.m.,
> a few white flags were unfurled on the mountain as the signal for revolt, while the armed

[95] B.-F. Leguével de Lacombe, *Voyages à Madagascar et aux îles Comores. (1823 à 1830)* (Paris:
L. Desessart, 1840), vol. 1, 20.

band of maroons came down. They were met by some soldiers. After firing a few volleys at random, they fled. Ratsitatane and twenty-five of his followers were captured. Ratsitatane and one Latulipe were executed and their heads exposed at their meeting-place. Laizaf was condemned to penal servitude for life, while the others had long sentences of hard labour passed upon them.[96]

There is an intriguing possibility that Ratsitatanina was the grandfather of the Merina King Radama II (1829–1863). Ratsitatanina's son, Andriamihaja, assisted in Ranavalona's seizure of power in 1828. Referred to in 1843 by one British economic analyst as 'a young handsome African',[97] Andriamihaja became one of the queen's lovers and, it is widely believed, was the father of Rakoto Radama – the future Radama II.[98]

In the tense atmosphere surrounding the escape, arrest, and execution of Ratsitatanina, the Merina envoys and the Madagascar Youths were popularly viewed with considerable suspicion, as they were widely believed to be sympathetic to, if not instigators of, Ratsitatanina's 'slave uprising'.[99] Ratsitatanina's death dampened this excitement, as did the high-profile government treatment of the Merina envoy, Rafaralahy (Rafaralahindriantiana/ Ifaralahindriantiana) (c.1797–1828). Rafaralahy was an *andriana* of the Zanakandriamasinavalona caste, which claimed descent from Andriamasinavalona, King of Imerina (r. 1675–1710), and was classified second in rank to the royal family. A favourite of Andrianampoinimerina, and relative of Radama, Rafaralahy was soldier of fabled strength.[100] In January 1822, Hastie requested the Mauritian government to pay 'Prince Farla' [Rafaralahy], the prince's secretary, and his interpreter $3 daily and his three servants $1 a day.[101] Farquhar ordered that Farla be given $583, and that he and his suite receive $505.50 for clothing. The governor also sanctioned Hastie to purchase a horse named Silver to enable Farla to ride throughout Mauritius to observe the island's arts and manufactures.[102] In April 1822, Farquhar commissioned Lysis Lemaire to paint a portrait of Rafaralahy and paid the artist an additional seventy-five piastres for 'a Copy

---

[96] Burgh-Edwardes, *History of Mauritius*, 60.

[97] John MacGregor, *Ottoman Empire, Greece, African States*, quoted in *Morning Chronicle* (27 Jul. 1843).

[98] 'Letter', Foulepointe, 3 Mar. 1829, in *Morning Chronicle* (29 Jun. 1829); Charles Brand, 'A Visit to the Island of Madagascar', *United Service Magazine* 2 (1829), 539; RA, 175, 186, 445; RH, 141–3.

[99] Albert Pitot, 'History', in Allister Macmillan (ed.), *Mauritius Illustrated. Historical and Descriptive, Commercial and Industrial, Facts, Figures, & Resources* (W. H. & L. Collingridge: London, 1914), 44.

[100] Campbell, *David Griffiths*, 717.

[101] Hastie to Barry, Port Louis, 8 and 14 Jan. 1822, HB 7, NAM.

[102] Hastie to Barry, Port Louis, 19 Jan. 1822 and Barry to Hastie, 'Resident Agent at Madagascar', Port Louis, 28 Jan. 1822, HB 7, NAM.

of the Bust of Prince Farla to be presented to him'.[103] During his time on Mauritius, Rafaralahy learned English 'sufficiently well to make himself understood'.[104]

By June 1822, Rafaralahy had returned to Antananarivo, and shortly afterwards he led a 2,000-strong expedition to create a model agricultural and commercial colony on the northeast coast around the port of Foulepointe, of which he became governor.[105] He had fully adopted European dress by the time Farquhar visited him in Tamatave in May 1823, aboard the *Menai*, under Captain Moresby, and conveyed him by ship to Foulepointe. Farquhar subsequently left definitively for Britain.[106] It was at Foulepointe, in mid-1828, that soldiers sent by the new queen, Ranavalona, executed Rafaralahy. Raombana records of his death,

the officers sent by Her Majesty came upon him suddenly in his house at Foulepointe, and speared him; but before he received his mortal wound, he sprung upon one of his murderers and seized him by his testicle, which nearly killed him for he held it so fast that after his death for to unclench his hand which still held it, they were obliged to cut away his fingers one by one.[107]

In sum, this chapter presents for the first time a review of the group of Madagascar Youths sent to Mauritius for education and training in the 1810s and 1820s. These comprised both princes and commoners, the first receiving tutorship in the mansion of Farquhar, governor of Mauritius, the remainder being allotted to various respectable Mauritian artisans and to Kyle, bandmaster of the 82nd regiment. There emerges from a patchwork of archival references a reasonably coherent picture of the history of these youths, although there remain some significant lacunae, notably relating to the experiences of the young female Malagasy members of the group.

As with the Madagascar Youths sent to Britain, the history of those despatched to Mauritius needs to be considered in the context of Britanno-Merina relations in the two decades following the British takeover of Mauritius in 1810. Farquhar, the first British governor of Mauritius, took the initiative in forging an alliance with Radama, king of the small highland kingdom of Imerina, in Madagascar. From the time of the first British embassy to Imerina in 1816, Farquhar sought to establish a system of exchange whereby 'British' (both Creole Mauritian and metropolitan British) agents established themselves in Madagascar as diplomatic and military aides, artisans, and missionary

---

[103] Barry to Hastie, Port Louis, 24 Apr. 1822, HB 7, NAM.   [104] Brand, 'A Visit', 529.

[105] Extract from Hastie's journal (10 Jun. 1822), in *Home Friend*, vol. 1 (London: Society for Promoting Christian Knowledge, 1854), 307–10.

[106] 'Civilization of Madagascar', *Morning Spectacle* (8 Sep. 1823); see also 'Journal of a Voyage Eastward of the Cape, &c.', *London Literary Gazette and Journal of Belles Lettres, Arts, Sciences* (27 Aug. 1825), 555.

[107] RA, 196; see also RA, 197; RH, 112, 151; Regis Rajemisa-Raolison, *Dictionnaire historique et géographique de Madagascar* (Fianarantsoa: Librairie Ambozontany, 1966), 279–80.

educators and members of the Merina ruling house and Malagasy youths travelled to Mauritius, at the expense of the colony's treasury, to be educated and trained under British supervision. The Malagasy who travelled to Mauritius under these auspices were triple the number of those who voyaged to Britain (some thirty-five plus as opposed to the twelve-strong embassy to Britain in 1820). The core focus of the Britanno-Merina alliance, as reflected in the 1820 treaty, was the ban on slave exports, hitherto the major source of revenue and arms for the Merina crown, in return for military aid and craft skills. Most youths sent to Britain were apprenticed in the armaments and textile industries, with the aim of boosting Merina military power and expansion and providing the basis for an export-based industry to replace the slave trade. Those sent to Mauritius were apprenticed in a wider variety of 'useful' trades, from that of gunmakers and silversmiths to mulberry and coffee producers. Of signal importance was the emphasis the Merina crown placed on training a military musical band. A few Malagasy girls were also sent to Mauritius learn the art of European domestic science.

Like those sent to Britain, the Madagascar Youths to Mauritius included individuals of different social rank, ranging from royalty to slaves. The last-named category, while little remarked upon in the literature, is of major significance given the centrality of the ban on slave exports to the 1820 treaty, for which Farquhar and his heirs were granted 'the dignity of a Baronet' in July 1821.[108] It reflects the continued widespread tolerance of slavery in British colonial society of the time, despite the growth of abolitionist sentiment in Britain, notably in parliament and among evangelicals. This sentiment mushroomed in scope and virulence in the 1820s, when attention previously focused on the Atlantic widened to include east African waters and Mauritius. From the mid-1820s, the British anti-slavery movement and its supporters in parliament brought serious accusations against British officials on Mauritius of colluding in clandestine slave imports and failing to implement regulations to improve conditions for slaves. In 1826, Thomas Fowell Buxton (1786–1845), by then the leading abolitionist in the British parliament, accused Farquhar and Telfair of participation in the slave trade.[109] The same year, a parliamentary Commission of Enquiry into slavery on Mauritius was established.[110] In 1827, Buxton claimed to possess sufficient evidence to prove that Farquhar had been complicit in breaking anti-slave trade laws and that he had willingly accepted that, during his governorship, 'the Slaves at the Mauritius have been treated with unparalleled cruelty'.[111] Changes in colonial office personnel, and

---

[108] *London Gazette* (28 Jul. 1821), 1555.
[109] Bathurst to Hay, 3 Aug. 1826, Loan ms. 57/178011.B., BL.
[110] Burroughs, 'Mauritius Rebellion of 1832', 246.
[111] [T.] Fowell Buxton to [Colonial Office], [Northrupps Hall, near Cromer], 21 Oct. 1829, CO 167/114, NAK.

his own ill health, prevented Buxton from pressing the issue until late 1829, when he alleged in parliament that there had been a massive illegal slave trade to Mauritius, in which local authorities and the colonists had colluded:

[D]uring a long series of years, those importers of Slaves have reaped most largely the benefits of their offense – have been enabled to quintuple the produce of sugar, and to obtain most evident advantages over all sugar growers who obeyed the law, and . . . this has been done at an incalculable expense of human life and misery.[112]

If found guilty, Farquhar and Telfair could have faced the death penalty. On 2 June 1829, Farquhar, who from 1825 was the member of parliament for Newton on the Legh, defended himself in the House of Commons against Buxton. Further, he accused all those calling for immediate emancipation on Mauritius of being visionaries with no understanding of the complexity of the issue:

Foiled in their wild attempts upon our established British colonies, they are now pouring forth their venom upon those which, by fate of war, have submitted to His Majesty's arms, and especially Mauritius, which from its position they think suitable for the trial of those visionary experiments which, if enforced, cannot fail to terminate in the same sad and awful catastrophe which we have witnessed already in other French colonies, and of which Bourbon and Mauritius have not been without symptoms of similar disturbances, but happily subdued since the conquest.[113]

In 1830, Telfair also published a book defending his position.[114] However, attacks upon them by anti-slavery advocates continued, and appear to have taken their toll. Farquhar died in 1830, and Telfair in 1833.[115]

The issue of the slave trade forms the context for the next chapter, which analyses a third batch of young Malagasy to receive training under the British outside Madagascar. These comprised the Madagascar Youths who in the 1820s served as apprentices aboard British naval vessels in the western Indian Ocean, a group as little recorded in the literature as those sent to Mauritius.

---

[112] [T.] Fowell Buxton to [Colonial Office], [Northrupps Hall, near Cromer], 15 Dec. 1829, CO 167/114, NAK.

[113] R. T. Farquhar, Address, House of Commons, 2 Jun. 1829 in response to Anti-Slavery Reporter no. 42, CO 167/114, NAK.

[114] Telfair, *Some Account of the State of Slavery.*

[115] For an example of the abolitionist perspective, see 'Picture of Mauritius Slavery Vindicated', *Anti-Slavery Monthly Reporter* 62 (Jul. 1830), 285–99; Anthony J. Barker, *Slavery and Antislavery in Mauritius, 1810–33: The Conflict between Economic Expansion and Humanitarian Reform* (London: MacMillan, 1996).

4   The British Navy

This chapter presents the history of the third group of Madagascar Youths, who Radama sent abroad as a result of the Britanno-Merina alliance. These comprised the youths who from 1824 served as apprentices on British naval vessels under the Cape Command, one of the main tasks of which was to counter the western Indian Ocean slave trade. The chapter examines the role of Madagascar in the regional slave trade, the strategy adopted by the British to suppress that trade, notably the desire that Radama build a navy to patrol Malagasy waters, and the training of a select group of Madagascar Youths aboard British naval vessels in the expectation that they would subsequently man Radama's fleet.

Britannia and the Indian Ocean Slave Trade

By the close of the French Wars in 1815, the British had established naval dominance in the Indian Ocean. Through its colonization of Penang Island in 1786, Singapore in 1819, and Malacca in 1824, Britain gained control over the Straits of Malacca and the eastern maritime route to India. Through the seizure of Sri Lanka in 1796, the Cape of Good Hope in 1806, and Mauritius in 1810, the British similarly secured the western maritime route to India via the Cape. However, the Indian Ocean is vast, and in order to maintain its naval dominance Britain was obliged to create within it different maritime spheres, each under distinct naval commands. Thus, the western Indian Ocean was divided into two zones, a northern sector under the jurisdiction of the Bombay Marine – called the Indian Navy from 1830 –and a southern one under the authority of the Cape Station.

The EIC built the Bombay Marine in the eighteenth century, primarily to counter pirates and French pretensions in India – which justified the Marine contributing five ships to the successful British assault on Mauritius in 1810.[1] Nevertheless, Mauritius subsequently fell under the jurisdiction of the Cape

---

[1] Len Barnett, 'The East India Company's Marine (Indian Marine) and Its Successors through to the Royal Indian Navy (1613–1947)', www.barnettmaritime.co.uk/mainbombay.htm (accessed 11/05/19); Anirudh Deshpande, 'The Bombay Marine: Aspects of Maritime History 1650–1850', *Studies in History* 11.2 (1995), 284–5.

Station, and it was upon the commander of the Cape Station that the British governors of Mauritius called when requiring naval assistance. Initially located in Table Bay, immediately to the west of Cape Town, the naval station was by 1814 relocated some 40 km distant to Simon's Town, on the eastern side of the Cape Peninsula.[2] Farquhar, the first British governor of Mauritius, used Cape-based warships to transport British emissaries and missionaries, and Malagasy emissaries and the Madagascar Youths, between Mauritius and Madagascar. He also summoned them, when requested by Radama or Hastie, to transport Merina troops along the Malagasy coast. Above all, he utilized them on anti-slave trade patrols in regional waters, where the traffic in slaves remained vigorous to the end of the nineteenth century. In the southwest Indian Ocean, the slave trade was conducted primarily by Europeans, who shipped African slaves chiefly to Brazil and African and Malagasy slaves to the Mascarenes, and by Swahili traders who exported Africans and Malagasy mainly to Muslim markets in the Gulf.[3]

Demand for slaves on the Mascarenes grew dramatically following the economic revitalization of the islands under from the 1730s. The closest and cheapest source of slaves was Madagascar, from which between 1610 and 1810 the Mascarenes procured 72,000 slaves (45 per cent of their total slave imports), compared to 64,000 (40 per cent) from East Africa.[4] As they were the closest to the Mascarenes, the preferred slave markets were in northeast Madagascar, where Foulepointe was in the late eighteenth century the major slave port, superseded from 1801 by Tamatave.[5] Both were within relatively easy reach of Imerina, the major source of Malagasy slaves. However, slave supplies from the highland interior of Madagascar were frequently interrupted by internecine strife in Imerina, and by trade disputes along the routes linking the interior to the northeast coast. Such insecurity encouraged middlemen, notably Swahili merchants from northwest of the island and Betsimisaraka from the northeast, to search for an alternative source of slaves.[6]

They found it in Iboina, the Sakalava kingdom in northwest Madagascar, notably in Majunga, the Boina capital, where most Madagascar-based Swahili traders resided. Majunga formed the base for an extensive coastal, regional, and

[2] W. L. Speight, 'The British Navy in South Africa', *Royal United Services Institution Journal* 77.506 (1932), 375; M. Marshall, 'The Growth and Development of Cape Town', MA thesis, University of Cape Town (1940), 59.

[3] Gwyn Campbell, "Madagascar and the Slave Trade, 1810–1895', *Journal of African History* 22.2 (1981), 203–5.

[4] Gwyn Campbell, 'Madagascar and Mozambique in the Slave Trade of the Western Indian Ocean 1800–1861', *Slavery and Abolition* 9.3 (1988), 166.

[5] George McCall Theal, *Records of South-Eastern Africa*, vol. 9 (Cape Town: Struik, 1964), 13, 50–2; Jean-Michel Filliot, *La traite des esclaves vers les Mascareignes au XVIIe siècle* (Paris: ORSTOM, 1974), 129–41, 157–9.

[6] Campbell, 'Madagascar and Mozambique', 168.

long-distance maritime network. Sakalava captains sailed 5–10 ton dhows along the entire western littoral of Madagascar and engaged in riverine trade. The Swahili, both in Madagascar (where they were called Antalaotra) and East Africa, primarily engaged in Western Indian Ocean commerce in dhows ranging from 30 to 200 tons, that could carry up to sixty men.[7] Indian merchants from Gujarat also annually sent a return fleet from Surat to northwest Madagascar and East Africa (see Map 4.1).[8] They had long-established links with mostly Khoja or Bohra Shia Muslims from western India who had settled in Madagascar probably from about the twelfth century.[9]

By the 1790s, Majunga boasted a population of 6,000 Indian and Swahili traders and their families.[10] Any Westerner wishing to trade on the Malagasy west coast was obliged to work through them.[11] The Indians and the Swahili imported mainly Surat silks and cottons, armaments (muskets, balls, flint stones, and gunpowder), glass, jewellery, and salt. In return, they exported Malagasy slaves, provisions (rice, live cattle, and smoked and salted meat), hides, precious woods, gum copal, ambergris, tortoise shell, and piastres to Mozambique, Arabia, and northwest India.[12] Indeed, prior to the 1820 treaty, of the estimated 120,000 piastres annually imported by European traders on the east coast to purchase export goods, the Merina transferred some 80 per cent to Indian and Swahili traders in payment for imports from the west coast. As Hastie remarked of Radama of Imerina in 1817, 'He exchanges chains [of silver] with the Arabs as they are stocked with slaves, and slaves with all European merchants.'[13]

[7] Gwyn Campbell, *An Economic History of Imperial Madagascar, 1750–1895: The Rise and Fall of an Island Empire* (Cambridge: Cambridge University Press, 2005), 50, 261 fn 86.
[8] Campbell, *Economic History*, 49.
[9] Frere, 'memo regarding the Banians ... in East Africa', in Frere to Granville, Gulf of Oman, 16 Apr. 1873; 'Memo', 31 Mar. 1873, in Bartle Frere, 'Correspondence Respecting Sir Bartle Frere's Mission to the East Coast of Africa, 1872–73', *House of Commons Parliamentary Papers* (London: House of Commons, 1873); see also Nancy Jane Hafkin, 'Trade, Society and Politics in Northern Mozambique c.1753–1913', PhD thesis, Boston University (1973), 85–8; Campbell, *Economic History*, 48.
[10] Vincent Noel, 'Ile de Madagascar: Recherches sur les Sakalava', *Bulletin de la société de géographie* 2.19 (1843), 275–95 and 2.20 (1843), 40–64; Alfred Grandidier, 'Souvenirs de voyages, 1865–1870' (1916), in *Documents anciens sur Madagascar*, vol. 6 (Tananarive: Association malgache d'archéologie, 1971), 28; Micheline Rasoamiaramanana, 'Aspects économiques et sociaux de la vie à Majunga entre 1862 et 1881', PhD thesis, University of Antananarivo (1983), 10–11, 35, 54.
[11] Campbell, *Economic History*, 51.   [12] Campbell, *Economic History*, 56.
[13] Hastie, 'Diary' (1817), 188, CO 167/34, NAK; see also Nicolas Mayeur, 'Voyage dans le nord de Madagascar' (1775), 86 – Add. 18128, BL; Nicolas Mayeur, 'Voyage au pays d'ancove, par le pays d'ancaye autrement dit des Baizangouzangoux', related by Dumaine (1785), 227 – Add. 18128, BL; Anon, 'Mémoire historique et politique sur l'Isle de Madagascar' [1790], 55 – Add. 18126, BL; Dumaine, 'Voyage à la côte de l'ouest, autrement dite pays des Séclaves' (1793), 294–7 – Add. 18128, BL; Hastie, 'Diary' (1817), 157, CO 167/34, NAK; Hastie, 'Diary' (1825), CO 167/78 pt. II, NAK; Samuel Copland, *A History of Madagascar* (London: Burton and Smith, 1822), 12–18; Samuel Pasfield Oliver, *Madagascar: An Historical and Descriptive Account of the Island and Its Former Dependencies*, 2 vols (London: Macmillan, 1886), vol. 2, 16–17;

Until the mid-eighteenth century, Europeans had occasionally sought slaves from Majunga. Thus, in 1743, a trader called Saveille obtained there a cargo of several hundred slaves.[14] However, by the late eighteenth century the demand for slaves from the Mascarenes was such that, in the context of periodic disruptions along routes between Imerina and the northeast coast, it stimulated a major investment in the regional slave trade by the Boina Sakalava, who launched what the British termed 'piratical expeditions' against the Comoro Islands and the Mozambique coast, primarily for slaves. According to James Prior (c.1790–1869), a surgeon aboard HMS *Nisus*, who was stationed at Mauritius in 1810–11, these expeditions started in 1786 and occurred on an almost annual basis.[15] They were primarily aimed at the Comoro Islands of Anjouan (Nzwani), Mayotte (Maore), and Moheli (Mwali) – avoiding Grande Comore (Ngazidja), the fourth island of the archipelago, because of its rugged topography. Sometimes, as in 1800, and from 1805–9, the Sakalava also attacked locations on the east African coast between Cape Delgado and Mozambique Island.[16] For example, in a five-month campaign from September 1808 to early January 1809, a Sakalava force ravaged the Mozambique coast from Ushanga, just north of the Lurio estuary, to Tungi, enslaving, 800 Africans, mostly women and children. However, so many of the Sakalava force contracted smallpox, to which many succumbed, that they were eventually forced to retreat.[17] Europeans weren't immune from the Sakalava attacks. In 1805, over 500 Sakalava warriors in twenty-five canoes sacked the Portuguese ship *Boa Mãe* in Domoni harbour, Anjouan; and in January 1806, the Sakalava 'pirates' slaughtered the seventy-man crew of the *Emboascada* in waters off the Cap d'Ambre, the northernmost tip of Madagascar.[18]

The Sakalava maritime campaigns started under the auspices of Ravahiny, queen of Iboina (d. 1808; r. c.1778–1808), and continued under her successor, Tsimalomoa (r. 1808–20).[19] James Prior received information from the Portuguese governor of Mozambique Island and from the Sultan of Anjouan that the

Alfred Grandidier and Guillaume Grandidier, *Histoire physique, naturelle et politique de Madagascar* (Paris: Imprimerie Nationale, 1908), vol. 4, book 1, 106, 160, 162, 171; Guillaume Grandidier, *Histoire physique, naturelle et politique de Madagascar* (Paris: Hachette, 1928), 260, 302–3, 322–3, 327, 332; Alfred Horn, *The Waters of Africa* (London: Jonathan Cape, 1932), 97;.

[14] Pierre Vérin, *Histoire ancienne du nord-ouest de Madagascar – Part 1* ([Antananarivo]: Université de Madagascar, 1972), 152.

[15] James Prior, *Voyage along the Eastern Coast of Africa: To Mosambique, Johanna, and Quiloa; to St Helena; to Rio de Janeiro, Bahia, and Pernambuco in Brazil, in the Nisus Frigate* (London: Richard Phillips, 1819), 62.

[16] Prior, *Voyage along the Eastern Coast of Africa*, 44, 56, 62, 64; Edward A. Alpers, 'Madagascar and Mozambique in the Nineteenth Century: The Era of the Sakalava Raids (1800–1820)', *Omaly sy Anio* 5–6 (1977), 38–9; Campbell, 'Madagascar and Mozambique', 168.

[17] Alpers, 'Madagascar and Mozambique', 40–1.

[18] Alpers, 'Madagascar and Mozambique', 39; Campbell, *Economic History*, 43.

[19] Prior, *Voyage along the Eastern Coast of Africa*, 64.

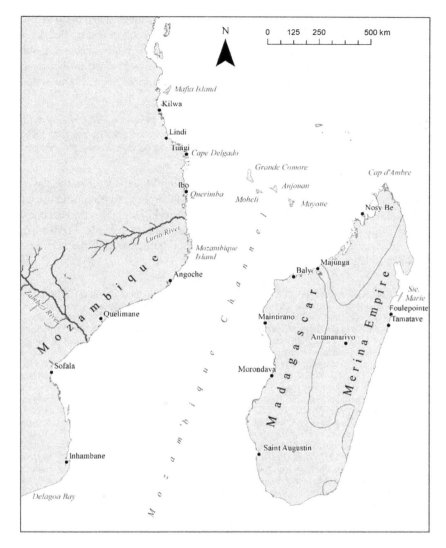

Map 4.1 Madagascar, Comoros, and East Africa
Source: Drawn by Kareem Hammami, © IOWC.

expeditions were organized between the months of August and October from Bombetoka Bay, where Majunga is located. Up to 40,000 Sakalava men, women, and children then gathered in the bay, from which fleets were launched carrying between 5,000 and 8,000 Sakalava warriors, allegedly armed with muskets purchased from French or Swahili traders. The raiders sailed in up to 300 outrigger canoes, the largest of which measured 10 m by 1.2 m and carried sixty warriors. If needed, two expeditions were despatched.[20] When successful, the raiders returned with enslaved captives who were initially detained in Iboina, in such numbers that François Albrand (1795–1826), governor of Sainte Marie, stated in 1820,

The people known as Sakalava have populated in the northwest of Madagascar with Anjouanais captives, and Jean Rene, sovereign of Tamatave, assured me that these foreigners, whose number increases every day, would soon become masters of this part of the island.[21]

This was an overstatement, for each dry season, from May to October, the slaves were dispersed. Some were retained in western Madagascar for domestic use by the Sakalava but most were marched overland by Swahili traders to the east coast ports of Foulepointe and Tamatave for sale to Mascarene merchants.[22] Indeed, in 1803, all slaves for sale on Sainte Marie, a French-held island off the northeast coast of Madagascar, hailed from Anjouan.[23]

[20] Anon, 'Mémoire historique' [1790], 60; Mayeur, 'Voyage au pays d'ancove' (1785), 54; Grégoire Avine, *Voyages aux isles de France d'Anjouan de Madagascar, de Mosambique, de Zanzibar et de la côte Coromondel*, (Paris: Mauritius Archives Publications, 1961 [1802]), 26–7; Prior, *Voyage along the Eastern Coast of Africa*, 62–4; Oliver, *Madagascar*, vol. 1, 38, 433, 435 and vol. 2, 38, 54, 101–2; Grandidier and Grandidier, *Histoire physique* (1908), vol. 4, book 1, 380–1.
[21] Quoted in Vérin, *Histoire ancienne*, 151.
[22] Nicolas Mayeur, 'Voyage au pays des Séclaves, côte de Madagascar', 86, 92–3, 97, 101, 103–5, 115, 121, 123 – Add. 18128, BL; Mayeur, 'Voyage dans le nord de Madagascar', 34, 37, 46; Mayeur, 'Voyage au pays pays d'ancove, autrement dit des hovas ou Amboilamba dans l'intérieure des terres, Isle de Madagascar' (1777), 176, 180 – Add. 18128, BL; Mayeur, 'Voyage au pays d'ancove' (1785), 221–2, 227, 233; Morice, 'Mémoire sur la côte oriental d'Afrique', Isle de France (15 Jun. 1777), edited by Joseph François Charpentier de Cossigny (1790), 100–6 – Add. 18126, BL; Anon, 'Mémoire historique' [1790], 95 – Add. 18126, BL; Dumaine, 'Voyage au pays d'ancaye, autrement dit des Bezounzouns, Isle de Madagascar' (1790), 278 – Add. 18128, BL; Dumaine, 'Voyage à la côte de l'ouest' (1793), 295, 297; Mayeur to Froberville, 4 Apr. 1806, in Jean Valette (ed.), 'Documents pour servir à l'étudè des relations entre Froberville et Mayeur', *BAM* 16.1-2 (1968), 89; Rondeaux, 'Mémoire' (1809) in Jean Valette, 'Un mémoire de Rondeaux sur Madagascar (1809)', *BAM* 44.2 (1966), 121–2; Copland, *History of Madagascar*, 12, 18; Duroche, 'Note sur Madagascar' (15 Mar. 1816) – Add. 18135, BL; Hastie, 'Diary' (1825); Noel, 'Ile de Madagascar'; Oliver, *Madagascar*, vol. 1, 272, 291, 323–4, 423; Charles Guillain, *Documents sur l'histoire, la géographie et le commerce de la partie occidentale de Madagascar* (Paris: Imprimerie Royale, 1845); Prud'homme, 'Considérations sur les Sakalaves', *Notes, reconnaissances et explorations* 6 (1900), 1–43; Grandidier and Grandidier, *Histoire physique* (1908), 160, 165, 315–16, 324; Grandidier, *Histoire physique* (1928), 260–2, 308; Horn, *Waters of Africa*, 97; Edmont Samat, 'Notes: La côte ouest de Madagascar en 1852', *BAM* 15 (1932), 61, 64; Jacques Lombard, *Le royaume Sakalava du Menabe: Essai d'analyse d'un système politique à Madagascar, 17e–20e* (Paris: ORSTOM, 1988).
[23] Filliot, *La traite des esclaves*, 153–4; Gill Shepherd, 'The Comorians and the East African Slave Trade,' in James L. Watson (ed.), *Asian and African Systems of Slavery* (Oxford: Blackwell, 1980), 74–6; see also James Walvin, *Slavery and the Slave Trade* (London: MacMillan, 1983), 66, 69.

From the first Mauritian embassy to Antananarivo in 1816, Farquhar pressed Radama to impose a ban on slave exports, with an emphasis on the major slave traffic from Imerina to the Mascarenes via Tamatave and Foulepointe. The ban was central to the Britanno-Merina treaty of July 1817. However, British attempts to protect East Africa from Sakalava attacks, as in August 1809 when a warship was positioned off the Mozambique coast, failed to stem the raids. Finally, following complaints from the sultan of Anjouan, a traditional provisioning base for EIC ships, the Supreme Court of Calcutta in 1817 petitioned Farquhar to end the Sakalava raids.[24] Thus, on 23 October 1817, as a result of pressure from Farquhar, Radama issued a proclamation 'for the Abolition of the Slave Trade' stating,

I command all my Subjects and Dependents, and invite all my Allies, to abstain from any maritime predatory excursion whatever; and more particularly neither to practise nor allow any attack or attempt upon the friends of our Ally the British Nation.

It has been usual to make an annual attack upon the Sultan of Johanna [Anjouan] and the Comoro Islands. Our good friend the Governor of Mauritius dissolved the meditated attack of last year; and we now join him in forbidding any further enmity to the King or inhabitants of the Comoro Archipelago, or other Islands on the coast of Africa or North Archipelago, under the pain of our most severe displeasure, and of incurring the punishment due to pirates, of whatever Nation or People they may be.

Such is my will; let it be known to every inhabitant of this Island: it is for their own happiness and their own safety to pay obedience to this Proclamation.[25]

After the renewal of the Britanno-Merina treaty in October 1820, Radama implemented an effective ban on slave exports from areas of Madagascar under Merina domination. However, slaves continued to be exported from Mozambique and areas of Madagascar independent of Merina rule. This is reflected in the growing numbers of Prize Negroes in the region.[26]

---

[24] Campbell, *Economic History*, 43.

[25] 'Proclamation of Radama, King of Madagascar, for the Abolition of the Slave Trade', Tamatave, 23 Oct. 1817, in Foreign Office, *British and Foreign State Papers, 1824–1825* (London: J. Harrison & Son, 1826), 461–2.

[26] And, as noted in Chapter 1, about 3,000 were landed on Mauritius between 1813 and 1827 – see Margaret Wilson, letter, Cape Town, 28 Nov. 1828, in John Wilson (ed.), *A Memoir of Mrs. Margaret Wilson, of the Scottish Mission, Bombay* (Edinburgh: Longman, 1844), 115; Christopher Saunders, 'Liberated Africans in Cape Colony in the First Half of the Nineteenth Century', *International Journal of African Historical Studies* 18.2 (1985), 224, 227; Joline Young, 'The Enslaved People of Simon's Town 1743 to 1843', MA Thesis, University of Cape Town (2013), 59–60, 65–7; Satyendra Peerthum Ally Hossen Orjoon, 'Liberated Africans in Nineteenth Century Mauritius', *L'Express* [Mauritius] 2 Feb. 2005, www.lexpress.mu/article/liberated-africans-nineteenth-century-mauritius (accessed 16/12/18). Overall, from 1808 to 1848, a minimum of 5,000 Prize Negroes entered service in Cape Colony – Saunders, 'Liberated Africans', 223.

A Merina Navy

It is in this light that the British fostered the idea that Radama should create a navy in order to quickly subjugate still independent regions of Madagascar, notably the Sakalava kingdoms, and to protect maritime commerce and ports, thereby both enhancing his revenues and ending all slave exports from the island. Radama had already made preliminary steps in that direction by consolidating his rule over the island's main port of Tamatave, captured in 1817, and utilizing it as a base to patrol coastal waters. In February 1822, keen to assist Radama in his efforts to stem slave exports, Farquhar approved Hastie's request for 'an Estimate for cordage and canvas required by Jean René, chief of Tamatave, Madagascar, for refitting his vessel to enable him to comply with the orders of Radama relative to the abolition of the slave trade, amounting to Four hundred and Eighty nine dollars'.[27] Shortly afterwards, in April 1822, Farquhar's secretary informed Hastie,

I have the honor to inform you that in consideration of the palpable and distinguished proofs given by the chief Jean Rene in seizing and confiscating two vessels laden with Mozambique slaves, and of the saving to the British government of a resident at Tamatave so long as Jean Rene co-operates with such vigour and good faith for the utter extinction of the slave trade; and more particularly of the signal blow he has given to this nefarious traffic by his conduct above adverted to, His Excellency is pleased to increase his Stipend from the British government from Fifty to one hundred Dollars per month, in hard Dollars.[28]

Farquhar additionally presented $325 worth of plates and knives to René.[29]

At the same time, Farquhar advised Radama to capture Majunga, the island's most important west coast port and a centre of the slave trade. Farquhar promised that a British warship would be present in Bombetoka Bay when Radama's army reached Majunga, in order to offer any necessary assistance. Farquhar noted that 'The paramount object [of his mission] still consists in the complete fulfilment of the Treaty abolishing the Slave traffic, for ever, in Madagascar, and the extension of the provisions of that Treaty to every portion of the population of that vast Island'.[30] However, conquest of the northwest coast would also promote foreign trade in which Farquhar envisaged British shipping would be paramount:

You will inform Radama that I am much pleased with his intentions of making settlements on the Coast, exclusively under his own power and authority, and which

---

[27] Barry to Hastie, Port Louis 14 Feb. 1822, HB 7, NAM; see also N. J. Kelsey, 'Abstract of the Expense incurred by the Government of Mauritius on Account of Madagascar' (26 Nov. 1827) in 'Slaves in Mauritius' 40–44, *Papers Relating to the Slave Trade* 26.2 (House of Commons, 1828).

[28] Barry to Hastie, Port Louis, 24 Apr. 1822, HB 7, NAM.

[29] Barry to Hastie, Port Louis, 24 Apr. 1822, HB 7, NAM.

[30] Farquhar to Hastie, Mauritius, 30 Apr. 1822, HB 7, NAM.

may serve not only for a ready and sure communication, at all times, between his Capital and this Island, but also as the means of opening a most advantageous commerce for the prosperity of his Country, and ultimately of a source of great revenue to himself . . .

A Country every way so Rich in its natural Productions, required only that protection to commercial enterprize and industry, which a strong and efficient Government can afford, to render its ports frequented by our Shipping, to carry off its produce and supply, in exchange, and in abundance, the manufactures of our own Country.[31]

In 1822, Radama led his army against Menabe, the Sakalava kingdom to the south of Iboina. In late 1822, in anticipation of a Merina advance on Iboina, two British warships sailed to Majunga under Commodore Nourse, who had recently been appointed commander of the Cape Station with the brief to suppress the regional slave trade. At Majunga, Nourse met Andriantsoly (c.1799–1847), king of Iboina. Given the show of British naval power, Andriantsoly could do little but acquiesce to Nourse's demand that he hoist over his residence a flag, sent by Farquhar, as a sign of the union of all Malagasy chiefs. Nourse also advised Andriantsoly to despatch an embassy to Antananarivo to conclude an alliance. The embassy was duly sent in December 1822. It reached the Merina capital during celebrations to welcome the return from Menabe of the Merina army under Radama, who had delayed his advance on Majunga. In Antananarivo, the Boina embassy learned that the flag Nourse had presented to Andriantsoly was none other than the Merina flag. The ambassadors protested but in February 1823 returned to Majunga with a message from Radama that he was the supreme leader in Madagascar and that he planned shortly to launch a military expedition against Andriantsoly.[32]

At the same time, exchanges with the British inspired in Radama the desire to establish his own fleet, independent of René. As a first step towards this, Radama wrote to Farquhar, probably in 1822 or early 1823, expressing his wish to purchase a vessel. As he noted to Hastie,

I informed you, My dear James Hastie that I am very happy to purchase a fine ship, and have just written to Mr. Farquhar to that effect. I told you that I am able to pay $10,000 in first-rate cattle delivered at Tamatave. If possible, I would be very pleased to have your response . . . I would very much like to possess that ship, for I have deeply considered Mr. Clarkson's letter concerning Madagascar. I believe that when I possess the ship everything will go well.[33]

The Clarkson referred to in Radama's letter was Thomas Clarkson (1760–1846), the celebrated English abolitionist, who in correspondence with Farquhar had recommended that Radama purchase a craft to engage in anti-slave patrols in

[31] Farquhar to Hastie, Mauritius, 30 Apr. 1822, HB 7, NAM.
[32] Guillaume Grandidier, *Histoire physique, naturelle et politique de Madagascar* (Paris: Imprimerie Paul Brodard 1942), 199.
[33] Radama to Hastie [1824?], HB 5, NAM.

Malagasy waters.[34] To encourage Radama, Farquhar informed him that Sayyid Said (1790–1856), sultan of Muscat and Oman, had recently agreed to an anti-slave trade treaty.[35] This was the Moresby Treaty – named after Fairfax Moresby (1786–1877), the senior naval officer at Mauritius who negotiated it. Signed in September 1822, the Moresby Treaty prohibited the sale of slaves by any of the sultan's subjects to any subjects of a Christian country.[36]

In May 1823, Radama accorded the British the right to seize any slave ships in Malagasy waters, but he hoped that he would soon possess an independent navy.[37] However, the 4,828 km coastline of Madagascar, first accurately surveyed in 1822–6 by British Naval Captain William Fitzwilliam Owen (1774–1857),[38] posed formidable problems to Radama in terms of conquest and control. Initially Radama concentrated on subjecting the northeast coast and securing control over Tamatave, the island's most important port. In 1823, he and Ratefy establish military dominance in the region, aided by the British, who transported Radama and his troops aboard HMS *Ariadne* from Vohibary to Hiarana (Vohimar/Amboanio) to establish a Merina garrison.[39] Shortly afterwards, Radama launched a military expedition against Iboina, to where Farquhar ordered Nourse's fleet in order to assist in the capture of Majunga (see Figures 4.1 and 4.2).[40] A newspaper report dated January 1824, probably written by a senior officer under Nourse, stated of the encounter between the Merina and Sakalava,

The *Andromache* arrived at Bembatooka on the 29th November [1823], fortunately at a time when two advancing armies were within a few days' march of each other – the army of King RADAMA, and of King ADANSAUL [Andriantsoly], of Bembatooka. The former is endeavouring to subjugate this fine island to his authority, with the exulting view of putting down that nefarious and inhuman practice, Slave traffic, and of substituting commerce and agriculture in its place.[41]

In December 1823, Nourse asked Hastie to enthusiastically encourage Radama to conquer Majunga in order that he might suppress the slave trade and regulate and tax the maritime commerce of the port with Bombay, Surat, Muscat,

---

[34] Papers of Thomas Clarkson, Add. 41265, BL.
[35] Farquhar to Hastie, Port Louis, 24 Oct. 1822, HB 7, NAM.
[36] Yusuf A. Al Ghailani, 'British Early Intervention in the Slave Trade with Oman 1822–1873', *History Research* 5.4 (2015), 226.
[37] Grandidier, *Histoire physique* (1942), vol. 5, book 2, 189, fn.
[38] A survey that was published in 1833 – James Sibree, 'History and Present Condition of our Geographical Knowledge of Madagascar', *Proceedings of the Royal Geographical Society and Monthly Record of Geography* 1.10 (1879), 658.
[39] RH, 119–20.   [40] Farquhar to Hastie, Port Louis, 24 Oct. 1822, HB 7, NAM.
[41] Letter from an anonymous sailor, dated Simon's Bay (Cape of Good Hope), 4 Jan. 1824, quoted in the *Morning Post* (5 Apr. 1824).

Figure 4.1 Majunga c.1840
Source: Personal collection.

Figure 4.2 HMS *Andromache*
Source: from a drawing by Captain Tobin RN, http://data.europeana.eu/con
cept/base/35.

Mozambique, and Zanzibar.[42] He further noted that Radama should take advantage of Majunga's significant boat-building capacity:

At Majungay [Majunga] they build Boats, from 10 to 20 Tons, the timber abounds in the Country, and the Iron is purchased from the Americans ... The beach at Majungay is excellent for building and launching, and there is a rise and fall of 14 feet water. Here, perhaps, Radama might give Birth to his Marine. All the N.W. Coast abounds in beautiful Harbours and Rivers, and there is little doubt, in the course of time, many valuable products will be found, that will render all that Coast of commercial importance ... There are a number of Slaves from the Coast of Africa; these people Navigate their boats, and I believe, build them, besides their usual occupations on shore.[43]

This observation was backed by Thomas Boteler (d. 1829),[44] first lieutenant and assistant-surveyor on the *Barracouta* during the 1822–6 survey of the western Indian Ocean by Captain W. F. Owen, who noted that Majunga was a major centre of dhow and other 'Arab' boat construction.[45]

A British naval fleet was present in Bombetoka Bay in mid-1824 when the Merina secured definitive control of Majunga.[46] Radama welcomed Nourse's invitation to inspect the British fleet,[47] and his suggestion that the king might procure a frigate.[48] Nourse also pushed further the project, conceived by Farquhar, of extending British informal hegemony over Madagascar. He drew up an agreement, signed by Radama in August 1824, whereby British subjects were in Madagascar granted virtual free trade and the right to settle, cultivate land, and move without hindrance:

Whereas having recently possessed myself of the Town of Mazungay and the Bay and harbours of Bembatok, and it appearing that various exorbitant and undefined sums have heretofore been extorted from British Vessels as well as others visiting this harbor for the purpose of trade or refreshment, And being desirous of manifesting on all occasions my high consideration for the British Nation and my friendship for Commodore Joseph Nourse C.B. commanding His Britannic Majesty's Ships and Vessels in those Seas, It is hereby ordered That all British Vessels visiting the said Ports and harbors for the purpose of, and engaging in lawful trade, shall have free liberty to do so, without let or hindrance of any kind, on payment of the sum of 'Fifteen Dollars' Anchorage money, and of 'Five per cent' duty on all articles, the produce of Madagascar, exported for the purpose of such trade and traffick, The said duty to be levied in the most equitable and convenient manner and no other duties or fees of any kind whatsoever to be imposed.

[42] Nourse to Hastie, HMS *Andromache* at sea, 11 Dec. 1823, HB 5, NAM.
[43] Nourse to Hastie, HMS *Andromache* at sea, 11 Dec. 1823, HB 5, NAM.
[44] John Marshall, 'Royal Naval Biography/Boteler, Henry', https://en.wikisource.org/wiki/Roya l_Naval_Biography/Boteler,_Henry (accessed 05.05.21).
[45] Thomas Boteler, *Narrative of a Voyage of Discovery to Africa and Arabia, Performed in His Majesty's Ships, Leven and Barracouta, from 1821 to 1826. Under the Command of Capt. F. W. Owen, RN*, vol. 2 (London: Richard Bentley, 1835), 118.
[46] RH, 124.   [47] RH, 122–3, 154.   [48] RA, 209–11.

That with a view to encourage the residence of British Subjects in my Dominions for the better Civilisation of my people and the introduction of various Arts and Sciences, I hereby assure them of my special protection and that they shall have free liberty to dwell therein, to build Ships and Vessels and Houses and cultivate Lands: to carry on lawful trade and trafick, to come and go at their own will and pleasure without let or hindrance of any kind and without payment of any duty or tax than before mentioned.[49]

Following the capture of Majunga, Radama felt no need to purchase many European ships. The port gave him control of a major boat-building centre, access to both west coast trade and the possibility of commandeering hundreds of Swahili dhows and Indian ships. Further, through the 1824 accord with Nourse, he might attract to Madagascar British boat builders whose skills he could utilize. Indeed, he had since at least 1823 envisaged building a fleet that would establish Merina predominance in Madagascar and extend Merina imperial sway over the entire western Indian Ocean by seizing the Comoros and even wresting the Mascarene Islands from British and French control.[50]

Merina Colours

The prospect of creating a Merina fleet raised the question of appropriate naval colours. In April 1824, Radama asked Hastie to have the British make for him a national flag with a 'Vourou Mahery' (*voromahery*) emblem.[51] This probably meant an eagle (*voromahery*), a royal symbol, although it might have referred to a special royal military corps whose members were drawn from the central Imerina region of Voromahery.[52] It was different from the usual royal Merina flag, which bore the sovereign's name in large black letters against a white background.[53] It might have been of the same design as that used by Radama II on ascending the throne in 1862, described as 'somewhat in the form of the broad pennant of our navy, with a narrow red border. At the broad end of the flag there was a red star of eight or ten points, with an inscription, Radama II., Mpanjaka ny Madagascar, 1862, and R.B. II in the centre.'[54] Possibly, as was

[49] Radama. 'Port Regulations' [Majunga?], Aug. 1824, HB 4, NAM.

[50] RH, 120, 122–3, 153–4.

[51] Hastie to [Sec] Govt Mauritius, Tananarive, 22 Apr. 1824 – 'private', HB 5, NAM.

[52] Gwyn Campbell, *David Griffiths and the Missionary 'History of Madagascar'* (Leiden: Brill, 2012), 752.

[53] In this case, 'Ranavalo Manjaka' – J. Ross Browne, *Etchings of a Whaling Cruise with Notes of a Sojourn on the Island of Zanzibar; and a Brief History of the Whale Fishery, in Its Past and Present Condition* (London: John Murray, 1846), 246; Joseph Barlow Felt Osgood, *Notes of Travel: Or, Recollections of Majunga, Zanzibar, Muscat, Aden, Mocha, and other Eastern Ports* (Salem: George Creamer, 1854), 4.

[54] W. A. Middleton, F. A. Marindin, Edward Newton, Edward Mellish, and J. Caldwell to William Stevenson, governor of Mauritius, Port Louis, 25 Nov. 1861, in 'Copies or Extracts of papers relating to the Congratulatory Mission to King Radama of Madagascar on his Accession to the Throne in 1861: And, of Correspondence and Papers relating to the Mission to Madagascar in

the case with later Merina flags, it was coloured red for the ancestors and white for the living – representing the pivotal role of the sovereign as the representative on earth of the supernatural world.[55]

Lowry Cole responded positively to the request but warned that the flag's manufacture would take time as only one embroiderer on Mauritius was capable of producing it.[56] This was a Mlle Coudrillier, who, contrary to the governor's expectations, had completer the flag by the start of August 1824. She claimed $89.33 in payment, which was provided by the Mauritius treasury, and the flag was delivered to Nourse to be presented to Radama.[57] Probably in 1825, Hastie also wrote to Hood Hanway Christian (1784–1849), from late 1824 Nourse's successor as commander of the Cape Station: 'I have the design of the flag he [Radama] has already chosen . . . Wouldn't it be best . . . to take the flag to the owner of the warship, who lives in London?'[58] Concerned that René was using a different banner, Hastie warned,

With reference to Jean Rene's purchase of a vessel and his flag, pray permit me to mention to you that from conversations that Radama has had with Commodore Nourse, Captains [Constantine Richard] Moorsom [1792–1861][59] and [Isham Fleming] Chapman [fl. 1808–1826], and other British Officers, and also with me, he has been led to believe that the English Government and consequently that of Mauritius would not acknowledge or countenance the flag of any subordinate Chieftain of Madagascar, yet I must say that he has not in my opinion been so particular as is necessary in defining the national symbol to those in command under him as the Flag sent to him by His Excellency is the only one he possesses and has been seen but by a very limited number of his subjects. Reflecting on the enquiry that occasioned me to write to you on the subject, I conclude he was not much flattered at learning that the Chief of Tamatave's flag was acknowledged by Government.[60]

He continued,

Again, with reference to Flags, I should mention to you that a day or two previous to my leaving Tananarivou, Radama received a letter from J. Rene acquainting him with the late arrangements in the maritime merchant service at Mauritius and soliciting permission to grant Radama's flag to vessels that should continue in the Madagascar trade, or be transferred by bills of Sale to residents in this country. I advised the King to defer a decision on so important a subject until he obtained more ample information. Of

1862, for the purpose of presenting the Portraits and presents sent by Her Most Gracious Majesty to King Radama' in House of Commons, *Accounts and Papers*, vol. 74 (1863).

[55] Campbell, *David Griffiths*, 557.

[56] [Dumeresq] to Hastie, Reduit, 20 Jun. 1824, HB 5, NAM.

[57] Barry to Hastie, Port Louis, 3 Aug. 1824, HB 5, NAM.

[58] Hastie to Captain Christian, [1825?], HB 5, NAM.

[59] It appears that all senior officers who met Radama engaged in a ritual exchange of presents with the king. In such an exchange, Radama presented Moorsom, with a flintlock – 'Weapons and Militaria', Whitby Museum, https://whitbymuseum.org.uk/whats-here/collections/social-history/weapons-militaria/ (accessed 13/05/19).

[60] Hastie [Sec to?] Govt Mauritius, Tamatave, 25 Feb. 1826, HB 4, NAM.

course, I am anxious to set him right, and beg you will have the goodness to give me an outline of what the regulations are, and say how far it would be consistent or otherwise for Radama to permit his flag to be used, as I must remark that the instances will be very rare of absolute transfers of Vessels to natives of this country.[61]

In May 1826, Hastie commented further to the Mauritian governor about the danger of foreign vessels, notably slavers, flying Radama's flag in order to escape notice by British anti-slave trade patrols and officials:

I mentioned to you in my letter of 25th February that Jean Rene had written to King Radama requesting his Flag for a Vessel then under British Colours (it was the *Philo*, Captain Herout) and as it was considered unsafe for the Vessel to await the King's answer at this anchorage, it appears that the Chieftain of Tamatave accorded par interim to the *Philo* the Flag under which the *Nancy* or *Courier de Tamatave* has been admitted at Mauritius. The *Philo* sailed from this [place] on 9th January for Port Louis and has subsequently been sold at Bourbon to a Monsieur Germain, and she arrived here on the night of the 3rd. inst.

Being apprized by King Radama that he did not authorize the act of Jean Rene with regard to the Flag, I required the Ships papers and annulled the Chieftain's passport, and I wrote to the Captain informing him that it would be at his own risque that he left the anchorage without efficient documents.

On an interview, I recognized the Captain to be a British subject, a Mr. Nicole who has a house near the Church at Port Louis, and some evasive answers on the part of the Supercargo, Mr. Gourdin (I think a borrowed name), and learning that Mr. Gonnet, a Slave dealer of Bourbon [Réunion], was on board, I was convinced that the Vessel tho' reported to be on a voyage to Vohemar to Salt Beef, was fitted out for the Slave trade. I therefore through Captain Dudoit of the *Coureur* [sic Courier] *de Tamatave* advised Nicole to leave the Vessel, and he being indisposed, I gave him a certificate of ill health to enable him to return to Port Louis.

I must remark that jean Rene's conduct with regard to the Flag merely merits the term indiscretion; he never anticipated the present voyage of the *Philo*, and I am sure he would not aid in any such project.[62]

Naval Youths

Radama's capture of Majunga and desire to create a Merina navy forms the context for the recruitment of a third group of some fifty Madagascar Youths apprenticed aboard British naval vessels in the western Indian Ocean. When Radama met Nourse in Majunga in mid-1824, the commodore stressed to Radama the importance not only of establishing a national fleet but also of training Malagasy to run it – an enterprise in which he offered his assistance. Boteler, who was present on this momentous occasion, stated,

[61] Hastie [Sec. to?] Govt Mauritius, Tamatave, 25 Feb. 1826, HB 4, NAM.
[62] Hastie to Viret, Sec. to Govt Mauritius, Tamatave, 10 May 1826, HB 4, NAM.

The day after the interview between the commodore and Rahdahmah, the latter, accompanied by his brother, Mr. Hastie, and several of the chiefs, repaired on board the *Andromache* to dine. He was received with a salute and a guard, and, as he had never yet visited so large a ship, he appeared lost in admiration as he walked round her decks. Nothing escaped his observation; and his remarks, if they were not pertinent and profound, were at least accounted so.

The commodore, in conversing with Rahdahmah, strongly impressed on his mind how admirably his island was situated, and how well adapted, from its numerous harbours, for the purposes of commerce. 'You want but vessels, he continued, 'seamen to navigate them, and trade will follow of course. Although I cannot supply you with the first, with the second I possibly may, if you give me but the means. Let me have a few of your young men; they shall be distributed among the squadron under my orders, and if they fail to learn at least something it must be their own fault.' Rahdamah approved the proposal, and with gratitude accepted it. 'A navy you would soon have, and believe me, nothing would yield me greater pleasure than to pay my respects to the Prince of Madagascar on the quarter-deck of a frigate of his own.' Rahdahmah half rose from his seat: his ecstasy at the idea was too great for utterance: it glistened in his expressive eye – it flushed on his cheek – he held his head down, as if wrapped in a pleasing reverie, and whined and rubbed his hands, as if unconscious of what he was doing.[63]

Thus, on 27 July 1824, immediately prior to signing the free trade agreement, Commodore Nourse agreed that twenty Madagascar Youths, aged from fifteen to eighteen years old, be selected from the ranks of Radama's army, ten to be placed aboard the *Andromache*, a frigate he commanded, and five each aboard the *Espiegle* and the *Ariadne*. Of the twenty initially selected, four were to join the ship's band – a reflection of Radama's passion for military music and penchant for grandeur.[64]

Boteler noted that although all the selected youths originated from Imerina, they were of different pigmentation:

The population of Ovah [Imerina] consists of Mulattoes and Blacks, the former of whom appear to be considered superior; though Rahdahmah [Radama] is anxious to do away with that distinction . . . It was on this account that Mr. Hastie, when presenting the Ovah [Merina] lads to Captain Vidal, to be trained up as seamen, earnestly requested that no distinction on account of colour should be made or permitted among them. They were habited in the becoming costume of their country, and were apparently from fifteen to eighteen years of age. They were fine intelligent-looking young men, and, like the rest of the people of Ovah, were more graceful than athletic, possessed a pleasing expression of countenance, and a handsome turn of features, for which those of the darkest dye were not less remarkable than the others.[65]

[63] Boteler, *Narrative of a Voyage*, vol. 2, 152–4; see also W. F. W. Owen, *Narrative of Voyages to Explore the Shores of Africa, Arabia, and Madagascar; Performed in HM Ships Leven and Barracouta*, 2 vols (New York: J. & J. Harper), vol. 2, 128–9.

[64] Hastie, 'Diary' (1824–4), entry for 27 Jul. 1824, CO 167/78 (part 2), NAK; Guillain, *Documents*, 84–5; Lyons McLeod, *Madagascar and Its People* (London: Longman, 1865), 72–3; Oliver, *Madagascar*, vol. 1, 37.

[65] Boteler, *Narrative of a Voyage*, vol. 2, 150–1.

In his turn, Raombana stated that the youths were either of the second-ranking *hova* caste or *Olomainty* (royal slaves).[66] On 14 August 1824, Captain Alexander Vidal (1792–1863) took a further six Madagascar Youths aboard the *Barracouta*, which had a crew of 24 youths, 926 seamen, and 4 bandsmen.[67] One of those selected for the *Barracouta* deserted on the eve of embarkation and returned on foot to Antananarivo. He had evidently attended a missionary school as he could already read and write English. On reaching home, his father surrendered him to the royal authorities who condemned him to death for desertion. However, prior to the date of execution, he died of malaria caught in Sakalava land.[68]

Recruitment continued, and by the end of May 1825, some fifty Madagascar Youths had been taken aboard British naval ships (see Table 4.1). Other Malagasy naval recruits, not listed in Table 4.1, included Ramiaramanana, an ex-mission scholar and student teacher.[69] Thus, 'three young persons, natives of Madagascar, the sons of Native Chiefs in that island' were placed under the protection of Lieutenant-Colonel Richard Kelly (fl. 1799–1845), during a voyage undertaken in the *Alexandra* in October 1824.[70] Given the close Britanno-Merina alliance of this period, the wording of this statement would seem to indicate that the youths referred to were the sons of chiefs from coastal areas under Merina control – most probably from Tamatave or Foulepointe.

Also, in late October 1826, after he broke with the British treaty, Radama negotiated an agreement with the Blancard brothers, Louis (1779–1853) and Jean, article 5 of which stipulated that 'Messrs. Blancard & Co. pledges to accept aboard each of their vessels the subjects that His Majesty Radama chooses in order to train them as sailors. They will be fed at the expense of Messrs. Blancard & Co.'[71] In the event, the Blancard agreement fell through in 1827, and no Malagasy youths were trained on their vessels.

Life Aboard the British Navy

The Madagascar Youths apprenticed aboard British naval ships were landlubbers from the high central interior of the world's fourth largest island. Conscripted into the Merina army, most first caught sight of the sea when marched overland 170 km to the east coast or 570 km to Majunga. It is unlikely

---

[66] RH, 122–3, 154.

[67] Hastie, 'Diary' (1824–4), entry for 14 Aug. 1824, CO 167/78 (part 2), NAK.

[68] Boteler, *Narrative of a Voyage*, vol. 2, 123–4.

[69] 'Appendix' in Arthur Frankland, 'Ten Weeks Leave of Absence: Cruise from Mauritius to Madagascar and East Coast of Africa', ref.216, PWDRO; Campbell, *David Griffiths*, 57, 59.

[70] 'Single Campaign Medals' #518, www.dnw.co.uk/media/auction_catalogues/Medals%20Strong%2018%20May%2011.pdf (accessed 04/08/18); see also www.bonhams.com/auctions/16881/lot/353/?keep_login_open=1 (accessed 13/05/19).

[71] Article 5, Agreement between Radama I and Louis Blancard, Tananarive, 25 Oct. 1826, HB 4, NAM; see also Campbell, *Economic History*, 279.

Table 4.1 *List of Madagascar Youths aboard British naval ships, 1825*

Stations at sea	Different trades	Proficiency in English	Music
Forstop	*Carpenters*	*1st class read pretty well*	*Can play musical instruments*
Benarivoa	Laimahrow	Quitounga	Quitrounga
Zatouvausandra	Quitounga	Ihaingio	Louhoutsy
Touby	Ihaingio	Louhoutsy	Mananquajaina
Mananquajaina	Miandry	Miandry	Touby
		Laimahrow	
Maintop	*Armourers*		
[...]itounga	Laingiany	*2nd class read not so well*	
Laimahrow	Maharow	Maharow	
Ihaingio	Louhoutsy	Tandrasana	
Maharow		Benarivoa	
	Sailmakers	Itranja	
Mizentop	Tandrasana		
Itranja	Touby	*3rd class cards with words of two and three syllables*	
Laingiany	Benarivoa	Touby	
Maroutsirafy		Mananquajaina	
Louhoutsy	*Coopers*	Maroutsirafy	
Miandry	Maroutsirafy	Zatouvausandra	
	Mananquajaina		
		Can write English	
	Ropemakers	Quitounga	
	Itranja	Ihaingio	
	Zatouvausandra	Laimahrow	
		Maharow	
		Tandrasana	
		Itranja	

Source: Hastie, List of Madagascar Boys, [May?] 1825, HB 4, NAM.

that any had ever before sailed aboard a vessel, let alone a warship. However, despite their apprehensions, the chosen youths undoubtedly realized their privileged status. The British Navy had established a reputation as the world's best during the French wars. Much of this was due to a culture of discipline, to which the Madagascar Youths would have needed to adapt.[72] However, whereas the war years had seen an enormous increase in naval vessels and almost unlimited possibilities for employment, peace in 1815 resulted, as in the army, with massive curtailment of ships and retrenchment of both ordinary

[72] Douglas W. Allen, 'The British Naval Rules: Monitoring and Incompatible Incentives in the Age of Fighting Sail', *Explorations in Economic History* 39 (2002), 204, 207–8, 209 fn 15.

seamen and officers. The British naval fleet was sharply reduced from 398 to 248 vessels between 1810 and 1820, by which time only 15 per cent of commissioned lieutenants retained their jobs.[73] Again, from 1815, the Admiralty removed the power of recruitment from captains and adopted a policy ensuring that new recruits were predominantly English, rather than Celts or youths from other parts of the empire. Moreover, they favoured 'gentleman', particularly those with connections to the nobility – although some such recruits grew up in financially challenged circumstances, often due to the death in the wars of their fathers. Until 1821, promotion to lieutenancy was largely based on service during the French wars, but as these older men retired, they were increasingly replaced by young gentlemen.[74] Many such recruits were already skilled in seamanship, or claimed appropriate skills, such as ability in mathematics, trigonometry, and foreign languages.[75]

Recruitment for the lower ends of the ship's hierarchy was also reorganized: the category of '3rd class boy' was eliminated and recruits for '2nd class' were to be aged fourteen or older and employed as officers' servants until they turned seventeen, when they could enter the ranks of '1st class boys', for whom the traditional three-year apprenticeship was abolished in favour of training as 'expert seamen or mechanics'.[76]

However, a high number of naval recruits perished. Roland Pietsch's study of ships' boys during the Seven Wars Year (1756–63) indicates that within that period at least a third of them died, got shipwrecked, or became 'unserviceable'.[77] In the southwest Indian Ocean, turbulent seas and currents took their toll on ships, but disease accounted for most deaths amongst ship's crews in tropical regions, obliging many captains take on foreign crew members as replacements. A case study of British naval ships off West Africa in the early 1840s indicates that about 20 per cent of the crew were Africans, mostly 'Kroomen' (adult males of a seafaring tradition from Liberia) but also ordinary Africans and ex-slaves.[78]

The daily routine of the Madagascar Youths aboard British naval ships was prescribed as follows:

Mustered with their Hammocks at 7 o'clock. All to see that their Hammocks &c. are in proper order.

[73] Samantha Cavell, 'A Social History of Midshipmen and Quarterdeck Boys in the Royal Navy, 1761–1831', PhD thesis, University of Exeter (2010), 346.
[74] Cavell, 'A Social History of Midshipmen', 341, 343–4, 348–9, 392–4.
[75] Cavell, 'A Social History of Midshipmen', 361, 364.
[76] Cavell, 'Social History of Midshipmen', 351–2, 355, 367.
[77] Roland Pietsch, 'Ships' Boys and Youth Culture in Eighteenth-Century Britain: The Navy Recruits of the London Marine Society', *The Northern Mariner/Le marin du nord* 14.4 (2004), 24.
[78] John Rankin, 'Nineteenth-Century Royal Navy Sailors from Africa and the African Diaspora: Research Methodology', *African Diaspora* 6 (2013), 184.

Mustered at half past 7 o'clock to see that the Boys are perfectly clean for the day.

At half past 8. All they are taught to read under the superintendence of the Ship's Corporal.

At half past ten o'clock they are sent to the different Tops under the directions of the respective Caps to be instructed in Seamanship.

At 1 P.M. they are sent to work under the superintendence of heads of the respective Trades, Carpenter, Sail Maker &c.

3 P.M. drilled at small arms by non-commissioned Officer of [Vessel].

N.B. When any thing particular is going on either by Carpenter, Armourer, Sail Makers &c., they are sent to such particular work in place of being sent into the Tops.[79]

Montagu Burrows (1819–1905), an English naval recruit aboard the *Andromache* when it sailed to Madagascar and the Comoro Islands in 1835, described the exercises the captain made the boys perform:

On our way to Mauritius my Journal describes our Captain's zeal in teaching us all gunnery and his officers seamanship. For the first, we put out a target, manoeuvred the ship round it under all sail and fired at it from all the guns; but not one hit it, and yet we were always exercising our guns. This at least taught us how difficult it was. We also had to fire a six-pounder on the quarter-deck at a target rigged out from the forecastle. For the second, we each of us were summoned to a formal examination in the art of tacking ship and in rigging a miniature bowsprit.[80]

Of the four Madagascar Youths sent aboard British ships to learn music, Hastie wrote to the governor of Mauritius in November 1825,

Previous to leaving the Mauritius, I took the liberty to write to you concerning four Boys that the late Commandore Nourse took on board the *Andromache* to receive some instruction in music. It was then expected that the *Owen Glendower* would make an early visit to the isle of France and I was desirous that the Boys might be sent down this year, but the season is now so far advanced that they would run so much risque of fever on the journey up the country that I am anxious for them to remain at Mauritius with the Band of one of the Regiments or on board if they receive any instruction in music, until the end of May next. May I entreat your Kind Offices on this account.[81]

In March 1826, Hastie wrote to the governor of Mauritius with reference to these youths:

With regard to the four Boys that were sent on Ship board to receive instructions in music, I should now mention to you that, as I have hopes that their services as mariners will possibly be required, and perhaps be more advantageous to their country than the object [for] which they shipped, I think if they have any opportunity of practising a little on board, and the Commodore will have the goodness to allow them to remain, it will be desirable that they should do so.[82]

---

[79] 'Madagascar Boys' in Capt. Moorson to Hastie, 20 May 1825, HB 4, NAM.
[80] Montagu Burrows, *Autobiography of Montagu Burrows* (London: Macmillan, 1908), 42.
[81] Hastie to Viret, Tananarive, 1 Nov. 1825, HB 4, NAM.
[82] Hastie to Viret, Sec. to Govt Mauritius, Tananarivou, 10 Mar. 1826, HB 4, NAM.

The Madagascar Youths were each allocated to a different eating mess.[83] This was commonly enforced by captains when taking aboard non-English speakers, in order to facilitate their learning the language and imbibing naval traditions and etiquette. For example, when at the Cape in July 1822, Captain Owen received as interpreters seven 'Kaffers' – Xhosa arrested by Boers for crossing into British territory on the Cape's eastern frontier – he placed them in different messes 'for the purpose of making them learn English'.[84] Boteler commented of the Madagascar Youths apprenticed aboard British naval vessels,

The conduct of these young men won the warmest approbation of the officers: mild, docile, and attentive to command, they manifested such good sense and integrity that they could be entrusted in any situation. As seamen they were emulous and active; and, in the fifteen months which they passed with us, made great progress as sailmakers and carpenters; but, from the constant occupation of all on board in the furtherance of the survey, they did not attain such proficiency in reading and writing as they otherwise would have done. For this backwardness they made ample amends after their removal to the *Owen Glendower* frigate, at the Cape, where leisure and means combined to assist them. Although so mild and obedient, yet with our seamen they maintained a conduct that gained them respect, and suppressed satirical observations on their colour or nation, to which they would by no means submit.[85]

Thus, 'Their skins were thrown aboard, their arms released, and in a short time there was no distinction between them and the rest of the crew in regard to food, dress, and treatment.'[86] It was also common practice for them to change ships, and thus become obliged to serve under different officers and mix with different crews. For example, in mid-1825, the Malagasy aboard the *Barracouta*, under Captain Owen, were transferred to another of the Cape station's ships.[87]

The provisioning of 'one blue jacket and a pair of trowsers' to each of the Madagascar Youths aboard the *Andromache* (they numbered fourteen by early 1825), became the centre of a naval scandal. In August 1825, after the ship reached Portsmouth from the Cape, Thomas Goble, its purser since January 1822[88] was accused on five counts of fraudulently overcharging for provisions. The last two charges were

4   For having in the month of June 1825, in a debtor and creditor statement rendered to C. R. Moorsom Esq., Captain of the said ship, of certain savings of provisions made by some Madagascar boys, forming part of the crew of the said ship, falsely charged the sum of £7.1s.8d to have been paid to Lieutenant Alexander Tait on account of the same boys.

---

[83]   Hastie, List of Madagascar Boys, [May?] 1825, HB 4, NAM.
[84]   Owen, *Narrative of Voyages*, vol. 1, 47.   [85] Boteler, *Narrative of a Voyage*, vol. 2, 151–2.
[86]   Boteler, *Narrative of a Voyage*, vol. 2, 15.
[87]   Owens to Hastie, Government Agent at Madagascar, HMS *Leven*, Port Louis, 28 Jun. 1825, HB 4, NAM.
[88]   'Andromache', Naval Database, www.pbenyon.plus.com/18-1900/A/00248.html (accessed 13/08/18).

5 For falsely and vexatiously imputing to the said Alexander Tait conduct unbecoming to an officer and a gentleman, by charging the said Lieutenant with having received the sum of £7.1s.8d which the said Lieutenant denied having received, and which in fact never was paid to the said Lieutenant.[89]

Goble was found guilty, court-martialled, and expelled from the Navy. Subsequently, he married and had six children, two of whom emigrated to Natal.[90]

The Madagascar Youths were exposed to Christian services held aboard ship[91] and to sailor subculture, language, and rituals – albeit in a context in which most British sailors they mixed with were of southern English origin and of high-class status.[92] They would certainly have witnessed, and possibly indulged in, drunkenness, which was common amongst seamen.[93] They would similarly have encountered homosexuality, which was openly tolerated on some ships. Certainly, it rarely appears in naval punishment records: between 1755 and 1831 only eleven charges of 'sodomitical practices' were brought against junior officers (5 per cent of all charges against them).[94]

Sailing the Western Indian Ocean

The Madagascar Youths aboard British naval ships sailed throughout the western Indian Ocean, between the Seychelles to the north and Cape Town to the south. For example, they participated in Owen's surveys of the East African coast. Some were aboard the *Barracouta* in 1828 when Vidal surveyed the Minnow Islands, off the west coast of Madagascar.[95] As Owen was keen to suppress slaving in the region, the Madagascar Youths also participated in anti-slave trade patrols.[96] British naval captains also noted a marked growth in the slave export trade from Mozambique, but as this was carried out chiefly under French colours they could do little, for international treaties restricted them from seizing slave vessels south

---

[89] 'Court Martial of Mr. Thomas Goble, Purser of HMS the Andromache', *Morning Chronicle* (26 Aug. 1825).

[90] 'Court Martial of Mr. Thomas Goble', www.goblegenealogy.com/data/SouthAfrica/gp57.html (accessed 13/05/19).

[91] John Gray, *The British in Mombasa 1824–1826* (London: Macmillan, 1957), 88–9.

[92] Pietsch, 'Ships' Boys', 23.

[93] John H. Dacam, '"Wanton and Torturing Punishments": Patterns of Discipline and Punishment in the Royal Navy, 1783–1815', PhD thesis, University of Hull (2009), 118–19.

[94] Cavell, 'Social History of Midshipmen', 416; Dacam, 'Wanton and Torturing Punishments', 155–6, 160–1.

[95] 'The Minow Islands, west coast of Madagascar, by Capt. A. T. E. Vidal & officers of HMS Barracouta & Albatross, under orders of Capt. W. F. W. Owen 1824'. Admiralty Chart 708 (1828), FO 925/1047, NAK.

[96] Although, from 1824–5, British warships from the Cape station captured no slaving ships – Extract of a Despatch from Lowry Cole to Bathurst, Mauritius, 4 Jun. 1826, No.2 in 'Correspondence Relating to the Slave Trade at the Mauritius', House of Commons, *Slave Trade: Papers Relating to Slaves in the Colonies*, vol. 22 (1826–7).

of the equator unless they were British.[97] And in 1830, a curious incident occurred, when Charles Schomberg (1779–1835), commandant of Cape Station from 1828 to 1832, arrested David Jones, a Welsh missionary, on the charge of running slaves from the southeast of Madagascar to Tamatave. However, Schomberg failed to make the accusation stick.[98]

The Malagasy naval apprentices were also involved in attempts by Owen to establish British protectorates in Delagoa Bay and at Mombasa. In June and August 1823, Owen negotiated protectorates on the south shore of Delagoa Bay with, respectively, Kapella, king of Temby, and the ruler of the neighbouring kingdom of Mapoota. He justified this move on humanitarian (promoting anti-slave trade measures; freeing Africans from Portuguese control), economic (favouring British trade), and political (countering Portuguese regional preten-sions) grounds. The Portuguese reacted by removing the British flags Owen had planted in the 'protectorates' and, in April 1825, seized the British brig *Eleanor* for unauthorized trading with the Africans of Mapoota. Owen pro-tested, claiming that the Portuguese had no authority beyond the precincts of their forts and warning the governor of Mozambique that the British would use force unless their wishes were respected. The governor of Delagoa Bay agreed to surrender the *Eleanor* only if the British paid a fine and compensated him for the value of contraband carried in the vessel. He further claimed that Delagoa Bay chiefs were under Portuguese authority and thus could not sell or cede land. On 28 August 1825, in an act witnessed by the Madagascar Youths, Owen compelled the Portuguese to surrender the *Eleanor*, whose captain, however, admitted to having asked the Portuguese for permission to trade – indicating that he had recognized their authority in the region. Owen also asserted the importance of a British presence to prevent French slavers who were active in Delagoa Bay. Nourse backed Owen on the grounds that British settlements in Delagoa Bay would also help counter French claims to Madagascar. However, the British foreign office insisted that it settle the affair directly with the government in Lisbon – discussions that collapsed with the outbreak of war in Portugal in 1828.[99] Of the Delagoa Bay incident, Boteler commented of the

---

[97] Patrick Harries, 'Slavery, Indenture and Migrant Labour: Maritime Immigration from Mozambique to the Cape, c.1780–1880', *African Studies* 73.3 (2014), 329.

[98] Schomberg to Colville, HMS *Maidstone*, Port Louis, 23 Dec. 1830, CO 167/153, NAK.

[99] 'Notice of cession of Lands of Tembé and Maputa to Crown of Great Britain, June 1, 1823', Inclosure 3 and 'Treaty of Commerce between Makasane, King of Mapoota, and the subjects of His Majesty the King of Great Britain', 3 Aug. 1823, Inclosure 7, in House of Commons, *Delagoa Bay: Correspondence Respecting the Claims of Her Majesty's Government* (London: Harrison & Sons, 1875), 21, 24; Owen to Botelho, Leven, 10 May 1825, Appendix 4, in House of Commons, *Delagoa Bay*, 16; Owen to J. W. Croker, HMS *Leven*, Delagoa Bay, 6 Sep. 1825, in Foreign Office, *British and Foreign State Papers, 1825–1826* (London: James Ridgway & Sons, 1848), 315; Naval Intelligence Division, *A Manual of Portuguese East Africa* (London: HM Stationery Office, 1920), 472; Raymond W. Bixler, 'Anglo-Portuguese Rivalry for Delagoa Bay', *Journal of Modern History* 6.4 (1934), 425–8; Mabel V. Jackson Haight,

Madagascar Youths that 'on one occasion, where there was a probability of our having recourse to force with the Portuguese of Delagoa ... they evinced the utmost satisfaction for displaying their national courage'.[100] In explorations of Delagoa Bay, the Madagascar Youths also witnessed hippopotami, elephant hunting, and inter-ethnic conflict.[101]

Between 23 October and 9 November 1823, the *Leven*, under Captain Owen, and the *Barracouta*, under Captain Vidal, with Madagascar Youths as crew members, conducted a survey of Mombasa.[102] At the invitation of its Mazrui rulers, threatened by the growing influence of Busaidi Arabs in East Africa, Owen declared a protectorate over the port settlement, promptly establishing there a colony of Prize Negroes, liberated from Swahili slaving vessels, that he put to work on plantations. The Madagascar Youths under his command witnessed the capture of one of a group of Swahili who tried to re-enslave some of the Prize Negroes. Owen had him whipped and banished to the Seychelles.[103]

Owen appointed Lieutenant Johannes Reitz (1801–1824) as the first British commandant of the protectorate. However, shortly after Owen left Mombasa, Reitz died, probably of malaria. Consequently, in early August 1824, the *Andromache*, under Commodore Nourse, with some Madagascar Youths aboard, sailed from the Cape, via Zanzibar and Pemba, to Mombasa. They arrived on 25 August, and three days later, Lieutenant James Emery (b. 1791) was installed as the new commandant, a position he held until July 1826. Emery used thirty liberated and salaried slaves to remove stones from Ras Serani fort, located south of Fort Jesus, to build a wharf, jetty, and customs house along the Mombasa waterfront and to construct a well.[104]

On 31 August, the *Andromache* sailed for Mauritius, and four days later, while at sea, Nourse died of malaria.[105] At Mauritius, Senior Lieutenant

---

European Powers and South-east Africa: A Study of International Relations on the South-east Coast of Africa, 1796–1856 (London: Routledge & Kegan Paul, 1967), 200–4.

[100] Boteler, *Narrative of a Voyage*, vol. 2, 150–2.   [101] Boteler, *Narrative of a Voyage*, vol. 2.

[102] Boteler, *Narrative of a Voyage*, vol. 2, 197; Gray, *British in Mombasa*, 85–6.

[103] Owen, *Narrative of Voyages*, vol. 2, 85, 92–3; *Official Gazette of the Colony and Protectorate of Kenya* (7 Jun. 1927), 691; Edmund H. Burrows, 'Queries', *Mariner's Mirror* 43.4 (1957), 344 n. 29; James Kirkman, 'John Studdy Leigh in Somalia', *International Journal of African Historical Studies* 8.3 (1975), 442; Brian Hoyle, 'Urban Renewal in East African Port Cities: Mombasa's Old Town Waterfront', *GeoJournal* 53.2 (2001), 193; Rosemary McConkey and Thomas McErlean, 'Mombasa Island: A Maritime Perspective', *International Journal of Historical Archaeology* 11.2 (2007), 117; Prita Meier, *Swahili Port Cities: The Architecture of Elsewhere* (Bloomington: Indiana University Press, 2016), 197, n. 54; J. P. van Niekerk, 'The Life and Times of Cape Advocate Dirk Gysbert Reitz: A Biographical Note', *Fundamina: A Journal of Legal History* 22.2 (2016), 314.

[104] Burrows, 'Queries', 344 n. 29; Kirkman, 'John Studdy Leigh', 442; Hoyle, 'Urban Renewal', 193; McConkey and McErlean, 'Mombasa Island', 117; Meier, *Swahili Port Cities*, 197 n. 54; van Niekerk, 'Life and Times of Cape Advocate Dirk Gysbert Reitz', 314.

[105] Anonymous letter, Mauritius, 10 Oct. 1824, quoted in *Caledonian Mercury* (8 Jan. 1825); *Morning Chronicle* (30 May 1825); Gray, *British in Mombasa*, 68, 70–2.

L. H. Wray assumed command of the *Andromache*, which he sailed to the Cape. There, on 26 March 1825, it was reported that

The only ships lying in this [Simon's] Bay are the *Andromache*, Commodore Moorsom, and the *Espiegle*, Capt. Wray. They will sail tomorrow for the Mauritius where the *Ariadne*, Capt. Chapman now is. The surveying ships *Leven* and *Baracouta*, and *Albatross* tender, are expected here next month from the Isle of Madagascar and the Seychelles on their voyage home. The King of Madagascar has sent twenty young men on board our squadron to learn the art of navigating ships. He appears very desirous of assimilating the manners of his people to the English character, and of making that fine Island an object of regard and attention with the British Government. We daily look for the arrival of the *Owen Glendower* and *Samarang* to relieve the *Andromache* and *Ariadne*.[106]

Subsequently, the Madagascar Youths aboard the *Andromache* were transferred to other vessels attached to the Cape station.[107] In January 1825, some of the youths were aboard two vessels that visited the Seychelles, where on numerous occasions slaves escaped to British naval ships to claim sanctuary and freedom.[108]

Sailing in the region carried with it major risks, notably from disease. From the late eighteenth century, the Admiralty instituted reforms to minimize threats to health aboard ship. These reforms concentrated on the provision of adequate sanitation, ventilation, food, clean clothing and bedding, and exercise and rest.[109] In the southwest Indian Ocean, malaria, endemic in Mozambique and Madagascar, was a major threat, killing probably 80 per cent of Europeans who contracted it and incapacitating the survivors.[110] In late January to early February 1822, while Owen was surveying the Maputo River in southern Mozambique, malaria decimated his crew and officers.[111] The following November, twenty-nine out of the crew of sixty aboard the *Cockburn*, again under Owen, died of malaria in Delagoa Bay.[112] In total, during the three and a half years that Owen was undertaking his survey of the African coast, he lost 85 per cent of his crew to 'fever' (a

---

[106] Report from Cape Town, 26 Mar. 1825, quoted in *Hampshire Telegraph and Sussex Chronicle* 1338 (30 May 1825).

[107] The *Andromache* then sailed for Britain, reaching Portsmouth on 1 August 1825. In 1828, the ship was sold for scrap and dismantled in Deptford – 'The Frigate *Junon*', https://shipsofscale.com/s osforums/threads/4th-of-february-today-in-naval-history-naval-maritime-events-in-history.2104/ page-12 (accessed 06.02.22).

[108] Owen, *Narrative of Voyages*, vol. 2, 98.

[109] Elise Juzda Smith, "Cleanse or Die': British Naval Hygiene in the Age of Steam, 1840–1900', *Medical History* 62.2 (2018), 180.

[110] Gwyn Campbell, review essay, *Feeding Globalization: Madagascar and the Provisioning Trade, 1600–1800*, by Jane Hooper, Athens, Ohio University Press, 2017, *International Journal of African Historical Studies* 51.2 (2018), 344.

[111] Boteler, *Narrative of a Voyage*, vol. 2, 208–14.

[112] Boteler, *Narrative of a Voyage*, vol. 2, 135.

common term for malaria).[113] Again, in August and September 1824, Nourse and eight of his officers succumbed to malaria.[114] 'Madagascar fever' was as notorious as that of Mozambique.[115]

Naval Plans Undermined

From 1825, Radama's hopes of creating a Merina navy were steadily undermined. By then, it had become increasingly clear that the British alliance was failing to deliver the anticipated economic and military benefits. British compensation for the loss of former slave export revenue proved inadequate, attempts to develop alternative export staples based on cotton and silk textiles and cash crops faltered, and the human cost of military expansionism within the island, due chiefly to disease and starvation, steadily mounted.[116]

Moreover, the optimistic plans laid in 1824 with the capture of Majunga for enhanced maritime exchange and trade revenues on the west coast and the creation of a navy comprising regional dhows, and dreams of imperial expansion over the western Indian ocean, were quickly crushed. First, Majunga remained Radama's sole major conquest on the west coast, and the Merina garrison established there faced continual attacks from the surrounding Sakalava. Second, whereas the 1820 ban on slave exports from Merina-controlled territory had led to a significant transfer of Swahili and Mascarene commerce to Iboina, the 1824 Merina conquest of Majunga and the application of Merina tariffs resulted in the flight of almost the entire population of the town to neighbouring independent regions and ports, depriving the Merina garrison of Sakalava manpower and the vital commercial services of the Indians and Swahili. Also, foreign traders, except for the British, who under the terms of the 1820 treaty paid 5 per cent ad valorem, were required to pay 10 percent customs duties in Merina-held ports. In consequence, many, notably from Réunion, transferred their activity from Majunga to independent Sakalava ports and to East Africa, where duties were cheaper and slaves readily available. The proportion of the Réunionnais merchant fleet trading in non-Merina ports increased from 42 percent in 1819 to a peak of 61 percent in 1823. The

---

[113] F. W. Chesson, 'The Dispute between England and Portugal', *St James's Magazine* 13 (1874), 494.

[114] Anonymous letter dated Mauritius, 10 Oct. 1824, quoted in *Caledonian Mercury* (8 Jan. 1825); *Morning Chronicle* (30 May 1825).

[115] Owen, *Narrative of Voyages*, vol. 2, 83; see also Gwyn Campbell, 'Malaria in Precolonial Imerina (Madagascar), 1795–1895', in Gwyn Campbell and Eva-Maria Knoll, *Disease Dispersion and Impact in the Indian Ocean World* (London: Palgrave Macmillan, 2020), 129–67.

[116] Gwyn Campbell, 'The Monetary and Financial Crisis of the Merina Empire, 1810–1826', *South African Journal of Economic History* 1.1 (1986), 99–118; Gwyn Campbell, 'The Adoption of Autarky in Imperial Madagascar, 1820–1835', *Journal of African History* 28.3 (1987), 395–411.

exception was American merchants, who, from 1824 to 1833, took advantage of the exodus of local and Mascarene traders to establish trading links with Majunga, which served as their chief transhipment centre for East African ivory and copal. Overall, however, the economic significance of Majunga, and thus its potential to boost Radama's revenues, dropped significantly.[117]

The exodus of Majunga's population also deprived him of the possibility of commandeering local dhows for naval duties. In 1825, Radama declared sovereignty over the seas within 12 nautical miles (22.22 km) of the island's coasts and threatened to confiscate any 'irregular' vessels found within that limit.[118] Nevertheless, he only controlled about one-third of the island and remained critically dependent upon British naval assistance. Thus, when in 1825 his forces at Fort Dauphin were faced with a revolt by local Malagasy, Radama was granted the use of a British ship to transport his troops to support the Merina garrison there.[119] Similarly, in late July 1825, when suppressing a Betsimisaraka rebellion in the Foulepointe region, Hastie enlisted the assistance of HMS *Barracouta* to carry some 200 Merina troops along the coast to crush the revolt.[120]

However, Radama lost major British supporters of his naval ambitions. In 1823 Farquhar resigned as governor of Mauritius and retired to Britain and, in September 1824, Nourse died of malaria. In August 1825, Lowry Cole, Farquhar's successor, demanded the repayment of $4,520 (currency) that had been advanced to Jean René to purchase and repair a schooner 'with a view to the more effectual suppression of the Slave trade'.[121] This placed Radama in acute financial difficulty, prompting Hastie to write to Christian:

In his agreement with the British government, king Radama guaranteed to ban the export of slaves from Madagascar and all places he governed. Since the date that he signed that accord, he has placed soldiers in eastern and western Madagascar, with the exception of the region to the south of the River Mainty, near St. Augustin. I think that this year he will also install soldiers there. Should Radama, a zealous soldier, dedicated to performing his duty, who knows how to observe this treaty, also obtain a ship to assist him, he will [be able to] do much more. He will be much stronger if he obtains a boat. In addition, a vessel might enable him to increase the transmission of information to his people on coasts far from his kingdom. By the same measure, he will be able to intervene more quickly to stop bad people and ensure that their words are punishable by laws.

I tell you that the wealth Radama has amassed is insufficient to pay for a boat, or the salary of its pilot, should he have one to protect the coasts and look out for slavers. As his

---

[117] Noel, 'Ile de Madagascar'; Grandidier, 'Souvenirs', 28; Rasoamiaramanana, 'Aspects économiques', 10–11, 35, 54; Campbell, *Economic History*, 70.

[118] Campbell, *Economic History*, 279.

[119] William Ellis, *History of Madagascar* (London: Fisher, 1838), vol. 2, 357.

[120] André Coppalle, 'Voyage dans l'intérieure de Madagascar et à la capitale du roi Radama pendant les années 1825 et 1826', *Bibliothèque malgache* 20 (2007), 11–13; *Morning Post* (9 Jan. 1826).

[121] Barry to Hastie, chief secretary's office, Port Louis, 30 Aug. 1825, HB 4, NAM; see also Kelsey, 'Abstract of the Expense incurred by the Government'.

subjects pay taxes chiefly in agricultural produce (not money), etc., that is all he has to pay for a ship and its captain's salary etc. [However] with this boat, he will occasionally export the products of the land to sell in Mauritius, and all profit from the sale of these products will help Radama pay the salary of the ship's pilot ... it's this kind of boat that could carry a Radama's pennant ...

It's preferable to have an English officer command the boat under Radama's colours. Someone ... who desires above all to prevent the slave trade and ... destroy all boats heading for a port that engage in this illegal trade ... Radama will punish them by destroying the boat and its cargo. Radama's order is that every boat that drops anchor should be inspected, and those seen to be approaching the coast. He will thus prevent slavers from arriving ...

I think a 250-ton boat will serve best ... with a very astute white officer and a white sailor aboard, but under the direction of a Malagasy. It's preferable that he also supplies soldiers, no matter how many, to help aboard ship.[122]

In a secret memo to Hastie, Christian advised against the use of a warship to carry commercial goods and informed him,

I think it's good to ask the British government to help Radama obtain a boat from Bombay or London ... Buying and selling is not suitable for an officer ... I know very well that he [Radama] wants a man who is really capable of running this boat, who will earn 500 francs for commanding the vessel ... and will gain a further 5000 [francs] if he succeeds in overcoming a French [slaving] ship, that will be his prize. A boat with ten guns is sufficient to achieve this goal.[123]

He noted further,

the French are very strong, and are insincere and dishonest, so the only option is to use warships. Only coercion can prevent or stop them ... If you can leave ... for Tamatave this Monday or Tuesday, I too will go there to settle this affair with Radama ... I am going to write to Earl Bathurst, and you must tell Sir L. Cole to write to me. And ask Lord Melville[124] to arrange this affair with the London-based proprietor of the warship. And when I know Radama's answer to how much money he can pay, and his stipulations, I'll write to inform him what he should do, and the amount he will need to pay the salary, etc. And if he appreciates my plans for him, I will ensure that he gets the best officer, a subject of George IV, and I will lend him my seamen, those aboard my vessel ... I will lend some to Radama to help stop the slave trade in his territories.[125]

A draft of a letter was also drawn up (probably corrected by Hastie) and sent to Lowry Cole proposing legislation for the creation of a Merina navy with the

---

[122]   Hastie to Captain Christian, [1825?], HB 5, NAM.
[123]   In Ratsisatraina [to Hastie?], [1825?], HB 5, NAM.
[124]   Robert Dundas, 2nd Viscount Melville (1771–1851), First Lord of the Admiralty 1812–27 and 1828–30.
[125]   'Copie de la lettre secrète écrite à M. Hastie par le commandant Christian', written by Rakoto, HB 5, NAM; see also Commodore Christian to Hastie n.d. [1825?], 'confidential', HB 5, NAM.

express purpose of suppressing the slave trade.[126] In February 1826, Hastie followed this up with a further letter to Cole, on the same theme, specifying a possible purchase:

When at Mauritius, I heard it rumoured that Government had some intention of selling the *Wizard*. She is a vessel, or one of her class, that would suit Radama, but to render her or any other useful, she should be commanded by <u>British Officers</u>, manned with a few good seamen, the Madagascar Boys that are now on board H.M. Ships and some others. Perhaps there may be some British Officers on half pay or so situated as to be at liberty to pass a few years from home, and who would be willing to bear Radama's commission. You know Radama's revenue is not a great burthen to him, but I have no doubt that he would willingly accord a fair Salary on this account. In fact, an industrious Commander should by mercantile pursuits with the aid and facility that would be afforded him in all the ports of Madagascar, make a vessel profitable to himself, of little expense to Radama and, at the same time, render great service to the country, and I have no doubt that a vessel so manned would give the most effectual blow to French Slave dealing that it has ever yet received: within a short period there has been four French vessels on this coast for the purpose of getting a few head of Cattle to enable them to go into port at Bourbon, each having landed her cargo of Slaves previous to coming here. Pray turn these matters over in your mind and give me your advice. Perhaps my scheme is not practicable, but it strikes me that a vessel bearing Radama's flag would be authorized to visit any vessel within a certain distance of his Shores. We could easily arrange the first cost and equipment of a vessel if the desired Officers are available.[127]

HMS *Wizard* was formerly *Le Succès*, a brig and former slaver, described as 'a most beautiful vessel' by Moresby when, as captain of HMS *Menai*, he captured it off the Almirante islands with 340 slaves that it had boarded at Zanzibar.[128]

However, the death of Hastie in October 1826 effectively ended any possibility that the British might supply Radama with a flagship and propelled him into negotiating with French traders for the use of their vessels. This may have formed part of the agreements Radama drew up that year with Napoléon Delastelle (1802–1856) and Jean Joseph Arnoux (d. 1829) – agents representing Julien Gaultier de Rontaunay (1793–1863), the largest Réunionnais merchant of the time. It was certainly central to the contract with the Blancard brothers of Mauritius, effective from 1 January 1827, whereby foreign shipping was restricted to twelve east coast ports in which their papers had to be presented to Merina officials. Radama stipulated that

Precise orders will be given to the offices of our ships to visit the vessels entering or leaving the ports and anchorages of our kingdom, and sailing in waters up to a distance of four leagues, and any captains of these vessels who fail to present the manifests and

---

[126] See Annex 2: Draft of a proposed letter from AB. Counsellor and Minister of Radama, King of Madagascar, to His Excellency Sir Lowry Cole &c., [n.d.], HB 5, NAM.

[127] Hastie [Sec. to?] Govt Mauritius, Tamatave, 25 Feb. 1826, HB 4, NAM.

[128] Gray, *British in Mombasa*, 24–5.

acquittals above mentioned ... will be escorted into the ports from which they have sailed under the suspicion of seeking to defraud the established impositions, and after an enquiry being made, should there be a contravention, a report will be immediately made stipulating a fine to double the amount of the levies or, depending on the gravity of the case, the confiscation of its cargo and even of the ship.[129]

Further, Radama acquired the use of Blancard's fleet. Thus article 4 of the 'Blancard treaty' stipulated, 'Messrs. Blancard & Co. undertake to place at the disposal of His Majesty [Radama] all vessels of theirs found in his harbours that he might find useful for royal purposes. He may use them for up to one month free of charge.'[130] Article 11 of the Blancard convention also stipulated that,

His Majesty [Radama] will grant his flag and commission two of MM. Blancard & Co's vessels which will be considered as His Majesty's Coast Guard and specially charged to execute all the regulations relative to navigation, and import and export duties, in all the ports and anchorages of the kingdom of Madagascar. Their captains will be considered to be officers of His Majesty. Consequently, they will be given all backing [main forte] by all military commanders. The purchase and all expenses incurred by these vessels will be the responsibility of the House of Blancard & Co.[131]

British authorities were alarmed at this development. Although residents of Mauritius, the Blancards were francophone and had strong commercial links with the French island of Réunion, the governor of which, seeking to promote French influence in Madagascar, might prove interested in providing Radama with naval ships under French command.[132] Consequently, Captain Owen advised Mauritian authorities to obtain for the Merina a steamship, the virtues of which Robert Lyall (1790–1831), Hastie's replacement as British agent in Madagascar, stressed when he first met Radama at Tamatave in late October 1827:

I described the nature and uses of a steam-boat to the King, with which he seemed delighted, especially when I indicated the facility and certainty with which, if he had one, he would be enabled to transport part of His troops along the coast, and thus suddenly to oppose and to quell His enemies. I afterwards presented to him a beautiful drawing of the Soho steam-boat, which attracted his minute attention.[133]

[129] Radama, proclamation, Tananarivou, 25 Oct. 1826, HB 4, NAM; 'Convention passé entre Sa Majesté Radama, Souverain de Madagascar, et le Sr. Louis Blancard, agissant au nom de M. M. Blancard & Co., Négociant de Maurice', Tananarive, 25 Oct. 1826, HB 4, NAM; see also Jones and Griffiths to [LMS], Antananarivo, 9 Nov. 1826, MIL B.2 F.3 J.D, SOAS/CWM. The twelve ports were Vohimara, Grand Mananara and Little Mananara [north and south of the Mananara river estuary?], Antongil Bay [Maroantsera], Fenoarivo, Foulepointe [Mahavelona], Tamatave, Vatomandry, Mahanoro, Mananjary, Mahela, and Fort Dauphin.
[130] Article 4, Agreement tween R1 and Louis Blancard, Tananarive, 25 Oct. 1826, HB 4, NAM.
[131] Radama, proclamation, Tananarivou, 25 Oct. 1826, HB 4, NAM.
[132] Georges-Sully Chapus and G. Mondain, 'Un chapitre inconnu: des rapports de Maurice et de Madagascar', BAM 30 (1951–2), 118; Campbell, David Griffiths, 70.
[133] Lyall, journal entry, 29 Oct. 1827, CO 167/116, NAK; see also Lyall, journal entry, 30 Oct. 1827, CO 167/116, NAK.

This was a reference to the internationally famous steamboat production at Boulton & Watt's Soho Foundry in Birmingham.[134] Lyall noted that

The King was delighted with the idea of having a Steam-Boat; as a great means of assisting the civilization of his people, as well as for the quelling of his enemies on the coast, by the speedy transport of troops; and to this subject he frequently reverted while I was at Tamatave.[135]

However, plans to obtain a British steamboat failed to advance, and when relations with the Blancards soured from mid-1827, Radama turned to other sources of naval assistance. By that time, the Majunga garrison had re-established relations with some Swahili and Indian traders and, in order to suppress revolt in Ambongo, a region to its north, despatched troops by sea in Swahili-managed dhows.[136] This might have rekindled Radama's ambitions to extend Merina imperial sway over the southwest Indian Ocean for, before his death in mid-in 1828, the king was planning an armada of 'canoes', carrying 12,000 soldiers, to invade central Mozambique. The venture was to be led by Aristide Coroller, who, from 1827, was Radama's *aide-de-camp* and secretary general.[137]

In sum, plans to create a Merina navy emerged out of the desire by Farquhar, the first British governor of Mauritius, to give Radama the means to enforce in Malagasy coastal waters the anti-slave trade ban, which formed a core clause of the 1820 Britanno-Merina treaty. British authorities initially supported the construction of a Merina fleet in the hope that it would relieve the Cape Station of some of its vast responsibility for anti-slave trade surveillance in the western Indian Ocean. It was envisaged that the bulk of the Merina fleet would comprise vessels either constructed in the newly captured west coast port of Majunga or commandeered from local Sakalava, Swahili, and Indians. Additionally, both the British authorities and Radama prioritized the purchase of a European vessel to serve as a flagship for the new navy and the training of Madagascar Youths, some fifty in number, to man the Merina vessels and form a naval band. For Radama, the creation of a national fleet was seen as vital not only to suppress the slave trade but to capture foreign trade in western Madagascar and to eventually carve out a maritime empire in the western Indian ocean.

However, a number of major obstacles arose. In 1824, the Sakalava, Swahili, and Indian inhabitants of Majunga fled Merina rule, while Mascarene

---

[134] Jennifer Tann and Christine Macleod, 'Empiricism Afloat – Testing Steamboat Efficacy: Boulton Watt & Co. 1804–1830', *International Journal for the History of Engineering & Technology* 86.2 (2016), 228–43.

[135] Lyall, journal entry, 30 Oct. 1827, CO 167/116, NAK.   [136] RH, 138.

[137] Pier M. Larson, 'Fragments of an Indian Ocean Life: Aristide Corroller between Islands and Empires', *Journal of Social History* 45.2 (2011), 380; Campbell, *David Griffiths*, 49.

merchants were deterred by the Merina imposition of high commercial tariffs in the port. American traders, from their Zanzibar base, seized the opportunity to increase their business with Madagascar, but this failed to compensate for the general loss of commercial activity and revenue. Also, the major British supporters of a Merina navy disappeared from the scene: Farquhar retired to Britain in 1823, the following year Commodore Nourse succumbed to malaria, and, in October 1826, Hastie, the British agent in Madagascar, also died. Faced with declining revenues and the rising cost of military expansion in the island, Radama pivoted, and following Hastie's death, abandoned the British alliance and instituted lower tariffs in Majunga. This attracted Swahili and Indian traders back to the port. Radama also negotiated a series of agreements with francophone traders through which he enjoyed access to their vessels. He thus revived his vision of forging a Merina fleet, and in early 1828 was planning to launch an armada to attack the Mozambique coast. However, Radama died in July that year, and his senior wife, Ranavalona, seized the throne and demanded the return of all Madagascar Youths under British supervision. The subsequent history of those youths apprenticed abroad to learn crafts and industrial skills forms the subject of the next chapter.

5 Industry

Following the 1820 Britanno-Merina treaty, the main aims of the Merina crown were to utilize the British alliance to create an island empire and to promote economic modernization through importing European skills and technology and exploiting the island's human and natural resources. Thus Radama sent a number of Madagascar Youths abroad to Britain and Mauritius to study British crafts and industrial techniques. He also encouraged an influx of 'British' military, agricultural, and craft specialists, chiefly British missionary and Mauritian Creole artisans, to whom he assigned Malagasy apprentices. He intended that the apprentices, both those sent abroad and those trained locally, would quickly replace European personnel. This imperative became more urgent from 1826, when Radama rejected the 1820 Britanno-Merina treaty and adopted autarkic economic policies, a decision endorsed from 1828 by his senior wife and successor, Ranavalona I. This change of policy had profound implications for relations with the British, for foreign artisans in Madagascar, and, upon their return, for the Madagascar Youths. This chapter examines the reasons for the rupture of the Britanno-Merina alliance, and in the context of the adoption of autarkic policies, assesses the Merina court's attempts to industrialize, and the role of the Madagascar Youths in such efforts.

Rejection of the British Alliance

Radama became disillusioned with the British alliance for its failure to produce the anticipated increase in revenue, speedy conquest of the entire island, and economic modernization. Following the 1820 ban on slave exports, royal Merina revenues slumped – from $32,927 in 1821 to $22,360 the following year. By 1824 they had increased to $50,000, but this fell far short of the crown's requirements.[1] This was in part due to inadequate 'equivalent' payments. In compensation for his ban on slave exports, Farquhar had

---

[1] Duhaut-Cilly, 'Notices sur le royaume d'Emirne, sur la capitale de Tananarivou et sur le gouvernement de Rhadama', in Jean Valette, 'Deux documents français sur Madagascar en 1825; les rapports Duhaut-Cilly et Frere', *BAM*, 66.1–2 (1968 [1825]), 238–9.

promised Radama an annual 'equivalent' of $20,000, backdated to 1817 (the year the draft treaty was drawn up), comprising $2,000 in cash and $18,000 in goods, chiefly military equipment.[2] However, in the first six years of the alliance (1820–6), Radama received a total compensation valued at $104,853, $95,147 short of that promised. Apart from lost export taxes, estimated at $1.25 m, the slave export ban depressed income, money supply, demand for imports, and total tax revenue on trade.[3]

Moreover, while the ban on slave exports from Merina-controlled territory was effective, efforts to promote 'legitimate' exports failed. Experiments with cash crop cultivation foundered chiefly because of a failure to appreciate Malagasy conditions. Attempts to grow European wheat, oats, and vegetables in the central highlands, which were characterized by laterite soil with low fertility, sharp climatic contrasts, hailstorms, and locust plagues, produced meagre results,[4] as did similar experiments at Foulepointe and Tamatave, on the east coast, due to humid tropical conditions that encouraged fungal infections, sandy saline soil, cyclones, the depredations of insects and wild boars, and malaria.[5] Despite the arrival of a number of skilled European artisans,

---

[2] Farquhar to Hastie, Instructions, Port Louis, 4 Sep. 1820, HB 13, NAM; Farquhar, 'Minute' respecting Hastie and the Madagascar Mission, 3 Sep. 1822, HB 7, NAM; article 3 of the 1820 Britanno-Merina treaty, detailed in *Papers relating to the Abolition of the Slave Trade in the Mauritius: 1817–1820*, vol. 18 (House of Commons, 1821), 360; Gwyn Campbell, *An Economic History of Imperial Madagascar, 1750–1895: The Rise and Fall of an Island Empire* (Cambridge: Cambridge University Press, 2005), 70.

[3] Nicolas Mayeur, 'Voyage au pays pays d'ancove, autrement dit des hovas ou Amboilamba dans l'intérieure des terres, Isle de Madagascar' (1777), 177–80, Add. 18128, BL; Hastie, 'Diary' (1817), 143, 148, 188, CO 167/34, NAK; Hastie, 'Diary' (1820), 484,493, 496, CO 167/50, NAK; Hastie, 'Diary' (1822), CO 167/63, NAK; Farquhar, 'Minute' on Madagascar (1822), CO 167/63, NAK; 'Expenses incurred by the Government on Mauritius on account of Madagascar', in House of Commons, *Parliamentary Papers*, 26 (1828), 72–82; Farquhar to Earl Bathurst, Port Louis, 29 Jul. 1822, CO 167/63, NAK; Hastie to Barry, Antananarivo, 22 Apr. 1824, CO 167/78, NAK; Jones and Griffiths to LMS, Antananarivo, 2 Jun. 1824, MIL B.2 F.1 J.A, SOAS/CWM; Duhaut-Cilly, 'Notices sur le royaume d'Emirne', 238–9; Alfred Grandidier, 'Property among the Malagasy', *AAMM* 22 (1898), 228, 230; Gwyn Campbell, 'Madagascar and the Slave Trade, 1810–1895', *Journal of African History* 22.2 (1981), 206, 208; Gwyn Campbell, 'The Adoption of Autarky in Imperial Madagascar, 1820–1835', *Journal of African History* 28.3 (1987), 400.

[4] Nicolas Mayeur, 'Voyage au pays d'ancove, par le pays d'ancaye autrement dit des Baizangouzangoux', related by Dumaine (1785), 224, Add. 18128, BL; Hastie, 'Diary' (1817), 160, 187; Guillaume Grandidier, *Histoire physique, naturelle et politique de Madagascar* (Paris: Hachette, 1928), 3–7, 11, 53, 60–1.

[5] Hastie, 'Diary' (1822), CO 167/63, NAK; Hastie, 'Diary' (1822–3), CO 167/66, NAK; Samuel Pasfield Oliver, *Madagascar: An Historical and Descriptive Account of the Island and Its Former Dependencies* (London: Macmillan, 1886), vol. 1, 285, 451–2; Alfred Grandidier and Guillaume Grandidier, *Histoire physique, naturelle et politique de Madagascar* (Paris: Imprimerie Nationale, 1908), vol. 4, book 1, 604 James Sibree, *A Naturalist in Madagascar* (London: Seeley, 1915), 53 Raymond Decary, 'Le voyage du lieutenant de Vaisseau de Semerville a l'île Sainte-Marie en 1824', *BAM* 16 (1933), 50–1; Charles Robequain, *Madagascar et les bases dispersées de l'union française* (Paris: Presses Universitaires de France, 1958), 50–1; Gwyn Campbell, *David Griffiths and the Missionary 'History of Madagascar'* (Leiden: Brill, 2012), 623.

efforts to develop craft production for export met with as little success (see next section).

Further, Merina imperial expansion proved costly. British officers formed a standing army that between 1822 and 1824 increased from 12,000 to 17,500 well equipped and trained soldiers. However, Merina forces despoiled much fertile territory in the provinces. Thus, the empire did not bring the anticipated bonanza of booty and revenue into the royal coffers. As Louis Blancard noted, 'Radama, having subjected almost all Madagascar, has been obliged to greatly increase his army, and keep it continually on a war footing. This increase in expenditure has necessarily forced him to [seek] an increase in revenue.'[6] Blancard's statement was unduly optimistic, for Merina forces failed to conquer more than one-third of the island and experienced high mortality, chiefly due to malaria and starvation. Thus, Hastie commented in March 1825, 'more than half the new enrolled troops perish chiefly by fever without attaining a year's service.'[7] Moreover, most of those who survived became impoverished, for *fanompoana* governed military service, with the result that all ordinary soldiers had to borrow to purchase the clothing, provisions, and medicine they required. On campaigns, which could last for six months or more, commanding officers purloined most spoils of war, and advanced credit to recruits to enable them to purchase provisions at famine prices. It was a vicious circle in which recruits were drawn from the peasantry (who also paid a special tax to support the army), leaving dwindling numbers, always the elderly and less able-bodied, to cultivate the land. Older people commented that Imerina was even more depopulated in 1825 than during the internecine wars of the late 1700s, a fact which had grave implications for the fragile agricultural base of the economy.[8]

At the same time, Radama feared that the British wished to make Madagascar at best a satellite power, at worst a colony. Farquhar's initial intention, evident in the initial version of the 1817 draft treaty, was to bring Radama under his informal influence and colonize Madagascar with British Mauritians.[9] In 1820,

---

[6] Louis Blancard to Governor of Mauritius, in Georges-Sully Chapus and Gustave Mondain, 'Un chapitre inconnu: Des rapports de Maurice et de Madagascar', *BAM* 30 (1951–2), 117; see also Hastie to Governor Mauritius, 22 Apr. 1824, HB 5, NAM; Duhaut-Cilly, 'Notices sur le royaume d'Emirne', 238–9.

[7] Hastie, extract from Report of the Examination of Schools (17 Mar. 1825), MIL B.2 F.2 J.A, SOAS/CWM.

[8] Hastie, 'Diary' (1820); Hastie to Barry, Antananarivo, 22 Apr. 1824, CO 167/77, NAK; William Ellis, *History of Madagascar* (London: Fisher, 1838), vol. 1, 119; James Cameron, *Recollections of Mission Life in Madagascar during the Early Days of the LMS Mission* (Antananarivo: Abraham Kingdon, 1874), 24–6; Oliver, *Madagascar*, vol. 2, 160; Grandidier and Grandidier, *Histoire physique* (1908), vol. 4, book 1, 371; Wenceslas Bojer, 'Journal', in Jean Valette, 'L'Imerina en 1822–1825 d'après les journaux de Bojer et d'Hilsenberg', *Bulletin de Madagascar* (Apr.–May, 1963), 23.

[9] Gwyn Campbell, 'The Role of the London Missionary Society in the Rise of the Merina Empire, 1810–1861', PhD, University of Wales, Swansea (1985), 103–9.

he appointed Hastie resident British agent at the Merina court, and in April 1822 ordered him to 'request of Radama to transmit to me copies of all communications which he may make to, or receive from other Governments, relative to the sovereignty of Madagascar or other public matters of transcendent interest to its prosperity'.[10] Further, Farquhar informed the Merina king that he was not essential to the British project in Madagascar and intimated that he might use force if attempts were made to undermine British interests in the island.[11] The threat of British economic and political domination was deeply offensive to Merina tradition and dashed Radama's dreams of using the British alliance to modernize the economy and create an island empire which, through the creation of a navy, might gain mastery of the western Indian Ocean and stand as an equal beside Britain and France.[12] The king was also aware of growing popular resentment of the economic consequences of the British treaty. As LMS missionary John Canham stated in November 1824, 'there is no money in the country, nor any channel to bring it. I am often told by the people that when they sold slaves they had plenty of money but since the slave trade ceased they are become impoverished.'[13]

Radama's pushback against British pretensions started in 1824 when he barred foreigners from holding freehold property. In 1825, he imposed ten-year residence permits on foreign residents and obliged them to obtain passports for any substantive journey made within the island. In December 1824, he established royal control over foreign craftsmen through five-year (renewable) contracts.[14] The following year, he placed British missionaries under Merina law and changed military commands from English to Malagasy.[15] Further, he adopted protectionist measures designed to rectify the unfavourable balance of

[10] Farquhar to Hastie, Mauritius, 30 Apr. 1822, CO 167/34, NAK.

[11] Farquhar, 'Minute' respecting Hastie and the Madagascar Mission, 3 Sep. 1822, HB 7, NAM; Farquhar to Hastie, Mauritius, 30 Apr. 1822, CO 167/34, NAK.

[12] Farquhar (1821) in [Edward Baker], *Madagascar Past and Present* (London: R. Bentley, 1847), 196, 198; Farquhar to Bathurst, Port Louis, 20 May 1823, and Darling to Bathurst, Mauritius, 16 Jun. 1823, CO 167/66, NAK; for the imperial ambitions of Radama I, see Hastie, 'Diary' (1817); RH, 79–95, 120; Hubert Deschamps, *Histoire de Madagascar* (Paris: Berger-Levrault, 1972), 151; Ludvig Munthe, Simon Ayache, and Charles Ravoajanahary, 'Radama I et les Anglais: Les négociations de 1817 d'après les sources malgaches ('sorabe' inédits)', *Omaly sy Anio* 3–4 (1976), 9–104.

[13] Canham to Burder, Ifenoarivo, 5 Nov. 1824, MIL B.2 F.1 J.C, SOAS/CWM.

[14] Chick to Burder, Antananarivo, 16 Dec. 1825, MIL B.2 F.2 J.C, SOAS/CWM; Chick to Burder, Antananarivo, 6 Jun. 1826, MIL B.2 F.3 J.A, SOAS/CWM; William Ellis, *Three Visits to Madagascar during the years 1853–1854–1856* (London: John Murray, 1859), 262–3; Oliver, *Madagascar*, vol. 2, 91; Georges-Sully Chapus, *Quatre-vingts années d'influence européennes en Imerina (1815–1895)* (Tananarive: G. Pitot, 1925), 201–2; Georges-Sully Chapus and Gustave Mondain (eds.), *Le journal de Robert Lyall* (Tananarive: Imprimerie Officielle, 1954), 171; HdR, 1062–3, 1066; Gwyn Campbell, 'Slavery and Fanompoana: The Structure of Forced Labour in Imerina (Madagascar), 1790–1861', *Journal of African History* 29.3 (1988), 463–86; Campbell, 'Role of the London Missionary Society', 245, 259, 262.

[15] Ellis, *History of Madagascar*, vol. 2, 366; Campbell, 'Adoption of Autarky', 407.

foreign trade and stimulate domestic industry. In 1825, he banned French arms imports and insisted that all non-British merchants, most of whom were French, pay export duties in cash, except for bullocks, which were taxed in cotton cloth.[16] In October 1826, immediately after Hastie's death, Radama signed a five-year exclusive commercial contract, effective from 1 January 1827, with the Blancard brothers. In return for annual payments of $30,000 in 1827 and $40,000 a year thereafter, cash loans, and the use of their fleet when required, Radama authorized the Blancards to purchase 4,000 bullocks annually at $6 each and granted them duty-free trade (except for bullock and rice exports, which carried a 100 per cent duty) in all east coast ports.[17] He also restricted other foreign ships to specified coast ports, in which a 25 per cent duty was to be imposed on all imports (except arms and ammunition, which could only be sold to the crown, and alcohol at $1 per velte – about 7.5 litres) and exports (except live bullocks, taxed at $5 a head, and salted meat at $6 per kg).[18]

The Blancard 'treaty' was roundly condemned on Mauritius, which imported some 2,000 Malagasy cattle annually.[19] Repeated protests by the governments of Mauritius and Réunion, and the tendency of European merchants to seek out the independent ports of the Malagasy west coast where duties were less, soon obliged Radama to lower export duties to 10 per cent ad valorem. This worked: for example, the proportion of Réunionnais ships trading through imperial Merina as opposed to independent ports rose from a low of 30 per cent in 1823 to 64 per cent by 1828.[20]

In May 1827, Governor Lowry Cole of Mauritius sent lieutenants Henry A. Cole (1800–1827), his nephew, and Charles William Mackenzie Campbell (fl. 1819–1840) to Madagascar as, respectively, special envoy and ad interim resident agent, in an attempt to persuade Radama to renounce the Blancard agreement, reiterate his allegiance to the British alliance, and reinstate minimal tariffs for British commerce.[21] Radama refused their demands.[22] Shortly afterwards, the king fell out with the Blancards but did not restore the British alliance. On 27 July 1828, four days before Lyall reached Antananarivo to take up his residency, Radama died, and Ranavalona, his successor, refused to recognize either the British treaty or Lyall as British agent.[23]

---

[16] Campbell, *Economic History*, 278–9.
[17] 'Convention passé entre Sa Majesté Radama, Souverain de Madagascar, et le Sr. Louis Blancard, agissant au nom de M. M. Blancard & Co., Négociant de Maurice', Tananarive, 25 Oct. 1826, HB 4, NAM; see also Jones and Griffiths to [LMS], Antananarivo, 9 Nov. 1826, MIL B.2 F.3 J.D, SOAS/CWM.
[18] Radama, proclamation, Tananarivou, 25 Oct. 1826, HB 4, NAM.
[19] Dupuy frères, to Cole, Port Louis, 13 Dec. 1826, HB 4, NAM.
[20] Campbell, *Economic History*, 408.
[21] Lowry Cole, 'Instructions for Lieutenant Cole', Mauritius, 7 May 1827, HB 4, NAM.
[22] C. W. Campbell, No. 1 [25 Jul. 1827], HB 22, NAM.
[23] Lyall, Journal (1828), Add.3408, BL.

Autarky and Industrialization

Considerable attention has been paid to the role that the technological innovations of the Industrial Revolution played in nineteenth-century European imperialism.[24] By contrast, relatively few studies have covered attempts by regimes indigenous to the Indian Ocean world to utilize such innovations to promote their own economic development. This is especially the case in Africa, where attempts at modernization are conventionally considered to have been largely limited to Egypt.[25] However, from the mid-1820s, following the rupture of the British treaty, Imerina also inaugurated an audacious but little-known attempt to industrialize that was contemporaneous with early industrial experiments in the West. As in Europe, the Merina experiment was based on a limited number of key industries, notably textiles, and military production – involving gunpowder, iron, and leather manufacture.

The Madagascar Youths trained in Britain and on Mauritius in crafts and industrial techniques, all of whom were immediately subject to *fanompoana* (unremunerated forced labour for the state) upon their return, were considered key to attempts to industrialize, and to replace European with indigenous personnel. However, initial efforts to modernize the economy were dependent upon the work of foreigners, notably LMS artisans and Mauritian Creole craftsmen (see Tables 5.1 and 5.2). In this respect, it is noteworthy that in sending missionary artisans to Madagascar, the LMS were in contravention of the British ban on the emigration of British craftsmen and machinery, which was fully lifted only on 21 June 1824.[26] Radama provided each foreign artisan with about 4,000 m² of land with access to water, a 2,000-strong *fanompoana* gang to level the ground, and additional skilled (mainly carpenters and thatchers) and unskilled (to fell and transport timber and other building material and provide construction labour) *fanompoana* to build a residence and workshop (see Map 5.1). These buildings were concentrated on low-lying land beneath and to the northwest of the hilltop capital of Antananarivo. There, the artisans enjoyed access to water in the form of fountains, streams, and, under Ranavalona, an artificial lake. The Merina court also assigned to each European craftsman a varying number of *fanompoana* 'apprentices'.[27] One

---

[24] See e.g. Daniel R. Headrick, *The Tools of Empire: Technology and European Imperialism in the Nineteenth Century* (New York: Oxford University Press, 1981); Michael Adas, *Machines As the Measures of Men: Science, Technology, and Ideologies of Western Dominance* (Ithaca, NY: Cornell University Press, 1989).

[25] Pablo L. E. Idahosa and Bob Shenton, 'The Africanist's "New" Clothes', *Historical Materialism* 12.4 (2004), 73.

[26] David I. Jeremy, 'Damming the Flood: British Government Efforts to Check the Outflow of Technicians and Machinery, 1780–1843', *Business History Review* 51.1 (1977), 18–19.

[27] Hastie to Sec. to Govt Mauritius, 5 Jun. 1825, HB 4, NAM.

Table 5.1 *Artisan members of the early LMS mission to Madagascar*

Name and Craft	Time spent in Madagascar	Notes
Thomas Brookes (1793–1822): carpenter	7 May–24 Jun. 1822	Died of malaria in Madagascar
John Canham (1798–1881): tanner and shoemaker, then became clerical missionary	7 May 1822–mid-1826 9 Aug. 1827–4 Aug. 1834	Later settled in South Australia where died of 'apoplexy'
George Chick (1797–1866): blacksmith	7 May 1822–20 Jul. 1835	In 1835 settled in South Africa where died
Thomas Rowlands (c.1804–1828): weaver	7 May 1822–4 Apr. 1828	Died of malaria in Madagascar
James Cameron (1800–1875): carpenter	2 Aug. 1826–20 Jul. 1835	In 1835 settled in South Africa, returning in 1863 to Madagascar where died
John Cummins (1805–1872): spinner	2 Aug. 1826–[6] Sep. 1828	Later, became minister in England where died
Charles Hovendon (1798–1826): printer	2 Nov. 1826–15 Dec. 1826	Died of malaria in Madagascar
Edward Baker (1805–1885): printer	[mid-Sep.] 1828–[early Jul.] 1832; 1 Jul. 1834–20 Aug. 1836	In 1836 moved to Mauritius, then South Australia where died

Source: Campbell, *David Griffiths*, 45–6.

missionary artisan described the apprentices allocated them by the crown as 'tractable and obedient, doing all they can to please us.'[28]

Textiles

By 1820, a considerable textile industry had developed in Madagascar. Cloth manufacture was a ubiquitous and mainly part-time female occupation, except among the Zanadoria and Zanadralambo clans of northern Imerina where the weaving of the highly valuable red silk shrouds used to wrap the dead of noble castes was a male prerogative.[29] Bark, leaves, raffia, hemp, cotton, and silk, all

---

[28] [An LMS artisan] to LMS, [Antananarivo], 30 Jun. 1822, in Thomas Smith and John Overton Choules, *The Origin and History of Missions: Containing Faithful Accounts of the Voyages, Travels, Labors and Successes of the various Missionaries who have been Sent Forth to Evangelize the Heathen* (Boston: S. Walker, and Lincoln & Edmands, 1832), vol. 1, 462; see also Keturah Jeffreys, *The Widowed Missionary's Journal* (Southampton: Printed for the author, 1827), 116.

[29] Mayeur, 'Voyage au pays d'ancove' (1777), 183; Mayeur, 'Voyage au pays d'ancove' (1785), 208; Anon., 'Mémoire historique et politique sur l'Isle de Madagascar' [1790], 62 – Add.18126, BL; Grandidier and Grandidier, *Histoire physique* (1908), vol. 4, book 1, 243–6, 250.

Table 5.2 *Non-missionary European and Creole artisans in early nineteenth-century Madagascar*

Name and Craft	Time spent in Madagascar	Notes
Louis Carvaille: Mauritian Creole, skilled tin-plate worker	22 Sep. 1821–?	Sold tools to Ranavalona in June 1830 and settled in Tamatave
Louis Gros (1790–1829): French carpenter (former soldier)	1821–[Jan./ Feb.] 1829	Married an Andriana woman, by whom he had a child, accepted traditional Malagasy religious beliefs, died in Tamatave
Jean Julien: carpenter, Creole from Mauritius	1821–[mid-1825]	[died in Antananarivo]
Charles Morillon [Mario?]: Mauritian tailor	1821–?	Faced stiff competition and after a short time probably returned to Mauritius
Gabriel Philibert [Fillicau/ Filleau]: Mauritian carpenter	1821–[mid-1825]	In 1822 Radama condemned him to irons for three years for the assassination of an associate; buried in a tomb in south Antananarivo
Savigny/Savinery: Mauritian weaver	1821–3	Faced too much competition from part-time Malagasy weavers and returned to Mauritius
Droit (Droite): French blacksmith	1832–Jun. 1835	Married sister of Augustine; expelled in 1835 and died shortly after in the Comoros
Vincent (d. 1835/6): French artisan	[1832?]–1835/6	Married Augustine, who inherited his considerable wealth; he died in Antananarivo
Jean Laborde (1805–1878): French master craftsman	1831–Jul. 1857; 1862–Dec. 1878	Highly successful; constructed industrial centre at Mantasoa, where buried

Source: André Coppalle, 'Voyage dans l'intérieur de Madagascar et à la capitale du Roi Radama pendant les années 1825 et 1826', *BAM* 7 (1909–10 [1827]), 28, 48;Carvaille to Jones and Griffiths [Antananarivo], 19 Feb. 1829, B.3 F.1 J.1; Freeman to Hankey, Tananarive, 28 Feb. 1829, MIL B.3 F.1 J.1, SOAS/CWM; Freeman to Hankey, Tananarive, 28 Feb. 1829, MIL B.3 F.1 J.1, SOAS/ CWM; Griffiths and Johns to LMS, Antananarivo, 28 Jun. 1830, MIL B.3 F.3 J.C, SOAS/CWM; RA, 307–8, 352, 362; RA, 307–8, 352, 362; Cameron, *Recollections of Mission Life*, 25, 27–8; Malzac, 'Ordre de succession au trône chez les Hova', 617; Grandidier and Grandidier, *Histoire physique* (1908), vol. 4, book 1, 537, fn. 1; Jean Chauvin, *Jean Laborde 1805–1878* (Tananarive: Imprimerie moderne de l'Émyrne, Pitot de la Beaujardiere, 1939), vii, 5–6; Adrien S. Boudou, 'Petites notes d'histoire malgache', *BAM* 23 (1940), 68; Bruno Hübsch (ed.), *Madagascar et le Christianisme* (Paris: Agence de cooperation culturelle et technique, 1993), 196; Didier Nativel, *Maisons royales, demeures des grands à Madagascar* (Paris: Karthala, 2005), 78; Campbell, *David Griffiths*, 611–2, 906.

of which grew wild and required little human attention, were used to make cloth. In Imerina, the main raw materials used were banana tree fibre, reeds, and hemp for coarser textiles, and cotton and silk for finer fabrics. Several different raw materials were often used in cloth production. For example, silk was frequently interwoven with other fibres and even tin. Production techniques were simple, using a wooden distaff to spin and a fixed heddle ground loom to weave.[30]

One of the first concerns of the Merina crown following the 1820 treaty was the production of European-style clothing. Radama welcomed the services of a Mauritian tailor, Charles Morillon [Mario?], to whom he assigned six Merina apprentices: Ratrimo, Ratompoaro, Ralambomiarana, Ratsilakamina, Ramanankoazy, and Rakotovala, who subsequently instructed slave and free Malagasy apprentices placed under them. They learned to make riding jackets and coats for the court and army elite, who, after Hastie introduced the first horses to Imerina in 1817, increasingly rode horseback on excursions, military campaigns, and hunting expeditions. Indeed, the growing import of horses from the Cape of Good Hope and Mauritius led to a decline in their prices from between $400 and $750 a horse in 1817 to between $100 and $150 by the mid-1830s. Even Ranavalona reviewed her troops on horseback.[31] However, after Ranavalona closed trade with Europeans in 1845, horse imports dropped precipitously, so that in 1863, French explorer and archaeologist

---

[30] Mayeur, 'Voyage au pays d'ancove' (1777), 165–6, 173, 175; Mayeur, 'Voyage au pays d'ancove' (1785), 223; Chardenoux, 'Journal du voyage fait dans l'intérieure' (1816), 175 – Add.18129, BL; Oliver, *Madagascar*, vol. 2, 80–2; Grandidier, *Histoire physique* (1928), 168; Georges-Sully Chapus and [André] Dandouau, 'Les anciennes industries malgaches,' *BAM* 30 (1951), 48, 50–1; Campbell, *Economic History*, 31–3; Sarah Fee, 'Historic Handweaving in Highland Madagascar: New Insights from a Vernacular Text Attributed to a Royal Diviner-Healer, c. 1870', *Textile History* 43.1 (2012), 63.

[31] Charles Theodore Hilsenberg and Wenceslaus Bojer, 'A Sketch of the Province of Emerina, in the Island of Madagascar, and of the Huwa, its Inhabitants; written during a Year's Residence', in William Jackson Hooker (ed.), *Botanical Miscellany; containing Figures and Descriptions of such Plants as recommend themselves by their Novelty, Rarity, or History, or by the Uses to which they are applied in the Arts, in Medicine, and in Domestic Economy together with occasional Botanical Notes and Information* (London: John Murray, 1833 [1823]), vol. 3, 273; 'Cape of Good Hope', *Morning Chronicle* (24 Oct. 1828); Freeman to Rutherford, [Antananarivo], 10 Mar. 1835, Bx.5 F.2 J.A, SOAS/CWM;Anon, 'Commercial Position of Madagascar, relative to India, Australia, and the Cape of Good Hope', *Perth Gazette and Western Australian Journal* (28 May 1842), 3; 'Magnificence of the Court of Tananarivo' *Morning Post* (14 Apr. 1843); David Griffiths, *Hanes Madagascar* (Machynlleth: Richard Jones, 1843), 25, 32; RA, 266; RH, 2, 90; James Sibree, *Madagascar et ses habitants: Journal d'un sejour de quatre ans dans l'ile*, trans. H. Monod and H. Monot (Toulouse: Société des Livres Religieux, 1873), 224; [Victorin] Malzac, 'Ordre de succession au trône chez les Hova', *Notes, reconnaissances et explorations* 1.1 (1900), 617–8; *HdR*, 1081–2, 1134; Manassé Esoavelomandroso, 'The "Malagasy Creoles" of Tamatave in the 19th Century', *Diogenes* 28 (1980), 58–9; Campbell, *David Griffiths*, 459.

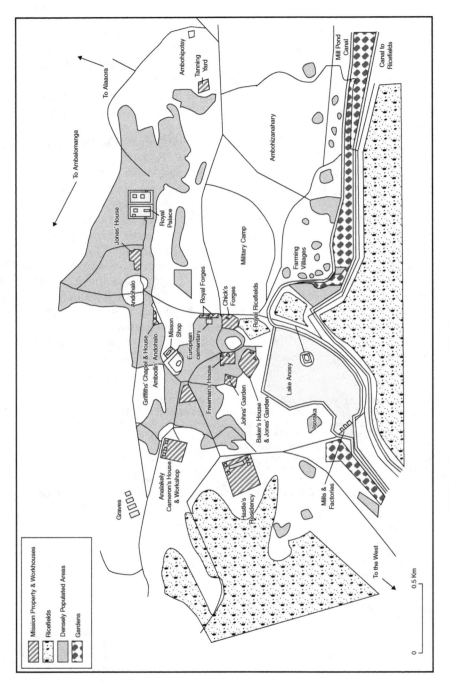

Map 5.1 Antananarivo: LMS residences and workshops 1822–35
Source: Adapted from Campbell, *Economic History*, 94.

Claude-Joseph Charnay (1828–1915) commented that horses were almost non-existent in Madagascar.[32]

After a short time, Morillon gave up, and probably returned to Mauritius. This may well have been due to competition from an enterprise established by Mary Griffiths (1793–1883) and Mary Anne Jones (née Mabille – b. 1801), wives of Welsh LMS missionaries David Jones and David Griffiths respectively. From 1824, they supervised from forty to fifty female pupils, who produced small, European-style overcoats of twilled calico and bordered woollen cloth, gowns, trousers, shirts, and kerchiefs. These products were placed in a mission shop in Antananarivo that operated from 1825 to 1829 and catered for the Merina elite, thus competing not only with Morillon but also with Mary Hastie, the British agent's wife, who sold imported velvets, silk, calico, and linen clothes to elite Malagasy females.[33]

After his arrival in Madagascar in 1822, Thomas Rowlands (c.1804–1828), a Welsh missionary weaver, planned to produce calico and other cloth at Antsahadinta. Rowlands hired a French carpenter [Le Gros?] to make two looms, which were operative by 1823, but he was frustrated by the lack of a spinner to supply him with yarn. Keturah Jeffreys (wife of missionary John Jeffreys) refused to assume the role of spinner assigned to her by the LMS, while Malagasy spinners worked on a seasonal basis so could not provide him with a regular supply of yarn. Rowlands therefore 'borrowed' spinners from Radama, but they deserted, probably because they were *fanompoana* and thus unremunerated. Hence Rowlands was obliged to purchase six female slave spinners, in addition to buying yarn from local 'free' spinners. However, his spinning machine possessed only thirty-six spindles instead of the hundreds required; and he faced strong local competition. As cotton and silk weaving were ubiquitous female activities, practised from June to August in the off-peak agricultural (dry) season when most festivals were held and demand for new clothes peaked, Rowlands simply could not compete with indigenous weavers, who had significantly less overheads. As a result, Rowland's two looms were running at only 25 percent of capacity by early 1824, and the project collapsed.[34]

The most serious attempt to establish a modern textile industry came in 1827, a year after Radama broke from the British alliance. He then ordered foreign traders to pay for cattle exports in cash, instead of cloth, in order to promote a Merina textile industry. Jones and Griffiths proposed a contract between the

[32] Claude-Joseph Desire Charnay, 'Madagascar a vol. d'oiseau' (1862), *Le Tour du Monde* 10 (1864), 198.

[33] Jones to Farquhar, Antananarivo, 25 Mar. 1822, CO 167/63, NAK; Ellis, *History of Madagascar*, vol. 1, 277–8; Griffiths, *Hanes Madagascar*, 29; RH, 6–7; Jean Valette, *Études sur le règne de Radama I* (Tananarive: Imprimerie Nationale, 1962), 321.

[34] Campbell, *David Griffiths*, 705–6.

LMS and the Merina court to erect a water-powered factory, equipped with British machines, with the capacity to produce 5,000 cotton pieces a year. James Cameron agreed to build a water mill, supplied by canal from the river Ikopa, and it was advocated that the LMS be asked to provide half the required investment, in return for 50 per cent of profits, until repaid by the crown. The factory was to be managed by Rowlands and by Raolombelona, a Madagascar Youth trained as a weaver in Manchester.[35] Raolombelona had left Britain in early 1826, reached Mauritius in May, and arrived back in Antananarivo in September in the company of Hastie, clerical missionaries Johns and his wife Mary, Cameron, and Cummins, a spinner who was to assist in textile production.[36]

In 1827, Rowlands moved to Ifody – a mountainous area east of Angavo in the eastern forest, some 80 km from Antananarivo – to initiate the large-scale cultivation of cotton, and of raffia and hemp (to produce sail cloth, for which he anticipated a large market).[37] In Manchester, Raolombelona was reported to have been 'a very good workman and far better acquainted with the principles of the art and preparation of the work, than many who earn their livelihood by weaving.'[38] However, in 1827, English missionary Joseph John Freeman (1794–1851), described him as a failure,[39] prompting Clunie, Raolombelona's educational and spiritual mentor in Manchester, to write to the LMS directors in April 1828 'on the subject of John Roloun Baloun disappointing the people in Madagascar as to his knowledge of the arts, which he came to learn in this country'.[40] Moreover, there is no indication that the LMS directors supported the proposal for textile manufacturing.[41] By then, they had become hostile to Jones and Griffiths, who they determined to replace as leaders of the Madagascar mission. The project was further

---

[35] Robin to Missionaries, 24 Jan.–14 Feb. 1827; Rowlands to Jones and Griffiths, Amparibe, 15 May 1827; Cummins to Jones and Griffiths, Amparibe, 17 May 1827; Cameron to J. and G. Brighton, 19 May 1827; Cameron to Arundel, 19 May 1827; Jones and Griffiths to Burder, Antananarivo, 30 May 1827 – MIL B.2 F.4 J.A, SOAS/CWM; Campbell, 'Role of the London Missionary Society', 205

[36] Ellis, *History of Madagascar*, vol. 2, 365; Rabary, *Ny Daty Malaza: Na Ny Dian' i Jesosy Teto Madagaskara* (Tananarive: LMS, 1930–1), 50.

[37] Campbell, *David Griffiths*, 708.

[38] In Barry to Hastie, Port Louis, 25 Apr. 1826, HB 4, NAM; see also Chapter 2; Robin to Missionaries, 24 Jan.–14 Feb. 1827; Rowlands to Jones and Griffiths, Amparibe, 15 May 1827; Cummins to Jones and Griffiths, Amparibe, 17 May 1827; Cameron to J. and G. Brighton, 19 May 1827; Cameron to Arundel, 19 May 1827; Jones and Griffiths to Burder, Antananarivo, 30 May 1827 – MIL B.2 F.4 J.A, SOAS/CWM; Campbell, 'Role of the London Missionary Society', 205.

[39] Freeman to Burder, Tananarive, 23 Oct. 1827, MIL B.2 F.5, SOAS/CWM.

[40] Meeting of Directors, 21 Apr. 1828, LMS Board Meeting, SOAS/CWM.

[41] 'Proposal to King Radama', read to LMS directors, 25 Feb. 1828, MIL B.2 F.4 J.C, SOAS/CWM.

undermined by the deaths in 1828 of Rowlands and Radama, following which Cummins gave up and left Madagascar.[42]

Following her ascension, Ranavalona prioritized armaments production, and thereafter the imported textile machinery was worked on a small scale by government weavers producing *lamba*, a kind of Malagasy toga.[43] The crown also monopolized the labour of males and females trained in the production of European-style clothing on Mauritius in the early 1820s, obliging them upon their return to form a *fanompoana* unit manufacturing clothes for the court elite. Girls similarly trained in Antananarivo by missionary wives were also forcibly incorporated into this unit. Thus, Raombana commented that 'since the [1820] Treaty, officers has splendid military uniforms, made by Tailors which has been sent to Mauritius to learn that profession.'[44] Additionally, a variety of foreign cloth continued to be imported, though such imports fell dramatically from 1845 to 1853 when Merina-controlled ports were closed to European trade. Otherwise, most cloth was produced on a traditional domestic handwork basis by chiefly female spinners and weavers.[45]

Military

Following the 1829 French invasion of the northeast coast, Ranavalona substituted for textiles the idea of a domestic armaments industry that would end reliance on the import of foreign armaments. In this context, military goods refer to a wide gamut of products for the Merina army, from boots and buttons to gunpowder and cannon.

Leather Products

Madagascar possessed vast herds of cattle, notably among the pastoral Bara and Sakalava of the southern and western plains. From circa 1795, with the unification of Imerina under Andrianampoinimerina, Merina armies started subjugating neighbouring provinces, enslaving captives, and seizing significant numbers of cattle from conquered pastoralists. By 1810, cattle raising had

---

[42] Rabary, *Daty Malaza*, vol. 1, 50, 59, 66; Valette, *Études sur le regne de Radama I*, 30; 'Extracts of the Minutes of the Madagascar Mission' (4 May–8 July 1829), MIL B.3 F.2 J.A, SOAS/CWM; Campbell, 'Role of the London Missionary Society', 206–7, 259–62.

[43] 'Extracts of the Minutes of the Madagascar Mission' (4 May–8 Jul. 1829), MIL B.3 F.2 J.A, SOAS/CWM; Rabary, *Daty Malaza*, vol. 1, 50, 59, 66; Valette, *Études sur le regne de Radama I*, 30; Campbell, 'Role of the London Missionary Society', 206–7, 259–62.

[44] RH, 6.

[45] Gwyn Campbell, 'The Decline of the Malagasy Textile Industry, circa 1800–1895', in Pedro Machado, Sarah Fee, and Gwyn Campbell (eds.), *An Ocean of Cloth: Textile Trades, Consumer Cultures and the Textile Worlds of the Indian Ocean* (Basingstoke: Palgrave Macmillan, 2018), 313–58.

spread to Antsihanaka, the Ankay, and parts of the uncultivated hilltops of Imerina and Betsileo. By 1814, Merina-ruled territory had quadrupled in extent, while cattle and slave raids continued on unsubdued peoples. By 1816, when one such expedition returned from southwest Madagascar with a booty of 2,000 slaves and 4,000 cattle, Imerina had gained sufficient cattle-grazing land to become an exporter of cattle to the Mascarenes.[46] However, the habit of firing grass to encourage new growth for cattle resulted in such erosion 'as to leave many acres totally inaccessible to cattle'.[47] Therefore, while sheep, goats, pigs, and fowl were a common sight in Imerina, cattle continued to be relatively rare and valuable.[48] Moreover, they were considered sacred and a symbol of wealth, were slaughtered generally only on ritual occasions, and the hide was usually consumed with the meat. Canham, an LMS tanner who arrived in 1822, was initially obliged to import hides from Mauritius – from Malagasy bullocks exported there. Lack of local supplies of lime also hindered the tanning process, obliging him to use bark as a substitute. When artisan wages were added to production costs, the price of the finished product was beyond the reach of ordinary Merina, while the local elite preferred imported luxury items.[49]

Nevertheless, some hides from slaughtered cattle were used to make belts, sandals, and drum and shield covers, and from 1822 the crown commanded all such hides to be delivered to artisans for tanning. Additionally, in 1822–3, the traditional taboo against goats within about 30 km of Antananarivo was lifted, leading to increased use of goatskin. In 1826, Radama entered a contract with Canham for the manufacture of leather goods and boots for the military. Canham was supplied with apprentices, and with hides, 50 percent of which were his, the other 50 percent belonging to the crown. He was to use the royal share to make shoes (for which he was to be paid $0.625 a pair), boots ($2.5 a pair), and military accoutrements ($0.625 a set).[50]

[46]   Gwyn Campbell, 'Commercialisation of Cattle in Imperial Madagascar, 1795–1895', in Martha Chaiklin, Philip Gooding, and Gwyn Campbell (eds.), *Animal Trade Histories in the Indian Ocean World* (Cham, Switzerland: Palgrave Macmillan, 2020), 188.

[47]   Hastie, 'Diary' (1824–25), CO 167/78, NAK.

[48]   Mayeur, 'Voyage au pays d'ancove' (1777), 166, 175; Hugon, 'Aperçu de mon dernier voyage à ancova de l'an 1808', 11 – Add.18137, BL; Chardenoux, 'Journal du voyage fait dans l'intérieure', 174; Grandidier, *Histoire physique* (1928), 117, 119, 127, 139–41, 143–4; HdR, 296–97, 404; Adolphe Razafintsalama, 'Les funérailles royales en Isandra d'après les sources du XIXe siècle' in Françoise Raison-Jourde (ed.), *Les souverains de Madagascar* (Paris: Karthala, 1983), 195; Campbell, *Economic History*, 24;.

[49]   Hastie, 'Diary' (1817) CO 167/50, NAK; Hastie, 'Diary' (1820) CO 167/50, NAK; Canham to Burder, 5 Nov. 1824, MIL B.2 F.1 J.C, SOAS/CWM; Oliver, *Madagascar*, vol. 1, 307, 318–9; Grandidier and Grandidier, *Histoire physique* (1908), vol. 4, book 1, 33; Gwyn Campbell, 'Labour and the Transport Problem in Imperial Madagascar', *Journal of African History* 21.3 (1980), 341–56; Campbell, 'Role of the London Missionary Society', 183; Campbell, 'Commercialisation of Cattle'.

[50]   Griffiths, *Hanes Madagascar*, 38.

On concluding the contract, Canham left for Britain, returning in 1827 with a wife, Mary Ann (née Metz – d. 1889).[51] From 1828, Ranavalona greatly promoted leather production, chiefly for the military. That year alone, Canham received over 16,500 hides and, utilizing bark for tanning, 'assumed his responsibilities with remarkable energy' at Amparibe, just outside Antananarivo.[52] Shortly thereafter, Cameron discovered lime on the Sirabe plain, in Betsileo, and tanning took off. Ranavalona ordered all hides of cattle slaughtered during the *Fandroana*, or Merina New Year celebrations, to be surrendered to the court, and established tanneries, supervised by Canham, at Ambohimandroso, Andoharano, and Vodivato (near Antananarivo). In addition to cattle hide, Merina tanners used goatskin, sheepskin, and dog skin to manufacture shoes, boots, hat linings, belts, bags, gunpowder pouches, and saddles. Treated hides from the central highlands were also carried in consignments of 45.5 kg per porter to the east coast for export. Subsequently, Canham moved to Anosifisaka, where his tanning industry, which relied on *fanompoana* labour, resulted in such a growth of population that its name was changed to Ambohimandroso ('Village of Progress').[53]

However, Canham aspired to become a clerical rather than artisan missionary; he became ordained in 1831, and subsequently devoted his attention chiefly to supervising schools and churches.[54] In mid-1833, he grudgingly agreed to the Merina court's demand that he devote his time to the dyeing of leather. However, he assured the LMS directors that he would 'spend but as little time as possible about it'[55] – an attitude which guaranteed that in 1834 the queen denied his request to renew his residence visa, obliging him and his family to leave Madagascar.[56]

Iron

Iron manufacturing in Madagascar, a male preserve, used traditional techniques introduced from the eastern Indian Ocean world. Imerina possessed high

[51] Campbell, *David Griffiths*, 691–2.
[52] Griffiths, *Hanes Madagascar*, 38; see also Chapus, *Quatre-vingts années*, 204.
[53] Etienne de Flacourt, *Histoire de la Grande Isle Madagascar*, edited and commentary by Claude Allibert (Paris: Karthala, 1995 [1658]), 114; Hilsenberg and Bojer, 'Sketch of the Province of Emerina', 252; Ralph Linton, 'Culture Areas in Madagascar', *American Anthropologist* 30.3 (1928), 368; HdR, 692, 996; Steven M. Goodman, J. U. Ganzhorn, and D. Rakotondravony, 'Introduction to the Mammals', in Steven M. Goodman and Jonathan P. Benstead (eds.), *The Natural History of Madagascar* (Chicago: University of Chicago Press, 2003), 1164; Campbell, *Economic History*, 29, 96 fn. 65; Campbell, *David Griffiths*, 455, 694.
[54] Griffiths, *Hanes Madagascar*, 53.
[55] Canham to Ellis, Ambohimandroso, 7 Jun. 1833, MIL B.4 F.4 J.B, SOAS/CWM. See also Johns, Freeman, and Canham to Ellis, Antananarivo, 28 May 1833, MIL B.4 F.4 J.B, SOAS/CWM.
[56] RA, 308; Campbell, *David Griffiths*, 94, 788–9.

quality iron ore; Alexandre Garnot (1792–1851), a Breton merchant who spent considerable time in Imerina in the mid-1830s, commented, 'Iron appears to some extent flush with the ground, and is excellent there: it is even superior to Swedish iron'.[57] Because of the need for firewood to smelt the iron, most ore was extracted from pits averaging 1 m² and 1.6 m deep in eastern Imerina, on the edge of the great rainforest. The furnaces were constructed of sandstone, in which the ore was laid between beds of charcoal, that were lit and fanned by bellows for some five hours until the ore had melted. Subsequently, the highest quality pig iron was selected for forging, the rest being re-smelted to eradicate impurities. Some 75 per cent of the ore was lost in smelting. Of the remainder, about 40 per cent was transformed into pure iron. Five men and two boy apprentices working one furnace produced an average of 18–25 kg of iron per session, although up to 408 kg has been recorded.[58]

After he arrived in Madagascar in mid-1822, George Chick, an LMS black-smith, established a workshop at Amparibe, close to Jones' gardens on land beneath the capital, and taught iron and metal work to several hundred Malagasy *fanompoana* apprentices. However, Chick found himself in compe-tition with specialist Malagasy blacksmiths. In particular, he suffered from the high cost of transporting to Amparibe supplies of iron ore and charcoal, whereas local ironworkers lived on the forest edge where there existed plentiful supplies of both. Hence, Chick concentrated on ironwork for the elite, employ-ing 250 or more apprentices to produce ornamental railings, although he also made utilitarian novelties such as hinges, screws, locks, rounded nails, and wire. The sale of these made him the only successful LMS artisan before the Merina crown broke with the British alliance in 1826. Radama died in mid-1828, and in mid-1829, following the period of mourning for the king, Chick signed a contract with Ranavalona to manufacture swords and bayonets, as well as to produce the ironwork for a gunpowder factory, for which he would be paid $2,500.[59] By the time he left Madagascar in 1835, Chick had under his supervision some 400 Malagasy apprentices, who Ranavalona subsequently used in special *fanompoana* units to fashion swords and bayonets for the army.[60]

[57] Alexandre Garnot, *Question de Madagascar traitée au point de vue de l'intérêt français et du droit publique européenne* (Bordeaux: P. Coudert, 1846), 30.

[58] Mayeur, 'Voyage dans le nord de Madagascar' (1775), 36 – Add. 18128, BL; Mayeur, 'Voyage au pays d'ancove' (1777), 174; Mayeur, 'Voyage au pays d'ancove' (1785), 210; see also Lescalier, 'Voyage à l'isle de Madagascar' (1792), 327–8 – Add. 18128, BL; Hastie, 'Diary' (1817), 169–70, 182–3; Decary, 'Le voyage du lieutenant de Vaisseau de Semerville'; Ellis, *History of Madagascar*, vol. 1, 307–9; Oliver, *Madagascar*, vol. 1, 343, 488, 492 and vol. 2, 88–9; RH, 15; Grandidier, *Histoire physique* (1928), 179, 181–3; Raymond Decary, *Coutumes guerrières et organisation militaire chez les anciens Malgaches* (Paris: Éditions maritimes et d'Outre-Mer, 1966), vol. 1, 29.

[59] Griffiths, *Hanes Madagascar*, 52; Campbell, *David Griffiths*, 648.

[60] Ellis, *History of Madagascar*, vol. 1, 311–3.

Gunpowder

In 1825, Verkey, who was a royal slave, returned from Britain where he had served an apprenticeship. Radama immediately put him to work on gunpowder manufacture, the techniques of which he had learnt at Waltham Abbey gunpowder manufactory.[61] However, Verkey initially proved incapable of producing gunpowder without the machinery he had employed in Britain. Radama therefore offered Cameron, who arrived in Madagascar in mid-1826, generous payment if he would manufacture gunpowder. Cameron, an LMS carpenter, 'declined undertaking such a dangerous, and [to him] untried, manufacture.'[62] Instead, on land Radama gave him at Ambatonakanga, then just to the west of Antananarivo, he built a large workshop and was assigned 600 youths to instruct in carpentry. Until Radama's death, most of Cameron's output was woodwork and furniture for local European consumption.[63]

However, with an end to the period of mourning for Radama in mid-1829, and the looming threat of a French attack – which occurred in late October that year – Ranavalona signed a contract with Cameron for the manufacture of gunpowder and to fully train Merina apprentices in the process. When Cameron's Ambatonakanga workshop burned down in August 1829, the crown authorized him to move to Analakely, a valley to the northwest of Antananarivo, and granted him a 1,600 *fanompoana* workforce to build there a gunpowder and gun cartridge factory.[64] The queen placed Verkey alongside Cameron, and from 1829 they supervised over 20,000 *fanompoana* in the erection of a large gunpowder mill at Isoraka (the site formerly earmarked for textile production), on Lake Anosy (see Figure 5.1), and the construction of a canal to the river Ikopa, the water from which both enlarged the lake and provided power for the mills.[65]

---

[61] Griffiths to Burder, Tananarive, 19 Dec. 1825 and Griffiths to Arundel, 'private', Tananarive, 20 Dec. 1825, MIL B.2 F.2 J.C, SOAS/CWM.

[62] Cameron, *Recollections of Mission Life*, 15; see also Freeman to Burder, Tananarive, 23 Oct. 1827, MIL B.2 F.5, SOAS/CWM; Cameron, *Recollections of Mission Life*, 14.

[63] Campbell, *David Griffiths*, 683–4, 707–8.

[64] Cameron to Arundel, Tananarive, 25 Sep. 1829, MIL B.3 F.2 J.A, SOAS/CWM; Freeman to Philip, Andevoranto, Sep. 1831, MIL B.4 F.1 J.C, SOAS/CWM; David Griffiths, *The Persecuted Christians of Madagascar: A Series of Interesting Occurrences during a Residence at the Capital from 1838 to 1840* (London: Cornelius Hedgman, 1841), 21; RA, 253; Anthony Tacchi, 'King Andrianampoinimerina and the Early History of Antananarivo and Ambohimanga', *AAMM* 16 (1892), 489; Campbell, *Economic History*, 87, 124, 126; Campbell, *David Griffiths*, 907.

[65] Griffiths to Burder, Tananarive, 19 Dec. 1825, MIL B.2 F.2 J.C, SOAS/CWM; Johns, Freeman, Canham and Atkinson to Clayton, Tananarivo, 5 Jul. 1832, MIL B.4 F.3 J.A, SOAS/CWM; RA, 253, 307–8; Griffiths, *Persecuted Christians*, 21; Tacchi, 'King Andrianampoinimerina', 490; Simon Ayache (ed.), *Raombana l'historien (1809–1855)* (Fianarantsoa: Ambozontany, 1976), 313; Campbell, *David Griffiths*, 487, 739.

Figure 5.1 Lake Anosy[66]

Hitherto, Verkey had been limited by the lack of equipment and raw materials. This was no longer the case. Cameron, who possessed a good understanding of the basics of chemistry, ordered from abroad the necessary equipment, including glass, indigo, copper, aluminium, acids, salt, and heating apparatus. Ranavalona contributed $318 to the cost.[67] The production of gunpowder involved four operations: the sourcing of local raw materials, preparation of charcoal at Analakely, crushing at Isoraka, and refining to the southwest of Ambohijanahary.[68] The requisite sulphur and nitre was obtained from local resources. For example, the queen issued a special proclamation concerning cattle urine, one of the ingredients used to make the saltpetre that ignited the gunpowder:

given that cattle urine is used in the preparation of gunpowder: I will consider you guilty if you do not bring the urine of your cattle. It serves to pacify the country and kingdom, to extend my authority over the entire island. Nevertheless, in making your arrangements for the transport of the urine, it will be widows who deliver it each Wednesday, and if you fail to send a jug of urine, I will fine you at the rate of 1 piastre per jug.[69]

---

[66] Samuel Pasfield Oliver, *Madagascar and the Malagasy: with Sketches in the Provinces of Tamatave, Betanimena, and Ankova* (London: Day & Son, 1865), 61.
[67] Cameron to Arundel, Antananarivo, 25 Sep. 1829, MIL B.3 F.2 J.B, SOAS/CWM; Joseph Freeman, 'Memorandum', 19 Aug. 1829, No. 2 in Lyall to James Smith, Acting Chief Sec. to Govt, Port Louis, 8 Apr. 1831, RA 438, NAM.
[68] *HdR*, 515.   [69] *HdR*, 692–3.

Oral traditions state further

Cattle were led from the villages to the locality where the urine was collected. It was mixed with soil, with the contents of the stomachs of slaughtered animals, and animal corpses. All these elements were mixed together there each week. This produced the saltpetre that served in the preparation of gunpowder. That is how it was made. The Marovatana delivered their supplies to Ambohidratrimo, the Tsimahafotsy to Merimandroso and Ambohimanarina, the Tsimiamboholahy to Ilafy, the Mandiavato to Ambohidrabiby, the Voromahery to Analakely, the Vakinisisaony to Ankadiefajoro, and the Ambodirano to Fenoarivo. The Vakinankaratra *fanompoana* was to prepare the sulphur, also used in the manufacture of gunpowder, and lime used to produce soap. That was why they were not obliged to carry cattle urine. The sulphur came from the region of Antsirabe in Vakinankaratra, and Madera in (western) Ambodirano. Eastern Ambodirano was subjected to the *fanompoana* of cattle urine, as was Vonizongo. Military garrisons were established in the localities where these products were developed, the soldiers of which were known as *fantsika* (lit. nails). There were also civilian *fantsika* there. Each [designated] population provided a quota of people to ensure the delivery and mixing of cattle urine, which was also surveyed by high ranking officers posted there.

Unmarried women were responsible for carrying the cattle urine. It was the heads of the 'hundreds' who imposed this task on them. Married women served their husbands in digging canals, transporting wood, and cutting stone, leaving the unmarried women the cattle urine *fanompoana* – they were subjected to that alone, none other, and these obligations were lifelong. It was the same throughout Imerina. This industry started in the reign of Ranavalona I. The manufacture of gunpowder led to unmarried women being subject to *fanompoana* for the first time.

When the saltpetre had been well mixed, it was heated in the same localities, and when the blocks were ready they were carried to Analakely. After delivery, they were sent to Raolanitra (in Ankatso, to the northeast of Ambohipo) where they were compressed. Once they had been well ground, they were taken to Isoraka to be turned, after which the saltpetre was taken [back] to Analakely.[70]

Cameron sourced soda and minerals for the manufacture of sulphur in southern Imerina and northern Betsileo.[71] Iron pyrite, which contains 16 per cent sulphur, and chalk, from which lime could be produced, was discovered at a location some 70 km southwest of Antananarivo [Manalalondo?], on the north side of the Vakinankaratra mountain range, and in Betsileo, probably at Antsolifara (from *solifara* – 'sulphur') to the south of Antsirabe.[72] From September 1829, these sites were mined and the pyrite

[70] *HdR*, 695–6. See also Joseph John Freeman and David Johns, *A Narrative of the Persecution of the Christians in Madagascar with details of the Escape of the Six Christian Refugees now in England* (London: John Snow, 1840), 45; RA, 357; Raombana, 'Livre' 13 B2, 29, AAM; Chauvin, *Jean Laborde*, 8.

[71] James Sibree, *Fifty Years in Madagascar: Personal Experiences of Mission Life and Work* (London: George Allen and Unwin, 1924), 314–6.

[72] Cameron to Arundel, Tananarive, 25 Sep. 1829, MIL B.3 F.2 J.A, SOAS/CWM; Ellis, *History of Madagascar*, vol. 1, 10; Jajosefa Rakotovao (ed.), *Voly Maitson'andriamanitra: Tantaran'ny*

carried to the capital.[73] Gunpowder manufacture proved so successful that by early 1830 it was reported that

Verkéy – who was taught the art in England – has been so fortunate as to make gunpowder from these materials, whose quality is said to equal that of the English powder formerly supplied as part of the equivalent to the Malagash Government. As they were totally dependent on foreigners for this highly necessary article of warfare, and as they expect, by and bye, to be able to supply themselves abundantly, great rejoicings took place at the Capital on the successful results of the trial of the said gunpowder.

Thus, Madagascar owes England another debt of gratitude – would that the Government, and natives, were sensible of it, and of its amount.[74]

The crown also ordered that the hoofs of slaughtered bullocks be delivered to Verkey and Cameron for the extraction of oil and gelatine, which was used to produce gunpowder and to maintain muskets in good order.[75] Additionally, the horns of cattle were used as gunpowder holders and bones to manufacture buttons.[76]

In December 1830, Rahaniraka reported that Verkey was producing gunpowder from the ingredients supplied by Cameron.[77] However, Verkey continued to feel stymied by the lack of appropriate machinery. As Cameron reported in April 1832,

The chief attention of the Malagasy at present seems directed towards establishing themselves as [a] Kingdom and it is with that view they chiefly employ us. The principal part of our employment at present in the wood way is some Machinery to be turned by water to be used for the Manufacture of Gunpowder. The Machinery &c. which Joseph Verkey has had hitherto being rather imperfect for that purpose.[78]

A year earlier, Verkey had asked the LMS board to send him the items he required from the Waltham Abbey gunpowder manufactory.[79] However, the directors refused. Again, in June 1832, by which time the canal, mill, and Analakely factory had been completed, Verkey requested from the LMS an updated book on chemistry and its practical applications, to replace the one

Fiangonana Loterana Malagasy 1867–1967 (Antananarivo: Trano Printy Loterana, [1967]), 78–9.

[73] Cameron to Arundel, Tananarive, 25 Sep. 1829, MIL B.3 F.2 J.A, SOAS/CWM; Campbell, *Economic History*, 95, 247.

[74] Lyall, 'Journal', 10 Apr. 1830, HB 20, NAK.

[75] *HdR*, 692; Sibree, *Naturalist in Madagascar*, 183–4; Campbell, *David Griffiths*, 456; see also Peter Lund Simmonds, *Animal Products, Their Preparation, Commercial Uses and Value* (London: Chapman & Hall, 1877), 166.

[76] James Wills, 'Native Products Used in Malagasy Industries', *AAMM* 9 (1885), 92. See also Hilsenberg and Bojer, 'Sketch of the Province of Emerina', 264.

[77] Rahaniraka to Hankey, Tananarive, 5 Dec. 1830, MIL B.3 F.4 J.C, SOAS/CWM.

[78] Cameron to Arundel, Tananarivo, 11 Apr. 1832, MIL B.4 F.2 J.B, SOAS/CWM.

[79] Verkey, 'letter', in Baker to Arundel, Tananarivo, 14 Jan. 1831, MIL B.4 F.1 J.A, SOAS/CWM; see also Baker to Arundel, Tananarivo, 14 Feb. 1831, MIL B.4 F.1 J.A, SOAS/CWM.

they had given him when he left Britain. It is uncertain whether the directors complied.[80]

Nevertheless, Merina apprentices under Chick's supervision constructed the necessary machinery,[81] and by 1834, Verkey and Cameron had made such progress that, through her officers, Ranavalona issued the following royal *kabary* (public proclamation):

Members of the same family must all carry out the same work, notably in ironwork. For in the case that people try to take our country, we will not be content with forty bullets or fight with a single lance; every person will need handfuls of bullets, and spears in reserve for each warrior. We must produce bullets that match the rifle, one model for English rifles and another for small rifles, lest we waste many; for larger bullets won't enter smaller rifles, and the small will not supply cannon. This is important because we exploit much iron when a large number of people manufacture bullets; it will therefore be as you wish; everything will be done if there is a lot of iron.[82]

The production process was not, however, without its dangers:

Many of the turners and grinders [of saltpetre] got burned at Ankatso and Isoraka. The products caught fire, causing many [fatal] victims amongst the population, while many survivors carried burns and body sores. [This almost caused] the queen to stop gunpowder manufacture. Burning coal or sulphur was used in the manufacture of gunpowder. The burning coals were prepared at Mantasoa, and the sulphur collected from Antsirabe. All ingredients for gunpowder manufacture had to be delivered to Analakely, for it was there, nowhere else, that it was manufactured. It has been produced there since the reign of Ranavalona I. Ravarikia II Honours, a Tsiarondahy, supervised the work, and on his death, R., a Tsmiamboholahy replaced him.[83]

Despite all obstacles, gunpowder production was perfected by February 1835, following which the manufacture of guns commenced.[84] Ranavalona subsequently pronounced to her closest ministers:

we learned how to make rifles, in Andriambé, and powder, in Isoraka; all rifles to be manufactured in the future will be marked in my name. May my successors never stop making them because they are the best guarantors of our power.[85]

This was a major step forward for the Merina crown, which in 1835 still imported from Mauritius 215 muskets for $825, 871 kg of lead and shot for $70, and 1,452 kg of gunpowder for $560.[86] That year, Ranavalona deprived

---

[80] Verkey to Directors, An Tananarivo, 12 Jun. 1832, MIL B.4 F.2 J.C, SOAS/CWM.
[81] Cameron to Arundel, Tananarivo, 11 Apr. 1832, MIL B.4 F.2 J.B, SOAS/CWM; see also Verkey, 'letter', in Baker to Arundel, Tananarivo, 14 Jan. 1831, MIL B.4 F.1 J.A, SOAS/CWM; Verkey to Directors, An Tananarivo, 12 Jun. 1832, MIL B.4 F.2 J.C, SOAS/CWM.
[82] Kabary of the officers of XI Vtr, 19 Alakaosy 1834, *HdR*, 1158.   [83] *HdR*, 696.
[84] Griffiths, *Hanes Madagascar*, 66.
[85] Quoted in Guillaume Grandidier, *Histoire physique, naturelle et politique de Madagascar* (Paris: Imprimerie Paul Brodard 1942), 318, fn.
[86] Campbell, *Economic History*, 206; see also *HdR*, 1157.

Rabenila/Rainisoa 10 *voninahitra* (honours), of his governorship of Majunga for having bought, without her authorization, a large cannon from a British or American ship. It took the queen one year to pay off the value of the cannon ($30,000) in kind (hides, gum copal, and beeswax).[87]

In March 1835, Ranavalona banned Christianity for her subjects, and most missionaries then left the island. The conventional view, based on the accounts of Freeman and Ellis, is that Ranavalona expelled the missionaries.[88] This was incorrect. Ranavalona indubitably welcomed the departure of Freeman, whom she knew to be a British spy.[89] However, she made it clear that all were welcome to remain until their ten-year visas expired, and to practise their own religion. Two of them, Johns and Edward Baker (1805–1885), the LMS printer, remained for another year preparing religious texts on the mission press,[90] while Griffiths left temporarily, returning in 1838.[91] Certainly, the queen wished Chick and Cameron to continue working for her. Due to the royal contracts, Chick had become a wealthy man.[92] However, the victim of recurrent attacks of malaria, he probably also suffered a stroke in November 1833 that temporarily paralysed the left side of his body. Although he recovered, he continued to be dogged by health issues, for which reason left Madagascar in July 1835 to settle in South Africa.[93] By contrast, Cameron was both healthy and wealthy, having received $6,250 for the powder mills, and $3,750 for the production of sulphur and nitre for gunpowder manufacture.[94] Indeed, in 1834, as the gunpowder mills were nearing completion, he negotiated a crown contract to take two Merina youths to Britain to spend a year studying the latest techniques of iron and glass manufacture, then return to apply those techniques in Madagascar.[95] It is probable that the decision by the LMS to neither sanction his manufacture of cannon nor pay for his planned trip to Britain was the decisive factor in his decision to leave Madagascar in 1835.[96]

This was where Verkey came into his own, as after Cameron's departure Ranavalona appointed him chief supervisor of gunpowder production at the Anosy sites. Verkey also managed Cameron's former apprentices, who from 1835 produced nitre and sulphur in workshops constructed in the garden of

[87] RA, 377–8.
[88] Ellis and Freeman, *Madagascar and Its Martyrs*, 33; Campbell, *David Griffiths*, 102, 199–200.
[89] Campbell, *David Griffiths*, 121, 154.   [90] Griffiths, *Hanes Madagascar*, 73.
[91] Campbell, *David Griffiths*, 103–13.   [92] Campbell, *David Griffiths*, 649.
[93] George and Mary Ann Chick to Ellis, Tananarivo, 11 Nov. 1833, MIL B.4 F.4 J.C, SOAS/CWM; [LMS], *Report of the Directors to the Fortieth General Meeting of the Missionary Society, usually called the London Missionary Society* (London: Westley & David, 1834), 103; Ellis to Cameron, London, 3 Mar. 1835; Ellis to Chick, London, 4 Mar. 1835, MOL, SOAS/CWM; Griffiths, *Hanes Madagascar*, 215; Campbell, *David Griffiths*, 195.
[94] Griffiths, *Hanes Madagascar*, 52–3; RA, 358.   [95] Ellis, *History of Madagascar*, vol. 2, 482.
[96] Ellis to Cameron, London, 3 Nov. 1834, 3 Mar. 1835 and 3 Mar. 1836, MOL, SOAS/CWM.

Griffiths' house at Ambodin'Andohalo.[97] In May 1836, Garnot visited Imerina, where Verkey showed him one of his worksites:

General Varky, commander-in-chief of the artillery, having the same evening informed Mr. Garnot that he was authorized by the queen to let him inspect in the greatest detail the powder mills placed under the direction of this officer; the following day was devoted to this examination. Mr. Garnot expressed his surprise on this occasion. He could hardly believe that the machines they used had been made in the country. These mills are moved . . . by the force of the water which has been channeled from far away by a canal [the building of] which has required a great deal of labour. These establishments are well maintained, but very little powder is manufactured there: No saltpetre quarry having yet been discovered in the island, they have been obliged to obtain it by artificial means; although sulfur is very abundant there.[98]

Verkey continued supervising the Isoraka powder mills until an explosion in November 1853 destroyed the works, killing Verkey (then called Rainimanana) and nine co-workers.[99]

Mantasoa: The Industrial Experiment

Ranavalona initiated an industrial experiment, contemporaneous with those of Western European, that almost succeeded. Its focus was a large-scale manufacturing site founded by Jean Laborde at Mantasoa, on the edge of the eastern forest.

In 1833, the queen had a musket factory and cannon foundry built at Andriambe, near Ilafy, 10 km from Antananarivo, supervised by Frenchmen Droit and Laborde, both of whom had arrived separately in Madagascar the previous year. They succeeded in boring muskets and manufacturing gunpowder at mills powered by water brought hydraulically from a dam they constructed on the river Mamba.[100] However, Droit was expelled in June 1835 for insulting Rainimaharo, one of Ranavalona's chief ministers,[101] and in 1837 Laborde, who had had a short-term contract with the crown, was forced to abandon the Ilafy site because of insufficient supplies of water to power the mills and wood for fuel. Laborde then negotiated a new contract with Ranavalona for the establishment of a cannon foundry at Mantasoa, some 40 km from Antananarivo, situated close to a series of lakes in the eastern forest.[102] Its location guaranteed it plentiful local sources of timber and water, although Laborde sourced limestone principally from the Sirabe plain, south of

---

[97] Griffiths, *Hanes Madagascar*, 108; Raombana, 'Manuscrit écrit à Tananarive (1853–1854)', trans. J. F. Radley, *BAM* 13 (1930), 4; Gerald M. Berg, 'Virtù, and Fortuna in Radama's Nascent Bureaucracy, 1816–1828', *History in Africa* 23 (1996), 48;.

[98] Garnot, *Question de Madagascar*, 16–17.

[99] Raombana, 'Manuscrit écrit à Tananarive', 4–5; Berg, 'Virtù, and Fortuna', 48.

[100] RA, 307–8, 352; Chauvin, *Jean Laborde*, vii, 5–6; Boudou, 'Petites notes d'histoire malgache', 68; Campbell, *David Griffiths*, 759–60.

[101] RA, 362.   [102] RA, 308, 446.

Table 5.3 *Skilled armaments and associated workers under Ranavalona*

Location	Supervisors	Occupation	Number	% total skilled *fanompoana*
Analakely	Cameron (1829–35); Verkey (1829–54)	Gunpowder and cartridge makers	1,621	37.45
Ilafy	Droit (1833–5); Laborde (1833–7)	Gunsmiths	303	7.00
Mantasoa	Laborde (1837–57)	Cannon founders	287	6.63
[Antananarivo]	?	Makers of military flags and clothes	165	3.81
Isoraka, Ilafy & Mantasoa	Verkey (1829–54); Laborde (1833–57)	Makers of gunpowder and explosives	124	2.86
[Mantasoa]	Laborde (1837–57)	Machine-gun manufacturers	42	0.97
Total			2542	58.72

Source: Campbell, *Economic History*, 124–5.

the Vakinankaratra, some ten days' journey to the south, and he imported sulphur. It is claimed that the felling of trees for the timber required to enlarge the site cleared the forest around Mantasoa by between 6.5 km and 8 km.[103]

By 1841, following the technical manuals published by Edme-Nicolas Roret (1797–1860), Laborde had constructed at Mantasoa 'a true industrial centre, a kind of Malagasy Creusot',[104] with 20,000 workers, equivalent to about 5 percent of the adult Merina male population, registered for *fanompoana* (see Table 5.3). He also employed a permanent workforce of 5,000 who comprised some 400 skilled workers, as well as condemned Christians and military and civilian *fanompoana*.[105] Additionally, local ironworkers were drafted to transport to Mantasoa surface iron ore from Ampihadiamby, Mararongotra, Andrangoloaka, and Ambohitrandriamanitra.[106] An aqueduct was built to convey water to the complex, where, in June 1843, the first blast furnace was lit and, thirteen months later, the first cannon was completed. By 1849, thirty small cannon had been manufactured and tested. They proved so good that Ranavalona ordered nineteen new buildings to be erected at Mantasoa and gave Laborde $10,000 to apprentice a number of officers.[107] She also had Laborde build a palace on the site, as one of

[103] Arthur M. Hewlett, 'Mantasoa and its Workshops; a page in the history of industrial progress in Madagascar' *AAMM* 2 (1887), 378.
[104] Chapus, *Quatre-vingts années*, 204.
[105] RA, 13, 18; Campbell, *Economic History*, 95, 247.   [106] Chauvin, *Jean Laborde*, 8, 18–19.
[107] Raombana, 'Annales', Livre 13, B2, 18, Archives de la République Malgache, Antananarivo, Madagascar (hereafter ARM); Chauvin, *Jean Laborde*, 20–2.

her country residences.[108] At its height, Mantasoa, the largest industrial project under autarky, comprised five factories containing forges, hydraulic machines, numerous craft shops, and blast furnaces that smelted iron ore in far larger quantities and more efficiently than the traditional Malagasy small-scale bellow furnaces (see Figure 5.2). The complex specialized in musket and cannon manufacture but also produced Congreve rockets, swords, gunpowder, grapeshot, copper, steel, lightening conductors, glass, pottery, bricks, tiles, silk, a variety of cloths, candles, lime, dye, white soap, and paper potassium, as well as processing sugar into sweets and alcohol and tanning leather.[109] In addition, a road was built connecting Mantasoa via Lohasoa to the east coast port of Mahanoro, which involved cutting through hills spanning valleys with 100 m-long embankments, 50 m high and 15 m wide.[110]

Visiting Mantasoa (also called Soatsimanampiovana) in June 1855, Marc Finaz (1815–1880), a Jesuit missionary, stated,

Soatsimanampiovana means 'beauty without change'. Its position is most agreeable. The country house is situated opposite a neat village, the residence of fifteen hundred workmen, whom M. Laborde directs, and with whom he has indeed created veritable marvels of industry. Some ten years since these localities were nothing but an uninhabited desert. Now amidst vast reservoirs of water formed by dams with sluices furnishing the various manufactories with abundant water power, there stands a blast furnace of cut stone for mineral smelting, and besides a cannon foundry, where there are now twenty field-pieces, ready for delivery, and a mortar which is now being bored. From here we pass to a pottery and glass factory, whilst the buildings constructed for silk manufacture and soap-making are at a little distance. Further on, in a retired corner, is the arsenal for Congreve rockets.[111]

Ranavalona's chief aim was, through import substitution, to remove dependence on foreign arms imports and domestically produce modern cannon, cannonballs, muskets, bullets, and gunpowder on a sufficient scale both to enable her army to achieve the military conquest of the entire island and to ward off any potential European attacks.

---

[108] Ida Pfeiffer, quoted in Antoine Jully, 'L'habitation à Madagascar', *Notes, reconnaissances et explorations* 2.2 (1898), 928.

[109] Raombana, 'Livre' 13 B2, 18, ARM; *Bristol Mercury* (7 Jan. 1837); Oliver, *Madagascar*, vol. 2, 107; RH, 13; RA, 305, 307–8, 352, 362; Samuel Pasfield Oliver, *The True Story of the French Dispute in Madagascar* (London: T. Fisher Unwin, 1885), 266–8; Jully, 'L'habitation à Madagascar', 928; Chapus, *Quatre-vingts années*, 204–5; Chauvin, *Jean Laborde*, vii–viii, 5–6, 7–9, 20–3; Boudou, 'Petites notes d'histoire malgache', 68; Campbell, *David Griffiths*, 759–60.

[110] Oliver, *Madagascar*, vol. 2, 107; Hewlett, 'Mantasoa and Its Workshops'; Alfred Grandidier, 'Souvenirs de voyages, 1865–70', in *Documents anciens sur Madagascar* (Tananarive: Association Malgache d'archéologie, 1971 [1916]), 38; Grandidier, *Histoire physique* (1928), 179, 186–7; Chauvin, *Jean Laborde*, 13–29; Chapus, *Quatre-vingts années*.

[111] Finaz, Jun. 1855, quoted in Oliver, *True Story of the French*, 265–6.

Figure 5.2 Blast furnace, Mantasoa[112]
Source: Photograph by author (1992).

Domestically produced arms were put to immediate use against internal opponents. In the dry season of 1835, a military expedition of 15,000 men was sent against St Augustin Bay and the Androy Sakalava equipped with muskets produced by Laborde and Droit.[113] Indeed, until 1853, Ranavalona launched almost annual military expeditions against non-Merina peoples, whose men were killed, women and children enslaved, and cattle seized. From 1820 to 1853, possibly 60,000 non-Merina (on average 1,622 per annum) were killed by Merina troops, whose own battle casualties were low because of their immense military and numerical superiority.[114]

The Merina also gained a major victory in 1845 over a combined Franco-British naval force under the commanders Romain Desfosses and William Kelly that attacked Tamatave. In 1834, following the unsuccessful 1829 French assault on the northeast coast, Ranavalona hired two Arab or Swahili engineers to construct a reinforced fort at Tamatave. Completed in the early 1840s, it was built of three successive circular walls of solid masonry.[115] In 1845, the governments of Réunion and Mauritius used long-standing protests

---

[112] See Élie Colin and Pierre Suau, *Madagascar et la mission catholique* (Paris: Sanard et Derangeon, 1895), 44.
[113] RA, 377.   [114] Campbell, *Economic History*, 154.
[115] [Baker], *Madagascar Past and Present*, 124, 127–8.

by European (predominantly Mascarene) traders of alleged ill-treatment by the authorities of east coast ports of Madagascar as a pretext to send warships to Tamatave to demand redress. The French and British fleets arrived independently but combined forces and on 15 June 1845 landed 350 troops to attack the fort. However, they encountered an unexpectedly robust Merina defence, due largely to the reinforced fortifications and the possession by Malagasy troops of firearms, some of them of undoubtedly domestic manufacture.[116] The fort, with about thirty guns, unleashed on the European force 'a shower of balls and grape-shot which committed great slaughter.'[117] The Merina killed seventeen French (another two wounded died later on board the French vessels) and five British soldiers. Following the retreat of the European soldiers, the Malagasy beheaded the dead they had left behind. The *Mauricien* reported that the heads were 'conveyed round the fort and village, amidst dances and songs of war. Now and then these hideous trophies were presented to the traitors and the natives, whilst the Hovas boasted of the great victory that had been obtained'.[118] Shortly afterwards, thirteen of these heads were stuck on poles fixed into the ground along the shore front, facing the sea.[119]

Fanompoana and the Failure of Modernization

Despite this major victory against arguably the two major world powers of the time, the attempted modernization in Madagascar, based on textile and armaments production, in which the Madagascar Youths trained by the British assumed significant roles, ultimately failed. As noted above, plans under Radama for large-scale textile production, using British technology and supervised by Raolombelona, failed due to the lack of funding by the LMS. However, the major underlying cause of the failure to modernize the Malagasy economy was *fanompoana*. *Fanompoana* derived from the principle of obligatory service to the sovereign. Initially, members of a caste or individuals chosen by the crown to perform a particular ritual task thereby gained special status.[120] Under Andriamasinavalona (r. c.1675–1710), at a time of environmental crisis, *fanompoana* was greatly expanded to include the obligatory labour of freemen in the collection of all 'first fruits', and their employment in state infrastructural projects, notably in the creation and maintenance of river dykes and irrigated

---

[116] [Baker], in the *Standard* (18 Oct. 1845); see also Baker to Ellis, Tamatave, 15 Jul. 1834, MIL B.5 F.1 J.C, SOAS/CWM.

[117] *Morning Post* (1 Sep. 1845).

[118] Quoted in *Freeman's Journal and Daily Commercial Advertiser* (29 Sep. 1845).

[119] *Morning Chronicle* (2 Sep. 1845); *Morning Post* (26 Sep. 1845); [Baker], *Madagascar Past and Present*, 95–143.

[120] Ellis, *History of Madagascar*, vol. 1, 175, 177–9; Jean-François Baré, 'Remarques sur le vocabulaire monarchique sakalava du nord', in Raison-Jourde (ed.), *Les souverains de Madagascar*, 167.

rice fields. To this end, he organized all Merina subjects into geographically fixed caste-based units (*foko*), which the crown could summon at will to perform obligatory labour. In his turn, Andrianampoinimerina incorporated the *foko*, into larger regional units (*toko*), six of which formed greater Imerina (Avaradrano, Marovatana, Ambodirano, Vakinisisaony, Vonizongo, and Vakinankaratra). The inherently passive nature of the caste structure facilitated its control by the crown, which claimed the labour of each male subject for six days each season (twenty-four days a year) for public works, notably in riziculture.[121] However, a radical change in the nature of *fanompoana* occurred as a result of the adoption of autarky in the mid-1820s. Thereafter, the dual aim of the Merina regime was to effect a swift military conquest of the entire island and generate economic growth through the exploitation of domestic resources, notably through forced labour. In the early 1820s, it reorganized and greatly expanded military and civilian *fanompoana*.[122]

Military

In the early 1820s, with British assistance, Radama organized a standing army comprising permanent military *fanompoana*. Further, in 1823 he established direct control over the LMS mission, transforming it into a machine for the recruitment of forced labour. Until the missionaries left Madagascar in 1835–6, the school system gave Merina youth basic literacy before channelling them into the imperial army or administration.[123] Rank and file soldiers were recruited directly through village-level conscription, and *deka* (aides-de-camp) via the mission schools. Army numbers grew from 12,000 in 1821 to 30,000 by 1830 and to a peak of 100,000 by 1852 (see Figure 5.3). Both village and mission school conscripts immediately became camp followers of senior army officers, who competed for the most gifted junior recruits, notably the mission-educated, who became their *deka*. Of the estimated 15,000 mission school graduates from 1821 to 1835, 4,000 became *deka*. Their literacy ensured accurate trans-empire communication, while those mastering foreign languages, notably English, became secretaries at court or to the governors of the major ports.[124] In addition, Merina craftsmen were drafted into the army in order to maintain weaponry and build roads, bridges, and forts. In all, state demand for both skilled and unskilled labour was such that Radama could not contemplate acquiescing to the request

---

[121] Campbell, *Economic History*, 121–2.   [122] Campbell, 'Adoption of Autarky'.
[123] Campbell, *Economic History*, 123.
[124] Johns, Freeman, and Canham to Ellis, Antananarivo, 18 Nov. 1833, MIL B.4 F.4 J.C, SOAS/ CWM; see also Ellis, *History of Madagascar*, vol. 2, 479; Freeman and Johns, *Narrative of the Persecution of the Christians*, 156; Finaz, 'Journal' (1855–7), 69 – Diaires II.20, Archives historiques de la Vice-Province Société de Jésus de Madagascar, Antananarivo (hereafter AHVP); Ellis, *Three Visits*, 2–3, 119, 279; Raombana, 'Manuscrit écrit à Tananarive'.

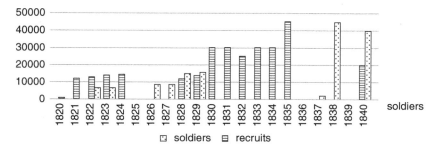

Figure 5.3 Estimated growth of the Imperial Merina Army, 1820–40
Source: Campbell, 'Slavery and Fanompoana', 470. Note: Gaps indicate
years and category for which data is missing.

from Mascarene planters for Malagasy contract workers, even though such
migrants would have earned badly needed foreign exchange and helped stem
the shift in foreign trade to the independent west coast.[125]

Moreover, while battle casualties amongst Merina troops was low, they
suffered from high mortality due to a combination of the enemies' scorched
earth tactics, the refusal of the Merina state to provision its troops, and the
spread of disease – facilitated by malnutrition and unsanitary conditions in
army camps. Indeed, up to 50 percent of military conscripts perished annually,
mainly through malaria and starvation. They had to be replaced to keep army
numbers from falling (see Figure 5.4).[126]

Civilian Labour

In the early 1820s, Radama also conducted a population census with the
express purpose of forming irregular civilian *fanompoana* units, each comprising between 10 and 1,000 men. To enforce participation, a royal edict of
January 1823 obliged anyone who claimed to be ill, upon recovery, to spend
a time corresponding to the length of their illness in public works *fanompoana*.
Radama and Ranavalona used this system to organize permanent industrial
fanompoana units, which were among the most exploited categories of unfree
labour. They included the *foloroazato* (lit. 'the 1,200') – comprising woodcut-
ters, 500–600 charcoal burners, 700 smiths and general ironworkers (in
June 1857, Ida Pfeiffer (1797–1858) witnessed a *fanompoana* unit of 1,000

---

[125] Hastie, 'Diary' (1820); Bojer, 'Journal', 23; Hastie to Barry, Antananarivo, 22 Apr. 1824, CO
167/77, NAK; Ellis, *History of Madagascar*, vol. 1, 119; Oliver, *Madagascar*, vol. 2, 160;
Cameron, *Recollections of Mission Life*, 24–6; Grandidier and Grandidier, *Histoire physique*
(1908), vol. 4, book 1, 371.
[126] Campbell, 'Adoption of Autarky'; Campbell, *Economic History*, 76.

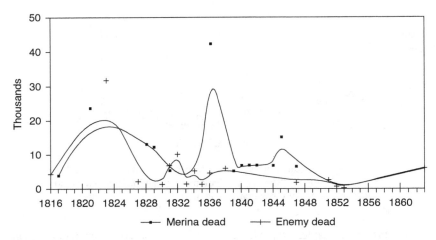

Figure 5.4 Merina military campaigns: estimated gains and losses 1816–63
Source: Campbell, *Economic History*, 155.

blacksmiths labouring in state forges), and many smaller *fanompoana* divisions, including gunsmiths, spear makers, gunpowder manufacturers, carpenters, seamstresses, tailors, tanners, curriers, and soap boilers. The LMS missionaries noted that such units were 'a sort of Government slaves', confined for life to their villages and occupations.[127] This was certainly the case for Merina workers who acquired European skills – including the Madagascar Youths.[128] In June 1836, the Malagasy apprentices, and other *fanompoana* assigned to European artisans, including the missionary artisans who left the island in 1835, were, except for hatmakers, barred from establishing themselves independently and severe limitations were placed upon their geographical mobility.[129] Baker noted in 1847,

Many hundred people are forced into learning a trade; but, when conversant with its minutiæ, instead of being allowed to offer themselves as competitors in its exercise, their labour is monopolised as the feudal property of the queen, by whom it is unceasingly put into requisition ... without any sort of requital. This principle runs through the entire catalogue of the mechanical arts. Again, the people think it a matter of exultation,

[127] Ida Pfeiffer, *The Last Travels of Ida Pfeiffer: Inclusive of a Visit to Madagascar: with a Biographical Memoir of the Author* (London: Routledge, Warne and Routledge, 1861), 267; Oliver, *Madagascar*, vol. 2, 89, 192–3.
[128] Freeman to Philip, Antananarivo, 19 Apr. 1832, MIL B.4 F.2 J.C, SOAS/CWM.
[129] For restrictions on skilled Malagasy workers see *HdR*, 164, 253–4, 303, 596, 885, 1158; ; Freeman and Johns, *Narrative of the Persecution of the Christians*, 78; [Baker], *Madagascar Past and Present*, 57, 60; Grandidier, *Histoire physique* (1928), 166, 175.

if she demands but one half of the men out of each hundred for perpetual unpaid servitude.[130]

And of the consequences of this system, Baker remarked,

The effect of this system [*fanompoana*] is, that the people universally execrate the period when they were instructed by the Europeans, and would view any new instructors presented to them, through their own government, as their enemies, rather than their friends.[131]

As noted, many Merina craftsmen were employed servicing the army during military campaigns. Others were drafted into the industrial workshops in the vicinity of Antananarivo and at Mantasoa, producing primarily armaments. For example, such was the demand established by the armaments industry in Antananarivo for blacksmiths alone that there quickly developed in the vicinity several *fanompoana* villages, composed entirely of smithies and their families.[132]

Much unskilled *fanompoana* was also imposed for military and industrial purposes. Such labour was utilized, for example, to cut and carry timber to construct the industrial sites. Large trunks, used as pillars and supporting beams, required between ten and forty porters each to carry from the eastern forest, a distance of 80 km to Antananarivo, much less for Mantasoa.[133] In response to continual rumours of a French assault, a massive *fanompoana* comprising both Merina soldiers and Betsimisaraka peasants was summoned in 1833–5 and again in 1847 to strengthen batteries at Tamatave and Foulepointe on the east coast, and in an unsuccessful bid to erect a barrage across the entrance to Tamatave harbour; while in 1846, a 30,000 strong *fanompoana* force was drafted for two weeks to carry stone and chalk from Sirabe, in Betsileo, to strengthen the fortifications at Ambohimanga.[134]

Unskilled labour was summoned in accord with imperial imperatives rather than those of the agricultural cycle. The result was periodic harvest shortfalls, famine, and growing vulnerability to disease. For example, in 1834, *fanompoana* so deprived agriculture on the northeast coast of the requisite labour that cheap Bengali rice had to be imported to avert mass starvation.[135] These risks were gravely aggravated during times of disputes with Europeans, as during the

---

[130] [Baker], *Madagascar Past and Present*, 77–8.

[131] Quoted in [Baker], *Madagascar Past and Present*, 62.

[132] Oliver, *Madagascar*, vol. 1, 228–9 and vol. 2, 86, 90; James Sibree, 'Industrial Progress in Madagascar', *AAMM* 22 (1898), 129–32; Georges-Sully Chapus and Emile Birkeli, 'Historique d'Antsirabe jusqu'en l'année 1905', *BAM* 26 (1944–5), 59–82.

[133] Ellis, *History of Madagascar*, vol. 1, 107–8.

[134] Johns to LMS, Tamatave, 6 Aug. 1838, MIL B.5. F.3. J.B, SOAS/CWM; Cartier, 'notes sur Madagascar' (1839–40), 12 – Clla, AHVP; Campbell, 'Slavery and Fanompoana'; Raombana, Livre 13, B2, 2.

[135] RA, 322, 346; see also Baker to Ellis, Ivohitsara, 30 Jul. 1834, MIL B.5 F.1 J.C, SOAS/CWM.

French attack and occupation of 1829–31, and from 1845 to 1853 when Merina-controlled ports were closed to European trade. At such times, the Merina regime intensified its exploitation of imperial subjects, and foreign trade, including the external supply of provisions, was curtailed. As *fanompoana* intensified, not only did the number of cultivators dwindle but, as young men were drafted into permanent or semi-permanent work for the state, the remaining peasantry increasingly comprised the older and less able-bodied members of the community. The state also imposed monetary demands on ordinary Merina. These included a tax to support the army and, under Ranavalona, special levies in 1835 to pay Laborde and Droit for teaching their Merina apprentices how to manufacture muskets. These raised $65,000, far more than the required sum, so the crown retained the surplus.[136] Two other taxes were imposed in 1837 to raise the $31,800 owed to Delastelle for imported European muskets and $100,000 to finance the construction of the Mantasoa industrial site. In order to meet these additional impositions, many subjects were forced to sell their slaves, who were thus increasingly transferred into the hands of the court elite, and to borrow at exorbitant interest rates from, or sell cattle to, members of the same elite, whose monopoly of cattle exports enabled them to dictate a sale price of $0.071 a bullock, which, when foreign trade was unhindered, they resold to European merchants on the coast for $15.[137]

Protest

Radama and Ranavalona faced incessant opposition from non-Merina peoples, both those who remained largely independent, such as the Sakalava and Bara of the western and southern reaches of the island, and those subjected to Merina rule, notably along the eastern littoral.[138] However, the greatest threat to the Merina court's autarkic policies, including attempted industrialization, came from Merina subjects burdened by increasingly oppressive *fanompoana*. Popular resentment of *fanompoana*, the militarization of Merina society, and the imperative to produce arms became progressively more palpable. A significant party, the 'Patriots' (see Chapter 7), even emerged in court circles opposed to the crown's policies that would 'oppress and destroy them [the people], instead of being for their defence and protection'.[139]

Much popular discontent was directed against Europeans. Thus, Raombana commented that 'the several Arts introduced by these [European] artisans has been the greatest scourge to the people of IMERINA, in-as-much as through them, the feudal services of the people

---

[136] RA, 360.   [137] Oliver, *Madagascar*, vol. 2, 196; Campbell, *Economic History*, ch. 6 and ch. 7.
[138] Campbell, *Economic History*, 153–5.   [139] Griffiths, *Hanes Madagascar*, 66.

were increased to the highest degree'.[140] Official abuse and exploitation was possibly greatest in and around Antananarivo, to which the government obliged many of those conscripted for military and industrial *fanompoana* to move. Thus, Baker commented in 1836,

General distress in Madagascar is extreme just in proportion to the proximity of a place to the capital. Immediately round An_Tananarivo every one is exposed to personal observation, and consequently Society presents but two faces, the one oppression, and the other its effect – wretchedness. The natives have only two methods of defending themselves – learning to deceive the oppressor, and the courage to flee from him. In the provinces, and amongst the hovas when sojourning there, the latter is often practicable, and many hundreds live like wild beasts in the deserts and woods. Around the capital, the former prevails, and pretended sickness, absolute poverty and nakedness, and selling themselves into slavery to each other, are the prevalent and daily modes of opposing the Government.[141]

Increasingly, the reaction of those subject to *fanompoana*, notably skilled craftsmen and those drafted into the army, was to resort to crime, resist conscription, or flee. For instance, Baker noted with reference to iron smiths and carpenters,

There are at least 800 smiths whose only means of subsistence is to steal the iron of Government brought on the same feudal system from the iron districts, work it clandestinely with the charcoal brought in the same way, and give the articles to their wives and relations for sale in the markets. The 300 to 500 carpenters steal the queen's wood on the same plan, so that peculancy has become universal.[142]

Those families who could afford to offered bribes to officials to prevent their younger male members being conscripted into the army – a practice so widespread that in 1840 Ranavalona arrested over 650 officers for accepting such inducements.[143] To avoid *fanompoana*, increasing numbers of potential recruits fled from central Imerina. A few managed to escape to the Mascarenes.[144] Many more fled to remoter regions of Madagascar – Baker asserting in 1840 that 'there are tens of thousands of persons in the woods who have escaped from the Queen, and who subside on roots &c.'[145] If such refugees were caught, they were severely punished, as were those who otherwise avoided *fanompoana*. Thus, in August 1834, it was commented of the 20,000 *fanompoana* workforce employed in the construction of the canal

---

[140] RH, 134.   [141] Baker, Memorial to Nicolay, Antananarivo, 20 May 1836, NAM, HB 9.

[142] Edward Baker, 'Restraint upon the Diffusion of knowledge under the Madagascar Queen's Government', La Chausée, Maison Mabille, Port Louis, 13 Sep. 1836, NAM, HB 9.

[143] Charles Mackenzie Campbell, 'Journal' (May–Aug. 1840)', *Studia* 2 (1963), 490; see also 79.

[144] Ramanasina to Nicolay, Tamatave, 17 Dec. 1838, NAM, HB 9; David Jones, letter [n.d.], [Port Louis], NAM, HB; Free Labor Association to John Irving and David Barclay (London), Port Louis, 18 Oct. 1841, NAM, IA 26.

[145] No. 11, Port Louis, 1–2 Mar. 1840, NAM, IA 28.

linking the river Ikopa to Lake Anosy and the gunpowder mills, 'the whole on an immense scale',[146] that 'some hundreds of people were sold into Slavery for not performing their portion of the labour in fetching the timber forming the Lake and Canal and preparing the materials and erecting the Mill for Powder.'[147] Indeed, such was the scale of resistance to *fanompoana* by those Malagasy instructed in European skills that in June 1836 Ranavalona passed a law:

That any persons happening to acquire a knowledge of the new arts introduced by the Europeans, and venturing to practice those arts for their own benefit, or out of the government premises, under any pretence, should be put to death.[148]

There was also open protest, albeit on a limited scale due to the court's network of spies[149] and military suppression. For instance, in March 1833, following a court *fanompoana* directive to district authorities to enlist 3,000 children in the mission schools, a petition was presented by 'the people' protesting against it. Freeman noted,

The fear of the School being made a mere introduction to the army, renders the Schools extremely unpopular with the mass of the population. Separation from home, – the loss of the children's services from agricultural labours – the dangers of war and the probable residence in a fever district at some Military outpost – these things make parents dread the thought of their children being summoned to the Schools.[150]

That the court halved the quota in response to the petition is an indication of the seriousness of the popular resentment of a school *fanompoana* that the court expanded to incorporate not only Imerina but also Vakinankaratra and Betsileo, plateau regions the south. However, when soldiers ordered to labour on a construction site under Laborde drew up a petition against the harsh conditions under which they worked, Ranavalona personally rebuked them.[151] So worried was the queen at the possibility of revolt within the army that she created a military secret police, drawn almost exclusively from the close relatives of her court favourites, Rainihiaro, Rainimaharo, and Rainiseheno.[152] They proved so efficient that at the end of 1842, or the start

---

[146] Freeman to Hankey, Antananarivo, 18 Jun. 1832, MIL B.4 F.2 J.D, SOAS/CWM; see also Freeman to Philip, Antananarivo, 19 Apr. 1832, MIL B.4 F.2 J.C, SOAS/CWM; Johns, Freeman et al. to Canham, Antananarivo, 5 Jul. 1832, MIL B.4 F.3 J.A, SOAS/CWM.

[147] Shipton to LMS, Tamatave, 10 Aug. 1834, MIL B.5 F.1 J.C, SOAS/CWM.

[148] Quoted in [Baker], *Madagascar Past and Present*, 60; see also Baker, Memorial to Nicolay, Antananarivo, 20 May 1836, NAM, HB 9; Edward Baker, 'Restraint upon the Diffusion of knowledge under the Madagascar Queen's Government', La Chausée, Maison Mabille, Port Louis, 13 Sep. 1836, NAM, HB 9.

[149] Gwyn Campbell, *The Travels of Robert Lyall, 1789–1831: Scottish Surgeon, Naturalist and British Agent to the Court of Madagascar* (Cham, Switzerland: Palgrave Macmillan, 2020), 121.

[150] Freeman to Wilson, Antananarivo, 26 Nov. 1833, MIL B.4 F.4 J.C, SOAS/CWM.

[151] Raombana, 'Livre' 13 B2, 23.   [152] RA, 286.

of 1843, a written protest against them was posted on the palace walls, for which the alleged culprits, army officers Andriantiana and Ratsitovana, were convicted of the crime of openly propagating 'European ideas' and publicly executed.[153]

Fires were not uncommon in Antananarivo, where buildings were constructed only in wood until the second half of the nineteenth century, but two disgruntled 'apprentices' set fire to Le Gros' Andohalo workshops during the night of 20 May 1826. They were caught and burnt alive.[154] Other aggrieved workers may well have been responsible for firing Cameron's Ambatonakanga workshop in early August 1829.[155] Certainly, in the 1830s, three soldiers carrying Cameron around the gunpowder mill site at Anosy, where thousands of *fanompoana* workers laboured under his direction, deliberately ditched him into the lake.[156] Cameron left for South Africa in 1835, but his return in 1853 for a brief visit prompted popular apprehension that it might result in increased *fanompoana*. As Raombana commented of *fanompoana* under Cameron prior to 1835, 'The labour of Mr. CAMERON though beneficial to Her Majesty and her government, proved to be one of the greatest scourges that could have been inflicted on the people of IMERINA.'[157] Disgruntled workers may also have caused the explosion at the Isoraka powder mills in 1853 that killed Verkey.[158] Inevitably, Mantasoa experienced worker protest. Although Laborde called his workers there *zazamadinika* ('little children'), built them housing, and granted them land for rice cultivation, the work regime and punishments he imposed were harsh, and the court appropriated half their rice crop.[159] In 1857, when Laborde was expelled from the island (see Chapter 7), the Mantasoa workforce, which at its peak numbered 20,000, destroyed the site's machinery, following which it is likely that most workers fled.[160] In 1861, after Ranavalona's death, her son and successor, Radama II, dismissed the 2,000 who remained at Mantasoa.[161]

[153] Griffiths, *Hanes Madagascar*, 122–3; RA, 287–90; see also Freeman, Edinburgh Witness (3 Jul. 1844), quoted in *The Madras Christian Instructor and Missionary Record* I (Jun.–May, 1843–4), 309.

[154] Edward Baker, 'Restraint upon the Diffusion of knowledge under the Madagascar Queen's Government', La Chausée, Maison Mabille, Port Louis, 13 Sep. 1836, NAM, HB 9.

[155] Cameron to Arundel, Tananarive, 25 Sep. 1829, MIL B.3 F.2 J.A, SOAS/CWM; Freeman to Philip, Andevoranto, Sep. 1831, MIL B.4 F.1 J.C, SOAS/CWM.

[156] RA, 359–60; Oliver, *Madagascar*, vol. 1, 238; Campbell, *Economic History*, 94.

[157] RA, 357; see also Raombana, 'Manuscrit écrit à Tananarive', 11–12

[158] Raombana, 'Manuscrit écrit à Tananarive', 4–5; Berg, 'Virtù, and Fortuna', 48.

[159] Hewlett, 'Mantasoa and its Workshops', 376; Chauvin, *Jean Laborde*, 27–8.

[160] RA, 308; Raombana, 'Annales', Livre 13 B2, 18 – ARM; Hewlett, 'Mantasoa and Its Workshops', 300; Idahosa and Shenton, 'The Africanist's "New" Clothes', 76–7; Chauvin, *Jean Laborde*, 33, 37.

[161] Hewlett, 'Mantasoa and Its Workshops', 378, 381; Raombana, 'Livre' 13 B2, 18.

In sum, the Madagascar Youths trained abroad in industrial and craft techniques, were employed on their return in an ambitious bid by the Merina crown to industrialize. The major focus was on textile and armaments production. Plans to create a modern textile manufacturing sector had failed by 1828, due to competition from local Malagasy, who produced excellent cloth, cheaply, on a domestic basis, and because the anticipated investment of funds by the LMS did not materialize. Thereafter, the Merina court abandoned the idea of large-scale textile production and concentrated on promoting a modern armaments industry. This achieved initial success, to which Verkey, a Madagascar Youth trained in Britain in gunpowder manufacture, contributed. Nevertheless, self-sufficiency was never achieved, the Merina crown continuing to depend on imported arms and gunpowder supplied by European and American traders.[162] More seriously, *fanompoana*, which governed all aspects of labour employed by the Merina regime, undermined its attempt to modernize the economy. Thus, the opportunity costs of *fanompoana*, expressed chiefly in terms of abandonment of crafts, neglect of agriculture, sabotage, flight, mortality, illness, and open protest, doomed the industrial experiment to failure.

The next chapter investigates the careers following their return to Madagascar of the youths apprenticed on Mauritius as musicians and aboard British naval vessels.

---

[162] Garnot, *Question de Madagascar*, 28; Marks to Raombana, Majunga, 6 Sep. 1852 in Ayache (ed.), *Raombana*, 323, 325, 329.

6   Musicians and Naval Ambitions

This chapter examines the history, following their return from overseas, of the Madagascar Youths sent to Mauritius to learn European music and those who served apprenticeships aboard British naval vessels. It surveys the history of traditional Malagasy music and, in that context, explores the role of the returning musicians at court. It also examines the history of the naval apprentice returnees in military and 'naval' duties, as well as – alongside other Madagascar Youths – in diplomatic roles, as representatives of the Merina crown in its relations with foreign powers.

Traditional Malagasy Music

In common with other regions of Madagascar, Imerina had a rich tradition of music. From an early age, Merina children learned to make and play musical instruments and to sing. They fashioned chiefly drums, guitars, and wind instruments. The drums included a kettledrum, formed of a piece of bladder stretched tightly across the rim of a broken earthenware water-pot and tied with raffia string. The guitars included the *jejileva*, an instrument with 'one or two strings, made of half of a pumpkin and a piece of wood running across and extending like the handle of a guitar',[1] and the *lokanga vava*, a mouth guitar made of a strong stalk of grass, which the child operated with one hand, hitting its chest – as a 'bass drum' accompaniment – with the other. They also made wind instruments, notably flutes or flageolets fashioned from various plants, in particular bamboo and rice-straw,[2] and the *farara*, a trumpet fashioned with a rice straw or *herana* (*cyperus latifolius*) reed leaves.[3] Adults fabricated primarily three instruments: the *valiha*, played mainly by non-slaves, the

---

[1] 'A native guitar having only one or two strings, made of half of a pumpkin and a piece of wood running across and extending like the handle of a guitar' – James Richardson, *A New Malagasy-English Dictionary* (Antananarivo: LMS, 1885), 300.
[2] Herbert F. Standing, *The Children of Madagascar* (London: Religious Tract Society, 1887), 152–4.
[3] Paul Camboué, 'Jeux des enfants malgaches', *Anthropos* 7 (1911), 669, 671.

lokanga, played chiefly by slaves, and the drum, used by both. William Ellis commented,

The *valiha* is a bamboo, having eight small slips cut from its rind between two of its joints, and then by means of small pieces of wood, used as bridges in a violin, elevated about a quarter of an inch. The player holds the instrument before him, and uses both hands in twitching the cords. The music thus produced is soft and plaintive; the tunes few, short, and extremely monotonous.

The *lokanga* is somewhat louder ... It is formed of a piece of wood, notched at one end so as to form three or four rests for the cord or string. One string is stretched upon it, and attached to the head of a hollowed calabash or gourd. The music, as might be supposed, is extremely feeble and dull ... Drums made in a form somewhat resembling those of Europe, are sometimes used. They are made of the hollow trunk of a tree, and are covered with untanned ox-hide, the ends being drawn together by thongs of the same material. They are beaten at one end with a stick.

A few inferior fifes are also used, as well as drums, but neither are well made or musical. Many of the latter are beaten upon the knee, or placed between the knees, and beaten with the hands instead of drumsticks, while the players are seated on the ground. They are chiefly used as an accompaniment to the females' clapping of hands and singing, and answer the purpose of assisting to keep the time.[4]

All classes in Imerina, from slaves to monarchs, relished traditional music. In January 1826, Coppalle commented of Radama's fondness for partying and indigenous music from all regions of the island,

Nighttime festivities resumed at the palace with renewed vigour, the Ambaniandre [Merina] tambourine, Sakalava cymbals, Antalaotra bagpipes, and Betsimisaraka antsoury in turn bursting the ears with their loud sounds.

Sometimes, we believe that in the midst of this appalling fanfare, arose lovely songs, and during the frequent insomnia caused by living near to the king, I had fun noting down some pleasurable tunes that I heard sung by the king's singers.[5]

Throughout their reigns, Radama and Ranavalona maintained groups of traditional Malagasy musicians, prominent among whom were the Sakalava, whose martial music and dancing the Merina sovereigns particularly enjoyed. Thus, Ellis commented of a celebration at the palace on 18 September 1856,

After waiting a short time on the outside we entered the large court before the palace, when the band played the national air, and the soldiers presented arms. The queen and her court, sixty or seventy persons, occupied the large open veranda or balcony in the centre of the palace. The queen sat beneath the large scarlet umbrella ... All the members of the court were in Arab costume. The prince wore an orange-colored silk robe, and a green silk turban, with a gold crescent in the centre.

---

[4] William Ellis, *History of Madagascar* (London: Fisher, 1838) vol. <pg>1, 272–3; see also James Sibree, *Madagascar and Its People* (London: Religious Tract Society, 1870), 234.

[5] André Coppalle, 'Voyage dans l'intérieur de Madagascar et à la capitale du roi Radama pendant les années 1825 et 1826', *Bibliothèque malgache* 20 (2007), 71–2.

The Frenchmen and myself were directed to chairs on the left in the shade … The queen's band and the prince's band were ranged on the right side of the square, beyond the members of the court. Behind them sat a large company of singing women, in front of whom stood three or four men blowing the turbo, or trumpet shell, and making a kind of bass to the women's soft and monotonous music in singing. The farther end of the court was filled with spectators, and the outside beyond was crowded with lines of lookers-on standing one above the other.

The dancing was commenced by the Sakalavas, inhabitants of the western parts of the island. The Sakalava band of native instruments included a large drum hollowed out of a solid piece of wood, with several smaller ones, and tomtoms or tambourines, apparently of Asiatic origin, the drum exactly resembling those I had seen in Ceylon. Four men arrayed as warriors, wearing singularly-shaped scarlet caps, having a broad scarlet lappet hanging down behind, with muskets in their hands, and powder-horns slung at their sides, and the Malagasy ornament or charm of silver crocodiles' teeth fastened in front of their girdles or sashes, followed this band, led by a sort of chief, whose business seemed to be to indicate the movements of the dance. The dancers were tall light-made men.

Commencing their performance as soon as they entered the court, they continued passing from side to side of the open space in the centre, making a sort of zigzag course until they came immediately in front of the queen. The musicians then gave three or four loud strokes on the large drum, while the dancers bowed before her majesty, and then retired to the side.

These were followed by four or five other sets of Sakalava dancers of four each, who, entering by the gate, danced along, each party with a different figure or step, until they came before the queen, when they bowed and retired. In addition to the musket in the right hand, one or two of the sets held a silk handkerchief or small scarf in the left. Their movements were light and easy; but for the most part measured and slow, except in those passages which appeared designed to represent the more exciting movements of battle, the assault, the strife, the pursuit, and the triumph. There was no shouting, and even those movements, though the muskets were sometimes thrown up in the air and caught as they fell, were restrained and moderate, according but little with the ideas we are accustomed to associate with the war-dance of the savage …

After the Sakalava dance, about a hundred females, connected, as I inferred from their air, their apparel, and the careful and elaborate dressing of their hair, with the officers and other respectable families of the capital, entered the open space. They ranged themselves three abreast and facing the queen, in a sort of open column. The line or column consisted of thirty-four successive threes. As soon as they were in position, they slipped the lambas or scarfs from their shoulders down to their waists, and thus exhibited their rich velvet, satin, silk, and muslin dresses, many of them trimmed about the body and sleeves with gold. The queen's band commenced a slow soft native tune. A dancing-master at the head of the column, and facing the queen, signalled the movements, and the dancing commenced – if dancing it could be called in which the feet covered by the flowing lamba appeared scarcely to move, for each dancer remained on the same spot, and the arms chiefly answered in easy and graceful motion to the measure of the music … The music consisted entirely of original native tunes remarkably soft and simple. After two or three dances they bowed to the sovereign and retired.[6]

[6] William Ellis, *Three Visits to Madagascar during the Years 1853–1854–1856* (Philadelphia: John E. Potter, 1858), 358–60.

European Music and Radama

Radama was eclectic in his musical tastes and from his first encounter with the British in 1816 was keen to have Merina apprentices learn European music, particularly martial airs, possibly in emulation of Napoleon, a figure he greatly admired.[7] The first group sent abroad specifically to learn European music was despatched to Mauritius in 1817. Others followed after the signing of the 1820 Britanno-Merina treaty. In May or early June 1823, after completing their 'apprenticeships', the Madagascar Youths who learned European martial music on Mauritius, under Kyle, sailed from Port Louis in an impressive convoy of seven British warships headed by HMS *Menai*, under Captain Moresby. The *Menai* also carried Farquhar and his wife, Maria. Farquhar commented of their arrival in Tamatave,

The young men whom Radama had sent, two years ago, to the Mauritius, for the purpose of learning martial music, and being formed as a band, under the tuition of Mr. Kyle (the master belonging to the 82nd regiment stationed there), accompanied us on board the *Menai*, and having been landed immediately after we anchored, the beautiful air of God Save the King was played for the first time, perhaps, in Madagascar, by a full military band, and with great execution and effect. These Madagascar youths, whose progress has been truly surprising, are now capable of performing all the tunes practised by the band of the 82nd regiment, and have acquired a very competent knowledge of music. The delight displayed by the assembled multitude on the beach was strikingly pleasing, and afforded an earnest [reflection] of the step to civilization, which this single acquisition to Madagascar must effect.[8]

The youths subsequently travelled to Antananarivo where their services were immediately monopolized by the crown. Hastie wrote to Lowry Cole, Farquhar's replacement as governor of Mauritius, commenting on a public performance they gave on 1 January 1824:

You will observe by my diary that Music had a powerful effect on the people at the assembly here on 1st Jany. It was the first time they ever heard a band. I send a Clarionet, one of 7 made here since that period, as a specimen of the ingenuity of the natives.[9]

In mid-1824, a British naval vessel, possibly the *Andromache*, carried a second group of Madagascar Youths trained by Kyle to Majunga, where Boteler commented of the king's first meeting with Commodore Nourse,

---

[7] J.-G. Prod'homme and Frederick H. Martens, 'Napoleon, Music and Musicians', *Musical Quarterly* 7.4 (1921), 579–605.

[8] Extract of a letter from Farquhar to R. Wilmot, Madagascar, 6 Jun. 1823, in House of Commons, *Papers: Relating to Captured Negroes; also to the Slave Trade at the Mauritius and Bourbon, and the Seychelles; Slave Population at the Seychelles &c.* ([London]: House of Commons, 1826), 150; see also *HdR*, 1087–8.

[9] Hastie to [Sec.] Govt Mauritius, Tananarive, 22 Apr. 1824 – 'private', HB 5, NAM.

The audience lasted about one hour, during which the commodore's band and that of Rahdahmah, composed of black men, alternately played; the latter having, if anything, the superiority. It was collected at the Isle of France [Mauritius] by Mr. Hastie, at the request of Rahdahmah, who supplied him with the requisite means for that purpose. The men were landed, on their arrival, unknown to the prince, and introduced among some troops about to be reviewed by him. He appeared; the band struck up a martial air; and Rahdahmah, equally astonished and delighted, stood entranced as it were with admiration. He hurried them over such pieces as he did not like, but carefully noted down the names of those that pleased him on a slip of paper, which he always carried in his watch-case for the purpose of writing notes on it.[10]

Radama valued the Mauritius-trained musicians so highly that he quartered them in the palace grounds in Antananarivo and had them accompany him on all excursions and military campaigns. In September 1825, Coppalle, who lodged in the palace, stated that it contained three distinct enclosures, the largest of which resembled 'a small town'. It housed, in addition to the king's wives, his musicians and singers, as well as the royal stables, armoury, and courtly school.[11] Coppalle noted that in late October, upon returning from a military expedition, Radama was greeted by a volley of cannon fire, then entered the capital

accompanied by his guard comprising some 3,000 men including the Tsi-mandoua [*Tsimandoa*] ('who have no heartache'), or bodyguards. All these troops, armed and dressed in English style, advanced in good order ... the artillery led the way, followed by the musicians, and then the companies of [royal] guards.[12]

Two days later, Coppalle noted that 'Early this morning, a bull and a cow were sacrificed, after which ceremony the King emerged with his musicians, singers, and Tsimandoua to go, I know not where, to fulfill some religious duty.'[13] And a week later, after remarking that Radama 'leads a very extraordinary life', Coppalle commented with some exasperation, 'The [royal] music plays continually throughout the day and a good part of the night. The dances sometimes stop around midnight, when there is a moment of calm, but suddenly the noise starts again.'[14]

The musicians played major roles at all royal ceremonies. Thus, on 16 March 1826, when Rasalimo, Radama's Sakalava bride, returned to Antananarivo from a country retreat (possibly Ambohimanga), where she had given birth to a baby girl called Raketaka, Coppalle wrote,

---

[10] Thomas Boteler, *Narrative of a Voyage of Discovery to Africa and Arabia, Performed in His Majesty's Ships, Leven and Baracouta from 1821 to 1826. Under the Command of Capt. F. W. Owen*, vol. 2 (London: Richard Bentley, 1835), 142–3.

[11] André Coppalle, entry for 25 Sep 1825, in Coppalle, 'Voyage dans l'intérieure', 55–6.

[12] André Coppalle, entry for 29 Oct. 1825, in Coppalle, 'Voyage dans l'intérieure', 62.

[13] André Coppalle, entry for 29 Oct. 1825, in Coppalle, 'Voyage dans l'intérieure', 63.

[14] André Coppalle, entry for 5 Nov. 1825, in Coppalle, 'Voyage dans l'intérieure', 63.

At 3 o'clock in the afternoon, the king and queens assembled at the entrance to the city, to meet the newly-born child, whose approach was heralded by a cannon fire. At 4 o'clock, the procession set off towards the palace, the king at the head accompanied by his leading officers and musicians, escorted by his Tsimandoua.[15]

It is of note that, on 27 March, the king also gave his musicians prominence at an official inspection of the mission schools, from which he drafted the top students into royal administration and army:

The most successful student received his award from the king who told them [the students] that he regarded this award as an incentive for them to work unceasingly to make themselves capable of being, subsequently, useful to their country and king. The band then played *God Save the King*, and the meeting ended.[16]

Radama had his Mauritius-trained musicians instruct other Malagasy, probably selected from the ranks of the army and from the *Olomainty*, or royal slaves. They taught them chiefly martial airs and to play European instruments, including the violin.[17] Thus Henry Cole (1820–1827), Lowry Cole's nephew, commented of the royal band that played when he had an audience with the king in Tamatave on 16 July 1827, 'the Music ... merits certain portion of praise, but as their numbers have been augmented considerably by new hands who have received their education at Madagascar only, a mixture of good and bad, true and false notes, necessarily struck the ear'.[18]

In his turn, upon first meeting Radama in Tamatave in late October 1827, Lyall noted, 'Having entered the Battery on horse-back, about 500 troops, all in English uniform, and drawn up around the square, presented arms to me, while the band struck up 'God save the King,' and I returned the Salute.' He commented on the continual presence of 'a band of forty black Musicians playing English, Scotch, and native airs'. He noted further, 'The music was tolerable, but still a number of false notes and an occasional want of concord struck the ear.' During an audience with Radama, Lyall noted that the band played 'God Save the King', 'Rule Britannia', 'The British Grenadiers', the tunes to several 'country' dances. They also accompanied Lyall when he sang 'Auld Lang Syne'.[19] And of a subsequent meeting with the king, to which he took Henry Morgan, his private secretary, Lyall wrote,

We drank some porter and wine, and then adjoined to the yard, to see the amusements. Radama conducted me into the middle of a circle of probably 150 men and women, arranged in bands of about 20 of each sex alternatively. In the centre were the musicians, seven in number: one beat with sticks upon a small brass pan; one beat upon a small

---

[15] André Coppalle, entry for 16 Mar. 1826, in Coppalle, 'Voyage dans l'intérieure', 80.
[16] André Coppalle, entry for 27 Mar. 1826, in Coppalle, 'Voyage dans l'intérieure', 83.
[17] *HdR*, 1063.   [18] Henry Cole, Memorandum, [Tamatave], Jul. 1827, HB 4, NAM.
[19] Lyall, journal entries for 29 and 30 Oct. 1827, Add. 3408, BL and CO 167/116, NAK.

oblong drum; one played upon a kind of simple coarse pipe (like the Russian Rojók); another played upon a kind of flageolet &c.

The noise was excessive, and so inharmonious, that it was sufficient to rupture the drums of one's ears.

The dancers went through a variety of steps and motions with joined hands, the whole immense circle moving, at the same time, to the sound of the music. Afterwards, the men entered the circle by pairs, and performed a not ungracefull kind of dance. Toward the conclusion, the large circle was converted into three or four smaller circles, one within the other, and we and the Musicians still in the centre. After about half an hour's duration, the ceremonies were ended by an uproarious cry, in compliment to the King.

We now sat down under the Veranda, and I desired Mr. Morgan to give us a few tunes solus upon the flute, as a contrast to the ear-rending noise we had just heard. He played 'God Save the King,' 'Auld Lang Syne' &c. &c., and concluded by a Country dance. During the latter, all the people, who had been very attentive, began to dance, and were very merry.[20]

Lyall also recorded the king's concern at popular opposition to the musicians:

My people ... even now ask me boldly why I forget the customs and manners of my ancestors; why I put on fine uniforms like white men ... why my soldiers are clothes and disciplined like Europeans; why I have foreign music; and such like questions; and they conclude by praying me to relinquish them all, and return to the days of yore.[21]

Nevertheless, by 1828, Radama had formed two military brass bands in Antananarivo, the first comprising musicians trained on Mauritius playing instruments imported from Britain, and the second local Malagasy, trained in the capital by those who had returned from Mauritius. Radama employed them often, and other members of the Merina elite also requested their services. These included performances for the royal ancestors. Thus, Lyall noted that

Andriamamba, one of the Chief Ministers, whom I have frequently maintained is a man, I should think, about sixty years of age. Sometime ago, he petitioned the late King to grant him his band of Musicians to play at his house, because Radama's father Andrianampouimerina had sent for him – of course from the other world. The monarch laughed heartily, sent Andriamamba a piece of money, and granted him his wish. Accordingly, the band played to the old man, long and loud, while he sat on a kind of coarse national palanquin (filasan) [filanzana] laughing and amusing himself with his jolly wives, children, relations and friends, who were awaiting his doom. But there had been some mistake in the matter, and he did not die at this period.

A short time afterwards, however, the dead Sovereign, Andrianampouimerrina, a second time sent for Andriamamba, and the same farce, to the great amusement of Radama, was gone through, and with a similar result. The Minister, to avoid the ridicule of the Court, wittily said: 'I believe I am mistaken, it was Radama and not Andrianampouimerina who sent for me.'[22]

---

[20] Lyall, journal entry for 2 Nov. 1827, Add. 3408, BL.
[21] Lyall, journal entry for 29 Oct. 1827, Add. 3408, BL.
[22] Lyall, journal entry for 4 Dec. 1828, Add. 3408, BL.

Radama was so fond of the bands that, in the first half of 1828, as his health grew progressively worse, he resisted pressure from his courtiers to have the *tangena* poison ordeal, the customary manner of disclosing acts of sorcery, from being applied to either the *Tsimandoa* (a group of royal slaves), or the musical bandsmen, in order to ascertain if they were responsible for the king's illness.[23]

Radama's death, on 27 July 1828, was initially kept secret. Indeed, the same day it was announced that the sovereign was feeling better, and music was played in front of the palace. From 30 to 31 July 'The chief judges organised competitions between the musicians; the *Tsimandoa* played the Arab drum and hit the bass drum which is used for dances; they fired muskets and danced.'[24] Only on 1 August was it announced that the king had died and that Ranavalona, his chief wife, was the new sovereign.[25] The bandsmen, always in dress, figured extensively in Radama's funeral celebrations. Thus, on 13 August 1828, the day that Radama was entombed, an eyewitness recorded that

During the whole of this day, while the chamber in the tomb was being prepared, the king's two bands of music, with drums and fifes, &c., were in the court, and played almost unceasingly, relieving each other by turns. The tunes were such as Radama most delighted in, many of the peculiar and favourite tunes of England, Scotland and Ireland, with waltzes, marches, &c. During intervals, cannon and musketry were fired outside the courts of the palace, and answered by musketry fired by the numerous soldiers inside the court.[26]

Ranavalona and European Music

Ranavalona fully embraced the musical bands, which, throughout her reign, remained a salient feature of royal ceremony. The queen dictated that the period of mourning for Radama, during which all festivals and non-essential activities were banned, would last for ten months until 27 May 1829. This ban included the playing of musical instruments, song, and dance.[27] Nevertheless, Ranavalona broke the interdiction by holding a party in the royal palace on the evening of 8 December 1828 in which the foreign-trained musicians played a prominent role. Lyall commented of the event,

---

[23] *HdR*, 1123.
[24] *HdR*, 1124; see also Guillaume Grandidier, *Histoire physique, naturelle et politique de Madagascar* (Paris: Imprimerie Paul Brodard 1942), vol. 5, book 1, 215.
[25] *HdR*, 1124; Grandidier, *Histoire physique* (1942), vol. 5, book 1, 215.
[26] George Bennet, 'Funeral of King Radama', *Asiatic Journal* (1 Sep. 1829), 362; *HdR*, 1126–30.
[27] Ellis, *History of Madagascar*, vol. 2, 398–9.

the Queen had all the individuals immediately attached to her, and of all ranks, not forgetting the servants – in a word, all within the palace yard – assembled, and they made merry in the manner of the Country – eating and drinking (but not of Spirituous liquors) &c. and listening to the music of the band, till one o'Clock this morning. They were warned, however, that though Her Majesty had ordered this joyful meeting to relieve their minds a little, who had so long mourned, yet that they were not to give way to mirth at home, nor at any time, without permission.[28]

On Friday 12 June 1829, under the direction of 'Lieutenant-Colonel Bena [or Benea]', the bands also performed at the coronation of Ranavalona.[29] It was noted of the occasion,

At the dawn of day on Friday the 12th . . . cannon were fired to give notice that the day for the coronation had arrived. At half-past ten the drums were beat and the trumpets were blown, as a sign to prepare for the grand ceremony. At twelve precisely the drums and trumpets were again flourished, to assemble the military officers of the first rank, and the bourgeois, in the courtyard of the palace called Tranavola.

The same was also the signal for those in the grand place of concourse [Andohalo], to put themselves in readiness to receive the Queen, who was about to appear for the first time before her subjects, and before the strangers (Missionaries and other Europeans). So soon as the first officers had entered the courtyard of the royal palace, orders were issued to Lieutenant-Colonel Benea, at the head of the royal band of music, and three hundred grenadiers, the Queen's body-guards, in full dress, in the style of British soldiers . . .

The Queen, surrounded by her guards, singers, attendants, &c. finely dressed, entered the public street through the north gate of the courtyard . . . Lieutenant-Colonel Benea marched at the head of the band of music taught at Tananarivo, then the grenadiers, then the whole infantry composing the royal guards. Afterwards the Hovan [Merina] bourgeois, according to the European mode; then the second band of music, taught at the Mauritius, playing on their new instruments from England . . .

Her Majesty having come to the south side of the stage, erected for her to stand upon and address the people, was then carried to the sacred stone, about one hundred yards west from the stage, preceded by five of her first generals, with their caskets in one hand, and their swords drawn in the other; she was then put down in her palanquin south of the holy stone. She got out of her palanquin without any aid, and mounted the stone. While this was being done, the national air was played by the two bands.[30]

As indicated, Ranavalona was as fond of the musicians as her predecessor, employing them on almost all publicly celebrated royal occasions. All of her subjects able to do so would be duty bound to attend. British army officer,

---

[28] Lyall, journal entry for 9 Dec. 1828, Add. 3408, BL; see also Grandidier, *Histoire physique* (1942), vol. 5, book 1, 217; Guillaume Grandidier, 'À Madagascar, anciennes croyances et coutumes', *Journal de la Société des Africanistes* 2.2 (1932), 193, 197.

[29] 'Coronation of Ranavalomanjaka' [mid-Jun 1829], MIL B.3 F.3 J.B, SOAS/CWM; Ellis, *History of Madagascar*, vol. 2, 422–3.

[30] 'Splendid Coronation of the Queen Ranovalo Manjaka, the Successor of Radama, Late King of Madagascar', *The Mirror of Literature, Amusement, and Instruction* 16 (1830), 116–19.

Samuel Oliver (1838–1907), noted the evocative nature of such an event in Antananarivo on 15 August 1862, one year after the death of Ranavalona, and which would have characterized many similar happenings during her reign:

About ten o'clock the Queen's filanzana [palanquin] stopped the way, and this broke up the party, which formed in procession and accompanied the King and Queen back to the palace. As it was an hour after gun-fire, the whole town was deserted and dark, but at the sound of the King's band of music the inhabitants rushed out of their houses all along our road with torches and lighted bundles of dry grass and straw. This rude impromptu illumination had a fine effect. Wherever the procession passed, men and women were ready with torches and firebrands, lighting them just as the head of the procession reached them, and extinguishing them directly after the rear of it had passed. The fixed bayonets and the brass instruments with the gilt appointments and accoutrements of the King and his court flashed in the red torchlight. The Queen and her attendants, whose gay ball-dresses were now covered with rich coloured silk lambas, were borne in their filanzanas, each surrounded by white-robed female slaves. The rattle of the drums with the clang of cymbals, and the ringing brass instruments, made the old streets rattle again with martial music, the whole forming a splendid though barbaric pageant. The rear was brought up by the screaming and clap-clapper, clap-clap, of the singing women, while the cheering of the crowds that lines the walls and houses, each person waving a flaming brand, was taken up in succession from street to street like a rolling wave, 'Trarantitra Ts-a-ra-a-a . . . a Tomp . . . qu-a-a Veloma Ra-da-a . . . ama!' ['May you live long, Radama'][31]

It was commented in 1846 that at the elite monthly balls which Ranavalona hosted at her palace, '*French dances* begin and open the ball to the sound of military music. This music, which was instituted by Radama, is quite passable.'[32] Her son, Rakoto, the heir apparent, formed his own band. Thus, in late August or early September 1856, when Rakoto invited visiting LMS Director William Ellis to Mahazoarivo, the royal 'country house' just outside Antananarivo, the party was led by 'the prince's band of nineteen musicians, including five clarionets, five flutes and fifes, one bassoon, four bugles, a bass and a smaller drum, and a triangle', playing European music, 'preceded and followed by two officers with drawn swords'.[33] Ellis had brought with him from Britain some newly composed pieces of music that he presented to the court, which was delighted with them.[34]

Ellis made no mention of the 'two or three military bands' and 'organs with a number of exchange cylinders' that a French newspaper claimed Delastelle had taken from France to Madagascar in 1843 as presents for Ranavalona.[35] Certainly in 1855, Joseph-François Lambert (1824–1873), a French trader and adventurer, who in 1854 had established close relations with the Merina court,

---

[31] Samuel Pasfield Oliver, *Madagascar and the Malagasy: With Sketches in the Provinces of Tamatave, Betanimena, and Ankova* (London: Day & Son, [1866]), 65.

[32] Alexandre Garnot, *Question de Madagascar traitée au point de vue de l'intérêt français et du droit publique européenne* (Bordeaux: P. Coudert, 1846), 7, fn. 1.

[33] Ellis, *Three Visits* (1858), 329–30.   [34] Ellis, *Three Visits* (1858), 345.

[35] Quoted in 'Magnificence of the Court of Tananarivo', *Morning Post* (14 Apr. 1843).

presented Ranavalona with a harmonium, invented and manufactured by Alexandre-François Debain (1809–1877) of Paris. The harmonium could be played 'in the manner of a barrel-organ by turning a handle or "manivelle"'.[36] At some point, Ranavalona was also presented with a piano. However, she found no one competent to play the instrument. In June 1857, after learning that visiting Austrian voyager Ida Pfeiffer was an accomplished pianist, Ranavalona commanded her to play the piano in the palace courtyard while she observed from her balcony. Despite the instrument being out of tune, and some keys difficult to move, Pfeiffer banged out a waltz and a march to the approval of the queen.[37] Sibree, during his first stint as an LMS missionary in Antananarivo from 1863 to 1867, noted that the crown owned the only piano in the country but that Merina craftsmen had made several harmoniums.[38]

As under Radama, so under Ranavalona, the new musical bands played a central role in all military manoeuvres. It was noted that

When the queen appears in the public eye and she attends a military parade, up close or from afar, she is accompanied by the red parasol. When she comes to attend a parade, the whole troop stands up to the command of the officers and presents arms to the Queen, at the same time as the music sounds. The sound of a fanfare is a customary practice, in the presence of the Queen, as a salute, at the same time that arms are presented ... After which the fanfare again sounded in honour of the Prime Minister ...

Here is the idea regarding music, each time it starts up: 'The Queen must be greeted by musical sound', even if she does not appear; this is the way to recognize it. The soldiers who are on guard inside the Palace also greet the Queen every day, without exception, with the 'Presenter Arms'; it's their way of recognizing it ... Officers of ten honours and above are saluted with a musical fanfare; it is a mark of respect that the queen shows them.[39]

Indeed, the bands were present, and played, at every royal occasion:

When she [Ranavalona] crosses a river, either over a bridge, or by canoe, or looks for ford, or simply frolics in the water, the brass band plays the *sidikina* (God save the Queen) or presents arms until the passage is made, that is to say until the queen is out of the water or difficult passage. The *sidikina* is also played when the queen chews tobacco. If she makes the slightest movement to leave or to move around a little, she is given the same honour.[40]

So closely associated were the European-style military brass bands with the crown that, by the close of Ranavalona's reign, every governor of a garrison within the Merina imperial domain possessed, or aspired to possess, one (see Figure 6.1).

---

[36] Ida Pfeiffer, *The Last Travels of Ida Pfeiffer: Inclusive of a Visit to Madagascar: with a Biographical Memoir of the Author* (London: Routledge, Warne and Routledge, 1861), 271; see also Joris Verdin, 'Les Grands moments de l'harmonium' Référence Harmonium (2011) – https://lirias.kuleuven.be/1916211?limo=0 (accessed 05/06/21); Arthur W. J. G. Ord-Hume, 'The Confused World of the Mechanical Organ', *Organists' Review* (Sep. 2019): 8–15.

[37] [Pfeiffer], *Last Travels*, 275–6.   [38] Sibree, *Madagascar and Its People*, 235.

[39] *HdR*, 363.   [40] *HdR*, 363.

Figure 6.1 Merina band and officers, Tamatave Fort, 1863
Source: *Illustrated London News* (8 Nov. 1863), 497.

Thus, in early 1863, a British army captain, W. Rooke noted of the garrison at Mahanoro, on the mid-east coast of the island,

Soon after taking possession of our quarters we heard strains of music proceeding from the Governor's residence at the battery ... About half an hour after our arrival he made his appearance, accompanied by his favourite wife, as also by his principal officers and their wives, a guard of honour and a brass band ...

Early the next morning, he came down to see us, accompanied by his officers and band, and remained upwards of an hour, examining our fire-arms and drinking brandy, the band meanwhile playing several English and Scotch tunes very well. At 5 P.M. we took our departure, the whole party coming down to see us of, and the band playing 'God save the Queen.'[41]

Military bands were retained by the Merina regime up to the French takeover of the island in 1895 when the new French colonial authorities incorporated the brass bands of the imperial Merina army into their own military.

Recall of the Naval Youths

When Radama died in July 1828, some Madagascar Youths were still being trained in seamanship by the British Navy, the world's premier naval force. Despite Radama's lack of success in forming a fleet, Ranavalona maintained her predecessor's vision that the naval apprentices should form the core manpower of a future Merina navy. Thus, on 7 October 1828, she wrote to five of them, Ranenja, Kanera, Razahara, Ramanankoriaisina, and Rainiaramanana:

And saith Ranavalomanjaka, when you know how to navigate a Ship, you will leave the whites. When you arrive, inform me, and we shall buy vessels in which you shall assume your positions. If your knowledge is still insufficient, continue to learn; and once your training is complete, inform me, and we shall buy ships in which you shall be placed. You must pay attention to all that you do. I succeed Andrianampoinimerina and Lahidama [Radama], and you need not fear me. Do you understand the language of the Whites? If any one of you wishes to inform me of something, write to me that I may know of it. Do not let the Whites or any of your comrades see this letter. This letter is for you.[42]

At the same time, she wrote to Captain Charles James Polkinghorne (fl. 1808–32),[43] asking, 'have the young men learned what has been taught

---

[41] W. Rooke, 'A Boat-Voyage along the Coast-Lakes of East Madagascar', *Journal of the Royal Geographical Society of London* 36 (1866), 58; see also Joseph Mullens, *Twelve Months in Madagascar* (London: James Nisbet, 1875), 33.

[42] Ranavalona to Ranenja, Kanera Razahara, Ramanankoriaisina, and Rainiaramanana, Tananarivou, 7 Oct. 1820, HB 20, NAM.

[43] [Admiralty], *The Navy List, corrected to the 20th December 1848* (London: John Murray, 1849), 66; Peter J. Howes (ed.), 'The Journal of Elizabeth Cozens', MA thesis, University of Cape Town (1993), 299, esp. fn. 103; John Marshall, 'Royal Naval Biography/Polkinghorne,

them?'[44] A year later, Lyall informed Charles Colville (1770–1843), governor of Mauritius from 1828 to 1834, that the queen

wished to be informed whether the said thirty Madagascar Youths are capable <u>alone</u> of navigating a ship from one part of the world to another – i.e. whether there are individuals among them who could act as Captains, Sailing –masters, Lieutenants, Midshipmen, mates, marines &c. &c ... I warned the [queen's] deputation that as the thirty youths were on board different ships, Your Excellency might be obliged to communicate with Admiral Schomberg.[45]

Lyall's comment reveals that by mid-1829, of the fifty Madagascar Youths chosen to be train as naval apprentices, only thirty remained aboard British naval vessels. They had served since 1824 on ships surveying the Mozambique and Malagasy coasts of the Mozambique Channel, regions where malaria was endemic. It was therefore highly likely that they had been exposed to the disease. Unlike the peoples of coastal Madagascar, highland Malagasy did not possess the sickle cell trait, so the Merina naval apprentices would have been as vulnerable to malaria as European sailors.[46] This may have formed the core of complaints by the Madagascar Youths to the Merina court and their parents, although some also felt slighted at being treated as if they were common seamen and not receiving a higher education. As Lyall informed the governor of Mauritius in July 1829,

In consequence of the discussions which have been lately agitated respecting the Madagascar youths on board the Cape Squadron, I deem it my duty to inform Your Excellency, that Louis had seven letters put into his hands by that part of them on board the *Maidstone* and the *Falcon*; some addressed to Andrimiady (the efficient King); some to Andianiss (another Youth in favor with the Queen of Madagascar and the Ministers of the old <u>reign</u>); and the rest to their parents. To Louis, they expressed much discontentment with their present situation, and a strong desire to return to their country, Imerina. They also complained that they are merely taught to be <u>sailors</u>, and added that when Captain Dunn was at Tamatave in 1827, he promised to Radama, on board the *Samarang*, that they should be taught '<u>every thing</u>'.[47]

To put this in context, British naval ships had limited means at their disposal to educate crew. Thus James Prior, of HMS *Nisus*, when sailing in the

James' – https://en.wikisource.org/wiki/Royal_Naval_Biography/Polkinghorne,_James (accessed 15/05/19).

[44] Ranavalona to Polkinghorne, Tananarivou, Oct. 1828, HB 20, NAM.

[45] Lyall to Colville, Tamatave, 9 Jun. 1829, CO 167/116, NAK.

[46] Ellis, *History of Madagascar*, vol. 1, 214; Elise Juzda Smith, '"Cleanse or Die": British Naval Hygiene in the Age of Steam, 1840–1900', *Medical History* 62.2 (2018), 181; Gwyn Campbell, 'Malaria in Precolonial Imerina (Madagascar), 1795–1895', in Gwyn Campbell and Eva-Maria Knoll, *Disease Dispersion and Impact in the Indian Ocean World* (London: Palgrave Macmillan, 2020), 129–67.

[47] Lyall to Colville, Bois Cherri, 28 Jul. 1829, HB 20, NAM; see also Lyall to Colville, Tamatave, 9 Jun. 1829, CO 167/116, NAK.

Mozambique Channel in 1812, commented, 'Often have we to lament the destiny that makes us strangers to general literature; for alas! A ship library, like sea education, is too strongly affected by imperious circumstances, to embrace the admixture of a great variety of subjects'.[48] Certainly Raombana reported that naval apprentices learned 'only a little bad English' – meaning swear words – in their time aboard British ships[49]

The French Attack of 1829–30

In early 1829, suddenly alert to the possibility of a French attack on Madagascar, Ranavalona ordered the return of the naval apprentices. The threat materialized when a frigate under Commandant Jean-Baptiste Gourbeyre (1786–1845) was in June 1829 despatched from Réunion with orders to eject the Merina from the northeast coast of Madagascar between Antongil Bay and Tamatave, a region to which France laid claim, and to occupy the port of Tintingue, near Manompana, in Antongil Bay. On 9 July, Gourbeyre, anchored off Tamatave, issued an ultimatum to the Merina governor of the fort there and, while waiting for a response from Antananarivo, sailed north to occupy Tintingue. When the Merina governor of Foulepointe responded by despatching soldiers to Taingitaingy (Pointe-à-Larée), close to Tintingue and opposite the French-held island of Sainte-Marie, Gourbeyre declared war.[50]

He sailed back to Tamatave, where, on 11 October, he blew up the Merina powder stocks and seized the port, forcing the Merina first to retreat some 30 km to the interior and, upon a further French advance, to flee. Although the French assault, in which some fifty Merina troops died, caused initial panic at the Merina court, Ranavalona quickly despatched 3,000 British-trained troops against the French.[51] Before that, on 13 October, HMS *Falcon*, under Captain Colpoys, arrived off Tamatave with twenty-three or twenty-four of the Malagasy naval apprentices.[52] Rather than risk confrontation, Colpoys sailed to Foulepointe where on 16 October he landed the

[48] James Prior, *Voyage along the Eastern Coast of Africa: To Mosambique, Johanna, and Quiloa; to St. Helena; to Rio de Janeiro, Bahia, and Pernambuco in Brazil, in the Nisus Frigate* (London: Richard Phillips, 1819), 45–6.

[49] RA, 211, 437.

[50] Coroller to Captain Colpoys (HMS *Falcon*), Ivondro. 12 Oct. 1829, quoted in James Holman, *Voyage round the World, including Travels in Africa, Asia, Australasia, America, etc. etc. from 1827 to 1832* (London: Smith, Elder, 1835), vol. 3, 156–7; Jean Louis Joseph Carayon, *Histoire de l'établissement français de Madagascar pendant la Restauration* (Paris: Gide, 1845), 102–12.

[51] RA, 228–32; Carayon, *Histoire de l'établissement français*, 113–15.

[52] James Holman, *Travels in Madras, Ceylon, Mauritius, Comoro Islands, Zanzibar, Calcutta, Etc. Etc.* (London: Routledge, 1840), 155.

Madagascar Youths.[53] Carayon considered that these men, the bulk of the remaining Malagasy naval apprentices, hugely bolstered Merina defences because of their 'British' discipline and anti-French zeal. On 27 October 1829, the French frigate *Terpishore* bombarded Foulepointe, forcing the retreat of the Merina troops, but the 200-strong French force that attacked the second Merina position was repulsed. Colpoys commented,

From Tamatave the French proceeded to Foule Pointe, where the inhabitants were better prepared to receive them, and where they were consequently repulsed on the first attack with considerable loss; upon this occasion the success of the Madagascans was imputed to the superior tactics of the young men who had served in the British squadron; and where they had learnt the exercise of the great guns with such advantage, that although they had only two small guns, they managed them so well that they sank one of the French boats, killed several persons in others, and finally compelled the assailants to return to their ships.[54]

However, upon visiting Tamatave in October 1830, an English officer aboard the *Jaseur* was told that fear of being burned alive, the punishment for desertion in the Merina army, was the greater motivation for the Merina defenders:

This accounts in a great measure for the determined resistance the French had recently met with at Foule Point ... Several of '*La Brave nation*' had their ears cut off at that attack and I found at Majunga a young man who said he had performed that operation on two or three before their heads were taken off – serve-um right too.[55]

For his part, Lyall noted that, overall, the biggest threat to the French during the 1829 campaign in Madagascar was not Merina resistance but the ravages of disease, notably malaria:

Were the Malagashes aware of the enormous losses of the french expedition, probably they would not have taken such precautionary measures.

General Death, as the late Radama well named that mortal disease, the endemical fever of the Island, is fighting the Malagashes' Battles more effectually than cannon, musquets, or sagayes.

One report gives us to understand that of 1,500 men originally under Gourbeyre's command, only four Hundred are now alive, and that many of these are sick!!!! If this be true, from the physical impossibility of its being successful, we may reckon that no fresh attack will be made by the French upon the coast of Madagascar this season unless the expedition be powerfully reinforced.[56]

---

[53] Freeman, 'Journal from 30th September, on leaving Tananarivo, to 6th November 1829; when he sailed from Tamatave, aboard the "Radama", for Mauritius', Journals B.2 1824–94, SOAS/CWM; *Colonial Times* (26 Feb. 1830), 3; Holman, *Voyage round the World*, vol. 3, 157.

[54] [Colpoys] quoted in Holman, *Voyage round the World*, vol. 3, 160; see also RA, 225.

[55] Arthur Frankland, 'Ten Weeks Leave of Absence: Cruise from Mauritius to Madagascar and East Coast of Africa', ref. 216, Plymouth and West Devon Record Office (hereafter PWDRO).

[56] Lyall, 'Journal', 17 Apr. 1830, HB 20, NAM.

Table 6.1 *Merina casualties in the*
Franco-Merina War, 1829

Location	Killed	Wounded
Tamatave	53	6
Ambatomany	51	5
Foulepointe	75	50
Pointe-à-Larée	125	55

Source: Gourbeyre, 10 Dec. 1829, in Anon, *Précis sur*
les établissements français formés à Madagascar
(Paris: Imprimerie Royale, 1836), 58.

However, the Merina considered the military engagements to have been a major triumph, despite their higher losses. In the battle at Foulepointe, seventy-five Merina were killed and fifty injured, as against eleven French killed and twenty-six wounded.[57] According to Coroller, a total of 304 Merina were killed and 116 wounded in the Franco-Merina hostilities along the northeast coast (see Table 6.1).

Some accounts reported that the French governor of Sainte-Marie was killed in the attack and his 'head was sent on a pole to the Queen of the Island',[58] while Griffiths commented,

When news of the victory reached Antananarivo, the queen and her coterie jumped for joy. Her closest advisers counselled her to resist the French to the bitter end, saying, 'We would all prefer to perish before seeing these pirates seize possession of one acre of our island. These white men are like frogs – in their element whilst in water, but to the contrary when upon land. Sea-bound in their ships they are invincible, but once they step ashore it is a very simple affair to defeat them.'[59]

The last five Madagascar Youths apprenticed aboard British ships missed action against the French. They left the Cape for Mauritius in June 1829 in a fleet that included HMS *Maidstone* and HMS *Falcon* commanded by Commodore Schomberg. At Mauritius, they were transferred, first to HMS *Helicon,* and then to the *Jaseur* (see Figure 6.2). While on the *Jaseur,* they served as interpreters when at Anjouan, on 28 August 1829, Captain John Lyons (who served on the Cape Station from mid-1828 to mid-1830) met Ramanetaka (c.1780–1841), cousin of Radama, and King of Moheli (r. 1830–

---

[57] Hastie, 'Diary' (1824–5), CO 167/78, NAK; Guillaume Grandidier, *Histoire physique, naturelle et politique de Madagascar* (Paris: Hachette, 1928), 163; Carayon, *Histoire de l'établissement français*, 116–18.

[58] *Colonial Times* (26 Feb. 1830), 3; see also *Caledonian Mercury* 16286 (12 Jan. 1826).

[59] David Griffiths, *Hanes Madagascar* (Machynlleth: Richard Jones, 1843), 55.

Figure 6.2 HMS *Jaseur*, standing in to Mauritius, 1830
Source: Frankland, 'Ten Weeks Leave of Absence'.

41),.[60] In late 1828, the people of Moheli, which is one of the Comoro Islands, had expelled the governor imposed by Abdallah bin Alawi, sultan of Anjouan from 1816, and elected as ruler one of their own. However, in September 1829, Lyons interceded on behalf of Abdallah and obliged the rebels to resubmit to his authority. Subsequently, Ramanetaka forced Abdallah to flee. In 1836, Abdallah launched an abortive invasion of Moheli, was shipwrecked, and was captured by Ramanetaka, who starved him to death. Abdallah's son, Alawi, briefly succeeded him as sultan of Anjouan (r. 1836–7).[61]

After their visit to Moheli, the Madagascar Youths aboard the *Jaseur*, 'constituting the remnant of all those who had been employed in the Cape squadron',[62] were taken to Mauritius and transferred onto the *Vittoria*, commanded by Lieutenant Nash. James Holman (1786–1857), the 'blind traveller', noted from Mauritius on 7 November 1829,

[60] Holman, *Travels in Madras*, 7; Nelson Lambert, 'Africa – HMS Maidstone, part 2', in *Acta Militaria* – http://nelsonlambert.blogspot.com/2011/06/africa-hms-maidstone-part-2.html (2011) (accessed 14/05/19).

[61] Holman, *Voyage round the World*, vol. 3, 20–34, 38–41; RA, 195; William Dallas Bernard, *Narrative of the Voyages and Services of the Nemesis* (London: Henry Colburn, 1845), 58–9; Bernhard Struck, 'An Unpublished Vocabulary of the Comoro Language', *Journal of the Royal African Society* 8.32 (1909), 415; H. A. Moriarty, *South Indian Ocean Pilot, for the Islands Westward of Longitude 80° East, including Madagascar and the Comoro Islands* (London: Taylor, Garnet, Evans & Co., 1911), 195; Jacques de Saint-Ours, '*Étude morphologique* et géologique de l'archipel des Comores', *BAM* 34 (1956), 8; Jeremy Prestholdt, 'Similitude and Empire: On Comorian Strategies of Englishness', *Journal of World History* 18.2 (2007), 129–31; Gwyn Campbell, *David Griffiths and the Missionary 'History of Madagascar'* (Leiden: Brill, 2012), 1077.

[62] Holman, *Travels in Madras*, vol. 3, 155; see also 108.

I accompanied Lieut. Nash of the *Tweed*, to take tiffin at the Government House, after which he embarked in the *Vittoria*, a merchant ship, bound to Madagascar with the people of that nation, who had been serving as supernumeries on board H.M.S. *Jaseur*, and who had been recalled by their Queen to their own country.[63]

Eleven months later, when HMS *Jaseur* visited Tamatave, a British officer aboard the vessel observed of a Merina official stationed at the port,

The Colonel of Artillery was one of those youths who at the request of King Radama, had been received on board the Men o' War of the Cape Station to be instructed in the arts of Navigation and Seamanship . . . Some of the lads were Princes, and others who afterwards distinguished themselves by working the Guns at 'Foule Point' against the French Squadron, were instantly promoted to the ranks of Captain, Major, Colonel &c. The young Militaire I have above alluded to, enquired after all the English Officers he had been serving under at the Cape and Mauritius, calling them over by their Surnames without giving them their Rank, as if he had been their most intimate friend. He told us we should go to 'Tananarivo' (the Capital) that place all same England must be, but when we came to 'Tamatave' all the same as me go board ship, but me Colonel and me make me happy like Captain man o' war who make all good for himself first, then take care Ships Company.

His uniform was red with blue velvet facings and a great quantity of gold lace. His Epaulettes, he gave us to understand, he had left at Tananarivo, he had several pair but that as he only came to Tamatave to inspect a few troops he had not thought it necessary to bring them. He wore also a curious pair of striped trousers and a cock'd Hat and Staff plume. All the officers seemed very proud of their dresses, one in particular with a rich gold laced coat and silver epaulettes, who came on board with some friends. It was highly amusing to see how annoyed he was when the skirts of his surtout coat hid the gold lace on his trousers, and he every now and then stuck out his legs half across the Gun Room in order that we might all see his finery. We asked our visitors to dinner, but the mention of that meal turned them all sea sick and they begged for a boat to go ashore in.[64]

On 22 October 1830, when HMS *Jaseur* anchored off Majunga, the same British officer commented,

We met at Majunga two more of those lads who had been serving in our Fleet. They had been placed on board the *Maidstone*. Both of them were suffering from the Madagascar fever and were too unwell to remain below where they had been conducted by the [Middies] to drink Grog. They were full Colonels.[65]

Ramaharo and Ramiaramanana

There is little in the archives about the subsequent careers of the naval return-ees, except for two individuals, Ramaharo and Ramiaramanana. In about 1836, Ramaharo, who Ranavalona had chosen to form part of the Merina embassy to Zanzibar, replaced Andrianavalona as governor of the port of Hiarana/

---

[63] Holman, *Voyage round the World*, vol. 3, 108.
[64] Frankland, 'Ten Weeks Leave of Absence'.   [65] Frankland, 'Ten Weeks Leave of Absence'.

Amboanio, on the northeast coast. However, he imposed such heavy *fanom-poana* on the local population, to create rice fields for him, and such higher taxes, that they rose in a revolt joined by the Sakalava of Nosy Be. During the uprising, a large number of Merina were killed including Andrianandrasana, Ramaharo's second in command.[66] Ramaharo married a daughter of Andrianatoro, a local holy man who reputedly possessed the power to control the sea from whence his ancestors originated. When Andrianatoro died, the Merina court appointed two of his sons – who claimed to possess the same powers as their father – to the garrisons at Tamatave and Foulepointe respectively in order to ward off possible attack from Europeans.[67] When Ramaharo died in 1846 or 1847, his brother, Rakabija (Rainikitovao), governor of Ambohitsara (Anonibe), on the east coast, fearing that the court might accuse him of sorcery because of the wealth he had accumulated, fled to Réunion. In consequence, Ranavalona confiscated the property of his family at Antananarivo where, in order to survive, Ramaharo's wife, a non-Merina, was reduced to prostitution.[68]

The other naval apprentice, Ramiaramanana, had attended a mission school in the early 1820s. He was then drafted into the army and, in 1824, chosen to serve aboard a British warship. In 1829, Ranavalona selected Ramiaramanana and Rahaingiomanana, a fellow former naval apprentice, for a special mission. They were sent to Mananjary, on the east coast south of Tamatave, to charter a vessel from the wealthy Réunion merchant, Rontaunay, who in the 1820s had forged commercial agreements with Radama I that were maintained under Ranavalona. The vessel was to sail to Fort Dauphin to seize the possessions of former governor Ramananolana (brother to Ramanetaka), whose execution Ranavalona had ordered in 1828, and return with them to Tamatave, from where they were to be transported to Antananarivo. Failing to charter a ship in Mananjary, Rahaingiomanana and Ramiaramanana travelled to Mauritius in early October 1830 and there hired the *Tiger* (owned by Captain Hunter) for $2,000 and took aboard missionary David Jones as interpreter. The *Tiger*, under Captain Thorn, sailed to Fort Dauphin, and then to Tamatave carrying Ramananolana's wives, some 490 (Raombana claims 900) of his slaves includ-ing many women and children, seven horses, twelve bullocks, and $20,000 in cash. After reaching Tamatave, Ramananolana's former possessions were taken to Antananarivo where Ranavalona retained half and distributed the rest to her paramours – although Raombana claimed that Rahaingiomana and Ramiaramanana also took a slice.[69]

---

[66] RA, 387–8.   [67] RA, 388.   [68] RA, 387–8.

[69] RA, 202–11; Lyall, Journal, 18 Oct. 1830, NAM; 'Case of the Tiger', CO 167/153, NAK; Alfred Grandidier and Guillaume Grandidier, *Histoire physique, naturelle et politique de Madagascar* (Paris: Imprimerie nationale, 1908), vol. 4, book 1, 659.

Of this incident, Arthur Frankland (d. 1843), aide-de-camp to his uncle, Charles Colville, governor of Mauritius, who visited Fort Dauphin aboard the *Jaseur*, commented in November 1830 that Ramananolana

was killed by order of the Queen and one of his Colonels, 'Ramanash' has stept into his shoes. The Spear heads of the Madagascar *Sagayes* are never riveted on to the Shaft. This enables the natives to make use of them at any time as daggers. On the occasion of Ramananoula's death, his attendants had concealed Spear heads under their Lambas [traditional Malagasy outer garment], and an officer, who I think had a share in the murder, shewed me how they approached him and did the deed ... All Ramananoula's goods have been taken away by sea to Tamatave, and his intimate friends, about Four hundred slaves and singing women, were at the same time embarked and claimed by the Queen as her own property. During the embarkation, a man was detected thieving in the village, upon which the present Governor sent him on board as an additional slave.

No one at Fort Dauphin dares to mention the name Ramananoula, but in talking of him they call him Adale (Adale [*adala*] signifies a Fool). On his being murdered, some said he would rise again, so they cut him into four, and buried him under the Flag staff where his own colours had been so lately flying. On his property being seized and carried away, his Flag was destroyed and her Majesty caused her own most extraordinary name to be hoisted in its stead.[70]

On 12 December 1830, upon its return to Port Louis, the *Tiger* was seized by Schomberg, commanding HMS *Maidstone*, who charged Thorn and Jones with slave running. They denied the charges. Thorn stated that all the passengers were Malagasy subjects – not Makua from Mozambique as alleged – and Jones testified that, although formerly slaves, they had upon the death of Ramananolana, become free subjects of the queen, albeit of the lowest rank. Lyall was asked to clarify the legal status of the passengers aboard the *Tiger* but deferred to Jones, whose word Schomberg was reluctantly obliged to accept.[71] In her turn, Ranavalona wrote to Colville in January 1831 stating that all the passengers were free, but that she had punished some who were guilty of rebellion.[72]

---

[70] Frankland, 'Journal of a Cruise in HM Sloop "Jaseur"', entry for 26 Nov. 1830, 216.1, PWDRO.

[71] Jones, 'A Brief statement of a painful but unforeseen Event connected with the voyage on board the Bark Tiger to Fort Dauphin'; Jones to Hankey, Port Louis, 18 Dec. 1830; Jones to Commodore, Port Louis, 21 Dec. 1830; Schomberg to Jones, HMS *Maidstone*, Port Louis, 22 Dec. 1830 – MIL B.3 F.4 J.C, SOAS/CWM; 'Case of the Tiger'; Colville to George Murray, Mauritius, 22 Jan. 1831; John Seddon [Capt of the Colonial Vessel the *Saucy Jack*], Instance Court of the Vice Admiralty, Mauritius, 12 Dec. 1830; Schomberg to Colville, HMS *Maidstone*, Port Louis, 23 Dec. 1830 – CO 167/153, NAK; RA, 333–5, 345–6.

[72] Ranavalomanjaka to Colville, Antananarivo, 22 Adijady (4 Jan.) 1831, CO 167/153, NAK.

In 1830, Ramiaramanana wrote from Antananarivo to Captain Lyons in a language and style which demonstrates that he had indeed received scant schooling in his time aboard British warships:

Sir,

Howar you (Sir) Ramiaramanana say that and is Father and Mother and is Country and is Friend, very glad indiar to you all my country when I tell you Like me very much and the Queen to, hear you Like me Mr Lyons, and fir the gune and the Solders ear the read cot and Below the Music and Dancing all the Off^f and Ferenc when we coming of the Queen sen the Letter to me she say is you Cornel is Right Done my name.

If you Please (Sir) very much Blass to you (Sir) Give me apolet Shod gold Lokhate any you gate Give me for I hav gate non tol

He say
Ramiaramanana

The meaning of the above letter is as follows:

Sir,

How are you (Sir)? Ramiaramanana says that, and his father and mother and his friends and countrymen felt very grateful on hearing how kind you have been to me. The Queen too heard that you like me Mr Lyons and fired the guns, and the Soldiers wore their red coats and blew the music and danced.

All the Officers and Generals were assembled when we approached the Queen's residence. After having remained three days there, the Queen sent me a letter in which she informed me that I was made a Colonel, and that she had written down my name as such.

If you please (Sir) I would be very much obliged to you, if you would give me some epaulettes, a Sword, and a gold-laced cocked Hat. Any you have got give me, for I have none at all.

He Say
Ramiaramanana[73]

The Issue of Ships

Like Radama, Ranavalona envisaged the creation of a Merina navy comprising commandeered boats and a European flagship manned by the Madagascar Youths apprenticed aboard British naval ships. Indeed, through contacts with Swahili and Indian merchants, she did form a temporary fleet at Majunga that was in action from October to November 1831. This 'navy', composed of

[73] Ramiaramanana to Lyons, An Tananarivo, 15 Mar. 1830, in Frankland, *Ten Weeks Leave of Absence*, annex.

dhows, supported 7,000 Merina soldiers, under the command of Ramaromisy, that marched northwards to suppress a Boina Sakalava uprising, led by Andriantsoly. The fleet confiscated the cloth cargoes and cannon of a number of 'enemy' dhows and at Nosy Be seized as slaves some 200 Sakalava – almost certainly women and children – who were subsequently kept at Majunga or sent to Antananarivo for sale.[74]

This event marked an improvement in Merina relations with Swahili and Indian merchants, most of whom had fled Majunga in 1824 following its capture by the Merina. Relations improved further during the closure of Merina-controlled ports to British and French trade from 1845 to 1853. Consequently, many Swahili and Indian merchants returned to Majunga, which, additionally, from the 1820s had become a base for New England traders and, after Nosy Be became a French protectorate in 1840, was also frequented by traders from Réunion. Thus, Majunga's economy revived, and its population increased rapidly – from an estimated 1,368 in 1842 to between 6,000 and 7,000 by the early 1850s.[75]

In addition, Ranavalona turned to her French commercial partners for the use of their ships. Thus, in c.1830, Delastelle transported three Merina generals and forty soldiers aboard *Le Voltigeur* from Mahela to St Augustin Bay to await the arrival of a larger force overland in order to seize the bay from the Sakalava.[76] Frankland, who that same year visited St Augustin aboard the HMS *Jaseur*, from Mauritius, on an anti-slave trade patrol, stated,

At St Augustines, Ranavalona is not acknowledged. They have two head men, King Baba and a savage rascally looking dog with only one eye calling himself the Prince of Wales. The latter came on board with one of his wives and suite. He was very anxious to get a present of a barrel of gunpowder and some muskets, saying that he would afterwards make one in return, but L____ was too well acquainted with the character of these fellows to give them more than a couple of thirty two pounder cartridges for which he got three sheep.[77]

The Merina failed to capture St Augustin, and in 1835 Ranavalona launched another expedition against it. For this, she again hired the *Voltigeur* from Delastelle to sail from Mahela with a detachment of fifty Merina troops commanded by three officers – former British Navy apprentices – and provisions, including rice and rum, to meet the troops marching overland. The land

---

[74] RA, 277, 282; Grandidier, *Histoire physique* (1942), vol. 5, book 1, 264–5.

[75] Joseph Barlow Felt Osgood, *Notes of Travel: Or, Recollections of Majunga, Zanzibar, Muscat, Aden, Mocha, and other Eastern Ports* (Salem: George Creamer, 1854), 7; Samuel F. Sanchez, 'Commerce régional et à longue distance dans l'ouest de Madagascar au XIXème siècle', *Tsingy: Revue de l'Association des professeurs d'histoire et de géographie de Madagascar* 9 (2008), 49–50.

[76] He was unable to remain because of the presence of many whaling ships in the bay – Grandidier and Grandidier, *Histoire physique* (1908), vol. 4, book 1, 659, fn. 1.

[77] Frankland, *Ten Weeks Leave of Absence*.

forces comprised 15,000 soldiers despatched directly from Imerina and 1,000 men from a 5,000-strong expedition under Rainijohary, one of Ranavalona's chief ministers and paramours, sent that year against the Bara of southern Madagascar. French master artisan Laborde constructed rafts to enable the troops to cross rivers and other expanses of inland water encountered en route. At St Augustin, the Merina commanders of the *Voltigeur* invited Sakalava chiefs, including Marotoetsa, son of the local king, aboard the ship – then promptly seized them. The prisoners were taken first to Fort Dauphin, then to Antananarivo where they were executed. The terrestrial forces returned to the Merina capital, a distance of some 1,000 km, decimated by disease and with little booty.[78]

In 1835, in an attempt to restore British influence in Madagascar, Colville's successor, William Nicolay, governor of Mauritius from 1833 to 1840, acquiesced to LMS missionary Freeman's request that the British present Ranavalona with a pleasure boat for royal use on Lake Anosy. However, porterage of the boat inland from Tamatave involved enormous forced labour for the local Bezanozano and Betsimisaraka. Moreover, it necessitated clearing a wide path through the eastern forest, which convinced Ranavalona that the gesture was a ploy to open an easy path for an invasion force. Immediately after the boat had reached the capital, she ordered that no cutting or burning of the forest be permitted until the path had been completely grown over and that traffic between the coast and Imerina pass along alternative routes.[79] There is no indication in the records that the boat was ever used – possibly out of suspicion that it had been bewitched by the English.[80]

In 1836, Ranavalona sent an embassy to Europe with $1,500 in cash to pay for the trip and buy a flagship for an envisioned Merina navy. She hoped to recoup the cost by using the purchased vessel both for military purposes and to export cattle to Mauritius, where by 1836 bullock prices had risen from $10 to between $30 and $40 a head. The embassy included Ramanankoraisana and Raneva, two former naval apprentices, and Raharolahy and Rasatranabo, two former missionary pupils employed by the Merina court to teach reading and writing to children of the Merina elite. Rasatranabo was married to Mary, the widow of James Hastie. The others were Ratsiohaina (Andriantsitohaina) and Andriantseheno. For the voyage, they chartered a ship, the *Mathilde*, owned and captained by Breton merchant, Alexandre Garnot.[81] Garnot claimed that one of the

---

[78] RA, 361; Grandidier, *Histoire physique* (1942), vol. 5, book 1, 276.   [79] RA, 358–60.
[80] For suspicion of the use of sorcery by British imperial agents, see Gwyn Campbell, *The Travels of Robert Lyall, 1789–1831: Scottish Surgeon, Naturalist and British Agent to the Court of Madagascar* (Cham, Switzerland: Palgrave Macmillan, 2020), 187–232.
[81] RA, 363, 379–80, 437.

embassy had earlier been enslaved for possession of a banned animal, the pig:

Upon the queen ascending to the throne ... it was again forbidden for any inhabitant of Antananarivo to own a pig. A breach of this order having been discovered, the Merina culprit, of superior noble birth, was condemned by the queen to be sold as a slave, an event which, following custom, took place publicly. This unfortunate Merina was immediately redeemed by his family. In 1837 he was one of the six Malagasy envoys sent to Europe.[82]

En route to Europe, the embassy met the governors of Réunion, Mauritius, and Cape Town. An idea of the importance accorded to them is given by a description of their visit to Réunion, where 'the ambassadors in full red uniform, gold braid, with colonel's epaulettes, were upon their arrival greeted by a twenty-one cannon salute, and escorted by troops to the governor's residence where a magnificent banquet had been prepared for them'.[83] The embassy sailed on to France, where in February 1837 the steamship *Monarch* took them from Le Havre to London. There, its members had interviews with Foreign Secretary Henry John Temple, 3rd Viscount Palmerston (1784–1865), who proposed a new treaty; Charles Grant, 1st Baron Glenelg (1778–1866) secretary of state for war and the colonies, and the LMS directors. Accompanied by Freeman, they also had audiences with Queen Adelaide (1792–1849) and William IV (1765–1837) (see Figure 6.3).[84] Further, Freeman took them to visit London Bridge, the Borough Road School, St Paul's Cathedral, the Mint, the Tower, London Dock, Woolwich, the British Museum, the Bank of England, and the House of Commons. In addition, they were treated to a three-and-a-half-hour train ride.[85] The embassy, which brought Madagascar back into the focus of British evangelicals,[86] then left for Paris. There, the Merina ambassadors met the British ambassador, Granville George Leveson-Gower, 2nd Earl Granville (1815–1891), as well as Louis Philippe (1773–1850), king of the French (r. 1830–48), and other French dignitaries including Nicolas Martin du Nord (1790–1847), minister of public works, agriculture and commerce (1835–9). They then travelled overland to Paulliac, in southwest France from where they sailed back to Tamatave aboard the *Mathilde*.[87]

In the event, the $1,500 Ranavalona had given them was insufficient even to pay for the expenses of her ambassadors, who were obliged to borrow $4,569.5 from Garnot. Upon their return, Garnot requested from the queen repayment of the capital of his loan plus $1,142 (25 per cent) interest. This infuriated

---

[82] Garnot, *Question de Madagascar*, 17, fn. 4.

[83] G. de Corlay, *Notre campagne à Madagascar: Notes et souvenirs d'un volontaire* (Paris: Tolra, 1896), 67; see also RA, 397, 404–7; Pier M. Larson, 'Fragments of an Indian Ocean Life: Aristide Corroller Between Islands and Empires', *Journal of Social History* 45.2 (2011), 382.

[84] Corlay, *Notre campagne à Madagascar*, 67; Arianne Chernock, 'Queen Victoria and the "Bloody Mary of Madagascar"', *Victorian Studies* 55.3 (2013), 425.

[85] RA, 408–23.   [86] Chernock, 'Queen Victoria', 426.   [87] RA, 430–5.

Figure 6.3 Merina embassy to Britain meet Queen Adelaide, 1836
Source: Painting by Henry Room (1802–50) – in the public domain.

Ranavalona, who paid the sum demanded but immediately cancelled the east coast trading monopoly Garnot had previously enjoyed and instead gave it to Delastelle.[88] Subsequently, Vieu, a French trader on the east coast, demonstrated interest in supplying the court with a boat but backed off when Ranavalona insisted that, prior to opening negotiations, he bring a new, three-masted ship to Tamatave.[89]

Thereafter, the court's interest in building a Merina navy dropped, and when required, the queen turned again to her French commercial allies. In about 1840, Delastelle established a shipyard at Mahela where 150 workers, comprising a carpenter, an iron-smith, and a cooper *fanompoana* unit, 'are occupied all year round constructing and repairing boats to serve us in the interior, and on the rivers and coast'.[90] Again, in 1852, William Marks, a favoured American

[88] RA, 378–85, 435–6, 457–9.   [89] RA, 436–7.

[90] Antoine Maurice Fontoynont and H. Nicol, *Les traitants français de la côte est de Madagascar – de Ranavalona I à Radama II* (Tananarive: Imprimerie moderne de l'Émyrne, 1940), 25; Gwyn Campbell, 'The Role of the London Missionary Society in the Rise of the Merina Empire, 1810–1861', PhD thesis, University of Wales, Swansea (1985), 297.

trader from Salem who supplied Ranavalona with cotton goods, guns, and gunpowder, lent Ranavalona a boat to carry troops to relieve the Fort Dauphin garrison, in return for the use of 1,600 Besimisaraka *fanompoana* as porters to carry his goods from Majunga, where he was based, to Antananarivo.[91] In July 1853, two Frenchmen, P. Lecordisy and H. Le Mierre, offered Ranavalona $54,000 and a boat for exclusive import and export rights in Madagascar. Ranavalona refused[92] and instead ordered Marks to bring a boat from America to enable her to enter into the cattle trade with the Mascarenes.[93] It appears that nothing came of this, and the court was again obliged rely on its local French trading allies. Thus, Ranavalona welcomed Lambert's offer in 1855 to carry provisions on his ships to Merina garrisons on the coast.[94] Indeed, not until the 1880s did the Merina regime acquire a sea-going vessel, the *Antananarivo*, which they used to carry rum, taken as import customs dues, to Mauritius for sale.[95]

In sum, the Madagascar Youths who had learned British martial music on Mauritius were upon their return to Madagascar monopolized by first Radama, then Ranavalona. They formed royal bands that played at all courtly events and invariably headed any royal procession. By contrast, those Merina youths who survived their apprenticeship aboard British naval ships had limited opportunity to demonstrate their skills of seamanship, as the Merina court did not have the means to build, purchase, or maintain a fleet. However, they did play a decisive role in repelling the French attack on Foulepointe in 1829. Moreover, Ranavalona made some use of them in relations with foreign powers, a role in which the twins Rahaniraka and Raombana, the only Madagascar Youths to receive an exclusively liberal education in Britain, were extensively employed. Their experience in Britain and their carers upon their return form the core focus of the next and final chapter.

---

[91] Raombana, 'Manuscrit écrit à Tananarive (1853–1854)', trans. J. F. Radley, *BAM* 13 (1930), 15, 17–18.

[92] Raombana, 'Manuscrit écrit à Tananarive', 7–8.

[93] Raombana, 'Manuscrit écrit à Tananarive', 18.

[94] R. E. P. Wastell, 'British Imperial Policy in Relation to Madagascar, 1810–96', PhD thesis, London University (1944), 304–5.

[95] Jeremiah Peill, 'Social Conditions and Prospect of Madagascar', *Journal of the Society of Arts* 1578.21 (1883), 280.

7   The Twins, Diplomacy, and British Allegiance

This final chapter examines the careers of two Merina princes tutored by Hastie on Mauritius in 1816–17 and those Madagascar Youths selected to be trained abroad as a result of the 1820 Britanno-Merina treaty, who, upon their return, were employed as court officials and diplomats for the Merina crown. It focuses in particular on the history of twins Raombana and Rahaniraka. They, alone of the youths sent to Britain, received a liberal education, with the specific intention that upon their return they might serve as royal counsellors and foreign secretaries. This chapter examines the experience of the twins in Britain and their subsequent roles in Madagascar, as well as the degree to which they, and the other Madagascar Youths, fulfilled the expectations of Farquhar, the missionaries, and the authorities in Cape Town and London that they would serve as steadfast proponents of British influence in Madagascar.

The Merina Princes

As noted in Chapter 3, Ramarotafika (Ratafikia) and Rahovy (Ratsimiovo), two half-brothers to Radama, returned to Madagascar from Mauritius in mid-1817, accompanied by their tutor, James Hastie, after having spent a year in the residence of Governor Farquhar on Mauritius imbibing English customs, manners, and education. Farquhar considered that they would play a pivotal role in future British relations with Imerina, possibly as Merina ambassadors to Mauritius. It was with this in mind that, after the signing of the Britanno-Merina treaty in late 1820, Farquhar invited them to make a return visit to Mauritius. In 1822, possibly regretting that he had not taken up Farquhar's invitation, Rahovy wrote to the governor:

I am quite well, and am continually thinking of you, and have been a long time expecting a letter acquainting me how you are. I hope you have not forgotten your friend, Rahove, who is longing to see you again, and shall never forget your kindness. We have a great number of soldiers now in Madagascar, and expect all the other powers will soon submit to King Radama's arms. Mr. Jones, Mr. Griffiths, and their wives are teaching the little children to read, write, and sew, very well; and I attend Mr. jones's school every day, as also my brothers Rataffe and Ratafik.[1]

However, Farquhar's plans for the princes were thwarted. Raombana claimed that during their time on Mauritius Ramarotafika and Rahovy had made negligible educational progress, signifying that they were of little diplomatic utility to the Merina crown.[2] More significantly, it would appear that Radama, who was constantly alert to the possibility of a palace coup, considered that they posed a political threat and, ostensibly for the 'crime' of incest (although Radama also slept with his own sister),[3] had them banished to the east coast where, within a year, Rahovy succumbed to malaria,[4] while upon her to ascension in 1828, Ranavalona ordered Ramarotafika at Mananjary to be starved to death.[5]

Ratefy, Radama's brother-in-law, who had accompanied the Madagascar Youths to Britain, met a similar fate under Ranavalona. While in London, Ratefy, who hitherto had worn his hair long as was the traditional Merina custom, followed local fashion and had his hair cut short. After Ratefy's return to Madagascar in mid-1822, Radama followed his example, and ordered his soldiers to do likewise.[6] This provoked a major popular protest, led by women, whose three ringleaders Radama executed.[7] Subsequently, Radama appointed Ratefy governor of Tamatave, in which role he led a number of military expeditions. On one of these, in early 1824, Ratefy's troops pillaged a number of probably Betsimisaraka villages, enslaving local people and seizing their cattle. Some even plundered graves for money and other valuables deposited in them. On learning this, Radama downgraded Ratefy by 1 *Voninahitra* (Vtr) (honour) and ordered that all stolen goods be returned and that the families of violated tombs be recompensed. The king nevertheless permitted Ratefy to command further military campaigns and appointed him chief judge of Mananjary and Tamatave in 1824 and 1826 respectively. By 1826, Ratefy was one of the four main Merina governors on the east coast, who, combined, had under them a 12,000-strong administration.[8] However,

---

[1] Rahovy to Farquhar and Mrs Farquhar, Tananarivoo, 15 Apr. 1822, encl. 3 in Farquhar to R. Wilmot, Madagascar, 6 Jun. 1823, House of Commons, *Papers: Relating to Captured Negroes; also to the Slave Trade at the Mauritius and Bourbon, and the Seychelles; Slave Population at the Seychelles &c.*, vol. 27 (1826), 156.

[2] RH, 90.   [3] RH, 168–9.   [4] HdR, 1097.   [5] RA, 201, AAM.

[6] Jeffreys to Arundel, Tamatave, 8 May 1822, MIL B.1 F.3 J.C, SOAS/CWM. Intriguingly, another Malagasy, called 'Steven', and his English wife, Elizabeth Stingo, returned on the same ship as Ratefy from London to Mauritius. They travelled to Antananarivo where Elizabeth died in early February 1822, Welsh missionary David Griffiths presiding over her funeral service on 8 February – Barnsley diary 1821–2, HB 7, NAM.

[7] RH, 106–7.

[8] James Montgomery (ed.), *Journal of Voyages and Travels by the Rev. Daniel Tyerman and George Bennet* (Boston: Crocker and Brewster, 1832), vol. 3, 253; RH, 120;

following Radama's death in mid-1828, Ranavalona ordered the execution of Ratefy and his wife Rabodosahondra, a sister of Radama. The queen also confiscated their possessions, including over 2,000 slaves, and distributed them to court favourites, notably her nephews Ramahatra and Ramonja and her niece Ramoma.[9]

Although he posed Ranavalona no political threat, she also killed Andriamahazonoro, who had accompanied Ratefy to London as a secretary. After returning to Madagascar, Andriamahazonoro initially remained in court circles in Antananarivo, but in 1828, believing him to be possessed by powerful forces, Ranavalona banished him to his home region of Matitanana, in the southeast of the island. For the same reason, when in 1831–2 the queen became very ill and subject to fits, she recalled Andriamahazonoro, along with four of his relatives, in order to treat her. They succeeded in alleviating her illness, and received royal presents, but were confined permanently to the palace.[10] In 1838, when Ranavalona forced four female Antanosy healers, again from the southeast, to enter her service at court, she ignored Andriamahazanoro's protests that he had faithfully served the Merina crown and subjected him and his relatives to the *tangena* poison ordeal – from which all died.[11]

Madagascar Youths and Christianity

Thomas Jarrold, a Manchester doctor, commented of the impact of an English education on the Madagascar Youths:

Men of every country are capable, almost equally capable, of receiving instruction. A Russian may be made as good a classic as an Englishman; for the memory is equally good in both, and instruction is little more than an appeal to this faculty. But information is not civilization. The Madagascar lads ... will return home well informed; but their civilization will, in a great measure, be the same as when they landed in this country. Their habits and their pleasures will be those of Madagascar: their education will be only so far valuable as it will enable the people to supply their wants, if they have any unsupplied. Their knowledge will not make them English: in feeling and in character they are Madagascan; and education cannot eradicate the character.[12]

Guillaume Grandidier, *Histoire physique, naturelle et politique de Madagascar* (Paris: Imprimerie Paul Brodard, 1942), vol. 5, book 1, 199, fn. 3; Regis Rajemisa-Raolison, *Dictionnaire historique et géographique de Madagascar* (Fianarantsoa: Librairie Ambozontany, 1966), 45; *HdR*, 1088, 1099; Gerald M. Berg, 'Virtù, and Fortuna in Radama's Nascent Bureaucracy, 1816–1828', *History in Africa* 23 (1996), 52–3.
[9] RA, 198–9.   [10] RA, 306–7.   [11] Raombana, B1, vol. 8, 8–10, AAM.
[12] Thomas Jarrold, 'Of the Influence of Early Impressions on the Future Character', *Monthly Magazine or British Register* 59.409 (1825), 304; see also Thomas Jarrold, *Instinct and Reason, Philosophically Investigated; with a View to ascertain the Principles of the Science of Education* (London: Longman, 1836).

In this context, it is interesting to investigate the degree to which, as the British authorities hoped, the Madagascar Youths would while abroad assimilate, and upon their return promote, the values of British civilization. The LMS was particularly interested in propagating its brand of Christianity, which by the late 1820s had shifted from being broadly international and ecumenical to London-based English Congregationalism. Moreover, the LMS was from 1831 under the tight, almost dictatorial, control of William Ellis, a virulently anti-Catholic Francophobe, fervent royalist, and advocate of English imperialism.[13]

The British and the LMS pinned their hopes particularly on those Madagascar Youths apprenticed in Britain who had converted to Christianity. British evangelicals trusted that these converts would promote their newly found faith in their homeland. Thus, in October 1824, after he had baptized Razafinkarefo, Verkey, and Ramboa, the Rev. John Angell James

pronounced a pathetic address, in which he exhorted the youths, on their arrival in their native country, not to be tempted to renounce those principles of the Christian religion, which had been taught them during their residence here, for the Pagan idolatries practised and followed by the majority of their countrymen.[14]

Shortly thereafter, the three youths embarked for Mauritius from where, on 19 February 1825, in a letter replete with biblical quotations and evangelical fervour, Verkey informed the LMS,

I have the opportunity, through the blessing of the Lord, to write to you these few lines about our arrival at the Isle of France. May they find you and your family well and happy!

On Monday, November 1, 1824, we left England at Gravesend, in the morning. In our going out of the Channel, between England and France, we had a gale of wind which blowed tremendously hard, so that the ship rolled about very much, by which means we were all sea-sick: we three were very weak on the next morning, so that we could hardly dress ourselves. Though we were weak and faint, yet the Lord was our relief and comfort: thus the Lord Jesus has been gracious to us in our trouble. In crossing the Bay of Biscay, (Nov. 14,) we again had stormy winds mixed with rain, so that the ship rolled very much, and we could not sleep in the night: every time when she rolled, I was fearful the ship would upset, for *the waves were lifted up*, as it is mentioned in the 107th Psalm, and verse 25: but, *though the waters thereof roar and be troubled, though the mountains shake with the swelling thereof*, we will not be afraid, *for the Lord of Hosts is with us, the God of Jacob is our refuge*. Ps. Xlvi.3, 11. Yea I say, *the Lord is mightier than the noise of many waters*, for He is the Creator and Preserver of all: He, even He only, can save from the uttermost danger, seen or unseen.

We bless and thank Almighty God for all His mercies. We have, through His kind Providence, escaped many dangers of which we are not aware, and from which no care

---

[13] Gwyn Campbell, *David Griffiths and the Missionary 'History of Madagascar'* (Leiden: Brill, 2012), esp. 146–53, 157–64, 807.

[14] 'Baptism of Three Madagascar Youths', *Morning Chronicle* (12 Oct. 1824).

of ours could have saved us. May our hearts feel the thankfulness which our lips express![15]

In mid-1825, the three youths sailed to Tamatave aboard HMS *Wizard*, captain Haskell.[16] Razafinkarefo and Verkey travelled immediately to Antananarivo. Ramboa, who died in early 1826 – of insanity, according to Raombana – may have remained in Tamatave.[17]

Razafinkarefo retained his Christian faith and remained closely involved with the missionaries who, he informed the LMS in September 1829, employed him as a 'visitor' inspecting mission schools. To assist him in this task, he requested that the LMS supply him with a watch, a compass, and a telescope.[18] In April 1831, he notified the society that he was working closely with Griffiths and fellow missionary David Johns. He probably assisted in translating Christian tracts and the remaining untranslated sections of the Old Testament, for he requested that the LMS send him a 'Comprehensive Bible and a Concordance'. The directors duly sent him the books and some stationery.[19] In addition, he received gifts from George Greatbach (1779–1864), from 1824 minister of the Independent Chapel, Eastbank Street, Southport, Lancashire, whom he had known when in Manchester.[20]

By contrast, the missionaries reported that Verkey was subject to temptation, irregular in chapel attendance, and by November 1826 had strayed from the Christian path.[21] LMS missionary David Johns reported that Raolombelona, who had arrived back in September 1826, had within two months abandoned Christianity and, by June 1827, risked being expelled from the missionary chapel for bad conduct.[22] However, Freeman noted in October 1827 that Raolombelona still occasionally attended church[23] and, in July 1828, that he

[15] Joseph Verkey to [Burder?], Mauritius, 24 Feb. 1825, in *Missionary Register* (Aug. 1825), 351.

[16] Samuel Pasfield Oliver, *Madagascar: An Historical and Descriptive Account of the Island and Its Former Dependencies* (London: Macmillan, 1886), vol. 1, 41.

[17] Verkey to LMS, Tananarivou, 12 Feb. 1826, in *The Evangelical Magazine and Missionary Chronicle* (Dec. 1826), 535; RH, 96–7; Simon Ayache (ed.), *Raombana l'historien (1809–1855)* (Fianarantsony: Ambozontany, 1976). 29.

[18] Razafinkarefo to [LMS], Antananarivo, [Sep. 1829], MIL B.3 F.3 J.B, SOAS/CWM.

[19] Razafinkarefo to Arundel, Antananarivo, 10 Apr. 1831, MIL B.4 F.1 J.A, SOAS/CWM; Meeting of Directors, 21 Nov. 1831, LMS Board Meeting, SOAS/CWM.

[20] Ellis to Freeman, Johns, and Canham, London, 14 Jun. 1833, MOL, SOAS/CWM; see also E. Bland, *Annals of Southport and District: A Chronological History of North Meols, AD 1086 to 1886* (Manchester: Abel, Heywood & Sons, [1887]), 83–4.

[21] Griffiths to Burder, Tananarive, 19 Dec. 1825 and Griffiths to Arundel, 'private', Tananarive, 20 Dec. 1825, MIL B.2 F.2 J.C, SOAS/CWM; Johns to Arundel, Tananarive, 26 Nov. 1826, MIL B.2 F.3 J.C, SOAS/CWM; Raombana, 'Manuscrit écrit à Tananarive (1853–1854)', trans. J. F. Radley, *BAM* 13 (1930), 4.

[22] Johns to Arundel, Tananarive, 26 Nov. 1826, MIL B.2 F.3 J.C, SOAS/CWM; Johns to LMS, Tananarivou, 16 Jun. 1827, MIL B.2 F.4 J.B, SOAS/CWM; see also William Ellis, *History of Madagascar* (London: Fisher, 1838), vol. 2, 365; Rabary, *Ny Daty Malaza: Na Ny Dian' i Jesosy Teto Madagaskara* (Tananarive: LMS, 1930–1), 50.

[23] Freeman to Burder, Tananarive, 23 Oct. 1827, MIL B.2 F.5, SOAS/CWM.

was the only Malagasy to have joined the church in Antananarivo,[24] although Johns reported that following Radama's death that month he abandoned Christianity and stopped communicating with the missionaries.[25] Nevertheless, in January 1829, the LMS presented Verkey and Raolombelona with religious books, including the Gospel of St Luke and a catechism.[26] Moreover, whereas Raolombelona failed to join the newly built chapel established by Freeman and Johns, with whom he evidently ceased relations, he continued to attend Griffiths' chapel at Ambodin-Andohalo, where, on Sunday 21 May 1831, Griffiths baptized eighteen Malagasy including Raolombelona's sister, Rangita.[27]

British Allegiance and Diplomacy

In a broader context, it is also important to examine to what degree the Madagascar Youths developed any allegiance to Britain and the role they played in diplomatic relations between the Merina court and the European powers following their return to Madagascar.

Ranavalona certainly valued the Madagascar Youths who had served in Britain for their fluency in English and knowledge of British customs. Verkey possessed the additional attributes of having earlier lived on Mauritius where he had also learned French. Immediately on ascending the throne, she conferred on him the status of 'colonel' and employed him alongside Raolombelona to represent the court in its relations with Lyall, who London appointed in 1827 as British agent to Madagascar. For example, in December 1828, Ranavalona sent a deputation, including Verkey and Raolombelona, to inform Lyall that although she refused the 'equivalent', and by implication the 1820 Britanno-Merina treaty, she would maintain the slave export ban.[28] In January 1829, the queen refused Lyall's request to have Verkey teach him Malagasy on the grounds that 'being much engaged, as Colonel in the Army and as one of the fixed deputation, She was sorry She could not spare him'.[29] A month later, she sent Verkey and Raolombelona to remove from Lyall's roof a flag he was using to measure wind direction.[30] Shortly thereafter, she accused Lyall of being engaged in sorcery, a process in which she again used Verkey and

[24] Freeman to [LMS], Tananarive, 13 Jul. 1828, Madagascar personal, B.2 F.3, SOAS/CWM.
[25] Johns to Arundel, Tananarivo, 30 Sep. 1829, MIL B.3 F.2 J.A and 19 Feb. 1830, MIL B.3 F.3 J. A – SOAS/CWM; RA, 300.
[26] Lyall, 'Journal' entry for 11 Jan. 1829, CO 167/116.
[27] Lyall, 'Journal' entry for 11 Jan. 1829, CO 167/116, NAK; Baker to [LMS, Antananarivo, Jun. 1831], MIL B.4 F.1 J.A, SOAS/CWM.
[28] Lyall, 'Journal' entry for 2 Dec. 1829, CO 167/116, NAK.
[29] Lyall, 'Journal' entry for 27 Jan. 1829, CO 167/116, NAK; see also Lyall to Ranavalona, Ambouni-Antsahatsiroua, 26 Jan. 1829. in Lyall, 'Journal', CO 167/116, NAK.
[30] Lyall, 'Journal' entry for 24 Feb. 1829, CO 167/116, NAK.

Raolombelona, and which resulted in Lyall's expulsion order in March 1829.[31] Lyall believed throughout that Aristide Coroller (1799/1802–1835), a Mauritian Creole, governor of Tamatave, and counsel to the Merina court, used Verkey to promote French over British interests in Madagascar.[32] In June 1829, Ranavalona also employed Raolombelona as interpreter in her communications with twins Rahaniraka and Raombana, who, newly arrived after eight years absence in Britain, initially found difficulty speaking Malagasy.[33]

The Madagascar Youths proved of critical importance in the Merina court's attempts to calm European imperial aggression in the wake of Lyall's expulsion and the failed French invasion of northeast Madagascar, both of which occurred in 1829. In February 1831, Ranavalona sent Verkey to Alasora to refuse the demand of Tourette, clerk of the French settlement at Sainte Marie, that she concede to France most of the eastern littoral of Madagascar.[34] In October 1832, the queen included Raolombelona, described as a 'civilian', and former naval apprentice Ramiaramanana, a lieutenant colonel, in a five-man embassy to Mauritius and Europe. Raombana remarked that Raolombelona spoke good English, but not Ramiaramanana. The embassy's brief was to assure Mascarene traders and the Europeans of her wish to trade and British authorities of her determination to uphold the slave export ban.[35] Ranavalona gave $300 to each member of the embassy, but as their foreign hosts afforded them free hospitality, she demanded they repay the money. When Raolombelona proved unable to do so, the queen sold him as a slave and confiscated his property (the combined value being estimated at $80). He died in 1851.[36]

In 1834, in response to a request from Said bin Sultan Al-Busaidi (1791–1856), sultan of Muscat and Oman (r. 1806–56), for an alliance and 2,000 Malagasy soldiers to help suppress 'rebels' at Mombasa, Ranavalona sent to Zanzibar a five-man embassy that included four former naval apprentices, Ramiaramanana, Rahaingiomanana, Ramaharo, and Ramanamalako. They returned in 1835 with presents from the sultan comprising over 400 muskets, an Arabian horse, and $10,000 worth of coral beads.[37] Ranavalona also used

[31] See e.g. Lyall, 'Journal' entry for 20 Mar. 1829, CO 167/116, NAK; Lyall to Freeman, Amboni-Antsahatsiroua, 28 Mar. 1829, in Lyall, 'Journal', HB 19, NAM; Lyall, 'Journal' entry for 26 Apr. 1829, HB 19, NAM.

[32] Lyall, 'Journal' entry for 12 Mar. 1829, CO 167/116, NAK.

[33] Simon Ayache, 'Un intellectuel malgache devant la culture européenne: L'historien Raombana (1809–1854)', *Archipel* 12.1 (1976), 109.

[34] RA, 257.

[35] The other members of the embassy were Lieutenant Colonel Rahandrara/Rahanrarasy 8 Vtr, Lieutenant Colonel Ratsiorimisa 8 Vtr, and Major Ramanga 7 Vtr – Ranavalona I to Gov. Mauritius, Antananarivo, 14 Alakarabo 1832 (12 Oct. 1832), HB 20, NAM; RA, 296–7.

[36] RA, 300.   [37] RA, 317–9, 330–46.

ex-naval apprentices to accompany high-ranking Europeans in Madagascar. In one case in mid-1856, when LMS director William Ellis visited the island, he was met in Tamatave by a middle-aged Malagasy who claimed to have spent some years in the 'Cape Corps' and to have been a 'servant' to Captain William Underwood, one of the aides-de-camp of Charles Somerset, governor of the Cape from 1814 to 1826. Ellis commented that his 'habits of drinking rendered my guide incapable of affording us much assistance' – a possible indication of the drinking culture to which he had been exposed during his time in the British Navy.[38] Ellis commented of Beoli, another ex-naval apprentice, appointed to supervise the bearers for his trip inland to Antananarivo,

A stout Betsimisaraka chief, named Beoli, belonging to the district, but who, from having been some years on board an English frigate, for the purpose of learning the duties of a sailor, spoke broken English, so as to be generally understood, and had been appointed by the authorities captain of the maromites, or bearers, came with a gun, and a powderhorn slung over his shoulder, to superintend the departure of the men with their burdens ...

When the bearers had taken charge of their packages, Beoli took me to the chiefs of each small party, which consisted of about ten men, and requested me to write down the names of these chiefs, who, he said, would be responsible for the safety of the packages carried by the men of their party.[39]

The Twins

The remainder of this chapter is devoted to the history of twins Raombana and Rahaniraka, both in Britain and upon their return to Madagascar (Figure 7.1). Theirs was an exceptional story. They were the only Madagascar Youths for whom Radama designated a full British liberal education. Their experiences are particularly well documented, in part because they became foreign secretaries at the Merina court, and were thus remarked upon by Europeans, and in part because, in secret and in English, Raombana wrote a history and kept a diary, both of which have largely survived to this day.[40]

The Malagasy often possessed several names and could change them over time. Raombana (1809–1855) was initially called Ratotozy and Rafaralahy, then Thotoos in Britain, and, after 1832, Raombana; while Rahaniraka (1809–1862) first carried the name Ravoalavo, was called Volave in Britain, and became known as Rahaniraka after his return.[41] The twins

[38] William Ellis, *Three Visits to Madagascar during the Years 1853–1854–1856* (Philadelphia: John E. Potter, 1858), 236; see also George Ross, *The Cape of Good Hope Calendar and Agriculturist's Guide* (London: T & J. Allman, 1819), 25, 121.
[39] Ellis, *Three Visits to Madagascar* (1858), 245.
[40] Ayache, 'Un intellectuel malgache', 95 fn. 1.
[41] J. T. Hardyman, 'Malagasy Overseas', PPMS63 J. T. Hardyman file 43, Bx.7, SOAS/CWM; Campbell, *David Griffiths*, 638.

Figure 7.1 Rahaniraka and Raombana
Source: Illustration by I. F. Mayoll (Brighton), in A. Siegrist, *Mademoiselle
Juliette: Princesse malgache* (Tananarive: Pilot de la Beau Jardière,
1937), 88.

were descendants of King Andriamasinavalona (r. c.1675–1710) through
their grandfather, Rafondrazaka, fief-holder of Tsimiamboholahy, a region
in Avaradrano province, to the east of Antananarivo. The twins' other
grandfather, Andriambao, changed sides in the Merina civil wars of the
late 1700s to support the eventual victor, Andrianampoinimerina, Radama's
father. Andrianavalona, Rafondrazaka's eldest son and the twin's father, was
also a veteran of the civil wars. He became a favourite of Radama, who
appointed him first commander of the British-trained Merina model army.
Because of their service to the crown, Raombana's family received a vast
fiefdom, were accorded the right to build a *trano masina* ('holy house') over
their tomb, and were exempted from both punishment by ordinary courts and
from *fanompoana*.[42]

---

[42] RH, 40–1; Berg, 'Virtù, and Fortuna', 45–6.

Radama took a special interest in Raombana, whom he introduced to Europeans at his court, where the child began to learn European languages.[43] He and his twin were thus natural choices for inclusion in the group sent to Britain after the 1820 Britanno-Merina treaty. Their father and Ratsifehera, their elder brother, initially opposed the royal decision but gave their consent after Radama promised that, upon the return of the twins, he would restore to them the principality of Hiaranandriana, in Sisaony district, that had formerly belonged to their grandfather.[44] More drama occurred when, as the chosen youths left Antananarivo in a convoy on 19 October 1820, Raombana fled with his slaves, who hid him in the countryside. However, Andrianavalona permitted royal agents to seize Raombana and force him to rejoin the group en route to Tamatave.[45] In this context, it should be added that when an unnamed member of the chosen youths claimed suddenly that he was too unwell to leave, Radama ordered that the boy receive fifty lashes and be suspended by his thumbs from a flag-staff until he relented.[46] At the twins' departure, their mother, Rataloha, mourned them as if dead and for five years refused to look at her image in a mirror.[47] Andrianavalona also wept, lamenting that he would never see the twins again. His premonition proved correct, but his wife lived to see them return. Shortly after the twins left, Radama appointed Andrianavalona governor of Hiarana (Vohimar) on the north-east coast,[48] and, in 1823, ordered him to lead an attack on rebel Sihanaka in Anosimboahangy, a village on an island in Lake Alaotra. The Sihanaka put up such a resistance that Andrianavalona fled, and in consequence, in accordance with a newly established martial law, Radama had him shot and burned. It was customary for the property of executed criminals to be seized by the crown, but in this case Radama accorded it to the twins, whom he made wards of a distant relative of theirs. By this act, Gerald Berg argues, Radama effectively adopted Raombana and Rahaniraka as his own sons.[49]

In Britain, alongside the other Madagascar Youths, the twins were taught elementary English and arithmetic at Borough Road School in London. At one board meeting, the LMS directors noted that Radama had instructed that Raombana subsequently be taught how to dye calico in Manchester.[50] However, Raombana later claimed that the king had designated the twins to learn 'polite literature', with which they might entertain him upon their return,[51] so that they

---

[43] Berg, 'Virtù, and Fortuna', 45.

[44] Raombana, 'Texts', in Ayache (ed.), *Raombana l'historien*, 2–3; see also Berg, 'Virtù, and Fortuna', 45–6.

[45] Ayache, 'Un intellectuel malgache', 105.

[46] J. T. Hardyman, 'Malagasy Overseas', PPMS63 J. T. Hardyman file 43, Bx.7, SOAS/CWM.

[47] Ayache, 'Un intellectuel malgache', 101–2.   [48] RH, 119–20.

[49] Grandidier, *Histoire physique* (1942), vol. 5, book 1, 197–8; Berg, 'Virtù, and Fortuna', 45–6; Ayache (ed.), *Raombana l'historien*, 53.

[50] Meeting of Directors, 11 Jun. 1821, LMS Board Minutes, SOAS/CWM.

[51] RH, 96; Raombana, 'Texts', in Ayache (ed.), *Raombana l'historien*, 1–2.

Table 7.1 *Expenses for*
Rahaniraka and Raombana
in Manchester 1825–8

Jan.-Jun. 1825	**£104.15.2**
Jul.-Dec. 1825	**£120.13.6**
Jul.-Dec. 1826	**£62.2.6**
Jan.-Jun. 1827	**£90.11.4**
Jul.-Dec. 1827	**£83.17.7**
Jan.-Jun. 1828	**£78.19.8**

Source: Meeting of Directors, 21
Feb., 27 Jun., and 26 Dec. 1825, 15
Jan., 25 Jun., and 31 Dec., 1827, 30
Jun. 1828 – LMS Board Minutes,
SOAS/CWM.

might 'reside with me ... to teach me how to rule my subjects'.[52] By contrast, Rainandrianampandry stated that Radama wished the twins to study civil law.[53] In the event, after Borough Road School, the LMS entered all Madagascar Youths into craft apprenticeships except for the twins, who were despatched to Manchester to receive a liberal education from Clunie paid for by the British government (see Table 7.1). Thus, in August 1823, Paul Dikkop, son of a Khoi chief and fellow Borough Road scholar, informed Scottish LMS missionary John Campbell (1766–1840), whom he had accompanied to Britain, 'The two Madagascar boys are gone to Manchester to learn Latin and Greek. I was very sorry when they went away'.[54] Of the twins, Bathurst stated to Lowry Cole in July 1824,

it will be the Object of the English Govt. to continue to them the same attention which the others have received, and it is my sincere hope that by proper treatment, and by their constitutions becoming more habituated to this climate, they may safely continue in this Country, and derive all the advantages that may have been anticipated from their residence in England.[55]

---

[52] Quoted in Simon Ayache, 'La découverte de l 'Europe par les Malgaches au XIXe siècle', *Revue française d'histoire d'outre-mer* 73.270 (1986), 15.
[53] Rainandrianampandry, quoted in L. Nogue, 'Étude sur École professionnelle de Tananarive' *Notes, reconnaissances et explorations* 1.1 (1900), 418.
[54] Paul Dikkop to John Campbell, Shacklewell, 2 Aug. 1823, in John Campbell, *Hottentot Children; with a particular account of Paul Dikkop, the son of a Hottentot Chief, who Died in England, Sept. 14, 1824* (London: Religious Tract Society, 1848), 43.
[55] Extract from a despatch of the Earl Bathurst [to Governor of Mauritius], 20 Jul. 1824, HB 4, NAM.

At Clunie's Leaf Square Academy (Rahaniraka called it a 'Grammar School') in Pendleton, just outside Manchester, the twins studied English, Geography, Arithmetic, Rhetoric, Geometry, History, and Chemistry.[56] In January 1825, Clunie reported to the LMS that their health, education, and conduct was 'satisfactory', in response to which the board presented them with 'an assortment of Small Books'.[57] In June 1825, Chenie, one of their teachers, informed the LMS that 'They are much more playful and volatile than Rolan [Raolombelona], but appear quite ingenious and affectionate. Indeed, they all do whatever they are ordered with pleasure and appear extremely happy.'[58] In the mid-1825 examination, Rahaniraka came fifth in his class.[59]

The twins were the only Madagascar Youths to remain in Britain after Raolombelona's return to Madagascar in May 1826. In January 1827, the LMS asked Clunie to give them French language lessons.[60] When in 1828 Raombana gained the Academy's silver medal for academic merit,[61] the *Missionary Gazetteer* announced that 'Volave and Thotoos, the Madagascar youths still remaining in this country, are making good progress in various branches of learning, and in the knowledge of useful arts: they conduct themselves with great propriety.'[62] By that time, the twins were also addressing evangelical gatherings in Manchester, through which they made a number of friends, including a Mr Jenkins, Woosnam from Llanidloes, Wales, Minshall from Oswestry, and Mrs Jones and Lacon from Liverpool.[63]

The surnames and place names mentioned indicate a strong Welsh connection. It would be impossible to trace a Jenkins or Jones. However, the Woosnams of Llanidloes were a well-established family, present in the area from at least 1684 and with numerous members, including Bowen Woosnam (1771–1841), a solicitor, appointed in 1825 first mayor of Glandwr, Llanidloes (following the 1835 Municipal Reform Act, a consequence of the 1832 Reform Act).[64] The Minshall referred to was probably Nathaniel Minshall (c.1780–1848) of

[56] Chenie to Arundal, Leaf Square, Manchester, 21 Jun. 1825 in Barry to Hastie, Port Louis, 25 Apr. 1826, HB 4, NAM; Ayache (ed.), *Raombana l'historien*, 359, 361.

[57] Meeting of the Board, 17 Jan 1825, LMS Board Minutes, SOAS/CWM.

[58] Chenie to Arundal, Leaf Square, Manchester, 21 Jun. 1825, in Barry to Hastie, Port Louis, 25 Apr. 1826, HB 4, NAM.

[59] Chenie to Arundal, Leaf Square, Manchester, 21 Jun. 1825. in Barry to Hastie, Port Louis, 25 Apr. 1826, HB 4, NAM.

[60] Meeting of Directors, 15 Jan. 1827, LMS Board Minutes, SOAS/CWM.

[61] Ayache (ed.), *Raombana l'historien*, 361.

[62] Charles Williams, *The Missionary Gazetteer* (London: Frederick Westley and A. H. Davis, 1828), 325.

[63] Ayache (ed.), *Raombana l'historien*, 361.

[64] Powys-Land Club, *Collections Historical & Archæological Relating to Montgomeryshire and Its Borders*, vol. 33 (Oswestry: Powys-Land Club, 1904), 45; E. R. Horsefall-Turner, *A Municipal History of Llanidloes* (Llanidloes: John Ellis, 1908), 99–100.

Oswestry, described in 1841 as a 'gentleman'.[65] The Minshall's were a strongly Nonconformist family, resident in the Hanmer district of Oswestry from at least the late 1600s. Nathaniel was raised in poor circumstances on a farm, then became a printer and bookseller who may have authored the first book in English devoted to bookbinding.[66] He subsequently became a solicitor. He was a staunch Congregationalist, a member of Oswestry Old Chapel under the ministry of John Whitridge from 1792 to 1826. In June 1822, Nathaniel offered free advice to the Primitive Methodist preacher, William Doughty (1798–1863), when he was arrested for open-air preaching in Oswestry. Nathaniel married Sarah (née Roberts), with whom he had eight children, two of whom, Thomas (1809–1890) and Margaret (b. c.1810), were about the same age as Raombana and Rahaniraka.[67] The Lacon reference may have been to Thomas Lacon, an ironfounder, who was probably related to William Lacon and John Lacon (b. 1790), both ironfounders originally from Oswestry.[68]

By 1827, it was noted that Raombana's health was 'delicate' (he was suffering from ulcers), and in December that year the LMS recommended to Bathurst his early return to Madagascar.[69] In mid-June 1828, after physician Thomas Jarrold confirmed Raombana to be in poor physical condition, the Colonial Office agreed to the LMS request that both Raombana and Rahaniraka be sent back to Madagascar 'without any avoidable delay'.[70] On 28 July, the board ordered that 'an assortment of Books adapted to their capacities, be purchased for the Madagascar Youths, also a small supply of Stationary and medicine'.[71] On 11 August, it was recorded that 'The youths about to embark for Madagascar, Volave and Thotoos, were introduced to the Board to take

[65] 'Nathaniel Minshall of Oswestry gentleman', ref. SRO 2847/7/230–231, Shropshire Archives – https://discovery.nationalarchives.gov.uk/details/r/cea449a0-3384-4d5d-834b-a3efceeaadce (accessed 18.06.21).

[66] *The Whole Art of Bookbinding, Containing Valuable Recipes for Sprinking, Makbling* [sic], *Colouring, &c.* (Oswestry, 1811) – see 'Recent Acquisitions Briefly Noted', *Yale University Library Gazette* 75.3/4 (2001), 190.

[67] *Solicitors' Journal and Reporter* 34 (1890), 461; H. B. Kendall, *The Origin and History of the Primitive Methodist Church* (London: E. Dalton, [c.1920]), 285–6; 'Nathaniel Minshall (abt. 1780–1848)' – www.wikitree.com/wiki/Minshall-199 (accessed 18.06.21); Chris Jones, 'Minshall Family Has Played a Huge Role in Oswestry's History', *Oswestry & Border Counties Advertizer* (21 Aug. 2017); 'The Register of Oswestry Old Chapel: 1780–1812' – www.melocki.org.uk/salop/OswestryOld.html (accessed 18.06.21).

[68] George Elwick, *The Bankrupt Directory* (London: Simpkin, Marshall & Co., 1843), 246; 'Joseph Lacon, 1842–1918' – www.myheritage.com/names/joseph_lacon (accessed 18.06.21); 'Newbridge Forge and Furnace' NPRN40431, Coflein – https://coflein.gov.uk/en/site/40431 (accessed 18.06.21).

[69] Meeting of Directors, 31 Dec. 1827, LMS Board Minutes, SOAS/CWM.

[70] Meeting of Directors, 16 Jun. 1828, LMS Board Minutes, SOAS/CWM; see also Meeting of Directors, 26 May 1828, LMS Board Minutes, SOAS/CWM.

[71] Meeting of Directors, 28 Jul. 1828, LMS Board Minutes, SOAS/CWM.

leave, when they were addressed by the Treasurer and Secretary and commended to God in prayer by the Rev. John Clayton.'[72]

The same month, unbeknown to the LMS, Ranavalona ascended the throne of Imerina and demanded that the British return the twins to Madagascar. She made her request to Lyall, who forwarded it to Governor Colville on Mauritius. Colville duly informed London but cautioned that if the twins were sent back, they might be killed because

I have been told, by a respectable and disinterested person, that Mr. Lyall has been misinformed with respect to the family and connexions of the two lads in question – and that they are in reality the sons of a once powerful Chief who, from his devotion to Radama's system of politics, has been put to death by order of the present Queen. If this be true, the object of Ranavaloona might be to get these youths into her power – and His Majesty's Government, therefore, may perhaps hesitate to comply with Her request; or, should Voolava and Totoos be sent from England, they could be detained here until affairs in Madagascar might assume a more settled and tranquil appearance.[73]

Colville had been misinformed for, as noted, it was Radama who had executed the twins' father, Andrianavalona.[74] Moreover, the British government had, independently of Ranavalona's request, arranged for the twins' return to Madagascar. On 12 September 1828, they left Dover aboard the *Childe Harold*, a 463-ton former EIC vessel, under Captain W. W. West.[75] On the voyage, the twins were supervised by Lachlan Grant, an assistant surgeon travelling to join the 49th Regiment of Foot on Mauritius.[76] On arrival in Port Louis in November 1828, Grant submitted a health report of the twins:

In transmitting to you a history of the cases of the Madagascar Youths placed under my charge during their voyage from England, great pleasure is afforded me in assuring you that their general health has been remarkably good. The youth [Raombana] to whom my attention was more particularly directed as labouring under a severe abscess on the left side of the sternum from the time of his embarkation to the present moment his appearance and general [health] have wonderfully improved.

Several small ulcers from time to time broke out in the vicinity of the abscess which were healed up by the application of Sulph. (Jinci gr.x ad Cerat Calaminaris Z1) The abscess did not attempt to heal up as I was confident the bone was not diseased at the

[72] Meeting of Directors, 11 Aug. 1828, LMS Board Minutes, SOAS/CWM.

[73] Colville to Huskisson, Mauritius, 1 Oct. 1828, CO 167/101, NAK.

[74] Grandidier, *Histoire physique* (1942), vol. 5, book 1, 197–8; Berg, 'Virtù, and Fortuna', 45–6; Ayache (ed.), *Raombana l'historien*, 53.

[75] Lloyds, *The Register of Shipping for the Year 1828* (London: W. Marchant, 1828): 'Ship Childe Harold' – https://eicships.threedecks.org/ships/shipdetail.php?shipID=891 (accessed 11.08.19); Charles Hardy, *Supplement to a Register of Ships Employed in the Service of the Hon. The East India Company, from the Year 1760 to the Conclusion of the Commercial Charter* (London: J. Hardy, 1835), 49.

[76] [J. McGregor] to W. Hay, Army Medical Department, 27 Apr. 1829, CO 167/113, NAK; Great Britain, War Office, *A List of the Officers of the Army and of the Corps of Royal Marines* (London: William Clowes, 1835), 221; Ayache, 'Un intellectuel malgache', 109.

same time conceiving it to be an effort of nature to prevent an attack of some more dangerous disease. The preparation of [Sarsaparilla] sent on board by Dr. Burder was used as directed by him, I am of opinion that beneficial effects were produced by it.

Attention was paid to the state of his hands more particularly when a change of climate took place. The other [Rahaniraka] had no illness while on board.[77]

In December 1828, Colville wrote to Horace Twiss (1787–1849), under-secretary for war and the colonies from 1828 to 1830:

I have had the honor to receive your letter of the 5th of Augt. last, brought by Volave and Thotoos, the remaining two of the Madagascar Youths, who had been sent to England for their instruction by Sir Robert Farquhar, and whose delicate health had rendered it necessary that they should return to their own Country . . .

I have caused Mr. Lyall to be informed of the arrival of Volave and Thotoos, and of the motives which have led to their leaving England; but, as the month of November is the commencement of the sickly season at Madagascar, and as it would be risking the lives of these Youths to send them home at this period, I shall detain them here until after April next. Meanwhile, I have placed them with Mr. Le Brun, a respectable Missionary Clergyman of this Colony, who will attend to their morals and education, and the gross expense of their maintenance will not, I trust, exceed Twenty pounds a month.[78]

The clergyman mentioned by Colville was Jean Joseph le Brun (1789–1865). Le Brun was born on Jersey in 1789, the son of Protestant parents from Saint-Malo, Brittany, who had fled the French Revolution. He was one of four monoglot francophones from Jersey who in 1810 the LMS accepted for missionary training. Initially earmarked for a mission in 'French Flanders', le Brun worked from 1812 to 1813 among French prisoners of war on Jersey and in Portsmouth before in 1814 being sent to Mauritius. His instructions were to engage in missionary work on Mauritius and Réunion and help prepare the LMS mission to Madagascar. Le Brun, who suffered constant ill-health and was intensely disliked by the local Creole society because of his opposition to slavery, refused Farquhar's repeated requests to found a mission in Madagascar. However, he provided a major service to missionaries David Jones and Thomas Bevan, who in 1818 attempted to settle on the northeast coast of Madagascar (in July 1821, Jones married Mary Anne Mabille, le Brun's sister-in-law). Le Brun continued to assist the mission to Madagascar and readily accepted the governor's request to lodge Raombana and Rahaniraka in his Port Louis home.[79]

[77] Lachlan Grant to James McGregor, Director General Army Medical Department, Isle of France, 22 Nov. 1828, CO 167/113, NAK.
[78] Colville to Horace Twiss, Mauritius, 1 Dec. 1828, CO 167/102, NAK; see also Meeting of Directors, 23 Mar. 1829, LMS Board Meeting, SOAS/CWM.
[79] Tyler Yank, 'Women, Slavery, and British Imperial Intervention in Mauritius, 1810–1845', PhD thesis, McGill University (2019); Campbell, *David Griffiths*, 607, 629.

When news of the twins' arrival on Mauritius reached Lyall in Antananarivo, he informed the Merina court,

In the evening [8 January 1829], I communicated the news of the arrival of Voalua and Totoos at the Mauritius to the Queen, and at the same time made known His Excellency, Sir Charles Colville's general sentiments and warm feelings toward this country. A message was sent in reply, with the Queen's regards, and thanks to the Governor, and a wish that the two Youths should be sent immediately to Madagascar. This led to a medical explanation of their situation, and of the danger of such a journey at too early a season.[80]

Ranavalona agreed that the twins should delay travelling to Madagascar until the start of the dry season in May.[81] She also passed news of the twin's anticipated arrival to their mother, who on 14 January 1829 paid Lyall a visit:

This morning Rafoulsiratoumpou [Rataloha], the Mother of Voaloa and Totoos, accompanied by the Queen's interpreters, presented herself in my chamber to return me thanks for the agreeable news I had communicated respecting her sons; and, at the same time, after the custom of the country, she made me a present of a couple of Ducks. She next requested me to present her kind regards to the Governor of Mauritius, and to make known her gratitude to His Excellency for his considerate attentions to Voaloa and Totoos. Amid so much gloom, and so much barbarism, it rejoices my heart that there is still some material affection and good feeling in the country. A letter is forwarded to Voaloa and Totoos, and another to Mr Jenkins from Rafoutsiratoumpou and Verke.[82]

The Jenkins referred to was almost certainly the same Jenkins the twins had encountered at Manchester. On 10 February, Lyall noted,

The mother of Totoos and Voalave was here again yesterday. She presents her respects to Your Excellency, and begs that you will deliver the accompanying silver chain to her sons; that you will inform them that their sister, two uncles, and family, were also here, and in good health; and that you will be pleased to order them to write to her immediately.[83]

In the event, the twins reached Tamatave on 17 June 1829. Rahaniraka immediately wrote to Viret, private secretary to the governor of Mauritius:

I take my pen in great haste to inform you of our safe arrival in this place, and I hope that this may find you in good health. We arrived here on the 17 inst. and were very well received by Mr. Reddington, who kindly gave us lodging in his house. Dr. Lyall gave us very good advice necessary for our journey, and if it was not for him and Mr. Reddington we would not have known how to act well. We are [preparing] to

---

[80] Lyall, 'Journal', entry for 8 Jan. 1829, CO 167/116, NAK.
[81] Ranavalona to Lyall, Antananarivo, 6 Adidzady (9 Jan.) 1829, in Lyall, 'Journal', CO 167/116, NAK.
[82] Lyall, 'Journal', entry for 14 Jan. 1829, CO 167/116, NAK.
[83] Lyall to Colville, Tananarivou, 10 Feb. 1829, in Lyall, 'Journal' (1829), CO 167/116, NAK.

begin our journey this morning. Please to remember us kindly to the Governor and his Lady &c. &c.[84]

Lyall, who had recently been ordered to leave Madagascar, was in Tamatave awaiting a boat to return to Mauritius. Reddington (d. 1834), also called Papay, who was a native of Manchester, where the twins had spent most of their time in Britain, had by 1827 settled as a merchant in Tamatave and married a Malagasy woman. Ranavalona appointed Reddington an *andriambaventy* – a judge – a status that gave him considerable prestige and material benefits. He rendered major assistance to the LMS missionaries, and by extension to Raombana and Rahaniraka, whom he informed that he had tried in vain to persuade Ratefy to flee to Mauritius to escape assassination by Ranavalona in mid-1828. When Reddington died in 1834, Baker, the LMS printer, adopted Reddington's second son and took him to Antananarivo to live with him and to educate. When, two years later, Baker left Madagascar definitively, the boy probably returned to Tamatave.[85]

The twins reached Antananarivo on 2 July from where, a week later, Rahaniraka wrote to Viret:

it is with great pleasure that I take my pen to inform you of our safe arrival in this place . . . The Country between Tamatave and Tananarive are beautiful, but the greatest part of the roads are most shocking compared with those at the Mauritius.

We had a pleasant journey to the Capital except 2 days when we were wet to the skin. At Anoosy July 2nd at 2 o'clock, we proceeded on our way to the Capital on horseback with 2 officers before and 2 behind, the cannons fired 7 times as we ascended the Hill for Tananarive, and at ½ past 3 o'clock, we were in the court yard.

The Queen showed us much respects – she promised that if we are faithful to Her, she will do anything for us, but if not the contrary, and to show, she said that she was glad at our arrival – She danced. There were about 200 persons dancing at once – their manners seemed very strange to us. The manner in which my Mother and our Friends received us, may better be conceived than described.

We are now at the end of our journey, and we hope that we may be useful to our Fellow-Countrymen. Please to excuse bad writing and all mistakes. Please to remember us kindly to the Governor and his Lady.[86]

This is the sole reference I have encountered to Ranavalona dancing, although Lyall noted that she thoroughly enjoyed swimming and games.[87] On 17 June 1829, Rahaniraka also sent a letter to the LMS, carried to Tamatave by 'our servants'–almost certainly slaves, announcing their safe arrival.[88]

[84] Volave to Viret, Tamatave, 20 Jun. 1829, HB 20, NAM.
[85] Campbell, *David Griffiths*, 719, 789, 995 fn. 5.
[86] Volave to Viret, Tananarive, 10 Jul. 1829, HB 20, NAM.
[87] Lyall to Colville, Tananarivou, 6 Nov. 1828, CO 167/116, NAK.
[88] Volare to [LMS], Tananarive, 10 Jul. 1829, MIL B.3 F.2 J.A, SOAS/CWM.

Rahaniraka's letter to Viret relieved the twins of any foreboding they might have felt due to the fate of their father. It demonstrated that Ranavalona and their mother were on excellent terms and that, provided they proved loyal and cooperative, they could expect the queen's blessing. Indeed, she confirmed that they would enjoy the noble privilege of being exempt from judgement in ordinary courts.[89] Ranavalona also permitted the twins to assume their *andriana* inheritance of a *menakely*, a fief granted by the crown, in Anosy (the location noted in Rahaniraka's letter to Viret) some 11 km north of Antananarivo. There, the twins maintained slaves and commanded the unremunerated servitude of the nominally free members of the lower *hova* caste.[90] In addition, Ranavalona favoured them with other domains, in Imerina, in Betanimena, and on the frontiers of Bezanozano and Antsihanaka 'because they are descendants from King Andriamasinavalona, ... their rank is the same as Duke in England, their people amount to 4000'.[91] The Bezanozano–Antsihanaka frontier was located at the top of the Mangoro Valley, a mountainous region where cattle were raised, in clearings surrounded by primary forest. The Merina court sent political exiles there as it was characterized by endemic malaria from which highlanders almost invariably soon perished.[92] The twins used their additional fiefs, run by slaves, to raise cattle for export to the Mascarenes – an enterprise that brought them great wealth.[93]

By all accounts, the twins valued their status, were devoted to the crown, and did not wish to see the pillars of the established order, such as the caste system and slavery, abolished.[94] They returned to Antananarivo at the height of tension between the Merina and European powers: with the British over the expulsion of Lyall and with the French, who a few months later attacked Tamatave and Foulepointe. At such a time, Ranavalona, who greatly valued the twins' fluent spoken and written English, anticipated that, as Radama had intended, they would act as court interpreters and counsellors on foreign, notably European, affairs. Although she was apparently illiterate, she prioritized written communication in her dealings with her officials and with foreigners (with the notable exception of Lyall).[95] As Raombana stated, with regard to the literacy spread by the missionary schools in the 1820s, 'Has no schools been established in IMERINA, no important business or affair could have been transmitted to the

[89] Ayache (ed.), *Raombana l'historien*, 54; Berg, 'Virtù, and Fortuna', 45–6.
[90] Ayache (ed.), *Raombana l'historien*, 10, 300.
[91] Meeting of Directors, 9 Feb. 1835, LMS Board Meeting, SOAS/CWM.
[92] Campbell, *David Griffiths*, 597, 746.   [93] Ayache (ed.), *Raombana l'historien*, 47.
[94] Ayache, 'Un intellectuel malgache', 97, 100, 103; Ayache (ed.), *Raombana l'historien*, 10.
[95] Gerald M. Berg, 'Writing Ideology: Ranavalona, the Ancestral Bureaucrat' *History in Africa* 22 (1995), 87; Gwyn Campbell, *The Travels of Robert Lyall, 1789–1831: Scottish Surgeon, Naturalist and British Agent to the Court of Madagascar* (Cham, Switzerland: Palgrave Macmillan, 2020).

Garrisons'.[96] However, it took some time before the queen could fully utilize them, for they had left Madagascar at the age of nine and after an absence of nine years initially had difficulty speaking their native tongue.[97]

As soon as the twins regained competency in Malagasy, they assumed the role of the queen's principal foreign secretaries and as such were privy to all important exchanges with Europeans, notably with the missionaries and LMS (see section below), and French and British political authorities. For instance, in mid-1840 they were present at a meeting in Antananarivo with C. M. Campbell, a representative of the Free Labour Association of Mauritius that, following the abolition of slavery in 1835 and a ban on the import of Indian indentured labour in May 1839, sought to recruit indentured Malagasy labour. The venture was fully backed by the governor of Mauritius. The twins translated Campbell's written proposal into Malagasy for Rainimaharo, chief secretary of state, and acted as interpreters throughout the meeting. However, the Merina economy rested on the exploitation of unfree labour, and the regime could not afford for Mauritius to gain access to its labour resources. Thus, the court rejected Campbell's proposal.[98] Again, Rahaniraka and Raombana assisted with the diplomacy that led to the reopening of imperial ports, closed after the 1845 Franco-British attack, following the payment in 1853 of a $15,000 indemnity by Mauritian traders.[99]

Their positions as chief secretaries did not preclude for Rahaniraka and Raombana military service, in which their elder brother, Ratsifehera had died in 1822, during an expedition to the southwest of the island.[100] In 1831, Raombana was promoted to the military status of 9 Vtr, or 'Honours', and commanded to select from newly conscripted soldiers those who were to participate in the next military expedition.[101] And in July 1834, Rahaniraka participated in a military expedition to Tamatave to counter the threat of an attack by French forces based on Sainte Marie.[102] The Vtr, introduced by Radama at the time of the British alliance, ran initially from grades 1 to 11. Ranavalona increased their number, first to 13, and in 1852 to 14.[103] In 1836, 1 Vtr signified a simple 'private', 7 Vtr 'captain', 8 Vtr 'major', 9 Vtr 'colonel', 10 Vtr 'marshall', and 12 Vtr a top-ranking 'general'.[104] As LMS printer

[96] RH, 134.   [97] Ayache, 'Un intellectuel malgache', 109.
[98] Charles William Mackenzie Campbell, 'Journal' (1840), HB 14, NAM.
[99] Raombana, 'Manuscrit écrit à Tananarive', 5.   [100] RH, 112–13.
[101] Ayache (ed.), Raombana l'historien, 11–16, 361.
[102] Baker to Ellis, Tamatave, 15 Jul. 1834, MIL B.5 F.1 J.C, SOAS/CWM; Ayache (ed.), Raombana l'historien, 115–16, 361.
[103] Raombana, 'Annales', Livre 13, 33, Fonds Résidence Générale de France, ARM.
[104] [Edward Baker], Madagascar Past and Present (London: R. Bentley, 1847), 97; Campbell, David Griffiths, 813.

Edward Baker explained in 1840, such honours were conferred in part as compensation to those, including women, requisitioned for *fanompoana*:

Eleven gradations of rank were created, above which was the King himself; and the 11th or highest was a Commander in Chief in the Military and a Chief Judge in the Civil Department. These have now been augmented to 13, and the officer of Government usually denominate themselves by their rank, as a Colonel calls himself the 9th Voninahitra, or faha 9, the 9th (i.e.) honor. This system has even been extended to the Women, making them Captains, Colonels, and so forth; and often are they called upon to do hard Service, such as collecting bees-wax, gum copal &c., and even carrying up luggage to the Capital.[105]

Sometime before 1838, Raombana was promoted to 10 Vtr, a rank he maintained until his death and which entitled him to more than seven *deka* (aides-de-camp).[106] In 1853, he led 5,000 soldiers to suppress a revolt in Vangaindrano in southeast Madagascar, in which, according to his brother, he gained a reputation because of his bravery, intelligence, 'and the compassion he showed to the poor prisoners and soldiers in the grip of famine'.[107]

The Twins, Christianity, and the Intra-missionary Dispute

Radama's decision in 1826 to break with the 1820 Britanno-Merina treaty accentuated a major intra-missionary rift in which, from their return in 1829, Raombana and Rahaniraka became deeply involved. From 1824, when Radama dictated that Welshmen Jones and Griffiths, instead of English missionary John Jeffreys (1792–1825), run the LMS schools in central Imerina, missionary activities were steadily brought under royal control. The following year, the king imposed ten-year residence permits on all European residents, instructed them where to reside, and obliged them to apply for passports in order to travel any distance.[108] This obliged the missionaries to choose between accepting crown control of the mission or abandoning Madagascar. Jeffreys left the island

---

[105] Baker to Lionel Smith, Pitou, Mauritius, 7 Aug. 1840, CO 167/229, NAK.
[106] Raombana, 'Annales' Livre 4, Fonds Résidence Générale de France, ARM; Ayache (ed.), *Raombana l'historien*, 115, 363.
[107] Rahaniraka, quoted in Ayache (ed.), *Raombana l'historien*, 363.
[108] Jean René to Farquhar, 4 Dec. 1821, in Jean Valette, 'Correspondance de Jean René à Sir Robert Farquhar', *BAM* 45.2 (1967), 83; Raymond Decary, 'Documents historiques relatifs àl'éstablissement français de Sainte-Marie sous la Restauration', *BAM* 13, 65; RA, 295; Ellis, *History of Madagascar*, vol. 1, 377–8; William Ellis, *Madagascar Revisited* (London: John Murray, 1867), 247–8; copies of correspondence between Freeman and Johns and Ranavalona I, MIL, B.4 F.3 J.C, and B.4 F.3 J.D, SOAS/CWM; Rabary, *Ny Daty Malaza*, vol. 1, 23, 26-7; HdR, 928; Gwyn Campbell, 'Labour and the Transport Problem in Imperial Madagascar, 1810–1895', *Journal of African History* 21.3 (1980), 341–3.

Figure 7.2 David Griffiths (1792–1863)
Source: Campbell, *David Griffiths*, frontispiece.

in June 1825, but Jones and Griffiths (see Figure 7.2) opted to remain and accept Radama's authority over their activities.[109]

The Welshmens' decision had some major advantages for mission work. First, by royal command, an Imerina-wide network of schools was established for which pupils were guaranteed. Second, the Merina court channelled older boy students into the government bureaucracy or army and older girls into arranged marriages with members of the court elite or into government sewing groups. The king also intended that Malagasy apprentices attached to European craftsmen would, once they had mastered the skills, replace the foreign artisans and manage workshops on the government's account. Over time, this ensured that missionary educated and trained Merina youths were placed in key positions where they might influence policy in favour of the mission.[110] More tellingly, Jones and Griffiths supported Radama in his

---

[109] David Griffiths, 'The Second report of the Madagascar Missionary School Society, 1828, Under the Patronage of His Majesty Radama', MIL B.2 F.4 J.D, SOAS/CWM; Campbell, *David Griffiths*, 83, 665, 668.

[110] Gwyn Campbell, 'Slavery and Fanompoana: The Structure of Forced Labour in Imerina (Madagascar), 1790–1861', *Journal of African History* 29.3 (1988), 466–74.

decision to reject the Britanno-Merina treaty of 1820 and thereby agreed to serve the Merina rather than the English crown. Jones, a native Welsh speaker who was also fluent in Malagasy, English, and French, accepted Radama's request to become his foreign secretary, thereby becoming intimately involved in Radama's relations with British and French traders and political authorities.[111] For example, he played an instrumental role as interpreter in negotiations leading up to the Blancard Agreement of October 1826 that undermined the free trade basis of the 1820 British treaty.[112]

The LMS directors in London were affronted by the stance of Jones and Griffiths, who they considered to be uncultivated Welshmen, hostile to English culture and imperial interests. Following Jeffreys' departure, they sought an educated Englishman to replace them as head of the Madagascar mission. In 1826, they offered Joseph Freeman, a man of refined education, an exceptional six-year contract with the brief to assume supervisory control of the Madagascar mission and act as the moral and spiritual counterpart to the British political agent at the Merina court. The directors considered that, for such a role, Freeman would not require a knowledge of Malagasy, instead sending him to France 'for the purpose of rendering himself competent to converse in the French Language' to use in his exchanges with Radama and visiting diplomats.[113]

Freeman, who arrived in Madagascar in August 1827, initially refused to engage in missionary activity.[114] Rather, he waited for the anticipated arrival from Mauritius in mid-1828 of Lyall, and of the LMS deputation comprising Tyerman and Bennet, to confirm his position as head of the mission. However, the hopes of Freeman and Lyall were dashed in mid-1828 by the deaths of Tyerman and Radama and the ascension to the throne of Ranavalona, who continued to acknowledge Jones and Griffiths as heads of the mission and expelled Lyall in 1829. When Jones left Madagascar in mid-1830 because of illness, Griffiths became the paramount object of the animosity of Freeman, Lyall, and the LMS.[115]

[111] Radama I to Cole, Tananarivou, 23 Oct. 1826, HB 4, NAM; Radama I to Cole, Tananarivou, 9 Mar 1827, HB 4, NAM; Jones to Hankey, Tananarivou, 15 Jun. 1827, MIL B.2 F.4 J.B, SOAS/CWM.

[112] Jones and Griffiths to [LMS], Antananarivo, 9 Nov. 1826, MIL B.2 F.3 J.D and Freeman to Hankey, Tamatave, 9 Aug. 1827, B.2 F.5 – SOAS/CWM; Radama I to Cole, Tananarivou, 15 Nov. 1826, HB 4, NAM; Campbell, *David Griffiths*, 686.

[113] LMS Board Minutes, 24 Nov. 1826, Home Correspondence, General, A, B.4 F.8 J.B, SOAS/CWM; LMS Board Minutes, 30 Oct. 1826; Freeman to LMS, [Kidderminster, 8 Nov. 1826], Home Correspondence. General. A, B.4 F.8 J.B, SOAS/CWM; Freeman to Arundel, Tamatave, 4 Nov. 1829, MIL B.3 F.5, SOAS/CWM; Freeman in 'Deputation to South Africa. Valedictory Service on the Departure of the Rev. J. J. Freeman', *Missionary Magazine and Chronicle* 151 (1 Dec. 1848), 184; Joseph John Freeman, *A Tour in South Africa, with Notices of Natal, Mauritius, Madagascar, Ceylon, Egypt, and Palestine* (London: John Snow, 1851), 5.

[114] 'Letter from Jones and Griffiths', 9 Nov. 1826, Africa and Madagascar, Committee Minutes, Meeting of Southern Committee, Monday 28 May 1827, SOAS/CWM.

[115] Campbell, *David Griffiths*.

It is in this context that the claims of Freeman, and fellow missionary David Johns, that Raombana and Rahaniraka had rejected Christianity should be evaluated. Certainly, despite their English liberal education, the twins praised Merina culture, including oral traditions that contrasted greatly with the book culture they had experienced in Britain. As Raombana stated,

what struck me most was their retentive memory, and the persuasive eloquence which every Hova [Merina] people seem to possess from the old men to the mere children that plays and romp about the streets, and in the public assembly or kabary, they display their eloquence in the highest degree. They speak without premeditation, and have a great flow of words, and no confusions are at all perceived in them ... the judges who are sent to hear or listen to the law suits of people in open courts rehearse them to the sovereign again, without I think so much as omitting the least circumstance, so that it is as good, as if what the contending parties had said, had been taken down in 'short hand'.[116]

The twins also embraced polygamy and slavery. Thus, Raombana took three wives, one an 'intimate relative of the Queen',[117] and possessed over 100 slaves.[118] In his turn, by the 1850s Rahaniraka had at least two wives.[119] In October 1830, reflecting the views of Freeman, Lyall commented,

It is painful to find that Tatous and Voalave, the two youths who lately returned from England to Madagascar, are already quite assimilated with their countrymen, in dress, and language, and, apparently, in manners. They are no longer English looking young men; and their means are inadequate for enabling them to support a high rank. In a paltry apartment, they give some instructions to their less informed brethren, but much of their time is said to be passed in trifling and idleness.[120]

The same year, Johns reported that the twins never attended church and actively opposed the 'Bible',[121] and Freeman that they had adopted 'licentious' ways. Freeman and Johns further claimed that the twins accused them of being political agents intent on imposing British rule over Madagascar.[122]

However, this reflected a malicious campaign orchestrated by Johns, Freeman, and Lyall, intended to undermine the reputation of the twins and, by extension, that of Jones and Griffiths. It was true that, unlike the other Madagascar Youths to visit Britain, Rahaniraka and Raombana had never been baptized, nor did they ever profess to being Christian.[123] However, they detested the *sampy*, or traditional Merina talismans, and, until Christianity was banned in 1835, maintained their

---

[116] RH, 6.
[117] Meeting of Directors, 9 Feb. 1835, LMS Board Meeting, SOAS/CWM; see also Ayache (ed.), *Raombana l'historien*, 104.
[118] Ayache (ed.), *Raombana l'historien*, 100, 102; Ayache, 'Un intellectuel malgache', 111.
[119] Ayache (ed.), *Raombana l'historien*, 104.
[120] Lyall, 'Journal', 18 Oct. 1830, CO 167/116, NAK.
[121] Johns to Arrundle [sic], Antananarivo, 19 Feb. 1830, MIL B.3 F.3 J.A, SOAS/CWM.
[122] Freeman to Hankey, Port Louis, 19 Jul. 1830, MIL B.3 F.3 J.C, SOAS/CWM.
[123] Ayache, 'Un intellectuel malgache', 113.

links with the mission church at Ambodin'Andahalo under Griffiths' supervision. Moreover, the twins consistently lauded the missionary endeavour to the LMS directors in London and Clunie in Manchester, to whom they regularly wrote, and from whom they received presents and news of their British friends.[124] In December 1830, the twins informed the LMS that Ranavalona had confirmed Radama's support of mission schools in which thousands of scholars had learnt to read and write.[125] In another letter, dated August 1831, they praised the work of Griffiths, whose chapel they attended and with whom they forged an intimate friendship, defending him against the attacks of Freeman and Johns.[126] In January 1832, they informed the LMS that Griffiths was not only at the heart of a Christian revival in Madagascar but was held in high esteem by the Merina crown:

We take the opportunity of writing to you to inform you that we and all the Europeans here are in good health and we hope that you are the same. By the efforts of your Missionaries, thousands here can read the word of God in their own tongue. Your Missionaries of which we are very glad to inform you (especially Mr. Griffiths) are indefatigable in their duties both to God and Man. Many of the boys these last 5 months have been baptized, and we think since the arrival of your Missionaries, the Malagasy has greatly improved. There are no less than 7 Prayer Meeting houses in AnTananarivo which are attended by Messrs. G[riffiths] and Baker. It is really affecting to see the Natives read the word of God and sing his praises in their own language. Does not this stimulate you to do all you can to send the Gospel of Jesus to all nations that all may read the word of God. Think that your country was once more superstitious than Madagascar, but by the introduction of Christianity it is now become the happy means of sending the Word of God to all parts of the world. Not a while ago, a little disagreeable dispute happened between Mr. Griffiths and all the other Europeans except Messrs. Baker and Baker [Brady?] who stood neutral. As they could not settle it among themselves, it was referred to the decision of Her Majesty, who decided that Mr. Griffiths was blameless. We were perfectly acquainted with what passed between them during their quarrel.[127]

In 1832, Rahaniraka and Rafaralahy also reacted to news that the LMS, influenced notably by Freeman, had decided to recall Griffiths, by informing the directors that if Griffiths left Madagascar, the mission would collapse:

Ever since we returned to Madagascar, we never heard of any complaint whatever against Mr. Griffiths by any of the Natives_ they consider him to be more entirely devoted to the Missionary labour than any of the Missionaries. His knowledge of the

---

[124] See e.g. Meeting of Directors, 19 Sep. 1831 and 9 Feb. 1835, LMS Board Meeting, SOAS/ CWM; Ellis to Kelsey, London 14 Jun. 1833, MOL, SOAS/CWM.

[125] Rafaralahy to Arundel, Tananarivo, 1 Dec. 1830, MIL B.3 F.4 J.C, SOAS/CWM; Rahaniraka to Hankey, Tananarive, 5 Dec. 1830, MIL B.3 F.4 J.C, SOAS/CWM.

[126] Rahaniraka and Rafaralahy to Hankey, Tananarivo, 20 Aug. 1831, MIL B.3 F.4 J.C, SOAS/CWM.

[127] Rahaniraka and Rafaralahy to Hankey, An Tananarivo, 12 Jan. 1832, MIL B.4 F.2 J.A, SOAS/CWM.

manners and language of the people here renders him truly useful. With these valuable acquisitions, the Natives are eager to hear him preach the Word of God and more inclined to talk to him on subjects that they cannot understand. But what was our surprise, when we heard that the Directors had recalled him, because there was a want of cordiality between him and the other missionaries. We hope that the Directors will recall back that order, because they must have been misinformed respecting Mr. Griffiths' character. If Mr. Griffiths leaves this place never to return again, we think that the Mission here in a few years will dwindle away. Without Mr. Griffiths' aid, how will they translate the Bible into a language that they do not perfectly understand. No Europeans whatever, whether Traders or Missionaries knows the Malagash Language so well as Mr. G. If Mr. G leaves this place the Directors will lose a most valuable Missionary.[128]

While the LMS directors remained adamant that Griffiths should leave, the twins were effective in promoting Griffiths at court, where their position as royal secretaries was unchallenged. This was particularly the case with Raombana, who, from 1832 until his death in 1855, was constantly in Ranavalona's presence, serving as her chief foreign and private secretary.[129] The twins were pivotal in persuading Ranavalona to grant Griffiths the right to stay in Madagascar when his ten-year residence visa expired in 1831: They persuaded Griffiths to deny that he was an agent of the British government, to abandon any claim to extraterritorial rights, and to become subject to local laws – effectively becoming a Merina subject. Further, they orchestrated all officers of 10 Vtr and many junior officers to present a 'verbal petition' to the queen in support of Griffiths.[130] In August 1832, they informed the LMS that Ranavalona had granted Griffiths the right to remain in Madagascar and urged them to express their gratitude to her:

After considering all the good that Mr. G. has done in Her Kingdom, his good behaviour to his countrymen, and his conduct to Her subjects, she has determined that he and his family should not leave Madagascar … We think that the Directors should rejoice and give thanks to God, for having a Missionary in the large island of Madagascar, who is admired by every class of people for his good conducts.

We think also that the Directors should write to Her Majesty to thank Her for permitting Mr. G. to remain in her Kingdom, after his time for staying here was expired. By the efforts of your Missionaries may this interesting Island, soon be turned into a garden of the Lord, and all Her sons look up to God as their Maker and Jesus as their Saviour. We can assure you, that the word of God has taken deep root in the mind of

---

[128] Rahaniraka and Rafaralahy to J. Arundel, An Tananarivo, 21 Jun. 1832, MIL B.4 F.2 J.D, SOAS/CWM; see also Rahaniraka and Raombana to Hankey, Antananarivo, 16 Jan. 1832, MIL B.4 F.2. J.A, SOAS/CWM.

[129] Ayache (ed.), *Raombana l'historien*, 363, 111; Ayache, 'Un intellectuel malgache', 97, 103.

[130] 'Baker to Clayton', Antananarivo, 18 Aug. 1831, MIL B.4 F.1 J.B, SOAS/CWM; see also Ranavalona to Griffiths, Antananarivo, 16 Jan. 1832, quoted in Rahaniraka and Raombana to Hankey, Antananarivo, 16 Jan. 1832, MIL B.4 F.2. J.A, SOAS/CWM.

many of the Natives, so that your missionaries have not laboured in vain. Ought not this to stimulate you to do all you can for the spread of the Gospel.

Her Majesty in a letter to the Directors (dated Antananarivo 13, Asombola 1832) told them that Mr. Griffiths' conduct during the late King's reign and Her reign was without blemish, and that the children he has taught had acquired a perfect knowledge of what they had learnt &c.[131]

Curiously given Freeman's animosity to Griffiths and to them, the twins intervened in mid-1833 to save him from Ranavalona's wrath. Freeman had returned from a visit to Mauritius carrying smallpox vaccine with which he inoculated Reddington and his family in Tamatave. This angered Ranavalona, who believed Freeman thereby intended to propagate smallpox. Consequently, she had him detained and banned the use of the vaccine.[132] However, Freeman was released upon the intervention of the twins and Griffiths, who explained the nature of vaccination.[133] Again, from May to June 1834, the twins assisted Freeman and Johns in printing the Malagasy to English and English to Malagasy dictionaries at the LMS press in Antananarivo.[134]

Following the ban on Christianity in March 1835, the twins were protective of indigenous converts, whose oratory skills sometimes impressed them. Thus Raombana wrote, 'Judge therefore my surprise … to hear this persuasive eloquence flow from the mouth of an indigenous Christian, whose words, I may say, were irresistible.'[135] They also honoured some Christmas festivals.[136] For example, in 1853, they celebrated Christmas Day at the residence of Laborde, in Andohalo, in the company of the Salem merchant, Marks.[137] The early Welsh missionaries did not acknowledge Christmas, which was traditionally ignored in Celtic Britain. However, it had a long tradition in parts of England, particularly in the north. Thus, in the 1820s, Liverpool workhouse paupers received an annual Christmas treat of roast beef and plum pudding, while in December 1828 a local paper in Manchester, where the twins studied, announced a Christmas season of pantomimes and other entertainment. Christmas became a major family event throughout England following the publication in 1843 of *A Christmas Carol* by Charles Dickens.[138]

---

[131] Rahaniraka and Rafaralahy to Arundel, Antananarivo, 14 Aug. 1832, MIL B.4 F.3 J.A, SOAS/CWM.

[132] Freeman to Ellis, Tamatave, 3 Oct. 1833, MIL B.4 F.4 J.B, SOAS/CWM.

[133] Freeman to Ellis, Vohitsara, 11 Oct. 1833, MIL B.4 F.4 J.C, SOAS/CWM.

[134] [Freeman], Report of the Madagascar Mission for the half year ending 3rd Apr 1834, MIL B.5 F.1 J.C, SOAS/CWM.

[135] Raombana, quoted in Ayache (ed.), *Raombana l'historien*, 109; see also 110.

[136] Ayache (ed.), *Raombana l'historien*, 110.

[137] Raombana, 'Manuscrit écrit à Tananarive', 15, 17–18.

[138] John Gillis, 'Making Time for Family: The Invention of Family Time(s) and the Reinvention of Family History', *Journal of Family History* 21.1 (1996), 9; Mark Connolly, *Christmas: A History* (London: Tauris, 2012), 3.

Moreover, despite banning Christianity, Ranavalona ordered the twelve senior teachers formerly in mission schools to continue their English studies and teach English to a class of forty children. She also authorized Raombana and Rahaniraka to assist in the revision of the New Testament, as well as to teach English to top officers and members of the royal family.[139] The twins thereby grew close to Rakoto Radama (the future Radama II), Ranavalona's son and heir, who they tutored in an 'English School' at court and who Rahaniraka continued to teach until 1862, the year he was crowned king.[140] The twins helped to shape Rakoto's pro-Christian stance, one that led him to initially declare himself a Christian and, even when he retreated from that position, to offer protection to clandestine Christians.[141]

Threat of Revolt

Following the 1835 ban on Christianity, the clandestine Malagasy church was a source both of refuge from and of protest against the Merina state.[142] Discontent among the growing band of Christians, and among members of the army and bureaucracy excluded from the inner court circle which enriched itself through pillage of the provinces and the widespread application of *fanompoana*, manifested itself in the form of a revolutionary 'Patriot' movement, which the twins joined. In 1837, one prominent Patriot, Rainihiova, fled Imerina with the intention of joining Ramanetaka on Moheli in rebellion against Ranavalona. He was captured at Mananjara and executed.[143] In 1840, when Campbell visited Imerina, he was approached by a fluent English-speaking Merina – possibly Raombana, who in his secret history called Ranavalona 'a fierce monster in the shape of a woman' and a usurper.[144] Decrying the destructive impact of *fanompoana,* the man requested that the British help Ramanetaka seize the Merina throne:

The Kingdom is rushing to its own destruction. All of the youth, whatever their social background, is being taken for the army, and everyone, everywhere, is being forced to work for nothing. Over three thousand officials are at this minute in jail for accepting bribes to release people from military service, and for stating that many people who are still alive, were dead. The country is tired of the two brothers, Rainihiaro and Rainimaharo [Ranavalona's chief ministers] – the latter being the worst. The two think of nothing but exploiting and plundering the people in order to fill their own coffers. Why don't you British, instead of the French, assist Ramanetaka to seize the throne in Madagascar? If he were placed over us, we would possess a good King. I'm

[139] Johns to Ellis, Antananarivo, 21 Nov. 1835, MIL B.5 F.2 J.C, SOAS/CWM.
[140] Ayache (ed.), *Raombana l'historien*, 117.
[141] Campbell, *David Griffiths*, 62, 68, 240, 803, 817
[142] See *Bombay Times and Journal of Commerce* (26 Jul. 1848) quoting *Le Mauricien* (3 Jul. 1848).
[143] RA, 448–9.   [144] RH, 35, 144–5.

certain that if the people heard that the *Angilis* [i.e. 'English'] were supporting him, hardly a sword would be raised against him.[145]

Again, writing shortly after his definitive departure from the island in 1840, Griffiths noted,

the inhabitants of the majority of provinces attempt to escape, in search of a refuge from the iron yoke placed around their necks. Some revolt against the government saying that, regardless of whether they are submissive or rebellious, their sons will be killed whilst the women and children will be sold like animals in the market place.[146]

Attempts were also made to foster links with anti-Merina movements elsewhere in the island. In the early 1840s, Andriamifidy, a high ranking *Olomainty*, fled to the 'south' to instruct provincial peoples in the art of fortifying villages, while a Merina officer, Andrianampaka, took flight to the west to offer the Sakalava instruction in British military discipline. However, both men were intensely distrusted by their respective hosts, who killed them.[147]

In 1845, the Patriots tacitly supported the Britanno-French naval assault on Tamatave. The attack caused Ranavalona to close Merina-controlled ports to the British and French, resulting in a slump in export earnings and sharp curtailment of the money supply. Consequently, people found it difficult to pay taxes, and there were further rumours of rebellion.[148] A foreign observer commented in 1848 that two unsuccessful attempts at revolt in Imerina had already been made, and many Malagasy would support armed intervention by Britain.[149] As there was no response from the British, the prominent Patriots Raharolahy and Razafinkarefo – one of the Madagascar Youths sent to Britain – hitherto major supporters of British influence in Madagascar, pressed Rakoto Radama to appeal, via Laborde, to Napoleon III (r. 1852–70) to depose Ranavalona and place him on the throne.[150] However, the 1848 revolution in France prevented any follow-up.[151] There is no further mention of Razafinkarefo until September 1862, when it was noted that he was aide-de-camp to the commander-in-chief of

[145] Extract from the Diary of Campbell, quoted in David Griffiths, *Hanes Madagascar* (Machynlleth: Richard Jones, 1843), 110– author's translation.

[146] Griffiths, *Hanes Madagascar*, 126 –author's translation.

[147] Raombana, 'Livre' 13 B2, 26–7; see also *Madagascar and the United States* (New York: Thompson & Moreau, 1883), 7.

[148] Raombana, 'Livre' 12 C1, 495, 501–2 – AAM; Raombana, 'Livre' 13 B2, 4; Oliver, *Madagascar*, vol. 2, 196.

[149] Samuel Shipton, 'Madagascar' (9 Jun. 1848), in House of Commons, *Parliamentary Papers* 37.23 (1849), encl. 1, 679.

[150] Raombana, 'Manuscrit écrit à Tananarive', 24; Laborde to Commander Febvrier des Pointes, Tananarivo, 6 Dec. 1848, in André Dandouau, 'Documents divers concernant J. Laborde', *BAM* 9 (1911), 144–7; Razafincarafe to Arundel, Antananarivo, 10 Apr. 1831, MIL B.4 F.1 J.A, SOAS/CWM.

[151] Raombana, 'Manuscrit écrit à Tananarive', 24; Dandouau, 'Documents divers concernant J. Laborde', 147–9; Grandidier, *Histoire physique* (1942), vol. 5, book 1, 289, fn. 2a.

Tamatave.[152] Raharolahy/Raharo (b. c.1811), another of the plotters, was one of the first three children to enter Jones' school in 1820. In the early 1830s, he continued his studies under Raombana, taught children to read and write Malagasy, and assisted Freeman and Johns with the dictionary. Tall and thin, he spoke fluent English and reasonable French. He later became a governor of Tamatave.[153]

By 1853, discontent among soldiers had reached such a pitch that, according to Raombana, the Merina army would have refused to defend the throne against a foreign invasion force.[154] Before the end of the year, Ranavalona abruptly ended the hitherto relentless campaigns against non-Merina peoples of the island and thus also the seemingly unlimited military conscription in Imerina. Further, she accepted a $15,000 indemnity from Mauritian merchants for the 1845 Franco-British attack and reopened her ports to foreign trade.[155] Nevertheless, non-military *fanompoana* continued to expand, and in 1857 Rakoto was part of a conspiracy to stage a coup, hatched by Laborde and other Europeans residents and visitors to Imerina, including Ida Pfeiffer and two Catholic missionaries, Finaz and François Webber (1819–1864).[156] The plot was discovered; Rakoto and Webber were spared punishment, but all the other Europeans involved were expelled from the island. Laborde returned after the death of Ranavalona to assume the post of French consul.[157]

[152] W. A. Middleton, F. A. Marindin, Edward Newton, Edward Mellish, and J. Caldwell to William Stevenson, Governor of Mauritius, Port Louis, 25 Nov. 1861, in 'Copies or Extracts of papers relating to the Congratulatory Mission to King Radama of Madagascar on his Accession to the Throne in 1861: And, of Correspondence and Papers relating to the Mission to Madagascar in 1862, for the purpose of presenting the Portraits and presents sent by Her Most Gracious Majesty to King Radama', in House of Commons, *Accounts and Papers*, vol. 74 (1863); see also Samuel Pasfield Oliver, *On and Off Duty, Being Leaves from an Officer's Note-Book* (London: W. H. Allen, 1881), 164; Oliver *Madagascar*, vol. 1, 94.

[153] LMS Board Minutes, 5 and 13 Mar. 1837, SOAS/CWM; RA, 379–80, 394, 397, 403, 404–5, 408–9, 430–5, 437; 'Genadwriaeth oddiwrth Frenhines Madagascar at Frenin Brydain', *Y Drysorfa* 7 (1837), 186–7; Joseph John Freeman and David Johns, *A Narrative of the Persecution of the Christians in Madagascar with Details of the Escape of the Six Christian Refugees Now in England* (London: John Snow, 1840), 39; William Ellis and Joseph John Freeman, *Madagascar and Its Martyrs: A Book for the Young* (London: John Snow, 1842), 33; RH, 123; ; James Cross Thorne, 'Elementary Education in Madagascar', *AAMM* 12 (1888), 28; A. Siegrist, *Mademoiselle Juliette: Princesse malgache* (Tananarive: Pilot de la Beau Jardière, 1937), 23–4, 101; Ayache (ed.), *Raombana l'historien*, 125.

[154] Raombana, 'Manuscrit écrit à Tananarive', 11.

[155] Campbell, 'Slavery and Fanompoana', 468–9; Gwyn Campbell, *An Economic History of Imperial Madagascar, 1750–1895: The Rise and Fall of an Island Empire* (Cambridge: Cambridge University Press, 2005), 337; Campbell, *David Griffiths*, 869–70.

[156] Paul Camboué, 'Les dix premiers ans de l'Enfance chez les Malgaches: Circoncision, nom, éducation', *Anthropos* 4.2 (1909), 375 fn. 2.

[157] H. H. Cousins, '*Tanghin*, or the Poison Ordeal of Madagascar', *AAMM* 20 (1896), 385–8.

Later Years

Rakoto Radama's association with the twins lasted until they died – Raombana in 1855, aged forty-six, and Rahaniraka in 1862 at the age of fifty-four.[158] Rahaniraka stated that Raombana died suddenly on 4 June 1855 either of apoplexy (a stroke) or epilepsy. The following Monday at 6.30 am the funeral celebrations commenced at Anosy, where he was buried in his ancestral tomb. The Merina often incurred significant debt in order to hold as lavish a funeral as possible for family members.[159] The proceedings, which lasted two days, were carried out with great official honours: forty-five cannon and 600 musket shots were fired, and a band of twelve musicians played. Some forty cattle were slaughtered, and the meat distributed to mourners, along with sheep, duck, geese, and rice.[160] Raombana's considerable fortune was divided among his many children.[161] News of his death moved those in Britain who had known Raombana from his Manchester days.[162]

Ranavalona died in August 1861. Rakoto Radama, who became king under the title of Radama II, immediately lifted the ban on Christianity, which led to the return of Christian refugees, and a surge in the number of Christian meeting houses and adherents. As part of this movement, almost every member of Rahaniraka's family publicly professed the Christian faith.[163] In 1861, Ellis, who had met Rahaniraka in Britain in the 1820s, and again when he acted as interpreter during Ellis' mid-1856 visit to Madagascar, travelled to Antananarivo to re-establish the LMS mission. He commented of Rahaniraka's family, who visited him shortly after he arrived,

The secretary's wife, his son's wife, and all his children – three sons, four daughters – came soon after, bringing, according to Malagasy custom, a present of food for the newly-arrived visitor. He said they were all Christians, and their conversation and demeanour accorded with this declaration. He then introduced his son-in-law, Ramaka, an apparently energetic man about forty years of age, who had been subjected to the ordeal of poison, and had, I was told, on account of his faith, been some years in prison, sometimes bound so tightly that his flesh was lacerated by the cords.[164]

Razanakombana, the eldest child of Raombana's favourite wife, Rabodo, also became a leading Protestant Christian, and all his children adopted European dress, at least following the death of Ranavalona (see Figure 7.3).[165] However, Rahaniraka refused to convert. Samuel Oliver, who met Rahaniraka in 1862, stated, 'Rahaniraka himself, on my inquiring about the

[158] Campbell, *David Griffiths*, 68.   [159] RH, 10.
[160] Ayache (ed.), *Raombana l'historien*, 363.   [161] See Appendix 2.
[162] Ayache (ed.), *Raombana l'historien*, 361.
[163] Ellis, *Madagascar Revisited*, 29; Ayache, 'Un intellectuel malgache', 113.
[164] Ellis, *Madagascar Revisited*, 29–30.
[165] Razanakombana died in exile on Réunion after the French takeover of 1895 – Ayache, 'Un intellectuel malgache', 111.

Figure 7.3 Rafetaka, Razanajaza, Razanakombana (Raombana's son), and
Ralefoka, Antananarivo, 1862
Source: Oliver, *Madagascar and the Malagasy*, 65.

progress of Christianity among the Hova, said, "Christianity is a good thing
for the *people*, – for the lower orders, – it is a good thing for them certainly,
but what good is it to us" (meaning the high Honours) – we do very well
without it.'[166]

In 1862, Radama II appointed Rahaniraka minister of foreign affairs and
employed him as interpreter with visiting Anglophone dignitaries, such as the
British ambassadors who arrived for the coronation and handed the king a letter
from Queen Victoria.[167] Ellis seized the opportunity to give both Radama II and
Rahaniraka an English-language Bible.[168] In return, three officers to whom
Rahaniraka taught English presented Ellis with a Malagasy–English vocabulary they had compiled, comprising almost 300 small octavo pages, with
illustrations and words in both languages. Ellis forwarded it to the LMS in
London to be printed and returned to Madagascar.[169]

---

[166] Oliver, *Madagascar and the Malagasy: With Sketches in the Provinces of Tamatave,
Betanimena, and Ankova* (London: Day & Son, 1865), 53.
[167] Oliver, *Madagascar and the Malagasy*, 55–6; Ellis, *Madagascar Revisited*, 131.
[168] Ellis, *Three Visits to Madagascar* (1858), 331; Ellis, *Madagascar Revisited*, 149, 331.
[169] Ellis, *Madagascar Revisited*, 6. Rahaniraka also sent Ellis a prospectus for a high school that
Radama II wished to establish in Antananarivo – Ellis, Madagascar Revisited, 41, fn.

Radama II sent Ellis a number of translators, including Ramaniraka, Rabearana and his brother Rabezandrina, Ralaitafika, and Rabetsarazaka, most of whom had learned English from Raombana and Rahaniraka.[170] Ellis also used Rahaniraka to translate scriptural texts or sermons he delivered to the king.[171] Additionally, when the French embassy was introduced to Radama, Ellis, who assumed the role of spiritual adviser to the king, had Rahaniraka translate a discourse he had prepared for the ambassadors.[172] Further, he berated the king and Rahaniraka after the king confirmed a concession of land to Lambert, made in secret in 1855 when they could have faced the death penalty, as under Radama I and Ranavalona it was illegal for foreigners to own land in Madagascar.[173] Rahaniraka was one of three Merina ministers (the others were Rainilaiarivony (1828–1896), the commander-in-chief, and Rainiketaka, minister of justice) to have signed a treaty with France on 12 September 1862 that reaffirmed the Lambert accord but which was rejected by the new government that followed the regicide of Radama II in May 1863 and the massacre of the *Menamaso* ('Red Eyes'), his closest advisers.[174] Had Rahaniraka not met a natural death, probably in early November 1862, shortly after Radama was crowned king (on 23 September), he would probably have been killed in the slaughter of the *Menamaso*. Ellis detailed Rahaniraka's death and funeral:

Rahaniraka, the foreign secretary, had been ill for about a week, and early in the morning after my return, hearing that he was dying, I hastened to his house. I found him unconscious and sinking. I had visited him daily during his illness and had spoken to him, and prayed with him when I had reason to suppose that he was conscious of what I said, which indeed was but seldom. The scene in his sick room was often deeply affecting. The members of his family were untiring in their kind attentions. In the room with him I often found one of the Catholic priests, while in the room adjoining, his sister, the wife of a judge, but not a Christian, would be employing the *sikidy* or divination for his recover. On this occasion I endeavoured to speak consolingly to his wife and family, some of whom were sincere Christians. I had prayed with them before I left, and about one o'clock in the day I received a message to say that the spirit had departed. The king and the two ministers, who were present when I went later in the day, appeared deeply affected by the unexpected suddenness of his removal. The king hinted his suspicions of foul play on the part of some enemy. I said I thought it was rather to be ascribed to ignorance on the part of those from whom he had sought the means of recovery, and to the loss of all stamina or power to resist disease. I took occasion to speak of the danger of delaying preparation for the great change common to us all, as the deceased had said the

[170] Oliver, *Madagascar and the Malagasy*, 47; Ayache (ed.), *Raombana l'historien*, 310–11.
[171] Ellis, *Madagascar Revisited*, 98, 102; Ayache (ed.), *Raombana l'historien*, 312-3; Ayache, 'Un intellectuel malgache', 101.
[172] Ellis, *Madagascar Revisited*, 123.
[173] Ellis, *Madagascar Revisited*, 162; Samuel Pasfield Oliver, *The True Story of the French Dispute in Madagascar* (London: T. Fisher Unwin, 1885), 28–30.
[174] Louis Simonin, 'La mission de Madagascar: Souvenirs d'un voyage dans l'Océan-Indien', *Revue des deux mondes* 50.4 (1864), 971–2.

last time I conversed with him, while he was sensible, that he hoped to become a Christian before he died.

The next day, when I paid a visit of condolence to the family of Rahaniraka, I found them exhausted with fatigue. The king's band was playing in the yard, the house was crowded with mourners. The wife of the commander-in-chief, the sister of the prime minister, Mary and others, were employed in decorating the bier and hearse, and numbers of cattle were being slaughtered. At seven o'clock next morning the funeral procession, which resembled that of Andriantsirangy, passed my house on its way to his village, Anosy, in the north, where the internment took place ... On the evening of the day before the funeral, the commander-in-chief came to ask if I could inform him what was the course pursued in England in reference to medals or decorations on the death of officers on whom the sovereign conferred such distinctions. Were they buried in the tomb with the deceased as was the custom in Madagascar, or did they descend, like other possessions, to the children? I said that in England I never heard of any being buried with the wearer. Some I knew were returned to the sovereign by whom they had been bestowed, others might be kept as memorials, or even heirlooms in the family, but I believed would not confer on the descendant the distinction enjoyed by the original recipient. Rahaniraka had received two decorations, one from the late queen, the other from the present king, and the inquiry made in reference to the mode of disposing of them, issued, I believe, in their being left with the eldest son, who succeeds to his father's position as head of the family, and also in association with his cousin as one of the English foreign secretaries.

In the course of the week the funeral ceremonies were over and the family returned. I was glad to see them more composed and tranquil since the first paroxysm of grief had subsided.[175]

Further, Ellis noted the attempt by thieves to steal from Rahaniraka's tomb:

A tomb had been prepared in the centre of the village of the deceased chief, Rahaniraka, not more than a yard or two from the houses. In this tomb, together with the body, many valuable articles of dress, &c., had been deposited, as it would be considered highly improper for any of the survivors to use or wear what had personally belonged to the deceased. A stone had been placed against the door of the tomb, and a large quantity of earth had been heaped up on the outside as a temporary protection until the tomb could be regularly finished and permanently secured. A night or two afterwards the family had been startled by the firing of muskets in the yard, and, on going out, they found that ten men had been discovered by the watch, who had fired upon them, attempting to violate the tomb; the robbers had fled, pursued by the watchmen and others, but without being overtaken. They had dug away the greater part of the earth from the door, but the stone had not been removed when they were disturbed by the firing of the watchmen. The young chief told me he had sent five men, armed with muskets, and provided with ball, to strengthen the guard left in the village until the tomb could be made secure by masonry.

Thieving among the Malagasy is extremely daring, and never more so than in the robbing of tombs. It is customary among the non-Christian part of the community, when they have little if any property to deposit in the grave, to place a few small pieces of

---

[175] Ellis, *Madagascar Revisited*, 212–14.

money in the mouth of the corpse, and unless well secured, the grave, even in this case, will perhaps be opened for the purpose of taking these few pieces of silver from between the jaws of the dead.[176]

The robbing of tombs, a reflection of growing impoverishment, became frequent from the 1830s. Thus, Raombana had noted a robber band led by a woman, Ibangozafy, that looted tombs of silk clothes and the traditional one-dollar coin placed in the corpse's mouth – as happened to the corpse of Rainiketaka, an unpopular judge.[177] Goods were buried in the tomb concomitant with the status of the deceased. For example, when Radama I died in August 1828, he was interred in a coffin of silver valued at $11,300 with many thousands of dollars, his finest horses, and his favourite female slave to serve him in the afterlife.[178] Again, in 1852, when Rainihiaro, the commander-in-chief, paramour of Ranavalona, and allegedly the richest man in Madagascar, died, he was entombed alongside many valued possessions and $50,000 in cash.[179] By the time of his death, Rahaniraka possessed at least $28,570 in cash, some of which was almost certainly interred with him.[180]

The Legacy

The twins' legacy was considerable. First, Raombana wrote a secret history of Imerina in English. His papers, which have in large part survived, constitute the first historical accounts written by a Malagasy that are imbued with both traditional oral traditions and European notions of source material and independent perspectives.[181] They remained unknown for many years, possibly because of Rahaniraka's concern about the reception they would have. Certainly some of Raombana's criticisms of royal policies, notably of *fanompoana*, would have infuriated Ranavalona and the Merina elite. For example, Raombana wrote of the massive *fanompoana* imposed in 1834 upon the Betsimisaraka to build coastal defences against a possible attack by Europeans:

The people every morning are compelled to rise by 3 o'clock for to fetch stones, red earths and fuels for the burning of the limes or mortars; and as they are to be brought from great distances off, they go twice a day to fetch them. As no Betsimisarakas were allowed to till and plant on account of the above works, which requires every body's hands, scarcity of food began to be manifested, and provisions began to be very dear, so

---

[176] Ellis, *Madagascar Revisited*, 214–15.   [177] RA, 362–3.
[178] RH, 156–7; see also Guillaume Grandidier, 'À Madagascar, anciennes croyances et coutumes', *Journal de la Sociétédes Africanistes* 2.2 (1932), 155.
[179] Raombana, 'Annales' Livre 13, 32–3, Fonds Résidence Générale de France, ARM.
[180] Ayache (ed.), *Raombana l'historien*, 104.
[181] Berg, 'Virtù, and Fortuna', 45; Didier Nativel, 'Les héritiers de Raombana: Érudition et identité culturelle à Madagascar à l'époque coloniale (fin XIXème siècle–1960)', *Revue d'histoire des sciences humaines* 1.20 (2004), 62.

that hundreds of dead Betsimisaraka were daily found in the woods, who has died through mere starvation and fatigues.[182]

Nevertheless, Rahaniraka was worried less at the reception of Raombana's works among the Malagasy, few of whom could read English, than by the British.[183] He feared that the descriptions of Malagasy traditions and mores might offend the sensibility of British Christians. Indeed, Raombana himself refrained from writing a full description of what occurred during circumcision ceremonies lest it offend Europeans –beyond stating that when, in 1844, Rakoto Radama was circumcised, the prince fainted twice from loss of blood.[184] Despite this, Raombana did not spare his readers detailed accounts of other traditions and events which his religious acquaintances in Britain would have considered vulgar. For example, he noted that at the close of the eighteenth century, Sakalava raiding parties to Imerina, knowing that the Merina feared them,

Used to ease themselves by farting without manifesting any shame at all, in the presence of the Hova men and women who are in the same house with them, and so fearful were the Hova people of incurring their displeasures if they were to say that the smell is bad, that in lieu of the above words, they say, 'that the smell are good and agreeable'.[185]

He was as candid when describing the assassination of Rafaralahy (see Chapter 3).[186]

In addition to leaving invaluable historical accounts, Raombana, with Rahaniraka, tutored a number of the children of the Merina elite, and thus had a considerable influence upon future Malagasy leaders. These included Rainilaiarivony, who from 1864 to 1895 was prime minister of the Merina government, and Rainandrianampandry (d. 1896), who became a major figure in the Merina administration.[187] At various times from 1851, they also taught English to other future statesmen, including Rainimaharavo, Rainitsimbazafy, Rabearana, Rabezandrina, Ralaitafika, Ramaniraka, Rainandriantsilavo, Ravoninahitriniarivo, Ramaharavo, Ratsimbazafy, and Razanakombana.[188]

In sum, Raombana and his twin brother, Rahaniraka, secured a lasting legacy through having been selected by Radama to go to Britain for a liberal education and their faithful service thereafter to Ranavalona, notably as foreign secretaries. These roles, and Raombana's historical writings, ensured that they figure prominently in the historical literature on nineteenth-century Madagascar. However, the twins were only two of some 100 Malagasy Youths sent abroad for education and training under British supervision in the 1810s and 1820s,

[182] RA, 322.   [183] Ayache (ed.), *Raombana l'historien*, 363.
[184] Raombana, 'Annales' Livre 12 C1, 481–2, Fonds Docteur Raoëly James, AAM.
[185] RH, 75.   [186] RA, 195–6.   [187] Ayache, 'La découverte de l 'Europe', 15.
[188] Ayache (ed.), *Raombana l'historien*, 310–11.

most as a result of the Britanno-Merina treaty of 1820. These comprised three main groups. One group, to which the twins belonged, travelled to Britain, another larger body was sent to Mauritius, and the third and most numerous group, numbering some fifty males, served apprenticeships abroad British naval vessels patrolling the waters of the western Indian Ocean. The British authorities involved, notably Farquhar, the first British governor of Mauritius, the LMS, and the British government, considered that through these youths the British might establish political, economic, and religious hegemony in Madagascar. The Merina crown had a different perspective and wished to utilize the youths and their training to advance its own interests, which, following the rupture of the British alliance in 1826, meant bolstering Merina independence, fostering autarkic policies, and keeping European imperial forces at bay. Possibly one-third of the youths failed to survive their overseas experience. All who returned in reasonable health were summoned to serve the Merina crown. Some used their overseas training to produce military goods. Others served as army officers, court officials and scribes, and diplomats. However, while the Merina crown directed the efforts of the Madagascar Youths to ward off European pretensions to the island, some of the youths joined a 'Patriot' movement that sought European military intervention to overthrow Ranavalona. Certainly, most former Madagascar Youths retained a strong attachment to the British and proved sympathetic to indigenous Christians, who from 1835 were persecuted by Ranavalona. This pro-British sentiment ensured that, following the death of Ranavalona in 1861, the reopening of the island to foreign investment, and the re-establishment of an LMS mission, the British again became the most dominant foreign influence, and remained so up to the French colonial takeover in 1895.

Appendix 1 The Britanno-Merina Treaty, 1817 (renewed 1820)[1]

HIS Excellency Robert Townsend Farquhar, Esquire, Governor and Commander in Chief, Captain General, Vice Admiral of the Islands of Mauritius and its dependencies;

By his Commissioners, Captain Stanfell, of the Royal Navy, commanding His Majesty's ship Phaeton, and Thomas R. Pye, Esquire, Assistant Agent for his Excellency's government at Madagascar, who are vested with full powers; and Radama, King of Madagascar and its dependencies, by his Commissioners, Ratzilika, Rampoole, Ramanon, and Racihato, representing the said Radama, and with full powers from his Majesty.

Article 1st
It is agreed by the parties to these present respectively, that the mutual confidence, friendship and brotherhood, which are hereby acknowledged to subsist between the contracting parties, shall be maintained and perpetuated for ever.

Article 2nd
It is agreed, and the two contracting parties hereby covenant and agree that, from the date of this treaty, there shall be an entire cessation and extinction through all the dominions of King Radama and wherever his influence can extend, of the sale or transfer of Slaves, or other persons whatever, to be removed off the soil of Madagascar into any country, island or dominion of any other prince, potentate, or power whatever; and that Radama, King of Madagascar, will make a proclamation and a law, prohibiting all his subjects, or persons depending on him or his dominions, to sell any slave, to be transported from Madagascar; or to

---

[1] Sources: *Papers relating to the Abolition of the Slave Trade in the Mauritius: 1817–1820* vol. 18 (House of Commons, 1821), 360; BL Add. 20131 f. 116.

240

aid or abet, or assist in such a sale, under penalty, that any person so offending, shall be reduced to slavery himself.

Article 3rd

And in consideration of this concession on the part of Radama, King of Madagascar, and his nation, and in full satisfaction of the same, and for the loss of revenue thereby incurred by Radama, King of Madagascar, the Commissioners on the part of his Excellency the Governor of Mauritius, do engage to pay Radama yearly, the following articles; viz.

> 1,000 Dollars in gold.
> 1,000 Dollars in silver.
> 100 Barrels of gun powder (100 lbs each).
> 100 English muskets and accoutrements complete.
> 10,000 Flints.
> 400 Soldiers caps.
> 400 Stocks.
> 400 Red Jackets.
> 400 Shirts.
> 400 Pair trowsers.
> 400 Pair shoes.
> 12 Serjeants regulation swords and belts.
> 400 Pieces of white cloth.
> 500 Pieces of blue cloth, India.
> One full dress coat, with two epaulets, cocked hat and dress boots for the king.
> Two horses.

Upon a certificate being received, that the said laws and proclamations have been enforced the preceding year; which certificate shall be signed by Radama and countersigned by the Agent of his Excellency Governor Farquhar, resident at the Court of Radama.

Article 4

And further, it is agreed by the contracting parties, mutually to protect the faithful friend and ally of England, the King of Johanna [Nzwani/Anjouan], from the predatory attacks to which he has been for many years annually exposed, from some of the smaller states of the sea coast of Madagascar, and to sue every means in their power, by their subjects, allies, and dependants, to put a final end to this system of piracy; and for this purpose, proclamations shall be made by Radama and the Governor of Mauritius, prohibiting all persons whatever from engaging in this piracy; and these proclamations shall be particularly distributed in all the ports of the sea coast of Madagascar.

Additional Article
The contracting parties agree in considering this treaty as provisional until ratified and confirmed by His Majesty's ministers, on the part of the King of Great Britain; which ratification will be forwarded, without loss of time, to the King of Madagascar, by his ambassador to that court. This formality, however, is not to prevent the stipulation of this treaty from being carried into full and complete effect, from the date hereof.

(Signed)	(Signed)
Francis Stanfell, Captain of H.M. Ship	Ratziliaka)
Phaeton, Senior Naval Officer and	Rampoole) Commissioners
Commissioner.	for Radama Ramanou)

(Signed)
T. R. Pye, British Agent and Commissioner.
Done at Tamatave, Island of Madagascar, the 23rd October 1817.

(Approved)
Signed, R.T. Farquhar

Annex 2 The Britanno-Merina Treaty, 1820[2]

No 2. – Additional Articles[3]

By virtue of the Treaty concluded between his Majesty Radama King of Madagascar, and his Excellency R. T. Farquhar, Esq. Governor and Commander in Chief of the Island of Mauritius and dependencies, Captain General, Vice Admiral, &c. &c. bearing date the 23rd October 1817, the abolition of the exportation of Slaves, shall from this day for ever be maintained and preserved inviolate; and the contracting parties severally bind themselves to fulfil all the articles and conditions contained in said Treaty, with most scrupulous care and attention.

In consequence of this Treaty, confirmed and ratified by command of His Britannic Majesty, and accepted this day by His Majesty the King of Madagascar, there has been agreed between Mr. James Hastie, agent of government on the part of His Excellency Governor Farquhar and King

---

[2] Additional to the renewal of the 1817 Treaty – see *Papers relating to the Abolition of the Slave Trade in the Mauritius: 1817–1820* vol. 18 (House of Commons, 1821), 360; BL Add. 20131 f. 116.
[3] *Papers Relating to the Abolition of the Slave Trade*, 356–8.

Radama that the said Mr. Hastie engages on the part of his government, to take with him, twenty free subjects of his Majesty King Radama, to be instructed in, and brought up to different trades, such as mechanicians, gold and silversmiths, weavers, carpenters, blacksmiths; or placed in the arsenals, dock yards, &c. &c. &c. whereof ten shall be sent to England, and ten to the Island of Mauritius, at the expense of the British Government.

It is further agreed upon between the two parties, that if on the arrival at Mauritius of the twenty individuals above-mentioned, accompanied by Mr. Hastie, the Governor should not consent to the instruction of the said twenty individuals, ten at Mauritius, and ten in England, then shall the Treaty become null, without compromising however the word of promise of King Radama.

It is understood by this article, that the British Government shall place the said twenty individuals with persons practising the various trades before mentioned; but that Government is not responsible for their conduct, or their want of capacity.

Mr. James Hastie further engages to take with him eight other individuals, to be instructed in music, for the purpose of being formed into a band for the regiment of guards of his Majesty the King of Madagascar.[4]

In consequence of this article, and the conditions before-stated, King Radama will make a proclamation, in which he will notify the said abolition of the exportation of Slaves from within his dominions; and will further invite all persons of talent or otherwise skilled in any trade or profession, to come and visit his country, promising to them his protection; and the said Proclamation shall be published in the Mauritius Gazette.

Given at Tanarivoux, this 11th of October, 1820.

Signed,
Radama Manzaka.

James Hastie,
Agent of the British Govt.

A true translation,
Nanin E. S. Viret,
Sworn Interpreter to Govt.

Following the signing of the 1820 treaty, a proclamation was issued by Radama I for release on Mauritius that read,

---

[4] They were put in the care of Charles Telfair: 'Believing in the influence of music in civilizing mankind, a vocal and instrumental band was formed among the Slaves, who, for above three years, learned the principles of this art, from the best European masters. During this time I gave up their services, for they were thirty miles distant from the estate. This hand assisted in teaching the musicians of Radama, king of Madagascar, under the superintendence of Mr. Kyle, the respectable Quarter-Master of His Majesty's 82nd Regiment.' Telfair, *Some Account of the State of Slavery*, 64.

Proclamation

Radama King of Madagascar

MOVED by the same principles of humanity which have animated the Sovereign of Great Britain and other powers to abolish and prohibit the exportation of Slaves, – By these present makes a Proclamation, in the which he forbids, in a solemn manner, all and every person to export the Natives of Madagascar, under the penalty of themselves in their Persons being reduced to Slavery.

The King Radama embraces the present occasion for calling upon all Persons of talent and profession to come and visit his Country in order to prosecute their enquiries and researches, as to the nature of its productions; and to whom he gives a sacred assurance of his protection in their efforts and undertakings.

Given at Tananarivoux this 11th October 1820

> (Signed)
> Radama Manzaka

A true Translation
Nanin E. S. Viret
Sworn Interpreter to Gov.

Annex 2

I have the honor to request, in obedience to the commands of my master Radama, king of Madagascar, that your Excellency will be pleased to transmit to your Government the enclosed edicts, one for the suppression of the Slave Trade throughout the dominions of Madagascar, and the other for creating a naval force for the suppression of that trade in the harbours and on the shores of that island.

I am desired to convey to your Excellency the assurance that His Majesty's zeal for the suppression of the Slave trade, the fertile source of anarchy and discord, remains unabated, as well as His Majesty's anxious desire to preserve by every means in his power, his commercial relations with His Britannic majesty's Colony under your Government.[5]

Draft of a proposed Edict for the more effectual suppression of the Slave Trade in the dominions of Radama, king of Madagascar.

Having resolved to preserve to my loving subjects by every means in my power the blessing of freedom and for the more effectual suppression of the Slave Trade in the Harbours and near the shores of my dominions, I do hereby ordain as follows.

---

[5] Draft of a proposed letter from AB. Counsellor and Minister of Radama, King of Madagascar, to His Excellency Sir Lowry Cole &c., [n.d.], HB 5, NAM.

That all Vessels of every sort and description who are in the pursuit of that abominable traffic approach the Shores (here specify some definite line of boundary) of my dominions shall be seized and condemned as prize and the proceedings thereof paid into the Royal Treasury.

Maritime Edict No. 1.

Draft of a proposed Edict for the creation of a maritime force in the Dominion of Radama, king of Madagascar.

I hereby decree and make known the creation of a Marine bearing my Flag on the same principles that have established the maritime Force of other nations and command a due observance to the laws which I have deemed it advisable to establish for the Government thereof.

Maritime Edict No. 2

Draft of proposed laws

1. Process of execution first, conforming as much as possible to the habits and manners of the country
2. Jurisdiction below Low Water mark
3. Treating seizure of all Vessel Slave dealing, smuggling or violating of law afloat
4. Officers, seamen and soldiers to be tried and punished according to the law of the land for crimes
5. Certain crimes and offences to be punished afloat by decision of Naval Officers only
6. Death alone excepted which must receive King's sanction except in cases of mutiny

Maritime Edict No. 3

Draft of Naval instructions

To be drawn up by the Officers who may first be appointed to the Command of a Man of War and submitted to the King. English Naval Instructions recommended as a basis but much must be left to the Officers first selected and a system must be gradually established that will combine Naval Discipline with whatever Military system now in existence. In short, for some little time, Radama must be brought to acknowledge the necessity that the only officer afloat must necessarily be invested with the same power when afloat as he exercises on shore.

Draft of a proposed letter from AB Counsellor and Minister of Radama, King of Madagascar, to Commodore Christian, Commanding [sic] in Chief His Majesty's Squadron at the Cape of Good Hope.

I am commanded by the King my Master to transmit to you copies of certain edicts, one made for the more effectual suppression of the Slave Trade, and the other creating a marine bearing His Majesty's Flag. I am also instructed to assure you that you may rely on receiving the cordial co-operation of all His Majesty's subjects in suppressing that horrid traffic.

Draft of a proposed Letter from Commodore Christian to the Lords Commissioners of the Admiralty.

I have the honor to transmit to you to be laid before my Lords Commissioners the enclosed Letters which I have received from Radama, King of Madagascar, covering certain edicts and, feeling satisfied that the measures Radama has adopted will tend to suppress the Traffic in Slaves, I beg leave to request their Lordships permission to assist and encourage Radama in his praiseworthy attempt to protect the shores of his Dominions from that abominable traffic

Private
Draft of a proposed Private Letter to Lord Melville the First Lord of the Admiralty.

Private
Draft of a proposed letter to Earl Bathurst, Secretary of State for Foreign Affairs.

Appendix 2   Raombana's Will[1]

How Raombana's Possessions Will be Divided

The children of Rasoahanta will inherit the ricefields that Raombana bought personally: the ricefield Ifanoharana cultivates to the north of Ivandry, and that which Ialaihitsihoaiza and his son cultivate to the west of Ivandru, and that located to the east of Morarano, and that at Anjezika, and that Itsianemenanan cultivates at Anjezika.

The children of Rabodo will inherit the ricefields Imaromanana and his wife cultivate to the west of Ivandry, at Imorarano and to the south of Ivandry, and those Imaromanana's mother cultivates to the west and north of Ivandry.

Raombana has rendered service to Radama; when barely weaned, he was sent to England [. . .] and when he dies, Ranavalmanjaka has ordered that he has the right to 12 rounds of cannon fire and two-and-a-half barrels of gunpowder, as well as 99 piastres in addition to that due to him for his rank; and the queen added to that two rounds of cannon fire and 200 rounds of rifle fire from the Palace Officers and the Tsimando [. . .] and a total of 12 musicians. That is what the queen has accorded him for the services he has rendered.

5 Anosy 29 Alahamady 1856
This is how Rahaniraka divided Raombana's possessions after the reading of the latter's will which conferred on Rahaniraka the power to divide his goods.

In the event that he died first, Raombana conferred on Rahaniraka, the care and protection of his children, and the conservation and growth of his personal fortune.

Thus Rahaniraka has divided the possessions of Raombana 12 Honours Off. D.P. (Ambodirano) as follows:

All fiefs, whether large or small, are to be divided into 3 equal parts – one third will go to his sons, Razanakombana, Andrianefananahary, and Rasolo; and

---

[1]   Dr Ranjeva, Private Archives, in Ayache, *Raombana l'historien*, 338–51.

two-thirds to his daughters, Rahamina, Razaoary, Rakaloanosy, Rangory, Ravaomihanta, Ranoro, Rafaravavy, and Ratomponiera [. . .]

Raombana's portion of the ricefields located to the west of the 'sacred stone' of Anosy, will be divided in two: Rabodo's chidren will receive the northern and Rasoahanta's children the southern half.

Raombana's portion of the Maitsoririnina ricefields is to be divided in two: Rabodo's children to have the northern and Rasoahanta's chidren the southern half.

The ancestral ricefield located to the south of the village of Anosy, that measures 58 fathoms [106.1 m] long and 8.5 fathoms [15.6 m] [wide] is to be divided in two: the eastern half to go to Rabodo's chidren, and the western to Rasoahanta's children.

The ancestral ricefield of Andohamandry (Anosy) measuring 22 fathoms [40.2 m] long and 7 fathoms [12.8 m] wide is to be divided into two equal parts: the eastern part to go to Rabodo's children, and the western to Rasoahanta's chidren.

The ancestral ricefield located to the southwest of Ilafy measuring 11 fathoms [20.1 m] long and 9 fathoms [16.5 m] wide is to be divided into two equal portions; the eastern portion to go to Rabodo's children and the western to Rasoahanta's children.

The ancestral ricefield of Andriamavo at Morarano measuring 40 fathoms [73.2 m] long and 32 fathoms [58.8 m] wide is to be divided on a north–south axis into two parts; the eastern portion to go to Rabodo's children and the western to Rasoahanta's children.

The 7 small portions of the ancestral ricefields of Andriamavo, located to the north of the village of Ivandry, will be divided as follows: Rabodo's children will have 3 portions, and Rasoahanta's children 4 portions.

Raombana's ricefields in Ambodirano [listed below] will be divided into two equal parts; Rabodo's children will inherit one half, and Rasoahanta's children the other half [. . .]

- Raombana's portion (the southern part) obtained from Rahamaly, of the ricefields located to the south of Ambatobe.
- The ricefield of Andranomahery cultivated by Ralaimahaiza's family.
- 1 portion of a ricefield located at Morarano purchased from Rainimaromandray and mortgaged for the sum of 5 piastres.
- 1 portion of a ricefield located to the west of Ivandry purchased from Ramanantsimitovy, measuring 44 fathoms [80.5 m] long and 7 fathoms [12.8 m] wide.
- The ricefield of Izehivola (only the southern portion), that Raombana received from Andriamalaiko.

Concerning the ricefields of Rabodo's children: At a later date, when they are divided, this is how they will be apportioned: they will be divided into 8 equal parts, 5 of which will go to Razanakombana and Andrianefananahary, and 3 to Ranoro and Ratomponiera.

The ricefields of Rasoahanta's children
- The ricefield Ratsiaboana cultivates at Anjezika
- The ricefield of Andranomahery, that which Ravita and his family cultivate
- The portion of a ricefield bought to the west of Ampangabe, that which was purchased from Rasoamanantany
- Two portions of a ricefield to the west of Ivandry, bought from Ratsitohaina, grandson of Andrianantsosa
- 1 portion of a ricefield at Morarano bought from Andriananja Off. D.P., measuring 50 fathoms [91 m] long and 26 fathoms [47.6 m] wide; the ricefield formerly cultivated by Ingahimanandrairoa

At a later date when the ricefields of Rasoahanta's children will be divided, this is how they will be allotted: they will be divided into 16 equal parts: 4 will go to Rasolo and the 12 others to Razaoary, Rakaloanosy, Rangory, Ravaomihanta and Rafaravavy.

Concerning Raombana's portion of the ricefields located to the south of Anjanahary, comprising half of the large section, the portion Ratsifoy cultivates, and the portion of the nursery situated at the west where one can sow ⅔ of a measure of rice – all that belongs exclusively to Razakombana and Andrianefananahary. Moreover, they receive that because they are male heirs, and because Raombana wishes it so.

As for the ricefields to the south of Anjanahary purchased from Rainmangorona for 35 piastres, they belong exclusively to Rasolo. He will own these as a supplement, because he is a male heir.

Rahamina's share of Raombana's ricefields are the ricefield of Anosibe, that purchased from Rabodmavo to the west of Anosy, and the ricefield of Itokotanitsara purchased from Ralaibongo.

Names of the Slaves that Rabodo's children have inherited from Raombana

1	Reninizanakombana	1	Reninitomponiera
1	Tsifotra	1	Ingita
1	Ihavantsiafoy	1	Imaromana
1	Indandeny	1	Itsimisazoka
1	Renininoro	1	Itsiandrainazy
1	Ilaihitafika	1	Rainisetroka
1	Itsira	1	Reninimaromanana
1	Ivoasa	1	Ramanankavana
2	Imanga and her child	1	Isoava
2	Itsihariva and her child	1	Iavomanitra
1	Itsimaninona	1	Itanantsara
1	Isendrandro	1	Ratsiananenana

At a later time when the slaves of Rabodo's children will be divided, they will be divided into 8 equal parts: 5 parts will go to Razanakombana and Andrianefananahary; and 3 parts to Ranoro and Ratompiera.

Names of the Slaves that Rasoahanta's children have inherited from Raombana

1	Ratsaratoniana	1	Iavorindrina
1	Itsimahory	1	Ranindraminia
1	Itsiambanindahy	1	Ibetsiratsy
1	Iketabao	1	Isikindreo
1	Itsimanova	1	Imiadana
1	Rafanoharana	1	Ifilanera
1	Itasy	1	Islama wife of Ibefihavy
1	Ilaihitsihoaiza	1	Rahova
1	Itsaratiana	1	Ratsara
2	Reninivaomihanta and her child	2	Reninboto and her child at Ibezano's home
1	Izanona	1	Iboneka
1	Renilaitsihoaiza	1	Raininahy
1	Itsoatoro	1	Imainty son of Itsaratoniana
1	Ratsieboana	1	Ikotokely son of Ramainty
1	Imahatoky	1	Ibefihavy

At a later time, the slaves of Rasoahanta's children will be as follows: They will be divided into 16 parts, 4 for Rasolo, and 12 for Razaoary, Rakaloanosy, Rangory, Ravaomihanta and Rafaravavy.

From Raombana to Ramasy: To Ravoanjo and his sister, grandchildren of Raombana:

1	Ramainty	1	Ramanankihantana
1	Rabehozaka	1	Itsiasanda

From Raombana to Rahamina: Given by Raombana while alive to Ramasy:

1	Ratiana	1	Inahindreo
1	Ifaralahimanohy	1	Iketaka, eldest daughter of Islama, wife of
1	Iandrongo, child of Tsimaninona		Ibefihavy

And those of Razanakombana: And those of Andrianefananahary:

1	Imanambato	1	Iambahive
1	Isambariaka	1	Ibekararavina
1	Ikavika	1	Ibotokely
1	Idaday	1	Itsarafodiana
1	Imanaovasoa	1	Itrafonkena
1	Itsiafenina		
1	Ilaka		
1	Itaibe, son of Ramainty, eldest son		

And those of Rahamina: And those of Ranoro:

1	Imampihanta	1	Imaronify
1	Itsiampitambazana	1	Imozezy
1	Itsimanohorariny	1	Imanambondrona

And those of Razaoary: And those of Rakaloanosy:

1	Isikimahefa	1	Itsimihambo
1	Itsarasaotra	1	Isarotrivaina
1	Ianhindreo	1	Ihavantsiavonana

And those of Rangory: And those of Ravaomihanta:

1	Imandrainohava	1	Itenimiera
1	Itsiambakaina	1	Ifianarana
1	Itsiavonana		

And those of Rafaravavy: Rasolo's portion:

1	Ifitia	1	Imaso
1	Itsimiorimpitia		
1	Isahafiana		

And the portion going to Ravoanjo, his grandson:

1 Isambaika

These are the slaves that Raombana has given while alive. Later, when Rahaniraka divides the money amongst Raomnaba's children, this sum will be divided into three equal parts. One third will go to his sons, Razanakombana, Andrianefananahary and Rasolo. Of the remaining two-thirds, 200 piastres will be given to his sons, and 30 piastres to Ramasy [The money of Raombana that has been recuperated has already been divided. The part for Razanakombana's brothers and sisters is conserved by Rabodo; the part for Razaoary's sisters by Rasoahanta, and that of Rahamina by Ramaka]

All that remains belongs to Rahamina, Razaoary, Rakaloanosy, Rangory, Ravaomihanta, Ranoro, Rafaravavy and Ratomponiera. And when Raombana's money is divided, it will start by deducting the 100 piatres that Razanakombana received before the general division takes place.

As for Raombana's cattle, and the later price of these cattle: they will be divided into three equal parts. One part will go to his sons Razanakombana, Andrianefananahary and Rasolo, and the remaining two-thirds to his daughters Rahamina, Razaoary, Rakaloanosy, Rangory, Ravaomihanta, Rafaravavy, Ranoro and Ratomponiera.

And the horses will belong to Razanakombana.

As concerns Raombana's houses and courtyards: those located in Antananarivo that have been occupied by Rabodo, will go to Rabodo's children, those occupied by Rasoahanta will go to her children, and those located at Ambaniavaratra will go to Razanakombana as these he received before the general division.

Rahanriaka has already divided the men's' clothes, and they shall be kept by those who received them.

Of the houses and courtyards at Anosy, the large house and its court to the south will belong toTazanakombana, and Imiandriosa and its court will belong to Rasoahanta's children.

Concerning the land at Tsarahonenana: the northernmost will go to Andrianefananahary, the next portion to Rasolo, that following (3 fathoms [5.5 m]) to Razanakombana, the next (3 fathoms) to Rahamina, and the remainder to Razaoary, Rakaloanosy, Rangory, Ravaomihanta, Ranoro, Rafaravavy, and Ratomponiera.

Raombana's field at Ivandry will be split into three equal portions, the two-thirds to the north going to Razanakombana and Andrianefananahary, and the third to the south, in addition to that located at Ifitodiana, at Anosy, will go to Rasolo.

And if, by mischance, some of Rabodo's children die without issue, Rabodo's living children will inherit the land of those who die. The same will be the case with Rasoahanta's children, and for Rahamina and her two children.

Raombana's lands cannot be sold; the exception being if the owners having engaged [mortgaged?] them, find it impossible to buy them back.

Those who have inherited Raombana's property are individually responsible for their inherited portions, whether it be in the form of ricefields or slaves &c.

As regards the money Raombana received from Mr Razafilahy, i.e. the sum in silver equivalent in weight to 200 piastres, and the 200 piastres in money – that goes to Rasoahanta's children.

This is how Rahaniraka has divided Raombana's property. If any of the heirs of Raombana fail to follow his written testament, they will inherit nothing from Raombana, and will have to pay 500 piastres, for in accordance with what has here been said the *hasina* has already been presented to the sovereign, and the witness stone has been erected.

Here follow the witnesses of these agreements:

Ravelo   13 Honours
Rahaniraka   12 Honours Off. D.P.
Rahanonjo
Ramaka   4 Honours
Ramaniraka
Razanakombana
Andrianefananahary
Ramasy

Ravahatra
Rasendra
Rasoamiato
Rabodo   wife of Raombana
Rasoahanta wife of Raombana
All Raombana's children
Ratsiralahy 8 Honours, aide de camp of Prince Rakoton'dradama 13 Honours Off.
              D.P.

Bibliography

Primary Sources

Archival

Archifdy Llyfrgell Genelaethol Cymru/Archives of the National Library of
Wales (ALGC)
- 11646B
- Casgliad J. Luther Thomas.
Archives de l'Académie Malgache, Antananarivo, Madagascar (AAM)
- Raombana, 'Annales' (1853)
- Raombana, 'Annales' Livre 12
- Raombana, 'Histoires' (1853).
Archives de la République Malgache, Antananarivo, Madagascar (ARM)
- Raombana, 'Annales' Livre 4
- Raombana, 'Annales' Livre 13
- Raombana, Livre 10.
Archives historiques de la Vice-Province Société de Jésus de Madagascar,
Antananarivo (AHVP)
- Clla; Diaires II.20
British Library, London, UK (BL)
- Add. 3408; Add. 18126; Add. 18128; Add. 18129; Add. 18135; Add.
18136; Add. 18137; Add. 20131; Add. 41265.
Council of World Mission/London Missionary Archives, School of African &
Oriental Studies, University of London (SOAS/CWM)
- Africa and Madagascar, Committee Minutes
- Home Correspondence
- J. T. Hardyman file 43, Bx7
- Journals Box 2 1824–94
- LMS Board Minutes (1821–31)
- Madagascar Incoming Letters (MIL)
- Madagascar Odds, Bx.4
- Madagascar Outgoing Letters (MOL).
Linnean Society Archives, London
National Archives, Kew, UK (NAK)
- CO 167/34; CO 167/50; CO 167/56; CO 167/63; CO 167/66; CO 167/77;
CO167/78; CO 167/101; CO 167/102; CO 167/107; CO 167/113; CO
167/116; CO 167/151; CO 167/153; CO 167/158; CO 167/173; CO
167/229
- FO 925/1047
- MS 11936/447/830309, 27 Apr. 1809.

National Archives, Mauritius (NAM)
  - BB 20; HB 4; HB 5; HB 7; HB 13; HB 14; HB 19; HB 20; HB 21; HB 22.
Plymouth and West Devon Record Office (PWDRO)
  - Arthur Frankland, 'Ten Weeks Leave of Absence: Cruise from Mauritius to Madagascar and East Coast of Africa', ref. 216
  - Arthur Frankland, 'Journal of a Cruise in HM Sloop "Jaseur" from Mauritius to Madagascar on Anti–Slave Trade Operations, 1830', 216.1.
Shropshire Archives
  - 'Nathaniel Minshall of Oswestry gentleman', ref. SRO 2847/7/230–231, https://discovery.nationalarchives.gov.uk/details/r/cea449a0-3384-4d5d-834b-a3efceeaadce (accessed 18. 06.21).

Printed

Books and Journal Articles

[Admiralty]. 1849. *The Navy List, corrected to the 20th December 1848* (London: John Murray).
Anon. 1883. *Madagascar and the United States* (New York: Thompson & Moreau).
    1836. 'Biographical Sketches: Dr. John Theodosius Vanderkemp'. *Foreign Missionary Chronicle* (Jun.): 81–2.
    1836. *Précis sur les établissements français formés à Madagascar* (Paris: Imprimerie Royale).
    1830. 'Splendid Coronation of the Queen Ranovalo Manjaka, the Successor of Radama, Late King of Madagascar'. *The Mirror of Literature, Amusement, and Instruction* 16: 116–19.
    1826. 'Commodore Joseph Nourse C.B.'. *Asiatic Journal and Monthly Register for British India and its Dependencies* 21 (Jan.): 34–8.
    1825. 'Journal of a Voyage Eastward of the Cape, &c.'. *London Literary Gazette and Journal of Belles Lettres, Arts, Sciences* (27 Aug.): 555–6.
    1824. 'Biographical Sketch of an Old Indian Chaplain [William Hirst]'. *Oriental Herald and Journal of General Literature* 2: 404–8.
    1823. 'Ordnance Estimates'. HC Deb (14 Mar.) Hansard, vol. 8, cc598.
Avine, Grégoire. 1961 [1802]. *Voyages aux isles de France d'Anjouan de Madagascar, de Mosambique, de Zanzibar et de la côte Coromondel* (Paris: Mauritius Archives Publications).
Backhouse, James. 1844. *A Narrative of a Visit to the Mauritius and South Africa* (London: Hamilton Adams & Co.).
[Baker, Edward]. 1847. *Madagascar Past and Present* (London: R. Bentley).
Beaton, Patrick. 1859. *Creoles and Coolies; or, Five Years in Mauritius* (London: James Nisbet).
Bennet, George. 1829. 'Funeral of King Radama'. *Asiatic Journal* (1 Sep.): 359–62.
Bernard, William Dallas. 1845. *Narrative of the Voyages and Services of the Nemesis* (London: Henry Colburn).
Biographicus. 1824. 'Biographical Sketch of an Old Indian Chaplain'. *Oriental Herald and Journal of General Literature* 2: 404–8.

Bland, E. [1887]. *Annals of Southport and District: A Chronological History of North Meols, AD 1086 to 1886* (Manchester: Abel, Heywood & Sons).

Bojer, Wenceslas. 1963 [1822–5]. 'Journal'. In Jean Valette (ed.), 'L'Imerina en 1822–1825 d'après les journaux de Bojer et d'Hilsenberg', *Bulletin de Madagascar* (Apr.–May): 23–9.

Bonne, Rigobert. [c.1771–85]. *Atlas moderne ou collection de cartes sur toutes les parties du globe terrestre* (Paris: Chez Lattré et Delalain).

Bontekoe, William. 1929. *Memorable Description of the East Indian Voyage 1618–1625* (New York: McBride).

Boothby, Richard. 1745. 'A Brief Discovery or Description of the Most Famous Island of Madagascar, or St Laurence, in Asia, near unto the East-Indies' [orig. pub. London, 1646]. In Thomas Osborne (ed.), *A Collection of Voyages and Travels*, vol. 2 (London: Thomas Osborne): 626–63.

Boteler, Thomas. 1835. *Narrative of a Voyage of Discovery to Africa and Arabia, Performed in His Majesty's Ships, Leven and Barracouta, from 1821 to 1826. Under the Command of Capt. F. W. Owen, RN*, vol. 2 (London: Richard Bentley).

Braddock, John. 1832. *A Memoir on Gunpowder, in which are discussed the Principles both of its Manufacture and Proof* (London: Richardson).

Brand, Charles. 1829. 'A Visit to the Island of Madagascar'. *United Service Magazine* 2: 529–40.

Browne, J. Ross. 1846. *Etchings of a Whaling Cruise with Notes of a Sojourn on the Island of Zanzibar; and a Brief History of the Whale Fishery, in Its Past and Present Condition* (London: John Murray).

Browne, John. 1877. *History of Congregationalism and Memorials of the Churches in Norfolk and Suffolk* (London: Jarrold and Sons).

Burrows, George Man. 1828. *Commentaries on the Causes, Forms, Symptoms, and Treatment, Moral and Medical, of Insanity* (London: Thomas and George Underwood).

1820. *An Inquiry into Certain Errors Relative to Insanity and Their Consequences, Physical, Moral and Civil* (London: Thomas and George Underwood).

Callet, François (ed.). 1974, 1978. *Histoire des Rois: Tantaran ny Andriana*. Trans. George S. Chapus and Emmanuel Ratsimba. Vols. 1–4 (Tananarive: Editions de la Librairie de Madagascar, 1974); vol. 5 (Antananarivo: Académie Malgache, 1978).

Camboué, Paul. 1911. 'Jeux des enfants malgaches'. *Anthropos* 7: 665–83.

1909. 'Les dix premiers ans de l'Enfance chez les Malgaches: Circoncision, nom, éducation'. *Anthropos* 4.2: 375–86.

Cameron, James. 1874. *Recollections of Mission Life in Madagascar during the Early Days of the LMS Mission* (Antananarivo: Abraham Kingdon).

Campbell, Charles Mackenzie. 1963. 'Journal (May–Aug. 1840)'. *Studia* 2: 463–99.

Campbell, John. 1848. *Hottentot Children; with a particular account of Paul Dikkop, the son of a Hottentot Chief, who Died in England, Sept. 14, 1824* (London: Religious Tract Society).

1815. *Travels in South Africa undertaken at the request of the Missionary Society* (London: Black and Parry).

Central Society of Education. 1838. *Papers* (London: Printed for Taylor & Walton).

Charnay, Claude-Joseph Desire. 1864 [1862]. 'Madagascar a vol d'oiseau'. *Le Tour du Monde* 10: 194–231.

CMS. 1826. *Proceedings of the Church Missionary Society for Africa and the East (1825–6)* (London: CMS).

Coates, Thomas. 1838. 'Report of a Visit to the Model School of the British and Foreign School Society in the Borough Road'. In Central Society of Education, *Papers* (London: Printed for Taylor & Walton).

Colin, Élie, and Pierre Suau. 1895. *Madagascar et la mission catholique* (Paris: Sanard et Derangeon).

Copland, Samuel. 1822. *A History of Madagascar* (London: Burton and Smith).

Coppalle, André. 2007 [1827]. 'Voyage dans l'intérieure de Madagascar et à la capitale du roi Radama pendant les années 1825 et 1826'. *Bibliothèque malgache* 20: 3–109.

——— 1910 [c.1826]. 'Les kimos de Madagascar'. *Bulletin de l'Académie Malgache* 8: 65–7.

——— 1909–10 [1827]. 'Voyage dans l'intérieur de Madagascar et à la capitale du Roi Radama pendant les années 1825 et 1826'. *Bulletin de l'Académie Malgache* 7–8: 30–46.

Corlay, G. de. 1896. *Notre campagne à Madagascar: Notes et souvenirs d'un volontaire* (Paris: Tolra).

Cousins, H. H. 1896. '*Tanghin*, or the Poison Ordeal of Madagascar'. *Antananarivo Annual & Madagascar Magazine* 20: 385–8.

Cousins, William Edward. 1894. 'Characteristics of the Malagasy Language'. *Antananarivo Annual & Madagascar Magazine* 18: 233–41.

——— 1884. 'Malagasy Dictionaries'. *Antananarivo Annual & Madagascar Magazine* 8: 43–51.

Curtis, Thomas. 1829. *The London Encyclopaedia*, vol. 22 (London, Printed for T. Tegg).

Dandouau, André. 1911. 'Documents divers concernant J. Laborde'. *Bulletin de l'Académie Malgache* 9: 143–56.

Drury, Robert. 1890 [1729]. *Madagascar; or Robert Drury's Journal, during Fifteen Years' Captivity on that Island* (London: T. Fisher Unwin).

Duhaut-Cilly, Malo. 1968 [1825]. 'Notices sur le royaume d'Emirne, sur la capitale de Tananarivou et sur le gouvernement de Rhadama'. In Jean Valette (ed.), 'Deux documents français sur Madagascar en 1825; les rapports Duhaut-Cilly et Frere', *Bulletin de l'Académie Malgache*, 66.1–2: 231–58.

Ellis, William. 1867. *Madagascar Revisited* (London: John Murray).

——— 1859. *Three Visits to Madagascar during the Years 1853–1854–1856* (London: John Murray).

——— 1858. *Three Visits to Madagascar during the Years 1853–1854–1856* (Philadelphia: John E. Potter).

——— 1838. *History of Madagascar*. 2 vols. (London: Fisher).

Ellis, William, and Joseph John Freeman. 1842. *Madagascar and Its Martyrs: A Book for the Young* (London: John Snow).

Elwick, George. 1843. *The Bankrupt Directory* (London: Simpkin, Marshall & Co.).

Flacourt, Étienne de. 1995 [1658]. *Histoire de la Grande Isle Madagascar*. Edited and commentary by Claude Allibert (Paris: Karthala).

1661. *Histoire de la grande isle Madagascar* (Troyes: Nicolas Oudot).

Foreign Office. 1848. *British and Foreign State Papers, 1825–1826* (London: James Ridgway & Sons).

1826. *British and Foreign State Papers, 1824–1825* (London: J. Harrison & Son).

Fox, Joseph. 1810. *An Appeal to the Members of the London Missionary Society, against a Resolution of the Directors of that Society; dated March 26, 1810; with Remarks on certain Proceedings relative to the Otaheitan and Jewish Mission* (London: Darton and Harvey).

Freeman, Joseph John. 1851. *A Tour in South Africa, with Notices of Natal, Mauritius, Madagascar, Ceylon, Egypt, and Palestine* (London: John Snow).

Freeman, Joseph John, and David Johns. 1840. *A Narrative of the Persecution of the Christians in Madagascar with Details of the Escape of the Six Christian Refugees Now in England* (London: John Snow).

Frere, Bartle. 1873. 'Correspondence Respecting Sir Bartle Frere's Mission to the East Coast of Africa, 1872–73'. *House of Commons Parliamentary Papers* (London: House of Commons).

Freycinet, Louis de. 1826. *Voyage autour du monde, entrepris par ordre du Roi, sous le ministère et conformément aux instructions de S. Exc. M. Le Vicomte de Bouchage, Secrétaire d'État au Département de la marine, executé sur les corvettes de S. M. l'Oranie et la Physicienne, pendant les années 1817, 1818, 1819 et 1820* (Paris: Pillet Ainé).

Galli, Henri C. 1897. *La Guerre à Madagascar. Histoire anecdotique des expéditions française de 1885 à 1895* (Paris: Garnier Frères).

Garnot, Alexandre. 1846. *Question de Madagascar traitée au point de vue de l'intérêt français et du droit publique européenne* (Bordeaux: P. Coudert).

Grandidier, Alfred. 1971 [1916]. 'Souvenirs de voyages, 1865–1870'. In *Documents anciens sur Madagascar*, vol. 6 (Tananarive: Association Malgache d'archéologie).

Grant, J. P. (ed.). 1844. *Memoir and Correspondence of Mrs. Grant of Laggan*, vol. 1 (London: Longman, Brown, Green, and Longmans).

Great Britain, War Office. 1835. *A List of the Officers of the Army and of the Corps of Royal Marines* (London: William Clowes).

Gregory, Olinthus, J. Handfield, and John Dyer (eds). 1815. *Memoirs of the Life of the Late Major-General Andrew Burn of the Royal Marines: Collected from His Journals, with Copious Extracts from His Principal Works on Religious Subjects*. 2 vols (London: W. Winchester and Son).

Griffiths, David. 1843. *Hanes Madagascar* (Machynlleth: Richard Jones).

1841. *The Persecuted Christians of Madagascar; A Series of Interesting Occurrences during a Residence at the Capital from 1838 to 1840* (London: Cornelius Hedgman).

1823. 'Journal'. *Missionary Register*: 178–81.

Guillain, Charles. 1845. *Documents sur l'histoire, la géographie et le commerce de la partie occidentale de Madagascar* (Paris: Imprimerie Royale).

Hamilton, William John. 1850. 'Abstract of MSS. Books and Papers respecting Madagascar during the Possession of the Mauritius by the French. Presented by Sir Walter Minto Townsend Farquhar to the British Museum'. *Journal of the Royal Geographical Society of London* 20: 75–88.

Hamond, Walter. 1640. *A Paradox. Prooving, That the Inhabitants of the Isle called Madagascar, Or St. Laurence, (In Temporall things) are the happiest People in the World* (London: J. Raworth, B. Alsop, T. Fawcet, and M. Parsons).

Hardcastle, Emma Corsbie (ed.). 1860. *Memoir of Joseph Hardcastle, Esq., First Treasurer of the London Missionary Society: A Record of the Past for His Descendants* (London: Alex Macintosh).

Hardy, Charles. 1835. *Supplement to a Register of Ships Employed in the Service of the Hon. The East India Company, from the Year 1760 to the Conclusion of the Commercial Charter* (London: J. Hardy).

Hewlett, Arthur M. 1887. 'Mantasoa and Its Workshops: A Page in the History of Industrial Progress in Madagascar'. *Antananarivo Annual and Madagascar Magazine* 2: 295–300.

Hilsenberg, Charles Theodore, and Wenceslaus Bojer. 1833 [1823]. 'A Sketch of the Province of Emerina, in the Island of Madagascar, and of the Huwa, Its Inhabitants; written during a Year's Residence'. In William Jackson Hooker (ed.), *Botanical Miscellany; containing Figures and Descriptions of such Plants as recommend themselves by their Novelty, Rarity, or History, or by the Uses to which they are applied in the Arts, in Medicine, and in Domestic Economy together with occasional Botanical Notes and Information*, vol. 3 (London: John Murray): 246–75

Holman, James. 1840. *Travels in Madras, Ceylon, Mauritius, Comoro Islands, Zanzibar, Calcutta, Etc. Etc.* (London: Routledge).

1834–5. *Voyage round the World, including Travels in Africa, Asia, Australasia, America, etc. etc. from 1827 to 1832*, vols. 2 and 3 (London: Smith, Elder).

Holyoake, George Jacob. 1909. *Sixty Years of an Agitator's Life*, vol. 1 (London: T. F. Unwin).

House of Commons. 1875. *Delagoa Bay: Correspondence Respecting the Claims of Her Majesty's Government* (London: Harrison & Sons).

1863. *Accounts and Papers*, vol. 74.

1849. *Parliamentary Papers* 37.23.

1828. *Papers Relating to the Slave Trade* 26.2.

1828. *Parliamentary Papers*.

1826–7. *Slave Trade: Papers Relating to Slaves in the Colonies*.

1826. *Papers: Relating to Captured Negroes; also to the Slave Trade at the Mauritius and Bourbon, and the Seychelles; Slave Population at the Seychelles &c.*

1821. *Papers relating to the Abolition of the Slave Trade in the Mauritius: 1817–1820* vol. 18.

1812–13. *Journals of the House of Commons* 68.

Jarrold, Thomas. 1836. *Instinct and Reason, Philosophically Investigated; with a View to ascertain the Principles of the Science of Education* (London: Longman).

1825. 'Of the Influence of Early Impressions on the Future Character'. *Monthly Magazine or British Register* 59.409: 301–5.

Jarvis, Charles. 1821. *The Life and Exploits of Don Quixote De la Mancha*, vol. 1 (London: W. Wilson).

Jeffreys, Keturah. 1827. *The Widowed Missionary's Journal* (Southampton: Printed for the author).

[Jesuit Mission de Madagascar]. 1860. *Ny Filazana ny Zavatra Nataony sy Nambara ny i Jeso-Kristy, Tompontsika, Zanak' Andriamanitra, sady Mpamonjy no*

Mpanavotra ny Olona (Ile Bourbon: Établissement malgache de Nôtre-dame de la ressource).

Jones, David. 1825. 'Extracts from Journal (1820)'. In Thomas Smith, *The history and origin of the missionary societies, containing faithful accounts of the voyages, travels, labours, and successes of the various missionaries who have been sent out, for the purpose of evangelizing the heathen,and other unenlightened nations, in different parts of the globe. Compiled and arranged from the authentic documents*, vol. 2 (London: Thomas Kelly and Richard Evans): 366–79.

Kelsey, N. J. 1828. 'Abstract of the Expense incurred by the Government of Mauritius on Account of Madagascar' (26 Nov. 1827) in 'Slaves in Mauritius' 40–4, *Papers Relating to the Slave Trade* 26.2 ([London]: House of Commons).

Lacombe, B.-F. Leguével de. 1840. *Voyages à Madagascar et aux îles Comores. (1823 à 1830)*, vol. 1 (Paris: L. Desessart).

Lasalle, Jacques de. 1898 [1797]. 'Mémoire sur Madagascar'. *Notes, reconnaissances et explorations* 2.2: 563–82.

Lewis, Locke. 1835. 'An Account of the Ovahs, a race of people residing in the Interior of Madagascar: with a Sketch of their Country, Appearance, Dress, Language, &c.'. *Journal of the Royal Geographical Society* 5: 230–42.

Löhr, Johann Andreas Christian. 1819. *Die Lander und Volker der Erde; oder, Vollstandige Beschreibung aller funf Erdtheile* (Leipzig : Fleischer).

[LMS]. 1834. *The Report of the Directors to the Fortieth General Meeting of the Missionary Society, usually called the London Missionary Society* (London: Westley & David).

— 1819. *Report of the Directors to the Twenty Fifth General Meeting of the Missionary Society, usually called the London Missionary Society, on Thursday, May 13, 1819* (London: F. Westley).

— 1818. *Report of the Directors to the Twenty Fourth General Meeting of the Missionary Society, usually called the London Missionary Society, on Thursday, May 14, 1818* (London: Williams & Co.).

— 1816. *Report of the Directors to the Twenty Second General Meeting of the Missionary Society, on Thursday, May 10, 1816* (London: S. McDowall).

— 1815. *Report of the Directors to the Twenty First General Meeting of the Missionary Society, on Thursday, May 11, 1815* (London: J. Dennett).

Lord, Thomas. 1900. 'The Early History of Imerina based upon a Native Account'. *Antananarivo Annual and Madagascar Magazine* 24: 451–75.

Lloyds. 1828. 'Ship Childe Harold'. In *The Register of Shipping for the Year 1828* (London: W. Marchant), https://eicships.threedecks.org/ships/shipdetail.php?ship ID=891 (accessed 11. 08.19).

Lyall, Robert. 1954 [1827–9]. 'Journal'. In Georges-Sully Chapus and Gustave Mondain (eds.), *Le Journal de Robert Lyall* (Tananarive: Imprimerie Officielle).

Malzac, [Victorin]. 1900. 'Ordre de succession au trône chez les Hova'. *Notes, reconnaissances et explorations* 1.1: 607–18.

Matthews, Thomas Trotter. 1881. *Notes of Nine Years' Mission Work in the Province of Vonizongo, North West, Madagascar, with Historical Introduction* (London: Hodder and Stoughton).

Montgomery, James (ed.). 1831. *Journal of Voyages and Travels by the Rev. Daniel Tyerman and George Bennet*. 2 vols. (London: Westley & Davis).

(ed.). 1832. *Journal of Voyages and Travels by the Rev. Daniel Tyerman and George Bennet*, vol. 3 (Boston: Crocker and Brewster).

Mullens, Joseph. 1875. *Twelve Months in Madagascar* (London: James Nisbet).

Murray, Hugh, William Wallace, Robert Jameson, W. Swainson, and Thomas G. Bradford. 1837. *The encyclopædia of geography: comprising a complete description of the earth, physical, statistical, civil, and political: exhibiting its relation to the heavenly bodies, its physical structure, the natural history of each country, and the industry, commerce, political institutions, and civil and social state of all nations* (Philadelphia: Carey, Lea, and Blanchard).

Noel, Vincent. 1843. 'Ile de Madagascar: Recherches sur les Sakalava [part 1]'. *Bulletin de la société de géographie* 2.19: 275–95.

——. 1843. 'Ile de Madagascar: Recherches sur les Sakalava [part 2]'. *Bulletin de la société de géographie* 2.20: 40–64

Oliver, Samuel Pasfield. 1891. 'Has There Been a Race of Pygmies in Madagascar'. *Antananarivo Annual and Madagascar Magazine* 15: 257–72.

——. 1888. 'General Hall and the Export Slave Trade from Madagascar: A Statement and a Vindication'. *Antananarivo Annual & Madagascar Magazine* 12: 473–9.

——. 1886. *Madagascar: An Historical and Descriptive Account of the Island and Its Former Dependencies*. 2 vols (London: Macmillan).

——. 1885. *The True Story of the French Dispute in Madagascar* (London: T. Fisher Unwin).

——. 1885. 'The French in Madagascar: Four Views of Madagascar'. *The Illustrated Naval and Military Magazine* 14 (August): 100–8.

——. 1881. *On and Off Duty, Being Leaves from an Officer's Note-Book* (London: W.H. Allen).

——. [1866]. *Madagascar and the Malagasy: With Sketches in the Provinces of Tamatave, Betanimena, and Ankova* (London: Day & Son).

Osgood, Joseph Barlow Felt. 1854. *Notes of Travel: Or, Recollections of Majunga, Zanzibar, Muscat, Aden, Mocha, and other Eastern Ports* (Salem: George Creamer).

Owen. W. F. W. 1833. *Narrative of Voyages to Explore the Shores of Africa, Arabia, and Madagascar; Performed in HM Ships Leven and Barracouta*. 2 vols. (New York: J. & J. Harper).

Peill, Jeremiah. 1883. 'Social Conditions and Prospect of Madagascar'. *Journal of the Society of Arts* 1578.21: 271–85.

Pfeiffer, Ida. 1861. *The Last Travels of Ida Pfeiffer: Inclusive of a Visit to Madagascar: with a Biographical Memoir of the Author* (London: Routledge, Warne and Routledge).

Philip, Robert. 1841. *The Life, Times, and Missionary Enterprises of the Rev. John Campbell* (London: John Snow).

——. 1840. *The Life and Opinions of the Rev. William Milne, D.D., Missionary to China* (New York: D. Appleton).

Prichard, James Cowles. 1855. *The Natural History of Man* (London: H. Baillière).

Prince, Mary. 1831. *The History of Marchy Prince, a West Indian Slave* (London: Frederick Westley & A. H. Davis).

Prior, James. 1819. *Voyage along the Eastern Coast of Africa: To Mosambique, Johanna, and Quiloa; to St Helena; to Rio de Janeiro, Bahia, and Pernambuco in Brazil, in the Nisus Frigate* (London: Richard Phillips).

Prout, Ebenezer. 1843. *Memoirs of the Life of the Rev. John Williams, Missionary to Polynesia* (Andover: Allen, Morrill & Wardwell).

Prud'homme, [Émile]. 1900. 'Considérations sur les Sakalaves'. *Notes, reconnaissances et explorations* 6: 1–43.

Raombana. 1976 [mid-19th century]. *Raombana l'historien (1809–1855)*, edited by Simon Ayache (Fianarantsoa: Ambozontany).

——— 1930. 'Manuscrit écrit à Tananarive (1853–1854)' (trans. J. F. Radley). *Bulletin de l'Académie Malgache* 13: 1–26.

Riaux, Francis. 1881 [1862]. 'Introduction: Notice historique sur Madagascar'. In Ida Pfeiffer, *Voyage à Madagascar* (Paris: Librarie Hachette): i–lxxv.

Richardson, James. 1885. *A New Malagasy-English Dictionary* (Antananarivo: LMS).

[Robert Howard & Co.] 1842. *A Catalogue of Tin, Japanned, & Zinc Wares: Sold by Robert Howard & Co* (London: J. H. Banks).

Rooke, W. 1866. 'A Boat-Voyage along the Coast-Lakes of East Madagascar'. *Journal of the Royal Geographical Society of London* 36: 52–64.

Ross, George. 1819. *The Cape of Good Hope Calendar and Agriculturist's Guide* (London: T & J. Allman).

Samat, Edmont. 1932 [1852]. 'Notes: La côte ouest de Madagascar en 1852'. *Bulletin de l'Académie Malgache* 15 (1932): 53–78.

Savaron, C. 1931. 'Contribution à l'histoire de l'Imerina'. *Bulletin de l'Académie Malgache* 14 (1931): 56–66.

Sibree, James. 1924. *Fifty Years in Madagascar: Personal Experiences of Mission Life and Work* (London: George Allen and Unwin).

——— 1923. *London Missionary Society: A Register of Missionaries, Deputations, etc. from 1796 to 1923* (London: LMS).

——— 1915. *A Naturalist in Madagascar* (London: Seeley).

——— 1898. 'Industrial Progress in Madagascar'. *Antananarivo Annual & Madagascar Magazine* 22: 129–36.

——— 1896. 'Malagasy Place-Names; Part 1'. *Antananarivo Annual & Madagascar Magazine* 20: 401–13.

——— 1892. 'Imerina, the Central Province of Madagascar, and the Capital, Antananarivo'. *Proceedings of the Royal Geographical Society and Monthly Record of Geography* 14.11: 737–53.

——— 1880. 'Relationships and the Names Used for Them among the Peoples of Madagascar, Chiefly the Hovas; Together with Observations upon Marriage Customs and Morals among the Malagasy'. *Journal of the Anthropological Institute of Great Britain and Ireland* 9: 35–50.

——— 1879. 'History and Present Condition of Our Geographical Knowledge of Madagascar'. *Proceedings of the Royal Geographical Society and Monthly Record of Geography* 1.10: 646–65.

——— 1879. 'Malagasy Folk-Lore and Popular Superstitions'. *The Folk-Lore Record* 2: 19–46.

——— 1873. *Madagascar et ses habitants: Journal d'un séjour de quatre ans dans l'ile*. Trans. H. Monod and H. Monot (Toulouse: Société des Livres Religieux).

——— 1870. *Madagascar and Its People* (London: Religious Tract Society).

Sibree, John, and M. Caston. 1855. *Independency in Warwickshire: A Brief History of the Independent or Congregational Churches in that County* (Coventry: G. & F. King).

Simmonds, Peter Lund. 1877. *Animal Products, Their Preparation, Commercial Uses and Value* (London: Chapman & Hall).

Smith, Thomas, and John Overton Choules. 1832. *The Origin and History of Missions: Containing Faithful Accounts of the Voyages, Travels, Labors and Successes of the various Missionaries who have been Sent Forth to Evangelize the Heathen* (Boston: S. Walker, and Lincoln & Edmands).

Standing, Herbert F. 1887. *The Children of Madagascar* (London: Religious Tract Society).

Stephen, Leslie (ed.). 1889. *Dictionary of National Biography*, vol. 18 (London: Smith, Elder & Co.).

Stone, John Seely. 1848. *A Memoir of the Life of James Milnor, DD: Late Rector of St George's Church, New York* (New York: American Tract Society).

Stuart, Martinus. 1806. *De mensch, zoo als hij voorkomt op den bekenden aardbol*, vol. 5 (Amsterdam: Johannes Allart).

Tacchi, Antony. 1892. 'King Andrianampoinimerina and the Early History of Antananarivo and Ambohimanga'. *Antananarivo Annual and Madagascar Magazine* 16: 474–96.

Telfair, Charles. 1830. *Some Account of the State of Slavery at Mauritius, since the British Occupation in 1810; in refutation of anonymous charges against Government of that Colony* (Port Louis: J. Vallet and V. Asselin).

Tyerman, Daniel. 1832. *Journal of Voyages and Travels by the Rev. Daniel Tyerman and George Bennet, Esq. deputed from the London Missionary Society to visit their various stations in the South Sea Islands, China, India, &c. between the Years 1821 and 1829*, vol. 3 (Boston: Crocker and Brewster).

Tyerman, Daniel, and George Bennet. 1841. *Voyages and Travels Round the World* (London: John Snow).

Wills, James. 1885. 'Native Products Used in Malagasy Industries'. *Antananarivo Annual and Madagascar Magazine*, 9: 91–9.

Wilson, John (ed.). 1844. *A Memoir of Mrs. Margaret Wilson, of the Scottish Mission, Bombay* (Edinburgh: Longman).

Yates, George. 1830. *An Historical and Descriptive Sketch of Birmingham* (Birmingham: Beilby, Knott, and Beilby).

Periodicals

- *Anti-Slavery Monthly Reporter* (1830)
- *Aristarque Français* (1820)
- *Asiatic Journal* (1826–9)
- *Bombay Times and Journal of Commerce* (1848)
- *Bristol Mercury* (1837)
- *Caledonian Mercury* (1825–6)
- *Christian Keepsake and Missionary Annual* (1835)
- *Colonial Times* (1830)
- *Commercial Directory* (1841)
- *Critical Review* (1810)
- *Derby Mercury* (1826)
- *Drysorfa* (1837)

- *Evangelical Magazine and Missionary Chronicle* (1818–26)
- *Freeman's Journal and Daily Commercial Advertiser* (1845)
- *Gentleman's Magazine* (1824)
- *Hampshire Telegraph and Sussex Chronicle* (1825)
- *Home Friend* (1854)
- *Illustrated London News* (1845, 1863)
- *Illustrated Naval and Military Magazine* (1885)
- *Juvenile Bethel Flag Magazine* (1848)
- *Juvenile Missionary Magazine* (1844)
- *Leeds Mercury* (1825)
- *London Gazette* (1821)
- *London Literary Gazette* (1825)
- *The Madras Christian Instructor and Missionary Record* (1843–4)
- *Magasin pittoresque* (1855)
- *Manchester Times and Gazette* (1832)
- *Mirror of Literature, Amusement, and Instruction* (1830)
- *Missionary Herald* (1824)
- *Missionary Magazine and Chronicle* (1848)
- *Missionary Register* (1822–5)
- *Missionary Sketches* (1821)
- *Monthly Magazine or British Register* (1825)
- *Morning Chronicle* (1817–43)
- *Morning Post* (1823–45)
- *Morning Spectacle* (1823)
- *Official Gazette of the Colony and Protectorate of Kenya* (1927)
- *Perth Gazette and Western Australian Journal* (1842)
- *Proceedings of the Church Missionary Society for Africa and the East* (1825–6)
- *Proceedings of the Royal Medical and Chirurgical Society of London* (1864)
- *Quarterly Chronicle of the Transactions of the London Missionary Society* (1821–4)
- *Solicitors' Journal and Reporter* (1890)
- *Standard* (1845)
- *Sunday at Home* (1859)
- *The Times* (1831–5)
- *Tour du Monde* (1861–4).

Secondary Sources

Anon. 1924. *The Arabian Nights: Tales from the Thousand and One Arabian Nights* (London: Hodder & Stoughton).
——— 1881. 'Man-Eating Tree of Madagascar'. *Antananarivo Annual & Madagascar Magazine* 5: 91–3.
Ackerman, Paul. 1833. *Histoire des revolutions de Madagascar, depuis 1642 jusqu'à nos jours* (Paris: Librairie Gide).
Adas, Michael. 1989. *Machines As the Measures of Men: Science, Technology, and Ideologies of Western Dominance* (Itahaca, NY: Cornell University Press).

Allen, Douglas W. 2002. 'The British Naval Rules: Monitoring and Incompatible Incentives in the Age of Fighting Sail'. *Explorations in Economic History* 39: 204–31.

Allen, Richard B. 2010. 'Satisfying the "Want for Labouring People": European Slave Trading in the Indian Ocean, 1500–1850'. *Journal of World History* 21.1: 45–73.

2002. 'Maroonage and Its Legacy in Mauritius and in the Colonial Plantation World'. *Outre-Mers: Revue d'histoire* 89.336–7: 131–52.

1983. 'Marronage and the Maintenance of Public Order in Mauritius, 1721–1835'. *Slavery and Abolition* 4.3: 214–31.

Alpers, Edward A. 1977. 'Madagascar and Mozambique in the Nineteenth Century: The Era of the Sakalava Raids (1800–1820)'. *Omaly sy Anio* 5–6: 37–53.

Anderson, Clare. 2008. 'The Politics of Punishment in Colonial Mauritius, 1766–1887'. *Journal of the Social History Society* 5.4: 411–22.

1997. 'The Genealogy of the Modern Subject: Indian Convicts in Mauritius, 1814–1853'. In Ian Duffield and James Bradley (eds.), *Representing Convicts: New Perspectives on Convict Forced Labour Migration* (London: Leicester University Press): 164–82.

Anderson, Daniel E. 1918. *The Epidemics of Mauritius* (London: H. K. Lewis).

Aujas, L. 1905–6. 'Notes sur l'histoire des Betsimisaraka'. *Bulletin de l'Académie Malgache* 4: 104–15.

Ayache, Simon. 1986. 'La découverte de l'Europe par les Malgaches au XIXe siècle'. *Revue française d'histoire d'outre-mer* 73.270: 7–25.

(ed.). 1976. *Raombana l'historien (1809–1855)* (Fianarantsoa: Ambozontany).

1976. 'Un intellectuel malgache devant la culture européenne: L'historien Raombana (1809–1854)'. *Archipel* 12.1: 95–119.

(ed.). 1980. *Raombana: Histoires* (Fianarantsoa: Ambozontany).

Baker, Philip, and Chris Corne. 1986. *Isle de France Creole: Affinities and Origins* (Ann Arbor, MI: Karoma).

Baré, Jean-Francois. 1983. 'Remarques sur le vocabulaire monarchique sakalava du nord'. In Françoise Raison-Jourde (ed.), *Les souverains de Madagascar* (Paris: Karthala): 154–73.

Barendse, R. J. 2002. *The Arabian Seas: The Indian Ocean World of the Seventeenth Century* (Armonk, NY: M. E. Sharpe).

Barker, Anthony J. 1996. *Slavery and Antislavery in Mauritius, 1810–33: The Conflict between Economic Expansion and Humanitarian Reform* (London: MacMillan, 1996).

Barnwell, Patrick Joseph, and Auguste Toussaint. 1949. *A Short History of Mauritius* (London: Longmans, Green & Co.).

Baron, Richard. 1890. 'A Malagasy Forest'. *Antananarivo Annual & Madagascar Magazine* 14: 196–211.

Benevent, Charles. 1905–6. 'Notes sur les Kimosy'. *Bulletin de l'Académie Malgache* 4: 101–3.

Berg, Gerald M. 1996. 'Virtù, and Fortuna in Radama's Nascent Bureaucracy, 1816–1828'. *History in Africa* 23: 29–74.

1995. 'Writing Ideology: Ranavalona, the Ancestral Bureaucrat'. *History in Africa* 22: 73–92.

1977. 'The Myth of Racial Strife and Merina Kinglists: The Transformation of Texts'. *History in Africa* 4: 1–30.

Bialuschewski, Arne. 2007. 'Thomas Bowrey's Madagascar Manuscript of 1708'. *History in Africa* 34: 31–42.

2005. 'Pirates, Slavers, and the Indigenous Population in Madagascar, c.1690–1715'. *International Journal of African Historical Studies* 38.3: 401–25.

Bidie, George. 1869. 'Effects of Forest Destruction in Coorg'. *Journal of the Royal Geographical Society* 39: 77–90.

Bixler, Raymond W. 1934. 'Anglo-Portuguese Rivalry for Delagoa Bay'. *Journal of Modern History* 6.4: 425–40.

Bland, E. [1887]. *Annals of Southport and District: A Chronological History of North Meols, AD 1086 to 1886* (Manchester: Abel, Heywood & Sons).

Bolt, Christine. 1971. *Victorian Attitudes to Race* (London: Routledge & Kegan Paul).

Bolton, W. Draper. 1852. *Bolton's Mauritius Almanac, and Official Directory for 1852* (Mauritius: Mauritian Printing Establishment).

Bontekoe, William. 1929. *Memorable Description of the East Indian Voyage 1618–1625* (London: RoutledgeCurzon)

Boudou, Adrien S. 1940. 'Petites notes d'histoire malgache'. *Bulletin de l'Académie Malgache* 23: 65–8.

Brown, Mervyn. 1978. *Madagascar Rediscovered: A History from Early Times to Independence* (London: Damien Tunnacliffe).

Burgh-Edwardes, S. B. De. 1921. *The History of Mauritius (1507–1914)* (London: East and West).

Burroughs, Peter. 1976. 'The Mauritius Rebellion of 1832 and the Abolition of British Colonial Slavery'. *Journal of Imperial and Commonwealth History* 4.3: 243–65.

Burrows, Edmund H. 1957. 'Queries'. *Mariner's Mirror* 43.4: 342–4.

Burrows, Montagu. 1908. *Autobiography of Montagu Burrows* (London: Macmillan).

Burton, Jim. 2017. 'Howard, Luke (1772–1864)'. *Oxford Dictionary of National Biography* (1 Sep.) www.oxforddnb.com/view/10.1093/ref:odnb/9780198614128 .001.0001/odnb-9780198614128-e-13928 (accessed 13.07.21).

Buxtorf, Marie-Claude. 1987. 'Colonie, comptoirs et compagnie: Bourbon et l'Inde Française, 1720–1767'. In *Les relations historiques et culturelles entre la France et l'Inde, XVIIe-XXe siècles*, vol. 2 (Sainte-Clotilde, La Réunion: Association historique internationale de l'Océan indien): 165–85.

Bynum, Helen. 2012. *Spitting Blood: The History of Tuberculosis* (Oxford: Oxford University Press).

Campbell, Gwyn. 2020. *The Travels of Robert Lyall, 1789–1831: Scottish Surgeon, Naturalist and British Agent to the Court of Madagascar* (Cham, Switzerland: Palgrave Macmillan).

2020. 'Malaria in Precolonial Imerina (Madagascar), 1795–1895'. In Gwyn Campbell and Eva-Maria Knoll (eds.), *Disease Dispersion and Impact in the Indian Ocean World* (London: Palgrave Macmillan): 129–67.

2020. 'Commercialisation of Cattle in Imperial Madagascar, 1795–1895'. In Martha Chaiklin, Philip Gooding, and Gwyn Campbell (eds.), *Animal Trade Histories in the Indian Ocean World* (Cham, Switzerland: Palgrave Macmillan): 181–215.

2019. 'Labour Migration to the French Islands of the Western Indian Ocean, 1830–60'. In Gwyn Campbell and Alessandro Stanziani (eds.), *The Palgrave Handbook of Bondage and Human Rights in Africa and Asia* (Basingstoke: Palgrave Macmillan): 83–104.

2018. 'The Decline of the Malagasy Textile Industry, circa 1800–1895'. In Pedro Machado, Sarah Fee, and Gwyn Campbell (eds.), *An Ocean of Cloth: Textile Trades, Consumer Cultures and the Textile Worlds of the Indian Ocean* (Basingstoke, Hampshire: Palgrave Macmillan): 313–58.

2018. Review Essay. *Feeding Globalization: Madagascar and the Provisioning Trade, 1600–1800*. By Jane Hooper. Athens, Ohio. Ohio University Press. 2017. *International Journal of African Historical Studies* 51.2: 341–6.

2016. 'Africa and the Early Indian Ocean World Exchange System in the Context of Human–Environment Interaction'. In Gwyn Campbell (ed.), *Early Exchange between Africa and the Wider Indian Ocean World* (London: Palgrave Macmillan, 2016): 1–24.

2012. *David Griffiths and the Missionary 'History of Madagascar'* (Leiden: Brill).

2005. *An Economic History of Imperial Madagascar, 1750–1895: The Rise and Fall of an Island Empire* (Cambridge: Cambridge University Press).

2005. 'Introduction: Abolition and Its Aftermath in the Indian Ocean World'. In Gwyn Campbell (ed.), *Abolition and Its Aftermath in Indian Ocean Africa and Asia* (Abingdon, Oxford: Routledge): 1–28.

2004. 'Madagascar'. In Shepard Krech III, J. R. McNeill, and Carolyn Merchant (eds.), *Encyclopaedia of Environmental History*, vol. 2 (New York: Routledge): 796–8.

1999. 'Imperial Rivalry in the Western Indian Ocean and Schemes to Colonise Madagascar, 1769–1826'. *Revue des Mascareignes* 1: 75–97.

1991. 'An Industrial Experiment in Pre-colonial Madagascar, 1825–1861'. *Journal of Southern African Studies* 17.3: 525–59.

1988. 'Slavery and Fanompoana: The Structure of Forced Labour in Imerina (Madagascar), 1790–1861'. *Journal of African History* 29.3: 463–86.

1988. 'Gold Mining and the French Takeover of Madagascar, 1883–1914', *African Economic History* 17: 99–126.

1988. 'Madagascar and Mozambique in the Slave Trade of the Western Indian Ocean 1800–1861'. *Slavery and Abolition* 9.3: 166–93.

1987. 'The Adoption of Autarky in Imperial Madagascar, 1820–1835'. *Journal of African History* 28.3: 395–411.

1986. 'The Monetary and Financial Crisis of the Merina Empire, 1810–1826'. *South African Journal of Economic History* 1.1: 99–118.

1981. 'Madagascar and the Slave Trade, 1810–1895'. *Journal of African History* 22.2: 203–27.

1980. 'Labour and the Transport Problem in Imperial Madagascar, 1810–1895'. *Journal of African History* 21.3: 341–56.

Carayon, Jean Louis Joseph. 1845. *Histoire de l'établissement français de Madagascar pendant la Restauration* (Paris: Gide).

Chapus, Georges-Sully. 1951–2. 'Le soin du bien-être du peuple sous le règne d'Andrianampoinimerina'. *Bulletin de l'Académie Malgache* 30: 1–9.

1925. *Quatre-vingts années d'influence européennes en Imerina (1815–1895)* (Tananarive: G. Pitot).

Chapus, Georges-Sully, and Emile Birkeli. 1944–5. 'Historique d'Antsirabe jusqu'en l'année 1905'. *Bulletin de l'Académie Malgache* 26: 59–82.

Chapus, Georges-Sully, and [André] Dandouau. 1951. 'Les anciennes industries malgaches'. *Bulletin de l'Académie Malgache* 30: 45–70.

Chapus, Georges-Sully, and Gustave Mondain (eds.). 1954. *Le journal de Robert Lyall* (Tananarive: Imprimerie Officielle).

1951–2. 'Un chapitre inconnu: Des rapports de Maurice et de Madagascar'. *Bulletin de l'Académie Malgache* 30: 111–30.

Chartier, Henri Le, and G. Pellerin. 1888. *Madagascar depuis sa découverte jusqu'à nos jours* (Paris: Jouvet).

Chauvin, Jean. 1939. *Jean Laborde 1805–1878* (Tananarive: Imprimerie moderne de l'Émyrne, Pitot de la Beaujardiere).

Cheke, Anthony, and Julian Hume. 2008. *Lost Land of the Dodo: An Ecological History of Mauritius, Réunion & Rodrigues* (London: T & A. D. Poyser).

Chernock, Arianne. 2013. 'Queen Victoria and the "Bloody Mary of Madagascar"'. *Victorian Studies* 55.3: 425–49.

Chesson, F. W. 1874. 'The Dispute between England and Portugal'. *St James's Magazine* 13: 492–501.

Connolly, Mark. 2012. *Christmas: A History* (London: Tauris).

Coppet, Marcel de (ed.). 1947. *Madagascar*. 2 vols. (Paris: Encyclopedie de l'Empire Francais).

Cornevin, Robert, and Marianne Cornevin. 1990. *La France et les Français outre-mer de la première Croisade à la fin du Second Empire* (Paris: Tallandier).

Couland, Daniel. 1973. *Les Zafimaniry, un groupe éthnique de Madagascar à la poursuite de la forêt* (Tananarive:Imprimerie Fanontam-boky Malagasy).

Davis, Ralph. 1972. *The Rise of the English Shipping Industry in the 17th and 18th Centuries* (Newton Abbot: David & Charles).

Decary, Raymond. 1966. *Coutumes guerrières et organisation militaire chez les anciens Malgaches*. 2 vols. (Paris: Éditions maritimes et d'Outre-Mer).

1953. 'Contribution à l'histoire de la France à Madagascar'. *Bulletin de l'Académie Malgache* 31: 49–58.

1933. 'Le voyage du lieutenant de Vaisseau de Semerville a l'île Sainte-Marie en 1824'. *Bulletin de l'Académie Malgache* 16: 17–21.

1932. 'La reddition de Tamatave à l'Angleterre en 1811'. *Bulletin de l'Académie Malgache* 15: 48–52.

1930. 'Documents historiques relatifs à l'établissement français de Sainte-Marie sous la Restauration'. *Bulletin de l'Académie Malgache* 13: 57–89.

Deissinger, Thomas. 2004. 'Apprenticeship Systems in England and Germany: Decline and Survival'. In Wolf-Dietrich Greinert and Georg Hanf. (eds), *Towards a History of Vocational Education and Training (VET) in Europe in a Comparative Perspective: Proceedings of the First International Conference, October 2002, Florence*, vol. 1 (Luxembourg: Office for Official Publications of the European Communities): 28–45.

Delivré, Alain. 1974. *L'Histoire des rois d'Imerina: Interprétation d'une tradition orale* (Paris: Klincksieck).

Deschamps, Hubert Jules. 1976. 'Tradition and Change in Madagascar, 1790–1870'. In John E. Flint (ed.), *Cambridge History of Africa*, vol. 5 (Cambridge: Cambridge University Press): 393–417.

1972. *Histoire de Madagascar* (Paris: Berger-Levrault).

1953. *Méthodes et doctrines coloniales de la France* (Paris: Colin).

1949. *Les pirates à Madagascar* (Paris: Berger-Levrault).

Deshpande, Anirudh. 1995. 'The Bombay Marine: Aspects of Maritime History 1650–1850'. *Studies in History* 11.2: 281–301.

[Dinan, Jacques]. 1972. *Industrie sucrière de l'île Maurice* ([Port Louis]: Le Bureau des relations publiques de l'industrie sucrière).

Dubois, Henri. 1938. *Monographie des Betsileo* (Paris: Institut d'ethnologie).

Durand, J. P., and J. Durand. 1978. *L'Ile Maurice et ses populations* (Bruxelles: Editions Complexe).

Duyker, Edward. 2008. 'Sydney's People: The Mauritians'. *Sydney Journal* 1.2: 58–62.

Ellis, Stephen. 2007. '*Tom and Toakafo*: The Betsimisaraka Kingdom and State Formation in Madagascar, 1715–1750'. *Journal of African History* 48.3: 439–55.

Esoavelomandroso, Manassé. 1980. 'The "Malagasy Creoles" of Tamatave in the 19th Century'. *Diogenes* 28: 50–64.

Etherington, Norman (ed.). 2005. *Missions and Empire* (Oxford: Oxford University Press).

Evers, Sandra. 1995. 'Stigmatization As a Self-Perpetuating Process'. In Sandra Evers and Marc Spindler (eds.), *Cultures of Madagascar* (Leiden: IIAS): 137–56.

Eze, Emmanuel Chukwudi (ed.). 2009. *Race and the Enlightenment: A Reader* (Malden, MA: Blackwell).

Fabian, Johannes. 2000. *Out of Our Minds: Reason and Madness in the Exploration of Central Africa* (Berkeley: University of California Press).

Fee, Sarah. 2012. 'Historic Handweaving in Highland Madagascar: New Insights from a Vernacular Text Attributed to a Royal Diviner-Healer, c. 1870'. *Textile History* 43.1:61–82.

Filliot, Jean-Michel. 1974. *La traite des esclaves vers les Mascareignes au XVIIe siècle* (Paris: ORSTOM).

Fisher, David R. 2009. 'Townsend Farquhar, Sir Robert Townsend'. In David R. Fisher (ed.), *The History of Parliament: The House of Commons 1820–1832* (Cambridge: Cambridge University Press). www.historyofparliamentonline.org/volume/1820-1832/member/townsend-farquhar-sir-robert-1776-1830 (accessed 30/04/19).

Fisher, Michael H. 1996. *The First Indian Author in English: Dean Mahomed (1759–1851) in India, Ireland, and England* (Delhi: Oxford University Press).

Fontoynont, Antoine Maurice. 1909. 'La légend des Kimosy'. *Bulletin de l'Académie Malgache* 7: 51–9.

Fontoynont, Antoine Maurice, and H. Nicol. 1940. *Les traitants français de la côte est de Madagascar – de Ranavalona I à Radama II* (Tananarive: Imprimerie moderne de l'Émyrne).

Forster, F. D., and Arnold Forster. 1957. *The Madagascar Pirates* (New York, Lothrup, Lee & Shepard).

Foss, Arthur, and Kerith Lloyd Kinsey Trick. 1989. *St Andrew's Hospital Northampton: The First 150 years, 1838–1988* (Cambridge: Granta Editions).

Freeman-Grenville, G. S. P. 1965. *The French at Kilwa Island* (Oxford: Clarendon Press).

Ghailani, Yusuf A. Al. 2015. 'British Early Intervention in the Slave Trade with Oman 1822–1873'. *History Research* 5.4: 225–38.

Gillis, John. 1996. 'Making Time for Family: The Invention of Family Time(s) and the Reinvention of Family History'. *Journal of Family History* 21.1: 4–21.

Goodman, Steven M., J. U. Ganzhorn, and D. Rakotondravony. 2003. 'Introduction to the Mammals'. In Steven M. Goodman and Jonathan P. Benstead (eds.), *The Natural History of Madagascar* (Chicago: University of Chicago Press): 1159–86.

Gordon, Charles Alexander. 1884. *An Epitome of the Reports of the Medical Officers to the Chinese Imperial Maritime Customs Service from 1871 to 1882* (London: Ballière, Tindall, & Cox).

Gourraigne, M. L. G. 1909. 'Les relations de la France avec Madagascar pendant la première moitié du XXe siècle'. In *Conférences publiques sur Madagascar faites à l'École Coloniale pendant l'année scolaire 1908–1909* (Paris:École Coloniale): 16–27.

Graham, Gerald S. 1967. *Great Britain in the Indian Ocean (1810–1850)* (Oxford: Clarendon Press).

Grandidier, Alfred. 1898. 'Property among the Malagasy' (trans. J. Sibree). *Antananarivo Annual and Madagascar Magazine* 22: 224–33.

Grandidier, Alfred, et al. (eds.). 1898. 'Republication of All Known Accounts of Madagascar', *Antananarivo Annual & Madagascar Magazine* 22: 234–5.

Grandidier, Alfred, and Guillaume Grandidier. 1905. *Collections des ouvrages anciens concernant Madagascar*, vol. 3 (Paris: Comité de Madagascar).

1908. *Histoire physique, naturelle et politique de Madagascar*, vol. 4, book 1 (Paris: Imprimerie nationale).

Grandidier, Guillaume. 1942. *Histoire physique, naturelle et politique de Madagascar*, vol. 5, books 1–2 (Paris: Imprimerie Paul Brodard).

1932. 'À Madagascar, anciennes croyances et coutumes'. *Journal de la Société des Africanistes* 2.2: 153–207.

1928. *Histoire physique, naturelle et politique de Madagascar* (Paris: Hachette).

1913. 'Le mariage à Madagascar'. *Bulletins et Mémoires de la Société d'anthropologie de Paris* 4.1: 9–46.

Gray, John. 1957. *The British in Mombasa 1824–1826* (London: Macmillan).

Grigg, E. R. N. 1955. 'Historical and Bibliographical Review of Tuberculosis in the Mentally Ill'. *Journal of the History of Medicine and Allied Sciences* 10.1: 58–108.

Grosbart, A. B. 1876. 'Madagascar Two Centuries Ago: A Proposal to Make It a British Plantation'. *Antananarivo Annual & Madagascar Magazine* 2: 51–6.

Grove, Richard H. 1999. *Green Imperialism: Colonial Expansion, Tropical Island Edens and the Origins of Environmentalism 1600–1860* (Cambridge: Cambridge University Press).

Gruchy, John de (ed.). 2000. *The London Missionary Society in Southern Africa, 1799–1999. Historical Essays in Celebration of the Bicentenary of the LMS in Southern Africa* (Athens, OH: Ohio University Press).

Haight, Frank 1941. *A History of French Commercial Policies* (New York: MacMillan).

Haight, Mabel V. Jackson. 1967. *European Powers and South-east Africa: A Study of International Relations on the South-east Coast of Africa, 1796–1856* (London: Routledge & Kegan Paul).

Hall, Catherine. 2002. *Civilising Subjects: Metropole and Colony in the English Imagination 1830–1867* (Chicago: University of Chicago Press).

Hardy, Georges. 1953. *Histoire de la colonisation française* (Paris: Librairie Larose).

Hardyman, James T. 1978. 'The London Missionary Society and Madagascar: 1795–1818. Part I: 1795–1811'. *Omaly sy Anio* 7–8:43–82.

Harries, Patrick. 2014. 'Slavery, Indenture and Migrant Labour: Maritime Immigration from Mozambique to the Cape, c.1780–1880'. *African Studies* 73.3: 323–40.

Hébert, Jean-Claude. 2001. 'Les "sagaies volantes" d'Andriamanelo et les "sagaies à pointes d'argile" des Vazimba: Un problème de critique de la tradition orale merina'. *Études océan indien* 31: 165–89.

Headrick, Daniel R. 1981. *The Tools of Empire: Technology and European Imperialism in the Nineteenth Century* (New York: Oxford University Press).

Herbert, J. C. 1979. 'Les Tribulations de Lebel, "négociant-voyageur" sur les hauts plateaux malgaches (1800–1803)'. *Omaly sy Anio* 10: 95–143.

Hervey, Frederick. 1785. *A New System of Geography*, vol. 1 (London: Printed for J. Johnson, and G. & T. Wilkie).

Hodgson, Jason A. 2016. 'A Genomic Investigation of the Malagasy Confirms the Highland–Coastal Divide, and the Lack of Middle Eastern Gene Flow'. In Gwyn Campbell (ed.), *Early Exchange between Africa and the Wider Indian Ocean World* (London: Palgrave Macmillan): 231–54.

Holding, John. 1869–70. 'Notes on the Province of Tanibe, Madagascar'. *Proceedings of the Royal Geographical Society of London* 14.5: 359–72.

Hole, Charles. 1896. *The Early History of the Church Missionary Society for Africa and the East to the End of AD 1814* (London: CMS).

Hollingworth, Derek. 1965. *They Came to Mauritius* (London: Oxford University Press).

Holmberg, Lars. 1962. 'Mauritius: A Study in Disaster'. *Economy and History* 5.1: 3–29.

Horn, Alfred. 1932. *The Waters of Africa* (London: Jonathan Cape).

Horsefall-Turner, E. R. 1908. *A Municipal History of Llanidloes* (Llanidloes: John Ellis).

Hoyle, Brian. 2001. 'Urban Renewal in East African Port Cities: Mombasa's Old Town Waterfront'. *GeoJournal* 53.2: 183–97.

Hübsch, Bruno (ed.). 1993. *Madagascar et le Christianisme* (Paris: Agence de coopération culturelle et technique).

Hugo, Abel. 1835. *France Pittoresque ou description pittoresque, topographique et statistique des départements et colonies de la France*, vol. 3 (Paris: Delloye).

Idahosa, Pablo L. E., and Bob Shenton. 2004. 'The Africanist's "New" Clothes'. *Historical Materialism* 12.4: 67–113.

Jenkins, Trefor, et al. 1996. 'ß-Globin Haplotype Analysis Suggests That a Major Source of Malagasy Ancestry Is Derived from Bantu-Speaking Negroids'. *American Society of Human Genetics* 58: 1303–8.

Jeremy, David I. 1977. 'Damming the Flood: British Government Efforts to Check the Outflow of Technicians and Machinery, 1780–1843'. *Business History Review* 51.1: 1–34.

Johnson, Charles [Daniel Defoe]. 1724. *A General History of the Pyrates* (London: T. Warner).

Jones, Chris. 2017. 'Minshall Family Has Played a Huge Role in Oswestry's History'. *Oswestry & Border Counties Advertizer* (21 Aug.).

Jully, Antoine. 1898. 'Notes sur Robin'. *Notes, reconnaissances et explorations* 3 (March): 511–16.

⸻ 1898. 'L'habitation à Madagascar'. *Notes, reconnaissances et explorations* 2.2: 499–910.

Kay, James. 2004. 'Étienne de Flacourt, L'histoire de le grand Île de Madagascar (1658)'. *Curtis's Botanical Magazine* 21.4: 251–7.

Keller, Conrad. 1901. *Madagascar, Mauritius and the Other East African Islands* (London: S. Sonnenschein).

Keller, Richard C. 2007. *Colonial Madness: Psychiatry in French North Africa* (Chicago: University of Chicago Press).

Kendall, H. B. [c.1920]. *The Origin and History of the Primitive Methodist Church* (London: E. Dalton).

Kiernan, V. G. 1972. *The Lords of Human Kind: European Attitudes to the Outside World in the Imperial Age* (Harmondsworth: Penguin).

Kirkman, James. 1975. 'John Studdy Leigh in Somalia'. *International Journal of African Historical Studies* 8.3: 441–56.

Koenig, Paul. 1914. 'Economic Flora'. In Allister Macmillan (ed.), *Mauritius Illustrated. Historical and Descriptive, Commercial and Industrial, Facts, Figures, & Resources* (London: W. H. & L. Collingridge): 102–9.

Kus, Susan, and Victor Raharijaona. 2015. 'The "Dirty"' Material and Symbolic Work of "State" Building in Madagascar: From Indigenous State-Crafting to Indigenous Empire Building to External Colonial Imposition and Indigenous Insurrection'. In F. G. Richard (ed.), *Materializing Colonial Encounters*. (New York: Springer): 199–227.

Kusimba, Chapurukha M. 2014. 'The Impact of Slavery on the East African Political Economy and Gender Relationships'. In Lydia Wilson Marshall (ed.), *The Archaeology of Slavery: A Comparative Approach to Captivity and Coercion* (Carbondale: Southern Illinois University Press): 230–54.

Laidlaw, Zoë. 2005. *Colonial Connections, 1815–45: Patronage, the Information Revolution and Colonial Government* (Manchester: Manchester University Press).

Larson, Pier M. 2011. 'Fragments of an Indian Ocean Life: Aristide Corroller between Islands and Empires'. *Journal of Social History* 45.2: 366–89.

⸻ 2009. *Ocean of Letters: Language and Creolization in an Indian Ocean Diaspora* (Cambridge: Cambridge University Press).

⸻ 2008. 'The Vernacular Life of the Street: Ratsitatanina and Indian Ocean Créolité'. *Slavery and Abolition*, 29.3: 327–59.

Lavondès, Henri. 1967. *Bekoropoka: Quelques aspects de la vie familiale et sociale d'un village malgache* (Berlin: De Gruyter).

Lewis, Charles Thomas Courtney. 1908. *George Baxter (Colour Printer) His Life and Work a Manual for Collectors* (London: S. Low, Marston & Co.).

Linschoten, John H. van. 1885. *Voyage to the East Indies*, vol. 1 (London: Hakluyt Society).

Linton, Ralph. 1928. 'Culture Areas in Madagascar'. *American Anthropologist* 30.3: 363–90.

Lombard, Jacques. 1988. *Le royaume Sakalava du Menabe: Essai d'analyse d'un système politique à Madagascar, 17e–20e* (Paris: ORSTOM).

Lombard-Jourdan, Anne. 1975. 'Des Malgaches à Paris sous Louis XIV'. *Archipel* 9: 79–90.

Lougnon, Albert. 1940. 'Vaisseaux et traites aux îles depuis 1741 jusqu'à 1746'. *Recueil de documents et travaux inédits pour servir à l'histoire de La Réunion* 5: 11–33.

Lovett, Richard. 1899. *The History of the London Missionary Society 1795–1895.* 2 vols. (London: Henry Frowde).

McConkey, Rosemary, and Thomas McErlean. 2007. 'Mombasa Island: A Maritime Perspective'. *International Journal of Historical Archaeology* 11.2: 99–121.

McKenna, Joseph. 2021.*The Gun Makers of Birmingham, 1660–1960* (Jefferson, NC: McFarland & Company).

McLeod, Bruce. 1999. *The Geography of Empire in English Literature, 1580–1745* (New York: Cambridge University Press).

McLeod, Lyons. 1865. *Madagascar and Its People* (London: Longman).

Macmillan, Allister (ed.). 1914. *Mauritius Illustrated. Historical and Descriptive, Commercial and Industrial, Facts, Figures, & Resources* (London: W.H. & L. Collingridge).

Malzac, [Victorin]. 1930. *Histoire du royaume Hova depuis ses origines jusqu'à sa fin* (Tananarive: Imprimerie Catholique).

—— 1900. 'Ordre de succession au trône chez les Hova'. *Notes, reconnaissances et explorations* 1.1: 607–18.

Martin, Robert Montgomery. 1839. *Statistics of the Colonies of the British Empire* (London: Allen).

Maynard, John. 1865. *The Parish of Waltham Abbey, Its History and Antiquities* (London: J. R. Smith).

Meier, Prita. 2016. *Swahili Port Cities: The Architecture of Elsewhere* (Bloomington: Indiana University Press).

Molet, Louis. 1958. 'Aperçu sur un groupe nomade de la forêt épineuse des Mikea'. *Bulletin de l'Académie Malgache* 36: 241–3.

Moriarty, H. A. 1911. *South Indian Ocean Pilot, for the Islands Westward of Longitude 80° East, including Madagascar and the Comoro Islands* (London:Taylor, Garnet, Evans & Co.).

Mosca, Liliana. 1980. *Il Madagascar nella vita di Raombana primo storico malgascio (1809–1855)* (Napoli: Giannini Editore).

Munthe, Ludvig. 1969. *La Bible à Madagascar* (Oslo: Forlaget Land og Kirke).

Munthe, Ludvig, Simon Ayache, and Charles Ravoajanahary. 1976. 'Radama I et les Anglais: Les négociations de 1817 d'après les sources malgaches ("sorabe" inédits)'. *Omaly sy Anio* 3–4: 9–104.

Murray, David. 1844. *Biblical Student's Assistant* (Edinburgh: Oliver & Boyd).

Myers, Norma. 1993. 'Servant, Sailor, Soldier, Tailor, Beggarman: Black Survival in White Society 1780–1830'. *Immigrants & Minorities* 12.1: 47–74.

Nativel, Didier. 2005. *Maisons royales, demeures des grands à Madagascar* (Paris: Karthala).

2004. 'Les héritiers de Raombana: Érudition et identité culturelle à Madagascar à l'époque coloniale (fin XIXème siècle–1960)'. *Revue d'histoire des sciences humaines* 1.20: 59–77.

Naval Intelligence Division. 1920. *A Manual of Portuguese East Africa* (London: HM Stationery Office).

Newitt, Malyn. 2005. 'Comoros: Before 1800'. In Kevin Shillington (ed.), *Encyclopedia of African History*, vol. 1 (New York: Fitzroy Dearborn): 289–90.

1984. *The Comoro Islands* (Boulder, CO: Westview Press).

Niekerk, J. P. van. 2016. 'The Life and Times of Cape Advocate Dirk Gysbert Reitz: A Biographical Note'. *Fundamina: A Journal of Legal History* 22.2: 310–46.

Nightingale, Benjamin. 1893. *Lancashire Nonconformity, Or, Sketches, Historical & Descriptive, of the Congregational and Old Presbyterian Churches in the County* (Manchester: John Heywood).

Nogue, L. 1900. 'Étude sur l'école professionnelle de Tananarive'. *Notes, reconnaissances et explorations* 1.1: 415–51.

Ord-Hume, Arthur W. J. G. 2019. 'The Confused World of the Mechanical Organ'. *Organists' Review* (Sep.): 8–15.

Ottino, Paul. 1982. 'The Malagasy *Andriambahoaka* and the Indonesian Legacy'. *History in Africa* 9: 221–250.

Parkinson, C. Northcote. 1937. *Trade in the Eastern Seas, 1793–1813* (Cambridge: Cambridge University Press).

Peabody, Sue. 2017. *Madeleine's Children. Family, Freedom, and Lies in France's Indian Ocean Colonies* (New York: Oxford University Press).

Pearl, Jason H. 2012. 'Desert Islands and Urban Solitudes in the "Crusoe" Trilogy'. *Studies in the Novel* 44.2: 125–43.

Peltier, Louis. 1903. 'La traite à Madagascar au XVIIe siècle'. *Revue de Madagascar* (August): 105–14.

Pickstone, John V. 1985. *Medicine and Industrial Society: A History of Hospital Development in Manchester and Its Region, 1725–1946* (Manchester: Manchester University Press).

Pietsch, Roland. 2004. 'Ships' Boys and Youth Culture in Eighteenth-Century Britain: The Navy Recruits of the London Marine Society'. *The Northern Mariner/Le marin du nord* 14.4: 11–24.

Pitot, Albert. 1914. 'History'. In Allister Macmillan (ed.), *Mauritius Illustrated: Historical and Descriptive, Commercial and Industrial, Facts, Figures, & Resources* (W. H. & L. Collingridge: London): 14–69.

Powys-Land Club. 1904. *Collections Historical & Archæological Relating to Montgomeryshire and Its Borders*, vol. 33 (Oswestry: Powys-Land Club).

Poyer, Lin, and Robert L. Kelly. 2000. 'Mystification of the Mikea: Constructions of Foraging Identity in Southwest Madagascar' *Journal of Anthropological Research* 56.2: 163–85.

Prestholdt, Jeremy. 2007. 'Similitude and Empire: On Comorian Strategies of Englishness'. *Journal of World History* 18.2: 113–38.

Prod'homme, J.-G., and Frederick H. Martens. 1921. 'Napoleon, Music and Musicians'. *Musical Quarterly* 7.4: 579–605.

[Dinan, Jacques]. 1972. *Industrie sucrière de l'île Maurice* ([Port Louis]: Le Bureau des relations publiques de l'industrie sucrière).

Rabary. 1930–1. *Ny Daty Malaza: Na Ny Dian' i Jesosy Teto Madagaskara* (Tananarive: LMS).

Rajemisa-Raolison, Regis. 1966. *Dictionnaire historique et géographique de Madagascar* (Fianarantsoa: Librairie Ambozontany).

Rakotovao, Jajosefa (ed.). [1967]. *Voly Maitson'andriamanitra: Tantaran'ny Fiangonana Loterana Malagasy 1867–1967* (Antananarivo: Trano Printy Loterana).

Rankin, John. 2013. 'Nineteenth-Century Royal Navy Sailors from Africa and the African Diaspora: Research Methodology'. *African Diaspora* 6: 179–95.

Razafintsalama, Adolphe. 1983. 'Les funérailles royales en Isandra d'après les sources du XIXe siècle'. In Françoise Raison-Jourde (ed.), *Les souverains de Madagascar* (Paris: Karthala): 193–209.

Razafy-Andriamihaingo, Jean-Pierre. 1997. *La Geste éphémère de Ranavalona 1re. L'expedition diplomatique malgache en Europe 1836–1837* (Paris: L'Harmattan).

'Recent Acquisitions Briefly Noted'. *Yale University Library Gazette* 75.3/4 (2001): 190.

Reigart, John Franklin. 1916. *The Lancasterian System of Instruction in the Schools of New York City* (New York: Teachers College, Columbia University).

Richards, Rhys. 2005. 'Manuscript XVII: Who Taught Pomare to Read? Unpublished Comments by a Missionary Surgeon on Tahiti in May 1807 to October 1810, and Journal Entries by an Able Seaman at Tahiti in 1811'. *Journal of Pacific History* 40.1: 105–15.

Robequain, Charles. 1958. *Madagascar et les bases dispersées de l'union française* (Paris: Presses Universitaires de France).

Robert, Dana L. (ed.). 2008. *Converting Colonialism. Visions and Realities in Mission History, 1706–1914* (Grand Rapids, MI: William B. Eerdmans).

Ross, Andrew C. 1998. 'Campbell, John'. In Gerald H. Anderson (ed.), *Biographical Dictionary of Christian Missions* (New York: Macmillan Reference USA): 112.

Rouhette, Annie. 1966. 'A Propos de la succession au trône de l'Imerina'. *Annales de l'Université de Madagascar – Droit* 3: 1–9.

Rouillard, John (ed.). 1866. *A Collection of the Laws of Mauritius and Its Dependencies*, vol. 3 (Mauritius: L. Channell).

Rowlands, Thomas. 1886. 'Notes on the Betsileo Dialect (As Spoken in the Arindrano District)'. *Antananarivo Annual & Madagascar Magazine* 10: 235–8.

Saint-Ours, Jacques de. 1956. '*Étude morphologique* et géologique de l'archipel des Comores'. *Bulletin de l'Académie Malgache* 34: 7–39.

Sanchez, Samuel F. 2008. 'Commerce régional et à longue distance dans l'ouest de Madagascar au XIXème siècle'. *Tsingy: Revue de l'Association des professeurs d'histoire et de géographie de Madagascar* 9: 44–56.

Saunders, Christopher. 1985. 'Liberated Africans in Cape Colony in the First Half of the Nineteenth Century'. *International Journal of African Historical Studies* 18.2: 223–39.

Scherer, André. 1966. *Histoire de la Réunion* (Paris: Presses universitaires de France).

Sédillot, René. 1958. *Histoire des colonisations* (Paris: Fayard).

Serva, Maurizio, Filippo Petroni, Dima Volchenkov, and Søren Wichmann. 2012. 'Malagasy Dialects and the Peopling of Madagascar'. *Journal of the Royal Society Interface* 9: 54–67.

Shepherd, Gill. 1980. 'The Comorians and the East African Slave Trade'. In James L. Watson (ed.), *Asian and African Systems of Slavery* (Oxford: Blackwell): 73–99.

Siegrist, A. 1937. *Mademoiselle Juliette: Princesse malgache* (Tananarive: Pilot de la Beau Jardière).

Simonin, Louis. 1864. 'La mission de Madagascar: Souvenirs d'un voyage dans l'Océan-Indien'. *Revue des deux mondes* 50.4: 968–1000.

Sinclair, Mick. 2007. *The Thames: A Cultural History* (New York: Oxford University Press).

Sivasundaram, Sujit. 2001. 'Natural History Spiritualized: Civilizing Islanders, Cultivating Breadfruit, and Collecting Souls'. *History of Science* 39.4: 417–43.

Slugg, Josiah Thomas. 1881. *Reminscences of Manchester Fifty Years Ago* (Manchester: Simpkin, Marshall & Co).

Smith, Bernard. 1960. *European Vision and the South Pacific 1768–1850: A Study in the History of Art and Ideas* (Oxford: Oxford University Press).

Smith, Elise Juzda. 2018. '"Cleanse or Die": British Naval Hygiene in the Age of Steam, 1840–1900'. *Medical History* 62.2: 177–98.

Smith, G. B. 'Farquhar, Sir Robert Townsend (1776–1830)'. *Oxford Dictionary of National Biography*, www.oxforddnb.com/view/10.1093/odnb/9780192683120 .001.0001/odnb-9780192683120-e-9180 (accessed 09. 04.21).

Smith, Thomas. 1825. *The history and origin of the missionary societies, containing faithful accounts of the voyages, travels, labours, and successes of the various missionaries who have been sent out, for the purpose of evangelizing the heathen, and other unenlightened nations, in different parts of the globe. Compiled and arranged from the authentic documents*, vol. 2 (London: Thomas Kelly & Richard Evans).

Somerset House. [1979?]. *The Somerset House Art Treasures Exhibition, 1979* ([London]).

Speight, W. L. 1932. 'The British Navy in South Africa'. *Royal United Services Institution. Journal* 77.506: 373–7.

Spence, Jonathan D. 1988. *The Question of Hu* (New York: Knopf).

Stanley, Brian (ed.). 2001. *Christian Missions and the Enlightenment* (Grand Rapids, MI: Wm. B. Eerdmans).

Starr, J. Barton. 2008. 'Morrison, John Robert (1814–1843)'. *Oxford Dictionary of National Biography* (3 Jan.), www.oxforddnb.com/view/10.1093/ref:odnb/97801 98614128.001.0001/odnb-9780198614128-e-19327 (accessed 14/07/21).

Stevenson, George John. 1885. *Methodist Worthies: Characteristic Sketches of Methodist Preachers of the several Denominations with Historical Sketch of each Connexion*, vol .4 (London: Thomas C. Jack).

Storey, William Kelleher. 1997. *Science and Power in Colonial Mauritius* (Rochester, NY: University of Rochester Press).

Stothers, Richard B. 1984. 'The Great Tambora Eruption in 1815 and Its Aftermath'. *Science* 224.4654: 1191–8.

Struck, Bernhard. 1909. 'An Unpublished Vocabulary of the Comoro Language'. *Journal of the Royal African Society* 8.32: 412–21.

Suzuki, Akihito. 2006. *Madness at Home: The Psychiatrist, the Patient, and the Family in England, 1820–1860* (Berkeley: University of California Press).

2004. 'Burrows, George Man (1771–1846)'. In *Oxford Dictionary of National Biography*, edited by H. C. G. Matthew and Brian Harrison (Oxford: Oxford University Press), www.oxforddnb.com/view/article/4114 (accessed 18/04/09).

Tann, Jennifer, and Christine Macleod. 2016. 'Empiricism Afloat – Testing Steamboat Efficacy: Boulton Watt & Co. 1804–1830'. *International Journal for the History of Engineering & Technology* 86.2: 228–43.

Teelock, Vijayalakshmi, and Abdul Sheriff. 2016. 'Slavery and the Slave Trade in the Indian Ocean'. In Vijayalakshmi Teelock (ed.), *Transition from Slavery in Zanzibar and Mauritius* (Oxford: African Books Collective): 25–43.

Theal, George McCall. 1964. *Records of South-Eastern Africa*, vol. 9 (Cape Town: Struik).

Thiébaut, Rafaël. 2017. 'An Informal Franco-Dutch Alliance: Trade and Diplomacy between the Mascarenes and the Cape, 1719–1769'. *Journal of Indian Ocean World Studies* 1.1: 130–48.

Thiriot, Jean Baptiste. 1882. *L'Ile Maurice, La Réunion et les productions de l'Inde, 1785*, edited by E. Génin (Douai: Imprimerie O. Duthillœul).

Thomson, Janice E. 1994. *Mercenaries, Pirates, and Sovereigns: State-Building and Extraterritorial violence in early modern Europe* (Princeton, NJ: Princeton University Press).

Thorne, James Cross. 1888. 'Elementary Education in Madagascar'. *Antananarivo Annual & Madagascar Magazine* 12: 27–40.

Thorne, Susan. 1999. *Congregational Missions and the Making of an Imperial Culture in Nineteenth- Century England* (Stanford, CA: Stanford University Press).

Toussaint, Auguste. 1967. *La route des Îles: Contribution à l'histoire maritime des Mascareignes* (Paris: SEVPN).

1966. 'Le trafic commercial entre les Mascareignes et Madagascar de 1773 à 1810'. *Annales de l'Université de Madagascar*, series Lettres et Sciences Humaines 5: 91–128.

1965. 'Le trafic commercial des Seychelles de 1773 à 1810'. *Journal of the Seychelles Society* 4: 20–61.

1953. 'Early American Trade with Mauritius'. *The Mariner's Mirror* 39.1: 45–56.

Townsend, William John. [1890]. *Robert Morrison: The Pioneer of Chinese Missions* (London: S. W. Partridge).

Turner, Iris. 2015. *The History of Borough Road School/College from Its Origins in 1798 until Its Merger with Maria Grey College to Form West London Institute of Higher Education in 1976* (London: Brunel University Press), http://bura.brunel.ac.uk/handle/2438/11435 (accessed 27.01.22).

Van Den Berg, Johannes. 1956. *Constrained by Jesus' Love: An Enquiry into the Motives of the Missionary Awakening in Great Britain in the Period between 1698 and 1815* (Kampen: J. H. Kok).

Van den Boogaerde, Pierre. 2009. *Shipwrecks of Madagascar* (New York: Strategic Book Publishing).

Valette, Jean. 1972. 'Contribution à l 'étude de la succession d'Andrianampoinimerina'. *Revue française d'histoire d'outre-mer* 59.214: 113–32.

1970. 'Rainandriamampandry, historien de Jean René'. *Bulletin de l'Académie Malgache* 48.1–2: 1–7.

1968. 'Documents pour servir à l'étude des relations entre Froberville et Mayeur'. *Bulletin de l'Académie Malgache* 16.1–2: 79–104.

1967. 'Correspondance de Jean René à Sir Robert Farquhar'. *Bulletin de l'Académie Malgache* 45.2: 71–98.

1966. 'Un mémoire de Rondeaux sur Madagascar (1809)'. *Bulletin de l'Académie Malgache* 44.2: 113–29.

1966. 'Un plan de développement de Madagascar: Le projet Bergsten (1825)'. *Bulletin de l'Académie Malgache* 40.2: 5–24.

1963. 'L'Imerina en 1822–1825 d'après les journaux de Bojer et d'Hilsenberg'. *Bulletin de Madagascar* (Apr.–May): 23–9.

1962. *Études sur le règne de Radama I* (Tananarive: Imprimerie Nationale).

Vaughan, Megan. 2005. *Creating the Creole Island: Slavery in Eighteenth-Century Mauritius* (Durham, NC: Duke University Press).

Vérin, Pierre, 1986. *The History of Civilisation in North Madagascar* (Rotterdam: A. A. Balkema).

1972. *Histoire ancienne du nord-ouest de Madagascar – Part 1* ([Antananarivo]: University of Madagascar).

Walter, Albert. 1914. 'The Sugar Industry'. In Allister Macmillan (ed.), *Mauritius Illustrated. Historical and Descriptive, Commercial and Industrial, Facts, Figures, & Resources* (W. H. & L. Collingridge: London): 208–32.

1914. 'Climate'. In Allister Macmillan (ed.), *Mauritius Illustrated: Historical and Descriptive, Commercial and Industrial, Facts, Figures, & Resources* (W. H. & L. Collingridge: London): 185–92.

Walvin, James. 1983. *Slavery and the Slave Trade* (London: MacMillan).

[War Office]. 1818. *The Army List for September 1818* ([London: War Office].

Wellesley, Arthur (ed.). 1878. *Despatches, Correspondence and Memoranda of Field Marshall Arthur Duke of Wellington K. G.*, vol. 7 (London: John Murray).

Whatley, Warren C. 2018. 'The Gun–Slave Hypothesis and the 18th Century British Slave Trade'. *Explorations in Economic History* 67: 80–104.

Williams, Charles. 1828. *The Missionary Gazetteer* (London: Frederick Westley and A. H. Davis).

Winters, William. 1888. *The History of the Ancient Parish of Waltham Abbey, or Holy Cross* (Essex: W. Winters).

1885. *Our Parish Registers; being three hundred years of curious local history, as collected from the original registers, churchwardens' accounts, and monumental records of the parish of Waltham Holy Cross* (Waltham Abbey: W. Winters).

Wright, Louis B. 1943. 'The Noble Savage of Madagascar in 1640'. *Journal of the History of Ideas* 4.1: 112–18.

Young, H. A. 2012. *The East India Company's Arsenals & Manufactories* ([Luton]: Andrews UK).

Yule, Henry, and Henri Cordier (eds.). 2014 [1298]. *The Travels of Marco Polo* (Adelaide: eBooks@Adelaide).

Zack, Naomi (ed.). 2019. *The Oxford Handbook of Philosophy and Race* (New York: Oxford University Press).

Theses

Boxen, Jennifer L. 2013. 'A Spirit of Benevolence: Manchester and the Origins of Modern Public Health, 1790–1834'. MA, Florida Atlantic University.

Campbell, Gwyn. 1985. 'Role of the London Missionary Society in the Rise of the Merina Empire, 1810–1861'. PhD, University of Wales, Swansea.

Cavell, Samantha. 2010. 'A Social History of Midshipmen and Quarterdeck Boys in the Royal Navy, 1761–1831'. PhD, University of Exeter.

Dacam, John H. 2009. '"Wanton and Torturing Punishments": Patterns of Discipline and Punishment in the Royal Navy, 1783–1815'. PhD, University of Hull.

Dugal, Sarah J. 2004. 'What's the Story with Vazimba? Oral History, Social Change, and Identity in Highland Madagascar'. PhD, Tulane University.

Hafkin, Nancy Jane. 1973. 'Trade, Society and Politics in Northern Mozambique c.1753–1913'. PhD, Boston University.

Howes, Peter J. (ed.) 1993. 'The Journal of Elizabeth Cozens'. MA, University of Cape Town.

Latsaka, Abraham. 1984. 'Politiques scolaires et stratégies concurrentielles à Madagascar de 1810 à 1910'. Doctoral thesis, University Lyon II.

Marshall, M. 1940. 'The Growth and Development of Cape Town'. MA, University of Cape Town.

Muller, Jennifer. 2015. '"Engines of Educational Power" – The Lancastrian Monitorial System and the Development of the Teacher's Role in the Classroom: 1805–1838'. PhD, Rutgers State University, New Jersey.

Rasoamiaramanana, Micheline. 1983. 'Aspects ´économiques et sociaux de la vie à Majunga entre 1862 et 1881'. PhD, University of Antananarivo.

Valentine, Barbara. 2000. 'The Dark Soul of the People: Slaves in Mauritius, 1835'. BA, Rhodes University.

Wastell, R. E. P. 1944. 'British Imperial Policy in Relation to Madagascar, 1810–96'. PhD, London University.

Yank, Tyler. 2019. 'Women, Slavery, and British Imperial Intervention in Mauritius, 1810–1845'. PhD, McGill University.

Young, Joline. 2013. 'The Enslaved People of Simon's Town 1743 to 1843'. MA, University of Cape Town.

Websites

'The 1832 Madhouse Act and the Metropolitan Commission in Lunacy from 1832', http://studymore.org.uk/3_06.htm (accessed 18/04/09).

Aapravasi Ghat Trust Fund. 'The Indenture Experience', www.aapravasighat.org/inden ture.htm (accessed 30/06/14).

'Apprenticeships', in Richard Evans, *A Short History of Technical Education*, https:// technicaleducationmattersorg/2009/05/13/chapter-3-the-guilds-and-apprentice ships (accessed 23. 04.21).

Barnett, Len. 'The East India Company's Marine (Indian Marine) and Its Successors through to the Royal Indian Navy (1613–1947)', www.barnettmaritime.co.uk/ma inbombay.htm (accessed 11/05/19).

'The Birmingham Gun Barrel Proof House', www.gunproof.com (accessed 05/10/2009).

'Borough Road College – Student List', www.brunel.ac.uk/about/Archives/Documents/Excel/Male-Students-at-BRC-Read-Only.xlsx (accessed 27/01/22).

Braine, Harriet. 'Thomas Boteler's African Adventure', Royal Museums Greenwich, www.rmg.co.uk/discover/behind-the-scenes/blog/thomas-botelers-african-adven ture (accessed 31. 07.19).

Carluer, Jean-Yves. 'John Jenkins 1', http://protestantsbretons.fr/protestants/john-jenkins-1 (accessed 15. 04.21).

Corrigan, Karina H. 2004. 'Chinese Botanical Paintings for the Export Market', *The Magazine Antiques* (June), www.themagazineantiques.com/article/chinese-botanical-paintings-for-the-export-market (accessed 12/02/22).

'Court Martial of Mr. Thomas Goble', www.goblegenealogy.com/data/SouthAfrica/gp57.html (accessed 13/05/19).

'A Fine Silver-Mounted Presentation Sabre', Bonhams, www.bonhams.com/auctions/16881/lot/353/?keep_login_open=1 (accessed 13/05/19).

'The Frigate *Junon*', https://shipsofscale.com/sosforums/threads/4th-of-february-today-in-naval-history-naval-maritime-events-in-history.2104/page-12 (accessed 06.02.22).

Hacking, Craig, and Daniel J. Bell. 'Solid and Hollow Abdominal Viscera', https://radiopaedia.org/articles/solid-and-hollow-abdominal-viscera (accessed 17. 07.21).

'Joseph Lacon, 1842–1918', www.myheritage.com/names/joseph_lacon (accessed 18.06.21).

'Joseph Nourse', www.thepeerage.com/p15954.htm (accessed 04/10/2009).

'Lady Maria Frances Geslip Hamilton [née de Latour]', www.lordbyron.org/persRec .php?&selectPerson=MaHamil1875 (accessed 09. 04.21).

Lambert, Nelson. 2011. 'Africa – HMS Maidstone, part 2', Acta Militaria, http://nelson lambert.blogspot.com/2011/06/africa-hms-maidstone-part-2.html (accessed 14/05/19).

Marshall, John. 'Royal Naval Biography/Boteler, Henry', https://en.wikisource.org/wi ki/Royal_Naval_Biography/Boteler,_Henry (accessed 05. 05.21).

'Royal Naval Biography/Polkinghorne, James', https://en.wikisource.org/wiki/Roy al_Naval_Biography/Polkinghorne,_James (accessed 15/05/19).

Mauremootoo, John. 2022. 'African Case Study II: Mauritius – A History of Degradation and the Beginnings of Restoration', www.researchgate.net/publica tion/267937347_African_Case_Study_II_Mauritius_-_a_History_of_Degradatio n_and_the_Beginnings_of_Restoration (accessed 08/05/19).

Mauritian Philatelic Blog, http://mauritianphilatelicblog.blogspot.com/2015/07/bicen tennial-of-arrival-of-reverend.html (accessed 15.08.19).

Mirza-Davies, James. 2015. 'A Short History of Apprenticeships in England: From Medieval Craft Guilds to the Twenty-First Century', House of Commons Library, https://commonslibrary.parliament.uk/a-short-history-of-apprenticeships-in-eng land-from-medieval-craft-guilds-to-the-twenty-first-century (accessed 23. 04.21).

'Nathaniel Minshall (abt. 1780–1848)', www.wikitree.com/wiki/Minshall-199 (accessed 18. 06.21).

'Newbridge Forge and Furnace', NPRN40431, Coflein, https://coflein.gov.uk/en/site/4 0431 (accessed 18. 06.21).

'The Register of Oswestry Old Chapel: 1780–1812', www.melocki.org.uk/salop/Osw estryOld.html (accessed 18. 06.21).

'Robert Farquhar', https://mauritiusislandhistory.wordpress.com/robert-farquhar (accessed 09. 04.21).

'Robert Farquhar', https://genealogie.mu/index.php/en/?option=com_content&vie w=article&id=225:login-register&catid=7&Itemid=321&lang=oc (accessed 12. 09.19).

'The Royal Gunpowder Mills – Waltham Abbey', Greater London Industrial Archaeology Authority, www.glias.org.uk/news/193news.html (accessed 04/10/ 2009).

Satyendra, Peerthum Ally Hossen Orjoon. 2005. 'Liberated Africans in Nineteenth Century Mauritius'. L'Express [Mauritius] 2 Feb., www.lexpress.mu/article/liber ated-africans-nineteenth-century-mauritius (accessed 16/12/18).

'Sibella Road Conservation Area Appraisal', www.lambeth.gov.uk/sites/default/files/ CA58SibellaRdAppraisal.pdf (accessed 28.01.22).

'Single Campaign Medals', #518, www.dnw.co.uk/media/auction_catalogues/Medals %20Strong%2018%20May%2011.pdf (accessed 04/08/18).

Stiles, H. Dominic W. 'Rev John Townsend (1757–1826), Founder of the London Asylum', https://blogs.ucl.ac.uk/library-rnid/2012/09/07/rev-john-townsend-175 7-1826-founder-of-the-london-asylum (accessed 23. 04.21).

'Townsend Farquhar, Sir Robert Townsend, 1st bt. (1776–1830), of 13 Bruton Street and 2 Richmond Terrace, Whitehall, Mdx', www.historyofparliamentonline.org/vol ume/1820-1832/member/townsend-farquhar-sir-robert-1776-1830 (accessed 09. 04.21)

Verdin, Joris. 2011. 'Les grands moments de l'harmonium', Référence Harmonium, https://lirias.kuleuven.be/1916211?limo=0 (accessed 05/06/21).

'Walter Farquhar Fullerton (b. 1801)), wearing blue Eton suit and white chemise with frilled collar by William Wood', www.bonhams.com/auctions/20767/lot/117 (accessed 09. 04.21).

'Waltham Holy Cross – Economic History and Local Government', www.british-history.ac.uk/report.aspx?compid=42719&strquery=powder (accessed 04/10/ 2009).

'Weapons and Militaria', Whitby Museum, https://whitbymuseum.org.uk/whats-here/ collections/social-history/weapons-militaria (accessed 13/05/19).

'William Buckland (1784–1856)', www.oxonblueplaques.org.uk/plaques/buckland .html (accessed 28.01.22).

Index

abolitionist, 47, 107, 117

accord, 1–2, 12, 18, 37, 118, 120–1, 123–5, 135, 137, 140, 145, 196, 225, 235, 252

acid, 158

Adelaide (1792–1849), queen of England, 201–2

agreement (*see* accord, contract)

agriculture, 7, 9, 18, 23, 32, 40, 78–81, 97, 118, 120–1, 142–3, 151–2, 171–2, 174–6, 196, 201, 237, 247–9

Africa, 4, 6, 10, 21, 50, 59, 63, 77, 120, 133, 146

    East, 3, 14, 78, 85, 107, 110–13, 115, 120, 130–5

    South Africa, 23–4, 147, 162, 175

    sub-Saharan, 22–3, 47

    West, 54, 127

African, 3–4, 6, 13, 47, 67, 107

    animals, 4

    plants, 4

Africans, 3, 12, 26, 46–7, 50, 53–4, 63, 67, 85, 105, 110, 112, 117, 131

aide-de-camp, 139, 168, 197, 223, 231

Alaotra (lake), 32, 213

Alasora, 210

Alawi, Abdallah bin, sultan of Anjouan (r. 1816–36), 194

Albatross, HMS, 133

Albrand, François Fortuné Joachim (1795–1826), governor of Sainte Marie, 114

Al-Busaidi, Said bin Sultan (1791–1856), sultan of Muscat and Oman, 210

alcohol (*see also* brandy, rum, wine), 31–2, 85, 145, 165, 211

Alexander, ship, 63, 68, 73–4

Alexandra, HMS, 125

Algoa Bay, 24

alliance, 1–2, 15, 17, 19, 21, 27, 33–5, 38, 40, 99, 106–7, 109, 115, 117, 125, 134, 140–2, 144–5, 152, 156, 210, 222, 239

ally, 30, 38, 115, 202–3, 241

Almirante Islands, 137

Alsace, 5

aluminium, 158

ambassador (*see also* embassy, envoy), 20, 46, 95, 117, 201, 205, 234–5, 242

Ambaniavaratra, 252

Ambatobe, 248

Ambatomanga, 32

Ambatomany, 193

Ambatonakanga, 157, 175

ambergris, 111

Amboanio (*see* Vohimar)

Ambodin'Andohalo, 150, 163, 209, 226–7

Ambodirano, 159, 168, 247–8

Ambohidrabiby, 74, 159

Ambohidratrimo, 32, 159

Ambohijanahary, 158

Ambohimanarina, 159

Ambohimandroso, 155

Ambohimanga, 28, 74, 171, 181

Ambohipo, 150, 159

Ambohitrandriamanitra, 164

Ambohitsara, 196

Ambongo, 87, 139

Ambositra, 32

Amboyna, 13

America, 22, 203

    South, 67

American Indians, 22, 63

Americans, 120, 135, 140, 176, 199, 202–3, 229

Ampangabe, 249

Amparibe, 155–6

Ampihadiamby, 164

Analakely, 150, 157–61, 164

Analamanga, 42

ancestor, 3–4, 122, 183, 196, 233, 248

ancestry, 3

Anderson, British naval physician, 75

Andohalo, 150, 175, 185, 229

Andohamandry, 248

Andoharano, 155

Andrangoloaka, 164

282

CPSIA information can be obtained
at www.ICGtesting.com
Printed in the USA
LVHW081903041222
734032LV00033B/495